Father of Rock & Roll

The Story of Johnnie "B. Goode" Johnson

Travis Fitzpatrick

Thomas, Cooke & Company
Houston

Copyright © 1999 by Travis Fitzpatrick

Thomas, Cooke & Company
Town Center Two
1330 Lake Robbins Drive, Suite 270
The Woodlands, Texas 77380
Ph: 281.364.9800

All rights reserved. No part of this book may be reproduced or transmitted in any form or by any means, electronic or mechanical, including photocopying, recording, or by any information storage and retrieval system, without permission in writing from the publisher, except by a reviewer who may quote brief passages in a review.

First Edition / First Printing

Endpapers: Johnnie at the Grand Piano
Frontispiece: Johnnie at the Upright Piano
Copyright © 1998 by Marc Norberg

Father of Rock & Roll® is a registered trademark of Johnnie Johnson.
Compact Disc: Copyright ℗ & © 1999 Father of Rock & Roll Piano Publishing

All photographs are copyrighted by the photographer and cited, all rights reserved. Every effort has been made to trace the copyright holders of the photographs used in this volume. Should there be any ommisions in this respect we apologize and shall be pleased to make the appropriate acknowledgements in any future printings.

Lyrics to *Leader of the Band* by Dan Fogelberg copyright © 1981 Sony Music

Library of Congress Cataloging-in-Publication Data

Fitzpatrick, Travis
    Father of rock & roll: the story of Johnnie "B. Goode" Johnson / Travis Fitzpatrick.— Ist ed.
    p. cm.
    Includes bibliographical references and index.
    ISBN 0-9672157-0-6
    I. Johnson, Johnnie, 1924 -   2. Rock musicians — United States — Biography. I. Title

BOOK DESIGN BY SPIKE LONGORIA

Printed in the United States of America

For my family, who always believed in me.
And to Jeanne Davenport, my seventh-grade English teacher,
who helped me believe in myself.

This book is dedicated to all the unknown masters of art who
never received their due. May you find glory with God.

CONTENTS

PROLOGUE / 3

I
SON'S DREAM / 7

II
BLUEHAND JOHNNIE / 37

III
BROWN EYED HANDSOME MAN / 65

IV
MAYBELLENE / 83

V
ROLL OVER BEETHOVEN / 111

VI
JOHNNIE B. GOODE / 139

VII
DYNA FLOW / 161

VIII
NO PARTICULAR PLACE TO GO / 185

IX
BYE BYE JOHNNIE / 213

X
I'M GOIN' FISHIN' / 235

XI
HAIL! HAIL! ROCK 'N' ROLL / 251

XII
FRANCES / 269

XIII
GEORGE'S JAM / 311

XIV
THROWING STONES / 337

XV
BLUE ON BLUE / 373

ACKNOWLEDGMENTS / 385

DISCOGRAPHY / 391

BIBLIOGRAPHY / 395

INDEX / 399

ABOUT THE CD / 409

CD LINER NOTES / 411

Father of Rock & Roll

The Leader of the Band is tired
And his eyes are growing old
But his blood flows through my instrument
And his song is in my soul
My life has been a poor attempt
To imitate the man
I'm just a living legacy
To the Leader of the Band

—Dan Fogelberg, "Leader of the Band"

There was no rock and roll before this guy.
It's that simple.
Johnnie Johnson built the bridge.
– Don Was

PROLOGUE

September 1, 1995
The Satellite Lounge
Houston, Texas

At half-past eight in the evening, a huge rig came rolling down Washington Avenue, billowing smoke and diesel fumes, and hissed to a stop in front of the Satellite Lounge. The growing crowd on the sidewalk turned to watch, perplexed by the rumbling misplaced monstrosity. Horns blared as a caravan of cars swerved wide to avoid the bulk of the vehicle and a few drivers yelled and gestured as they passed. Then all at once the engine died, the cab door burst open and a cowboy jumped out onto the pavement.

He was a small man, but wiry tough. His boots clacked on the pavement as he made his way to the passenger side and he tipped his wide-brimmed Stetson at the crowd as he pulled himself up with one quick motion and opened the door. He disappeared for a moment into the darkness then reemerged holding something long and weighted in his right hand. The bouncers next door at Rockefeller's, where Bobby "Blue" Bland was scheduled to perform, craned their necks suspiciously and moved forward. But the cowboy was not interested in seeing Bobby "Blue" Bland. He lowered himself carefully this time and gently guided the object with undisguised tenderness to a safe descent. As he turned to face the crowd, they saw that it was a guitar.

The guitar was nothing special: like the man himself it was road-weary and scarred from use. But from the way he held the instrument, there could be no doubt that he would sooner sell his soul than give up that guitar, and his right shoulder turned in to protect her as he made his way purposefully through the crowd and towards the Satellite. The waiting line stretched around the block, yet not a single soul moved to stop him as he pushed to the front and approached the doorman. He met the cowboy's eyes and the cowboy nodded. Then with a slow and almost painful movement, the cowboy brought his guitar to chest level, cradled it for a moment uncertainly, then offered the instrument to the doorman. When he spoke, the voice that drawled out held the sincerity of a firm handshake and a working man's integrity.

"I was passin' through on 59 when I heard over the radio that Johnnie Johnson, the piano man, was gonna be playing here tonight. S'at right?"

The doorman nodded.

"Well, sir, I don't have no money to get in your club and I can't stay 'cause my truck's parked out there in the middle of the street. But I was wonderin' could ya do me a favor?"

"Depends on what you want," the doorman answered dryly.

"Well, that man you got playin' in there tonight is a hero of mine. I don't have many heroes, and I ain't the type that goes around huntin' for autographs. But I was wonderin', could you take this guitar of mine back there and have Mr. Johnson sign it for me? That's all I ask. Then I'll get back in my truck and get it out of the way of your club."

The doorman was starting to shake his head when another man in a black shirt came forward and greeted the cowboy. The cowboy nodded.

"You want Johnnie to sign your guitar?" the man in the black shirt asked.

"I'd appreciate it quite a bit."

"Well I'll do you one better. I'll take you back to meet him."

For the first time, the cowboy's sturdy demeanor broke and a jubilant grin crossed his leathery face, exposing tobacco-stained teeth. He reached out, still holding his guitar, and shook the man's hand firmly.

"You would do that for me?" he asked, cocking his head ever so slightly. He peered up at the man in the black shirt with incredulous eyes.

"Yeah, I'll do it for you. He's in the back, now come on."

The man led the way through the dark belly of the club and the cowboy strutted behind, bow-legged in his tight Wranglers, the guitar still cradled in his arms. Security stepped aside as they recognized the man in the black shirt and held the door open for them as the pair entered into the backstage area. They eyed the cowboy. The cowboy nodded.

The dressing room was small and Johnnie Johnson, dressed in a red shirt and his usual white hat, was chatting with the drummer when the two men came towards him. He looked up from the couch and grinned.

"There he is! Hey, George!" Johnnie chuckled and put down his orange juice to shake hands with the man in the black shirt. "This is my good friend George," he said to the drummer. George and the drummer exchanged greetings. Meanwhile the cowboy seemed to melt unobtrusively into the background as George and Johnnie talked for a few moments. Johnnie didn't even notice him. Then George gestured and the cowboy came forward. This time he didn't nod but took his hat off and held it in his left hand, his right still held the guitar. Sweat plastered his thinning hair in a crescent shape around his head.

"Johnnie, this man was driving his eighteen-wheeler through town when he heard on the radio you were going to be here. He got off the freeway and came down here just to see you. He was wondering if you would sign his guitar."

Johnnie smiled again and reached out for the guitar, took a marker from George, and in a careful scrawl inscribed his name on the well-used surface. There were no other names on the guitar. Then as Johnnie started to return the instrument, the cowboy suddenly dropped to one knee and took the black man's massive hand into his own, thin and calloused, as if he were intent on proposing marriage. The cowboy's eyes were red-rimmed as he spoke.

"Mr. Johnson," he said, "I've been listenin' to your music my whole life. Since I was a kid. It is an honor to meet you. I never would have dreamed I'd be in the same room talkin' to you."

"Thank you," Johnnie said warmly.

The cowboy lowered his eyes for a moment then looked back up at the old man sitting before him.

"I know the truth," he said and the room fell silent. "I know it was you."

With that the cowboy stood, brushed off his jeans, and put his hat back on. Johnnie handed him his guitar and he held her for a moment at arms length, admiring the signature with childish wonder. Then he shook hands with George, gave a quick nod to the rest of the room, and headed back to the highway.

I

SON'S DREAM

"He had a left hand like God. He didn't even know what key he was playing in, but he played them all. He would play the ragtime stride bass, but it bothered him because his stomach got in the way of his arm, so he used a walking bass instead. I can remember when I was thirteen—this was 1896—how Turk would play one note with his right hand and at the same time four with his left. We called it 'sixteen'— they call it boogie-woogie now."
—Eubie Blake on unschooled pianist William Turk from *A Left Hand Like God: A History of Boogie Woogie Piano* by Peter J. Silvester.

Johnnie Johnson wants to show me something. Rising from his seat, he shuffles to the piano like a slow blues, his feet never leaving the ground. He pulls out the bench, slightly askew, and rests his bulk behind the keys. "This is one of the first songs I learned to play," he says in his deep and quiet voice. "I taught myself from the record."

The left hand comes alive first and begins to pump out the bass line to "Cow Cow Blues," a 1925 boogie-woogie by the late Charles Davenport. Then with no deviation in his left, the right hand joins in to play the melody. Johnnie doesn't use the pedals, but one heavy black-shoed foot taps out a steady rhythm on the hard tile floor. *Clack. Clack. Clack. Clack.* Watching the expression on his face, at once a mask of quiet detachment and boundless joy, I realize that he is enjoying the show as much as I am. There is something scary about that. Something that chills me. For the hands, huge and thickly muscled, dance about separately, each with it's own agenda. And Johnnie watches as if he has no control of their movements— as if he is only the guardian of the hands, the body that keeps them fed and alive, while they await their chance to dance on the keys. Johnnie catches my eye and chuckles softly. He knows exactly what I am thinking. "Look at 'em go," those eyes say like a proud and delighted child with a pair of interesting pets. "Look at 'em go." Then he is finished and the hands return to his lap to wait once again.

"I haven't played that one in a long time," he laughs.

"When did you learn to play 'Cow Cow Blues,' Johnnie?" I ask him.

"Six years old," he says matter-of-factly, without even noticing the surprise on my face. Six-year-olds don't play boogie-woogie.

"Who taught you?"

"Nobody. I taught myself."

"Nobody helped you at all?"

"Well, my momma helped some." There is the answer.

"Did she play?"

"Oh no. Nobody in my family was musical. She'd just put the record on for me 'cause I was too young to do it myself. It was an old Victrola, the kind you had to wind up, and she'd start it and stop it for me while I got the song together."

He smiles more to himself than me, and I know at that moment he is a child again, a skinny little boy in overalls, feet dangling from the too-tall bench, mutely picking out chords as his momma strings beans on the back porch, stopping every so often to rewind the record. *That sounds good, baby. Keep playing for Momma.*

"What did your mother think about the fact that you could play all these songs so young?"

"She said I had a gift from God. That's what she called it—a gift from God." With that, the hands return impatiently to the keys, and as he has done for seventy years, Johnnie Johnson begins to play.

* * *

Johnnie Clyde Johnson was born on July 8, 1924, in Fairmont, West Virginia, a small town of 23,000 located between Morgantown and Clarksburg near the Monongahela River. The labor was not difficult; his mother, Priscilla Banks Johnson, was a big woman, country strong, and the boy drew his first breath a little after nine o'clock that sweltering summer evening, just as darkness fell and the lightning bugs began to glow.

Buddy Johnson, a coal miner, stomped in moments later, covered in coal dust and blacker than the night itself. They had sent word to him down in the tunnels that his wife was in labor, but he could not leave until his shift had finished. He spent the next few hours praying under his breath as he swung his pick into the rock. He prayed as he did every day in the wee hours before dawn, when he and the other men took the long, slow ride into the bowels of the earth. *Lord don't let the air run out down there, don't let them timbers crack, don't let me die down here in the ground. Just let me see that sunset at the end of this day, Lord.* And when he had finished his shift he had run. All the way home in his heavy boots, he had run. When he finally burst through the door, he was just in time to hold his infant son. He whispered to him then, as he had with all his children, breathing into the boy's ear as he squealed and screamed his birth cry. *Let my boy be strong, Lord. Let him live.* Then he bent down and placed the squalling infant on his mother's breast and kissed her on the forehead, leaving a soot stain on her damp skin. He turned his back to her, just in time to see two wide-eyed round faces disappear around the corner. Smiling, he called to them in his rich rumbling voice.

"Pless! Jack! Come on in here and see your brother."

The boys crept in, hesitant at first, with Pless, the oldest, leading the way. He was tall for his age and thin, the Sears Roebuck overalls hanging off his body yet scarcely clearing his spindly calves. His brother was shorter, thicker, with a big round head and curious countenance. His given name was Willie Vaughan, but the family called him Jack for his resemblance to Jack Johnson, the first black heavyweight boxing champion. However, this Jack was no fighter like the Galveston Giant. He was a gentle boy and he smiled a gap-toothed grin as he reached out to touch his brother's tiny grasping hand.

"What you gonna name him?" Pless asked.

"Well..." Buddy hesitated.

"Johnnie," said Priscilla from her bed, "with an ie at the end. Just like his daddy."

Buddy laughed at his sons' questioning stares. No one called him Johnnie anymore, though that was his given name. He'd always been Buddy.

"Don't worry, that's me," he reassured them. "Just like we all call Willie here, 'Jack.' My momma named me Johnnie, but they've been callin' me Buddy since I can remember."

"We gonna give him another name, too?" Jack asked, pointing to the sleeping bundle in his mother's arms.

"I got a feeling we'll just call him, Johnnie," Buddy answered. "Johnnie Johnson. That's a good name for a boy."

* * *

The sky is crying in St. Louis. The tears roll down from the heavens and onto the street where Johnnie Johnson sits on his porch and watches in silence. His eyes are impossible to read behind the dark sunglasses, although it appears he is focusing on someplace far away. For the last half-hour, a steady drip of water has filtered through the shingled roof, each drop barely missing the rim of his coal black baseball cap. He seems not to notice and makes no effort to move. Suddenly, I realize he's asleep.

"Johnnie?"

The only sound is the hum of the air conditioner in the window behind us and the pattering of rain. I hesitate to speak any louder. Then his head turns slightly, and through the shades I can barely make out the heavy lids of his eyes as they slide slowly open to survey the scene.

"Mmmmhmmm?"

"How long did you live in Fairmont?"

"Seventeen years."

"Ever think about going back?"

He doesn't falter, but he turns to the street again before he answers.

"No I don't. I don't ever think about going back."

* * *

No one expected Priscilla Johnson to die. It just happened. She wasn't sick and she'd made it through the labor six months before with no ill effects. Then one evening after supper she went to bed early and never woke up. Her death was attributed to an attack of acute indigestion— apparently her system was unable to process the large amount of cabbage she had eaten during the meal. She was only thirty years old.

The death of his wife devastated Buddy Johnson, who now found himself grief-stricken and alone with a six-month-old baby. This posed a serious problem. Neither Pless nor Jack was old enough to be trusted with the care of an infant, and Buddy was gone all day underground.

Desperate for a solution, Buddy approached his sister, Cora, and her husband, Ernest Williams, about taking Johnnie until he could find a better arrangement. Cora accepted, knowing full well that, despite her brother's good intentions, he would never come back for the boy. She was right. Less than a year later, Buddy Johnson found work twenty miles away in the mining town of Osage, West Virginia, and left for good. Pless and Jack, coming up on school age, were sent to live with other relatives in Fairmont, not far from the Williamses.

From the moment Buddy dropped little Johnnie in her arms, Cora became his mother and he her son. "She was the only mother I ever knew," Johnnie says of his father's sister. "She raised me from the time I was a baby 'til I was seventeen. I called her Momma and Mr. Williams, Daddy."

Elvira Sims, a cousin of Johnnie's, and at ninety-five, his oldest living relative, remembers Cora Williams as a stern but good-hearted woman who dedicated herself fully to raising her brother's child.

"She didn't have no children of her own," says Sims, "and she didn't expect to get one. But she loved that boy like her own and she did what any mother would do tryin' to bring him up best she could. And she raised him up right 'cause he was a good boy back then and he grew into a good man. She was real proud of Johnnie."

For Ernest Williams, raising a child was something entirely new, but he handled it as he did everything else in his life—with a resolute and quiet strength. Like Buddy Johnson, Williams also worked the mines from sunup to sundown, and he did so without complaint. At five-ten, he was not particularly large, but his toughness went unquestioned and his cool demeanor was legendary. Everyone in the black community knew him as "Mr. Williams" and nobody crossed him.

"He wasn't afraid of anything," Johnnie remembers of the man who raised him. "Man, beast, whatever. Daddy used to grab copperheads, water moccasins, big ol' black snakes by the tail and snap their heads off like a whip. I'll never forget 'cause I was afraid of snakes back then and I still am today. Seeing them just makes me turn cold. I couldn't understand how he could touch them, but he did, and it wasn't like he thought about it when he did it. We'd just be walkin' along and next thing you know, he'd reach down real quick and pull one up then, 'SNAP!' Half the time I wouldn't even see the snake 'till he had a hold of it. Daddy said that was bad, 'cause if you was gonna walk around in the woods, you had to watch out for snakes and be careful not to get bit.

"Another thing, he didn't want nothing to do with no superstitions. He laughed at superstitious people like they was fools. Kids used to come to the house all the time talkin' 'bout 'Mr. Williams! Mr Williams! That house is haunted over yonder! I bet you won't go in!' They did it just to challenge him, and also 'cause they really were scared and wanted to find out what was inside without havin' to meet up with somethin' nasty themselves. Daddy always went. He'd walk all through the house laughin' and teasin' them saying, 'If there be any ghosts in here, you best come out 'cause Mr. Williams is here, and if he see you he's gonna whip your ass.' He just didn't have no fear, and he was always cool.

"Only one time I ever saw him lose it, and that was when this travelin' magician made a snake come out of his shirt. I guess he'd heard about how Daddy wasn't afraid of anything superstitious, so he was tryin' to scare him. That was a mistake. When Daddy saw that snake crawl out of his shirt, his eyes got real wide. Then he went home and got his gun. When the magician heard where Mr. Williams was going, he hit the road and we never saw him again."

* * *

In January of 1925, when Johnnie came to live with them, the Williamses were living in what was known as a "shotgun house," so named because one could fire a shotgun through the front door and the shot would exit through the back door. Most of their neighbors occupied similar dwellings in the rural areas outside of Fairmont, farming small plots and living off the land. "It was a close-knit group back in Fairmont," Johnson remembers. "There weren't too many black people in the area, so we all sort of stuck together."

Like most of rural America at that time, the Fairmont of the late twenties and early thirties was a town living far above its means. Although the coal industry had prospered during the first part of the century, it was soon plagued by union strife and market fluctuations—the first signs of the Great Depression to come. West Virginia has always been one of the poorer states, and its fragile economy would all but crumble in the coming years, leaving many without jobs.

For black men in Fairmont like Ernest Williams, there was little opportunity even before the Depression. Segregation was a way of life and they accepted what they could get with little protest. Because of scarce numbers, blacks did not pose a threat to their white neighbors and for this reason were not persecuted, but treated with a quiet disdain.

As a young boy, Johnnie quickly became aware of the differences between his family and the white families nearby. In order to receive an education, he and the other children, whose families could afford to spare them from full-time work, were forced to walk nine miles to and from the only "colored school" in the area. The first of these schools was built in 1869, with a grant from the Freedman's Bureau, and needless to say, convenience was not a major concern. Johnson and the other black children, including his older brothers, spent their mornings and late afternoons dodging vicious dogs and angry bulls from neighboring pastures on the trek to school and back.

"We learned to be careful real quick," Johnnie recalls of his harrowing trips to school. "The worst part of it all was bad weather, especially durin' the winter. The teachers used to let us out an hour early in order for us to get home before dark since it took so long walkin' in that snow. I bet we did ninety miles of walkin' a week."

Growing up in the country, Johnnie did a lot of walking—and a lot of running. As a youngster he was notorious for misadventure, and he was hardly out of diapers before trouble became a constant pursuit. "I must have gotten a whippin' every day for being wild," he laughs. "Tippin' over outhouses, stealin' ice off the ice truck, all kinds of foolishness a young boy could get into, I was into up to my neck."

On weekends and during the summer months, Johnnie occupied his time fishing for bluegill and bass in the creeks around his area. The peace and quiet afforded by the solitude of fishing was pleasing to him, and the fish he caught were welcome additions to the dinner table as food, especially meat, was becoming scarce. Like most children, Johnnie had little patience when the fish weren't biting, and lulls between catches often found him indulging in some curious pursuit of his own device.

"I used to visit my grandmother on the weekends and she'd take me fishin' with her, which was wonderful for me," Johnnie says. "My first love then and now was fishin', and I'd spend all day down by the banks with my homemade pole and string.

"There was one afternoon I wasn't catchin' anything, so I started foolin' around, throwin' stuff in the water and whatever. I took a big rock and tied it on my line then dropped it in the water, just to see what would happen. Well, the rock went to the bottom all right—and pulled me in with it!

"I couldn't swim, and as soon as I fell in I started drownin', so I grabbed onto a piece of dead tree and held on for dear life! Meanwhile my grandmother had seen I was gone, so she started looking for me screamin' and hollerin', 'JOHNNIE...JOHNNIE!' She liked to have fainted when she caught sight of me down there in the water. I just popped my head up and said, 'Here I am, Grandma!' Let me tell you, she beat the tar out of me. We had a lot of weepin' willow trees in West Virginia, and she took three willow branches and braided 'em together before she whipped me with it.

"Anyway, the first thing she says when she's done is, 'Johnnie, don't tell your mother about what happened or she'll never let you come back and visit again.' So I promised her I wouldn't tell and went on playin' in the yard until Momma came to get me around supper time.

"Well, you know how little ones are. I guess I must have forgotten my promise, 'cause as soon as I saw Momma, I ran up to her with a big grin on my face and said, 'Guess what Momma? I almost drowned!' I got two whippin's that day!"

Perhaps the most notorious family story involves Johnnie's perilous first brush with creativity. Left alone in the living room while the adults played cards in the kitchen, Johnnie grew tired of his usual games and moved towards the fire. What followed was an experience he would never forget.

"There was one time...oh I must have been three or four, old enough to walk and talk," he says. "We had this fireplace near the back of the house, and I was sittin' there by myself heating up the iron poker and starin' at all the pretty reds and oranges as it got hotter and hotter. Then for some reason I decided to draw some designs on the wallpaper with that poker. I just sat there burnin' designs in the wall and watchin' the paper curl up and blacken. I didn't mean no harm—I was just tryin' to make somethin' nice.

"After a while, I got bored and went in to the livin' room where my parents and some neighbors were playin' cards. Sure enough, 'bout five minutes later, my mother starts sniffin' around talkin' 'bout how she smelled smoke. I just looked at her like it wasn't no big deal and said, 'Course you smell smoke, Momma. I just set the house on fire.'

"Well, you should have seen the commotion...cards flyin', chairs overturned...all the screaming and hollerin'. Neighbors all out in their yards. It was quite a show watchin' all these grown folks runnin' around actin' crazy. They finally put that fire out without too much damage to the house, and everything was saved but my behind.

"Naturally, I knew what was coming next. So when evenin' came around, I just sort of snuck off to bed hopin' that Momma would forget. Not a chance. I hadn't even pulled the covers up yet when she walked in and told me to go get a switch from the trees out back. I could tell right away she meant business, so I went to get a switch while Momma sat on the porch and watched me. I'd never been that scared 'cause I'd never seen Momma so mad. For a second, I thought about runnin'. Then I looked down by her feet and saw that old clothes iron—the old-fashioned kind that really was made of iron—and I knew if I took off she would throw that thing at me. Wasn't no doubt in my mind. I had no choice but to take my whippin'.

"As soon as I got back, she told me to take down my pants. The whole time I was beggin' her not to whip me. But it was no use. As soon as I had my pants down, she laid into me worse than she'd ever done before. I thought that whippin' would never end. It hurt real bad and believe me, I never went near that fireplace again!"

Johnnie Johnson's search for a non-destructive creative outlet came to an early end during his fifth summer when Cora Williams spontaneously purchased an upright piano. To this day, Johnnie still wonders what drove the normally reserved Cora to spend hard earned money on a musical instrument when no one in the family had demonstrated any ability or desire to learn. She never fully explained her reasons, and the family gave up asking long before her death fifty years later. "We never figured it out," Johnnie says. "It just wasn't like her to do something like that 'cause Momma was always tight with that dollar and for good reason—money was hard to come by in those days. But one day these movers came to our home with a piano. She told us she bought it cheap and thought it would be a nice decoration—somethin' to go with the rest of the furniture in the house. Neither of my parents were musical at all. They liked it sure enough, my mother loved piano music, but playin' it was a different story."

The piano, he remembers, "was nothing special, just a regular old upright." But Johnnie was fascinated. "It just seemed so natural to touch those keys. I climbed right up on the stool and started playin' 'Chopsticks.' Everyone in the room recognized the song, and Momma just burst into tears. She said I had a gift from God."

From that moment on, the piano became young Johnnie's passion—his obsession—and he progressed rapidly. Without the benefit of formal lessons, he taught himself by ear, copying his mother's Bessie Smith and Ethel Waters records on the windup Victrola and absorbing the sounds of the Big Band Era through late-night radio.

"All day long they played country music and I liked that fine," he says. "But at night there was this radio station out of Pittsburgh—KDKA—that played a lot of the jazz and blues stuff. I used to fall asleep listening to people like Count Basie and Glenn Miller on this show called 'Dawn Patrol.' My favorites were the big bands and orchestra leaders like Basie, the ones who were piano players. I loved Avery Parrish from the Erskine Hawkins Orchestra, especially when he did 'After Hours.' I learned to play that song just like him. And Meade Lux Lewis. I didn't know his name then but I knew his music. You talk about a boogie pianist, boy, he was something else."

Sitting up alone at night, Johnnie would listen intently to the tones and rhythms, practicing mentally as opposed to on the keyboard so as not to wake his family. The skill came in handy during the years to come when he could not afford a piano of his own to practice on.

"I learned to listen to a song and hold it in my head 'til I could get to the piano," says Johnnie. "While I was hearin' it I was seein' the keys in my head and figurin' out where the music was. The next mornin' I'd get up and play the songs I'd heard the night before, and nobody could figure out how I knew them without practicin'. I told them I practiced in my head, but they didn't believe me 'til I started doing it all the time. I'd come up with new songs every mornin'; just sit right down and play them after breakfast. After that it wasn't no surprise to them at all."

As Johnnie grew older and more experienced, he began to develop his own style, based partly on country music but more so on the jazz and big-band swing he'd absorbed through late-night radio. While this style would continue to change and expand throughout the years to include a variety of influences, jazz and big-band swing would always remain the nucleus of Johnnie's music. As he recalls, "My parents, living in West Virginia, were big country music fans—everyone I knew listened to it, white or black—and I learned a little of that. But my first love has always been jazz. I loved playing old standards like 'Love for Sale' and 'Green Dolphin Street.' I'll do 'A-Train.' See, jazz was and is my favorite thing to play. In fact, if you listen to the music I did with Chuck Berry, it's got a lot of that big-band jazz in it. It swings."

Word of little Johnnie Johnson's precocious talent spread quickly through the black community, and it wasn't long before neighbors began asking Clara to bring her son over to play piano at parties and gatherings. The boy had developed quite a repertoire of popular tunes and skillfully picked them out, complete with his own improvisations, to the delight of family and friends alike. "My family really enjoyed my piano and they'd help me learn new songs by stoppin' and startin' records while I tried to play each part of the song. I remember my mother playin' these records over and over on the Victrola until I could play 'em all by memory. Wasn't long 'til we wore them records out. But I was learnin' more and more songs and gettin' pretty good."

A few months after his eighth birthday, radio station WMMN in Fairmont heard about Johnnie through an employee and invited the boy to play during one of the broadcasts. The following weekend, Ernest and Cora got up early, dressed Johnnie in his brother Jack's hand-me-down suit, and drove the family's rusty Ford truck down the dirt roads and into town.

"I remember bein' real excited," Johnnie recalls. "And I remember Daddy tryin' to play it off like it was just another trip to town. But he was proud. Both my parents were proud, especially, they said, 'cause I was careful 'bout sayin' 'Yes, sir' and 'No, ma'am' to the people at the station and being respectful and quiet. But I was always quiet, so I knew it was 'cause I was on the radio that they were so happy."

When Johnnie made his debut on local radio it was a thrill to the black community, most of which had little or no chance of being recognized for anything positive. "It gave them somethin' to be proud of," Johnnie says of his spot on the air. "Nothin' ever came of it, but the folks in my neighborhood were real excited—especially the family. I remember after that show my uncle started wakin' me up in the middle of the night and sneakin' me out of the house so I could play at fish fries and neighborhood parties. You could say that wasn't any place for a young boy to be with all the cussin' and fightin' and drinkin', but people liked seein' this little kid up there playin' piano, and it made them feel good. Things were rough with the Depression and all, so there wasn't much for entertainment. Everyone was down."

An anonymous black man once said of the Depression, "The Negro was born in depression. It only became official when it hit the white man." Nevertheless, the Depression had just as marked an effect on the Afro-American if not more so. Black unemployment was at an all-time high, and by 1932 had reached fifty percent—twice the national level. Those who managed to retain their jobs found their wages cut in half at best. Ernest Williams was one of the majority. Out of work and low on money he began farming to survive.

"We lived off the land," says Johnnie of his family. "Most folks did in our area. We sold some of what we grew, but most of the crop and the animals went to keepin' the family fed. We'd pick strawberries and walk all the way to town in order to get a little extra money. The average black farmer back then wasn't makin' but $200 a year. We didn't have much of anything, and what we did have we shared. My brothers and I had one suit and it was passed down from oldest to youngest. You wore it 'til you outgrew it and then the next one got it. By the time my turn came around, the whole thing was worn to the threads."

In 1935, Franklin Roosevelt proposed the Emergency Relief Appropriation Act in order to help those Americans who were still jobless. Roosevelt's plan involved a record $4.8 billion budget–the majority of which went to the Harry Hopkins-led Works Progress Administration (WPA), the largest work-relief program in history. It was through this program that Ernest Williams was finally able to find work, as a ditch digger. "We were all relieved when Daddy got that job," Johnson remembers. "He started making thirty dollars a month, which kept food on the table."

But the relief the family felt was short-lived. Less than a year after starting his new job, Ernest Williams succumbed suddenly to the respiratory disease known as "black damper" or "black lung." Caused primarily by the inhalation of coal dust, black lung was common among miners, many of whom spent upwards of eighteen hours a day below the earth. Although he had not worked in the mines for years, Mr. Williams had already damaged his body beyond repair from a lifetime underground.

Johnnie is solemn when he speaks of Williams' death. "The only time my daddy saw the sunlight was durin' the weekend," he says. "Otherwise he was down in them mines. I remember him workin' in cold water that was up to his knees with bad arthritis and comin' home black as night all covered in coal dust from head to toe. Those miners never did breathe no fresh air. That type of life was bound to kill him early and it did."

Ernest Williams was only forty-five when he died.

* * *

"They sent me to live with my real father after that," says Johnnie. "Up in Osage."

The wind has picked up, and although it is summer, a cool breeze blows in from the street and wets us with an earthy mist. A single car glides past and Johnnie raises his hand to wave. The driver, an older man, responds with a wave of his own and a close-lipped smile. Sabu, Johnnie's little dog, eyes the car warily from behind the screen door and lets out a perfunctory series of barks before settling back down on his front paws. Johnnie tells him to hush.

"It was my momma's idea," he continues. "She said I needed to get to know my real father, especially with Daddy gone, and 'sides that she needed to get back on her feet again. I was real sad about goin' and kind of scared. I'd seen my father a few times, and I remembered him as a giant with a bass voice who was always tryin' to pick me and my brothers up. Truth was, he was more stout than tall, but that was how I remembered him when I saw him pullin' up to our house—a giant."

* * *

The boy stands in the doorway as the truck clambers to a stop, stirring dust and dead leaves in the Autumn sun. He hides behind his mother who pushes him forward. The driver door opens and the big man steps out into the yard. The boy tries to stand up straight and tall, but he is frightened and casts his eyes downward as he walks out onto the porch.

"Hey boy," the man says. "Come here and give Buddy a hug."

He complies half-heartedly and feels the solid arms engulf his body then lift him painfully off the ground.

"You getting big, boy! What you been eatin'? You're momma feeding you good?"

He smiles. The boy stares at his feet. The man shifts awkwardly then lays a hard, calloused hand on the boy's shoulder.

"I'm sorry about your daddy, boy. Ain't no one more sorry than me. But we gonna have a good time together, you and me. So don't you worry none, all right?"

The boy nods.

"Now go on and give your momma a kiss and c'mon so we can get back on the road."

* * *

"He didn't expect me to call him Daddy 'cause he knew Mr. Williams had raised me." Johnnie brushes a bug off his sleeve and coughs into a ham-sized fist.

"He said I should just call him Buddy and that was perfectly okay with me. We got into Osage not too long after we left 'cause it wasn't but twenty or thirty miles from Fairmont. Buddy lived by hisself in a little house, but he had a girlfriend who used to come around a lot—I can't remember her name right now—but she helped him out with cookin' and takin' care of the place. She had supper waitin' for us when we got in. I guess I knew then that things would be all right."

The following Monday, Johnnie started seventh grade at a school called Beech Church, which serviced Osage and some of the smaller communities nearby. Quiet and unassuming, Johnnie blended in without any problems, and in fact found that his status as the "new kid" afforded him certain advantages with the opposite sex. Before long he had found a potential girlfriend.

"I met a girl in school named Dorothy Johnson and we hit it off pretty good," Johnnie remembers. "Then one night I was walkin' back home through the woods after visitin' at her house, feelin' good, you know, when a little kitten crossed my path. It was pretty dark, but I bent down and tried to pet her sayin' 'Hey, kitty-kitty!' and all that. Well, all the sudden that 'kitty' turned around and puffed out her tail real big and I felt this liquid shoot all over my face and clothes. I knew right away that it wasn't no kitty—I'd tried to pet a skunk.

"I walked all the way home tryin' to keep from losin' my dinner and 'bout to pass out. I don't know if you've ever been sprayed directly by a skunk, but it will like to kill a person. I went in the house and sat down by the window waitin' for Buddy to get home from work. Didn't even change my clothes. Well, he must have smelled it out in the yard 'cause he walked in and said 'Whew, you smell that, Johnnie? Somebody done hit...' He turned around and walked over to me. 'Goddamn, boy! You get sprayed by a skunk?' He told me to take off all my clothes and then he made me bury them and after that he had me take a bath, the whole time he was cussin' up a storm. He finally had to go outside 'cause I smelled so bad.

"Next mornin', I figured the worst of it was over and went to school as usual. I was sittin' by the radiator thinkin' that nobody would notice when Ms. Waters comes up to me and says, 'Johnnie, did you get sprayed by a skunk last night?' I said, 'Yes, ma'am.' She said, 'Well you better get down to the office. We can't have this, you're about to kill everybody in here.'

"Well, the principal said he couldn't have that in the school and he made arrangements for me to stay out of school until I could get rid of that smell. We tried everything—different kind of soaps, washin' powders—Buddy's girlfriend even brought over some of her bath oils, but nothin' could get that smell out. I even ended up shavin' all my hair off, but that didn't work either. I was out of school for almost a month, and naturally, that was the end for me and Dorothy. Don't nobody want to date a person who smells like a skunk!"

Years later, Johnnie remembers that he didn't experience much teasing from the incident. "I was a loner," he recalls. "Bullies didn't have no interest in me. The other kids either liked me or didn't pay no attention one way or the other."

Before Johnnie moved to Osage, he had never been in a serious altercation. "Just the usual playground stuff, wrestlin' around and shovin'," he says. "No one ever got seriously hurt or bloodied up."

Then it happened. One day after school, he and a few friends were shooting marbles when an older, bigger boy pushed his way into the circle and tried to steal all the marbles. As Johnnie had done particularly well, the boy approached him first. "He reached down, pushed me back and took all the marbles I had won. Then he laughed and said, 'What you gonna do about it?'" Johnnie remembers. "The other kids grabbed up all the marbles they could and started to run, but I was stuck with this fool in my face tellin' me how he was gonna whip my ass. He was bigger than me and I knew he was probably a lot stronger. So I grabbed the first thing I could find—which was a railroad spike—and I hit him just as hard as I could in the head with it.

"That was the end of the fight. The blood just sprayed all over the place and he fell like he'd been shot. They took him to the hospital and bandaged up his face, and everybody started talkin' 'bout how I had almost killed this boy. I don't think nobody messed with me after that. All I remember was bein' worried about what Buddy would do 'cause he'd never whipped me or anything like that. But all he said was, 'The boy had it comin'. He shouldn't been tryin' to take your marbles.' That's the way Buddy was, and the way most of the men I grew up around was. My daddy would have said the same thing if he'd been alive. You didn't get in no trouble for protectin' yourself, but if I had started that fight or tried to steal someone else's marbles, I would have gotten it good. That's how it was back then. I guess after that things went pretty smooth and I made it through the school year without any more problems."

As summer approached, Johnnie began longing for the familiarity of his old stomping grounds in Fairmont and both Cora and Buddy decided it would be better for the boy if he returned home. At the end of the school year, he said good-bye to his father and returned to Fairmont to begin the eighth grade.

"I liked it up in Osage, but I was ready to come home," Johnnie recalls. "Buddy wasn't hurt or nothin'. He gave me a hug, shook my hand and said I could come up and stay with him anytime I wanted. Then he took me back down to Fairmont and had supper with Momma, Pless, Jack, and me before he took off again, 'cause he had to be at work the next mornin'. I felt sad when I watched him drive off, 'cause we had gotten pretty close and had a lot of good times together. But I was glad to be back home with Momma. When Buddy left, he waved to us as he turned onto the road and we all waved back and watched him drive off."

He would never see his father again.

*   *   *

"The black damper got him," they said in the kitchen. "Damn black damper."

The boy listened from the other room. The same thing that got his daddy had got Buddy, too. Got him down in the mines. Crept right up out of the rock and jumped down his throat.

The boy cried silently to himself. He was too old to be crying with Momma and the other women. What would Pless and Jack think? They'd call him a girl. He was fourteen now and almost a man. Pless had already left town to make his living and Jack was saving up to go himself. They were men: both of them in their Sunday clothes they'd bought themselves, looking solid, comforting Momma and Buddy's girlfriend, talking with the other men in the yard about baseball and farming and mining.

"Wasn't nothing wrong with him when I was up there," the boy thought. "He was fine, just as strong as he ever was. Didn't see him short of breath or hear that wet cough that Daddy got before he passed." He didn't understand how it could have happened so quick. Just like that.

"I was angry after Buddy died," Johnnie remembers. "I'd always been the type who tried to keep the peace and get along with everybody, but after he passed I started gettin' a real short fuse."

The anger was justified. By age fourteen, Johnnie Johnson had lost both his natural parents and the man who had raised him. He felt confused, bitter, isolated. "I'd fight at the drop of a hat," he admits shamefully. "I was good at it."

One afternoon, while in a particularly foul mood, he got into a brawl with a local boy "over something stupid" and ended up smashing the boy's nose with a horseshoe. The sight of blood brought Johnnie to his senses as he recalled the incident nearly two years before when had hit the bully with the railroad spike and nearly killed him. As the young man lay bleeding on the ground, Johnnie decided he wasn't cut out for a life of violence. "I knew I was eventually gonna kill somebody or get killed," he remembers. "I decided that street fightin' wasn't for me."

Instead, Johnnie channeled his energy and aggression into music, specifically the piano, which he had all but abandoned during his stay in Osage. During that time puberty had set in, and with it came drastic changes which were both strange and confusing, but in some cases beneficial. Upon returning to the keyboard, the teenage prodigy became aware of a distinct physical advantage that he had not had as a smaller boy—the size of his hands. By the time he was fourteen, Johnnie Johnson's hand span covered eleven white keys and he needed a size thirteen ring. He could play a full octave (seven keys) effortlessly, without even stretching, and he fit snugly between the black keys when playing flats. In addition, he noticed that he no longer had to use his whole body to play loudly, that just his wrists and hands alone could produce a full, powerful sound when playing boogie, or relate the proper intensity on songs like Avery Parrish's 'After Hours,' which required an attacking solo.

"Having big hands," says Johnnie, "gives me a heavier sound when I play and lets me get around the keys a little easier. When I was little there was just some things I couldn't play 'cause I couldn't stretch far enough or fast enough to make it sound right. It wasn't nothing I had control over, but it sure helped me to become a better piano player."

* * *

In September of 1938, Johnnie started Dunbar High School as a freshman. He had spent the remainder of the preceding summer practicing piano with a religious fervor, as if trying to make up in a single month the entire year he had missed in Osage. The practice paid off. Before long, he had reestablished himself as the top young piano player in town, joining his uncle at the fish fries and juke joints where he dazzled his elders with his amazing ability and repertoire. Word was getting around. It wasn't long before Johnnie was invited to join his first band.

Shortly after his first day of classes at Dunbar, Johnnie was approached by Clifford Brown, an older student who led a seven-piece combo called the Blue Rhythm Swingsters that played dances and socials around the area. Brown was in need of a pianist and felt Johnnie could more than fill the role. Johnnie had his doubts, since he had always played unaccompanied, but at the same time he was more than ready to test himself within the parameters of a rehearsed band. He told Clifford he would show up whenever they needed him.

"I had just started gettin' into the piano again when Clifford asked me to join his group," Johnnie remembers. "We rehearsed at school and got to be pretty good although we wouldn't have won any Battle of the Bands contests. It was fun getting up there and playing in front of the school and our friends. If we got paid two dollars a man at the end of the night with tips, that was good money!"

Music seemed to offer a way out for the teenage Johnnie, and it would seem logical that he would aspire for a life on stage. But this was not so. For despite his talent and the love he had for music, Johnnie could not imagine playing the piano for a living. Fairmont was hardly a hotbed of musical talent, and as members of a poor community, young men were expected to find jobs and contribute to the family. Music was considered a hobby, something fun to pass the time. No one actually took it seriously as a career option, including Johnnie.

"See, there just wasn't much of a music scene in Fairmont," he recalls. "I can't name a single musician who ever made it big. Sometimes a local booking agent would bring in the Dorseys or some other big band into the Fairmont Armory, and those of us who were interested would pay a dollar to check them out. Other than that, you joined the drum and bugle corps at school or played around town for fun. I did both and kept up my practicin' at home whenever I could."

In addition to music, Johnson also became involved in athletics, participating in football, baseball, basketball, and even boxing. The latter would bring him early success, and for a short time he toyed with the prospect of becoming a fighter, an idea that did not appeal at all to Cora Williams.

"She hated me fightin'," he remembers. "But I had a good reason. See, I pitched for the Elks and played basketball and football for the school. At that time I was strong as a bull but clumsy as an ox. I could press two hundred pounds easily, but I was always trippin' over my own feet. I guess that's what got me into boxin', and I did pretty good for a while. I won all my fights by knockout—not a single decision—and I started to get cocky. Well you know how it is when you get to thinking your better than you really are. I ran into this boy from Star City—a left-hander named Levi Scott—and he whipped me so bad, I couldn't see straight. When I got home, my Momma begged me to quit. She said I was liable to end up catchin' rainwater in my nose if I kept fightin'. I took one look at my face and realized she was right. That ended my boxin' career right there."

A typical teenage boy, Johnnie began to take notice of the opposite sex but found his quiet personality detrimental to his efforts to actually attract them. Shy and awkward around girls and too nervous to approach them, Johnnie and friend Donald Montgomery, the son of the football coach, would often sneak up to the gym in order to watch the girls during P.E. class. It was during one of these expeditions that he first laid eyes on Marguerite Rolls. "It was love at first sight—she was beautiful. I told Donald right then and there that I was gonna marry her," Johnson remembers.

Spirited and outgoing, Marguerite was the perfect companion for the reserved, soft-spoken Johnson, and it was with much trepidation that he finally found the courage to ask her out. She accepted, and before long they were an item. Years later, Marguerite remembers their dates as "pretty standard."

"We went to movies and dances and took long walks," she says of their courtship. "We did a lot of things together, had a lot of fun with each other talking and laughing."

In the evenings and on weekends, Marguerite often went to where the Blue Rhythm Swingsters were playing to listen to Johnnie play piano. As she recalls, "Whenever I went to see their little group, Johnnie would always make sure to play 'After Hours' for me because he knew it was my favorite. He won me over playing that song. To this day, whenever I hear 'After Hours,' I think of Johnnie Johnson."

"Marguerite and I had a good relationship back in high school," remembers Johnnie. "I guess you could say we was in love—we did a lot together. Movies and dances, or whatever. Everyone figured we was gonna get married."

Life had taken a turn for the better for Johnnie Johnson. He had his music, he had a girlfriend, and he was active in school with sports and the drum and bugle corps. But the carefree days of high school would be short-lived for Johnnie, and adulthood would arrive all too early.

In 1941, after his junior year, Johnnie was faced with a decision. The meager amount of life insurance money Cora Williams had received after her husband's death was nearly gone. She had saved and rationed, but the money had not stretched far enough, and now she was nearly broke. Johnnie knew it was up to him. Cora had taken care of him, raised him from an infant, now it was time to pay her back.

"When Momma told me what was going on, I knew what I had to do," Johnnie remembers. "I quit school the summer before my senior year and went lookin' for work."

Jobs in Fairmont were scarce at that time, especially for a young black man. Johnnie searched in vain for any sort of regular work, and although he found a few odd jobs, he was unable to make enough to get by.

Then a family friend named Jim Davis informed Johnnie that he could arrange a job for him in Detroit, Michigan, working for the Ford Motor Company. The pay wasn't great, but it was far more than he could make in Fairmont. Johnnie swallowed the lump in his throat and took the job. "I was sad to go," he recalls, "but we needed the money, and I wasn't about to let Momma starve."

* * *

Johnnie Johnson arrived in Detroit, a wide-eyed country boy of seventeen. He had never seen a big city, and there was little time to get acquainted before he was forced into the drudgery of the working world. He found a room on a Sunday and immediately went to work on Monday, clocking in at three in the afternoon and going home in the early hours of the next morning. Overtime was unlimited and even encouraged, and Johnnie took advantage of every opportunity to make extra cash, sending home part of each paycheck to support Cora Williams and spending only enough to survive.

"I would have loved to get into the club scene back then," says Johnnie of his first year in Detroit, "'cause I missed playing with a band. But there just wasn't no time for anything but work and sleep, and I barely had time for that. Momma needed the money, and I wasn't about to lose my job foolin' around on the piano. Three years later I wouldn't have said that, but back then I was all about work. I'd never known anyone who made any money as a musician. It was just a foolish dream of a lazy man who didn't want to work. I didn't want folks to look at me like that. So I put the piano on the shelf."

When war broke out in 1942, Johnnie found himself on the assembly line of a weapons plant, watching as his fellow workers received their draft notices and headed off to join the fight. By then he knew his own induction was inevitable and was not surprised when after a few months, he was given orders to report for the draft.

"They were gonna send me to the Army but I beat them to it," Johnnie laughs. "I joined the Marines. People ask me sometimes why I chose the Marines, and I have to say that back then it was mainly 'cause I liked those dress blue uniforms. The Army was just too plain for me and I wasn't much into the Navy either. Everyone joined the Army or Navy. The Marines were different and I respected them. I had to pass an I.Q. test to get in and take some other exams, but I made it. I got my uniform and went off to war. We were the first black company in World War II and I was one of the first 1500 black soldiers allowed in the Marines so I was getting to represent my people and my country at the same time. We started with forty-seven platoons and ended up with something like 148. In the beginning, all our drill instructors, what we called D.I.'s, were white men. But pretty soon, after we got the hang of things, we started having our own D.I.'s. I became a corporal and won a few medals for service and sharpshooting—nothing heroic. I was just proud to be part of it all."

As a member of a special weapons crew, Johnnie spent thirty-one months in the South Pacific assigned to secure captured territory—most of which he spent in the Marshall Islands building airstrips and pulling M.P. duty.

Nevertheless, despite a relatively tame tenure in the armed forces, the young G.I. had two close calls during those three years that almost took his life—neither of which involving actual combat.

"I had some free time one afternoon and we were all getting thirsty," he recalls of his first brush with death. "So I decided to start buildin' steps up a palm tree so I could get to the coconuts at the top, and then we could drink the juice. I did this by nailin' slats to the tree one by one and climbin' like a ladder. Anyway, I made it to the top and started twistin' off those coconuts, when all of the sudden, the slat I was standin' on broke and sent me face-first down the tree and into the coral rock. I don't know if you know anything about coral rock, but it's hard, thick, and sharp as razor blades. I was messed up bad, covered in blood, but the doctors were able to fix me up, and they did a damn good job, 'cause to this day I only have a small scar on my face from one nasty fall."

The second incident happened just a few months before the end of his tour. Johnnie and some other soldiers were finishing construction on an airstrip when an enemy plane, a Japanese Zero, made a surprise pass at the troops while they were absorbed in their work. Caught unawares, the Americans were sitting ducks and could only watch helplessly as the plane bore down upon them. "We'd just finished and were about to clear out," Johnnie recounts, "when a plane came down and fishtailed, the way pilots did to signal that they was an ally. We didn't think nothin' of it until one of us looked up and saw that the plane was a Zero. He didn't drop any bombs, and we found out later that he was either reconnaissance or a kamikaze pilot who had lost his nerve at the last minute. Can't say I'd blame him, and I'm sure glad he changed his mind."

With the exception of these two incidents, Johnnie's tour of duty remained relatively danger-free throughout. He was relegated to the motor pool, where he was assigned a variety of jobs. After going through what he called "the circle," including K.P., M.P., guard duty, and other menial tasks with great success, the young soldier was asked by a commander where he felt he might fit in best. Hungry for a chance to play his piano, Johnnie asked for a spot in the company band.

"After I took my I.Q. test, they put me in the motor pool," Johnnie laughs "which was perfectly okay with me. But when they gave me a choice and asked me what I wanted...well, there wasn't any fishin' duty, so I said I wanted to get into music 'cause that's what I was best at. That's how I got in with the Barracudas."

The Barracudas, were a twenty-two-piece orchestra led by a Lieutenant named Troop. Featuring members of Glen Miller's, Tommy Dorsey's, and Count Basie's orchestras, they were an elite group made up of some of America's finest jazz and swing musicians. As a premiere military band in World War II, they were assigned to many of the U.S.O. functions, including backing up such stars as Bob Hope and Betty Hutton. Troop and his confidants chose each musician from the hundreds of aspiring players who periodically tried out for positions in group auditions. "There were lots of guys who wanted in the band," remembers Johnnie. "Piano players were a dime a dozen."

Nevertheless, Troop and the other members of the Barracudas were impressed with the nineteen-year-old's abilities and chose him along with a pianist from Chicago to fill the vacant keyboard spots. For Johnnie, playing side-by-side with the players whom he had heard years before on the radio in Fairmont was a dream come true. He exulted in his position, missing shows and rehearsals only for guard duty and other required services.

"It was big-band swing, jazz, everything I love to play and then some," says Johnnie. "We did U.S.O. shows behind Bob Hope, Joe Stafford, and other big names. I remember those days as the most fun I've ever had on a piano. Here I was, nineteen, a small-town boy from West Virginia, playin' with cats from Lionel Hampton's band, Glenn Miller's band, even some of Count Basie's regulars. I learned a lot about performance and picked up things from the older fellas who had been around. We did several shows during that time and we had guys who played the same instruments and just switched in and out. There wasn't much pressure, but you had to pick things up quick, and of course they watched me 'cause I was so young. I had to prove myself to them and I did."

As would often be the case in years to come, Johnnie was the only member of the band who could not read music. The score sheets distributed before shows were meaningless to him, unintelligible marks on a page. While the other band members could simply reproduce note-for-note what they read on the page, Johnnie was totally dependent on his memory and improvisational ability. Learning by ear, uncorrupted by the rules and limitations of a formal musical education, allowed him a unique perspective on performance. For Johnnie Johnson's mind, while limited scholastically, was virtually an endless store of riffs and melodic patterns. He absorbed every song he heard and could, with split-second intuition, pick and choose from this vast library to suit his needs. Each performance promised something new as Johnnie would joyfully wend his way through a song, embellishing when appropriate, holding back when necessary, depending entirely on his mood. Even then, his music was unique. The late Ben Harris, a member of the Barracudas and a friend of Johnnie's, often remarked that even at age nineteen, "No one played like Johnnie. He had a style all his own."

"I did things differently 'cause I was self-taught and 'cause of what I had heard growin' up," notes Johnnie. "I never had anyone tellin' me, 'you have to play this way or that way.' I just did what I felt 'cause that's the only way I knew how to play."

In the end, Johnson found his tour in the Marines a rewarding experience. While he missed the States, he was grateful to have gotten the chance to serve his country during the war, a chance few blacks had during the segregated 1940s. Moreover, he was proud of being a Marine, and he relished their beliefs, their traditions. Even the painful ones.

"In the Marines we had a tradition that when you crossed the equator you became a 'Son of the Father Neptune'," Johnnie recalls. "The older soldiers would sit you down on the toilet and stick a needle through your left ear. Course, we had nothin' to numb the pain, so you just gritted your teeth while they stuck that needle in and followed it up with a broom straw which they kept turnin' until the hole got big enough for an earring. It hurt like nothin' else, but you stayed quiet 'cause you was a Marine and proud of the traditions. I still have my ear pierced to this day."

In 1946, Johnnie Johnson, twenty-two, returned home with a couple medals, a hole in his ear, and a firm grasp on what he wanted to do with his life. His tenure with the Barracudas had awakened a desire in him that he could not ignore, despite the hardships he knew he would suffer for the pursuit. He had found his place, and that place was on stage behind a piano. Looking out over the crowd and seeing the enjoyment on their faces—the smiles, the excitement, the feelings he himself had experienced when listening to the music— that was where he wanted to be. And he knew that if he could somehow transmit even a fraction of the joy he felt behind the piano to the audience, he would find his serenity.

Standing in a Detroit bus station, still dressed in his uniform, Johnnie felt exactly as he did the day he first sat down behind a piano—the moment when the shackles of his inborn shyness were cast off and he was able for the first time to express, to emote. He felt young. He felt alive. He felt free.

"I knew that no matter what, I was born to play the piano," he says, "and I would do whatever it took to make music my life. It wasn't about choosin'; this was something I had to do and I was gonna do it if it killed me. I can tell you now...it damn near almost did."

II

BLUEHAND JOHNNIE

"Johnnie Johnson is undoubtedly the best blues pianist in the world today." —Ahmet Ertegun, 1997

"I'll never forget the first time I really heard the blues," Johnnie Johnson says as he sips his Diet Coke. We are in Portland, Oregon, just the two of us, before a show with the legendary John Lee Hooker. The men are sharing a trailer, and with Johnnie's set finished, we have nothing to do but wait until Hooker arrives. As the subject turns to blues, I listen intently, for Johnnie, in the manner of the truly modest, holds his history closely, surreptitiously, like a straight flush in a high-stakes poker game. Any unsolicited divulgence on his part is a rare treat, not to be muddled by questions.

"It was back in Detroit," he continues, "must've been about 1947—late in the evenin'. I was downtown lookin' to hear some jazz and I walked by this place called the Cozy Corner. That's what they called it. But it didn't look cozy to me 'cause there was all kind of people dancing and carryin' on all the way out on the sidewalk. Spillin' their drinks everywhere. I was about to walk on past when I heard this guitar over top the rest of the music and it stopped me dead in my tracks. I said, 'I don't know where I'm goin' or if I'm stayin', but I'm gonna find out who's playin' that guitar.'"

He pushes his way through the mass of twisting bodies and finds a space near the bar where he can get a clear view of the stage. A woman sidles up to him, blocking his view with her considerable girth and drapes flabby arms around him. "You wanna buy me a drink, sugar?" Her breath is a fetid mix of booze, onions and stale cigarettes. He shakes his head. She dismisses him with a wave of her hand and stumbles into the arms of the man next to them who nearly topples over as he attempts to steady her. "Get your hands off me, goddamn it!" she screams. Everyone laughs. But not Johnnie. He doesn't even see it happen. He is watching the man with the guitar.

The band has finished whatever they were doing— something fast, a jump blues. Now the man with the guitar calls for the group to slow it down. He is small and not particularly handsome, the kind of man you would pass on the street without so much as a sideward glance. But this is not the street. On the bandstand he is a commanding presence, and the group of musicians falls in behind him as he strums his guitar softly and begins to sing.

> *They call it stormy Monday*
> *But Tuesday's just as bad*
> *Yes, they call it stormy Monday*
> *But Tuesday's just as bad*
> *Wednesday is worse*
> *And Thursday's oh so sad*

The club is a sea of swaying heads. Some men pull their women tight while others stare longingly into the amber depths of watery drinks and dream. The guitar has sliced through the rancorous night and the souls of each man and woman lay bare under the hazy blue lights.

> *The eagle flies on Friday*
> *And Saturday I go out to play*
> *Yes, the eagle flies on Friday*
> *And Saturday I go out to play*
> *Sunday I go to church*
> *And I kneel down and pray*

"T-Bone Walker," says Johnnie, shaking his head. "That man was bad. Had the whole club under a spell. He was doing 'Stormy Monday' and went off into this vamp and you could've knocked me over with a feather. I had never heard anything like what he was playin'. He could do things with a guitar no one had ever seen before—not until B.B. King came along at least. And it wasn't just his guitar playin'—it was his music, the whole band, it was all new to me. I said to myself, 'I am gonna learn to play the blues like this.'"

He smiles whimsically and empties the rest of his soft drink into a plastic cup, a task awkward for him because of his poor eyesight and the fact that the eight-ounce cup is almost invisible in his huge right hand. A small runner of cola leaks from his fingers and he quickly dabs it with a napkin.

"I guess I was taken with the blues from that point on," he recalls, "which wasn't too good, because I was supposed to be raising a family. I got back with Marguerite right after I got out of the service and we got married on February 22, 1946. She'd waited for me all that time while I was overseas. Since I had my job waiting for me in Detroit, that's where we moved, and it wasn't too long after that we had ourselves a baby boy. We named him John David."

With a growing family to support, Johnnie took his old job back at Ford and left Marguerite at home with the baby. For the first few months, he was more than up for the challenge of fatherhood. He prided himself on the fact that he was a dutiful husband and father and, although he did not make much of a salary, he was nonetheless able to provide for his family.

All things considered, the Johnsons led what most would consider an ideal domestic existence—an existence most men might have been content with. But not Johnnie. He lay awake most every night thinking about what he had left behind. There were other women, sure, and the freedom of being single and unattached. Yet it wasn't those temporal corners of his being that haunted him incessantly. It was the music: the fact that he'd forsaken his piano for the sake of practicality, when he knew in his heart that music was his destiny. He tried to push the thoughts out of his head, to rationalize, and reason, and pretend that he was happy with his life. In the end, his attempts were futile. When the music called to him again that night in 1947, Johnnie followed. His heart presented no other choice.

"The blues took my family away," he remembers. "Blues and alcohol. Same old story. Once I heard T-Bone and started gettin' into the blues and that whole late-night club scene in Detroit, that was where it all went wrong. I started goin' out at night. At first it would be only on the weekends—Fridays after work, then maybe Saturday. But after a while, I started goin' out during the week and stayin' two or three nights in a row while Marguerite was home taking care of our baby. She didn't want no part of that kind of life, and she told me so every time I came crawlin' back in from them clubs smellin' like beer. But I was a kid and I wouldn't listen. I just kept on goin' out. I wish I could say that it was only for the music, but I'd be lyin' if I did. Music was only half the reason I went out so much. The other half was so I could get drunk. I'd been drinkin' since I was seventeen, but I really started goin' heavy once I got into the clubs. It was just part of the whole scene. Drinkin' and the blues walked hand-in-hand."

He started drinking because he saw other men doing it. On the porch after work, in the juke joints, at the fish frys. It was something the men did. He didn't like the taste at first—the whiskey burned, the beer was sharp, the wine sour. But he kept on drinking because, he discovered, it made him happy. Because he could come out of his shell and be the life of the party He never got teary-eyed or mean like he saw some men get when they were on a drunk. He never got sick. He just talked and laughed and had a good time and everyone loved him. How could there be anything wrong with that?

"Most of the time you wouldn't have no idea just how much you had drank until you tried to stand up at the end of the night," recalls Johnnie. "That's when it hit you that maybe you had too much. That, and when you walk outside and the sun's shinin' in your face and you realize you've been out all night. You knew then you might be doing somethin' wrong. But the next night you be right back making the same mistake again 'cause it felt good while you was makin' it."

He shakes his head plaintively. Outside, the Paul DeLay band finishes up to a swell of applause which ebbs slowly as they leave the stage and the roadies start preparing for the next act. The P.A. system kicks back on halfway through some nameless blues that ends quickly and anonymously atop the restless chattering.

Then suddenly from the speakers, a familiar sound rings out, spilling over the grounds like an antediluvian dust. To me it is the sound I'd expect to hear faintly echoing from the musty bowels of some long abandoned Mississippi cabin in the dark and lonely hours of a sweltering summer night. The tin of a well-worn acoustic guitar and then the high mournful voice, an eerie falsetto that seems to come from far away in a place best left undisturbed.

I went to the crossroads
Fell down on my knees
I went to the crossroads

Fell down on my knees
Asked the Lord above, Have mercy, now
Save poor Bob, if you please

Robert Johnson—perhaps it's his legend, the mysterious nature of his death, and tales of his self-professed deal with the devil that chills me each time I hear his music. Then again, maybe it is the picture, not the posed, smiling, dandied-up portrait on the front of his anthology, but the other less-publicized grainy black-and-white featuring him in his natural state, cigarette drooping from disdainful lips, spidery fingers tensed on the fretboard. There is a distinct duality of Robert Johnson's countenance in that particular photograph. The right side of his face is sad and doleful, a naive country boy, while the left is cold, calculating, sociopathic—the kind of man who could slit your throat and watch you die while he ate his supper. Perhaps it was the devil in him.

"That's Robert Johnson," I say aloud, hoping to elicit a response from Johnnie, who has also tuned in to the music filtering in from outside. "Well if he's here, too," Johnnie replies, "I'm leavin'!" We both laugh. Johnnie nods towards the door.

"See, that's what I'm talkin' about—havin' feelin' in your playin'," he says. "The way Robert Johnson plays. Some folks can play all the notes, but it just don't sound the same as someone who has feelin', or what we call soul. The blues is all about putting your feelings out in the keys you playin'—whatever you play, even if it's a kazoo—music comes from inside. That's the soul."

* * *

In 1940s post-War Detroit, where a young John Lee Hooker spent his nights boogie chillin' down on Hastings Street and his days sweeping floors at Comco Steel, soul was a plentiful commodity. What mattered was if you had the chops and if you could play what people wanted to hear. Johnnie Johnson certainly had the chops; his playing had greatly improved during his stint with the Barracudas, but the nearly three years spent overseas playing big-band swing had left him ignorant of the new trends and completely out of the developing music scene. Upon returning to Detroit, he found that his beloved swing music had been replaced by bop and the raw sound of electric blues, a style pioneered by the virtuoso he had seen on stage at the Cozy Corner, Aaron Thibeaux "T-Bone" Walker.

A direct disciple of Blind Lemon Jefferson, for whom he had collected tips as a small boy, Walker had a firm grasp on the fundamentals of Delta blues and the shuffle beat. Along with this knowledge he combined the precision of jazz soloing, a skill he acquired through stints with bandleaders Lawson Brooks and Count Biloski. Ironically, it was Walker's departure from Brooks's band that allowed Charlie Christian to take his place and become the second great electric jazz guitarist. The first was T-Bone himself.

In terms of the electric guitar and its evolution in popular music, T-Bone Walker was a pioneer, a genius, with a mind for experimentation the likes of which would not be seen again for nearly thirty years, when Jimi Hendrix began working his magic with feedback and distortion effects. His tone was clear, the notes precise, the delivery self-assured and flawless, even when exploring the outer limits of what was then possible in live musical performance. He was a master of his craft and his performances reflected both limitless skill and unbridled passion.

Johnnie Johnson dreamed of someday playing on stage with the likes of Walker. But at twenty-two, he lacked the experience necessary to join a band, much less secure a regular gig in Detroit's highly competitive club scene. As an aspiring musician, he had two choices: to stick with the jazz clubs on the east side near Gratiot Avenue, or try his luck in a seedy area known as the "Black Bottom," where questionable establishments like the menacingly monickered Bucket of Blood offered raucous rhythm and blues and a fair share of trouble for a small-town boy with little street sense and a head full of liquor. Johnnie chose the jazz clubs.

"You could get yourself killed down in the Black Bottom," Johnnie remembers. "I'd go down there once in a while, but for the most part I stayed up on Gratiot and tried to set in with some of the jazz bands. I loved the blues, and I'd go down there to listen. In fact, I think that's where I met John Lee for the first time. But when it came to sittin' in, I was strictly jazz. At that time, the blues was called 'old man's music' and there wasn't too many places outside the Black Bottom where folks wanted to hear it. I found out soon as I started goin' to the clubs that if you wanted to get jobs, you had to play jazz. So that's what I did. 'Course they had to know you before they even gave you a chance to sit in at them jazz clubs. Jazz players can be kind of uppity 'bout who they let play with them. But after a few months of goin' to the clubs at night, gettin' up courage, I finally got my chance to play with some of the bands.

"Now I could play all kinds of big-band jazz and boogie, but they didn't care nothin' 'bout that. Big band was out and boogie was for the house parties. They was into Dizzy Gillespie, Charlie Parker, Art Tatum, and all that new-style jazz. I didn't know nothin' 'bout all that. There was this song 'Honeydripper' that was popular in them days. By the time I got into the scene it'd been out for a couple of years; everybody knew 'Honeydripper,' but I was just hearin' it for the first time. That's how far out of it I was. I didn't even know what was happenin' two years before!

"When I finally got to sit in, I only knew one popular song, 'September in the Rain,' that I tried to play like Errol Garner. And I tried a lot. After the first time, when I got a little applause from the crowd, I kept comin' back almost every night. It used to drive them jazzmen nuts. They used to say, 'Here comes Johnnie Johnson again. Just let him play his one song and leave.' I'd get up on stage, play 'September in the Rain,' then sit back down in the audience.

"At first it was kind of a joke, but then they got tired of me askin' and would make up excuses when they didn't have the patience to let me up on stage. I knew what they was doin', but I kept coming anyway. Then they started tryin' to embarrass me by changin' the tempo or key in the middle of the song. I looked like a fool more than once, but I kept on comin'.

"Finally," he remembers, "they stopped lettin' me play at all—wouldn't even let me on stage. They'd just ignore me until I went away or tell me to go on and get lost.'You ain't gettin' up here, man. Just sit down.' I heard that quite a bit. It broke my heart and I felt real bad for a while, but I was determined to show them that I could play them songs as good as anybody."

The blatant rejection by the local talent was a first for Johnnie. He took it hard. Not once in seventeen years of playing piano had his ability been called into question. Now as feelings of self-doubt wormed their way into his consciousness, he found temporary solace in alcohol and imbibed more frequently than ever, escaping into blissful forgetfulness and the dark and empty sleep which often follows.

But when morning came and the cold slap of sobriety awakened him from his binge, only two things remained: a dull ache in his head and the unflagging desire to learn the new music and prove them all wrong. In the end, he would not be deterred.

"I disappeared," Johnnie says candidly. "For a whole year I just disappeared altogether from the big clubs. Where I'm from, when you go back and start workin' on improvin' yourself, that's what we call 'goin' back to the woodshed.' That's what I did. I went back to the woodshed."

For the next twelve months, Johnnie practiced with religious fervor. There was no money for a piano, but he found one at the local musician's union, where he spent hours upon hours working out the popular standards. He kept tabs on the current trends, bought new records whenever possible and promptly stored them in his head, as he had done as a boy, until he could get to the piano.

"The whole year I was either workin' or practicin', which didn't sit too well with Marguerite," recalls Johnnie. "She'd had another baby, Connie, and with two kids at home, I should have been there helpin' out more. Of course, I didn't think nothin' 'bout that. I just kept thinkin' how bad I wanted to play and how them jazzmen was laughing at me. I'd stay up nights thinkin' 'bout it. All I wanted to do was play with a real band, and after a year of practicin', I finally got to where I could."

* * *

The drummer sees him first, near the back of the club. "Ain't that fool Johnnie Johnson?" he asks, pointing to the young man approaching the stage. The alto saxophonist looks up, blinks twice, then nods. "That's him all right." He picks up his instrument from where he has laid it between sets and pretends to fix the mouthpiece.

Johnnie stands before them as always, head down, hands in his pockets, his voice barely audible in the din of the club. "You fellas mind if I set in for a song or two?" he asks.

The alto saxophonist smirks but doesn't look up. The drummer opens his mouth to tell him to take a hike when the tenor saxophonist, the leader of the group, cuts in.

"Johnnie Johnson! Where you been, man? We figured you must have give up and left town."

Someone stifles a laugh. The hands in the young man's pockets clench into fists, but he answers calmly.

"I've been around."

"Well, we ain't seen you. You hit the big time already?" He winks at the drummer.

The young man ignores the comment, but feels his anger rise. He knows when he is being ridiculed.

"Well, you ought to come on up and show us how it's done, man. We gonna start the next set real soon. You don't mind if Johnnie sets in, do ya?" He turns to the pianist who giggles as he gives up his seat.

"Naw, man. Be my guest."

The young man climbs on stage and sits down behind the piano, barking his shin on the bench and nearly tripping on an amplifier. He keeps his head down in a vain effort to block out the titters and whispers from the crowd, most of whom recognize him. The tenor saxophonist walks to the microphone.

"Y'all are in for a treat now, 'cause we got the man over here on piano gonna do his thing. Ain't that right, Johnnie?"

The crowd bursts into laughter.

"September in the Rain?" The bassist asks.

The young man doesn't answer, but begins to play, his fingers picking out the intro to 'How High the Moon.' The drummer raises his eyebrow, then joins in, the rest of the band following suit. A minute into the song, the young man suddenly changes the tempo, and the drummer winces at what he thinks is a mistake. Irritated, he clambers to catch the signature, then starts when the young man changes the key and then changes it again. At that moment, they all know this is a different pianist than the one they had hoped to send home shamed once and for all.

Before long he has broken into an entirely different song and there is tension on the tenor saxman's face as he scrambles to figure out the key. The song is brand new. They have not rehearsed it. Finally he catches on and they are in sync again, if only for a moment. The alto sax fixes the tenor with a worried glance. He turns to the bass player, but the man is occupied by the youngster's left hand, his eyes never leaving the keyboard as he follows the notes on his bass. Nobody laughs. Not anymore. They are too busy trying to keep up.

"You should have seen the looks on their faces," Johnnie smiles at the memory, a rare moment of pride for a man known to be humble to a fault. "Then they started askin' me if I knew any others. I said, 'If you can play it, I know it.' The work had paid off. All the sudden, I had all these bands beggin' me to join up with them. It was great! I think it was after that night I really became a piano player and not just some kid tryin' to play."

He turns to face me. The smile is gone.

"'Course, I never forgot what it felt like to be kicked off the stage," he says. "I was never bitter towards the fellas who did it, 'cause I knew the reasons for them doin' it. Those were lean times for musicians, and they didn't have no time to fool around with me not knowin' what I was doin'. But that don't mean I agree with it, though. There's been a lot times that I've been the one up on the bandstand and some kid, or maybe just someone who ain't that good, wants to come up and play with me. If it's up to me, I'll let them come on up. This is because I remember how I felt back when I was tryin' to sit in and learn. Ain't no reason to embarrass somebody. They might embarrass themselves, but you let 'em 'cause that's how they'll learn. You have to give folks a chance."

* * *

A few minutes later, John Lee Hooker arrives with his entourage in tow. "There he is!" Johnnie calls out as the door opens and the elder statesman of the blues steps in. This is the first time that I have seen Hooker in person and I am surprised at how small he is physically. The growling persona he portrays on stage truly belies his actual size. His manager, Mike Kappas, leads him to the couch and he settles on his throne, surrounded by an array of bandmates, aids, and well-wishers. Someone asks him to autograph a guitar, and he graciously complies, signing the Gibson ES135 with a quavering child-like scrawl. The ancient hands are racked with tremors as he writes, and when he speaks there is a distinct stutter in his voice.

Watching him, I realize that this man should not be able to sing like he does or even hold a guitar, much less play it with such dexterity and skill. The fact that he can still perform at such a level is incredible. John Lee Hooker is a living testament to the power of the human spirit.

As he finishes, I reach out to shake his hand, but he is occupied by the instrument on his lap. He turns it this way and that, examining the neck and body, the finish. Finally, with undisguised tenderness, he returns the guitar and I shake his hand. Like many musicians, Hooker's is a gentle handshake, with only a hint of the strength it possesses. In his case, it is more than I could even comprehend.

When I return to our side of the trailer, Johnnie is halfway through his second Diet Coke.

"He sure does have a lot of friends," I say.

"That's John Lee all right," Johnnie answers between gulps. "Everybody loves him."

"When did you first play with him?" I ask.

"Well, like I said, I met him in Detroit, but I first played with him back in Chicago, not that he'd remember. I moved there in 1949 after things got too tough in Detroit. Too much backstabbing and politics going on behind the scenes. Too much competition. You'd get hired for twenty dollars and there'd be ten other piano players better than you who would do the gig for fifteen dollars. Everyone was desperate for work. Besides music, my marriage was also falling apart. With my drinking and late hours, I was always gone and I lost a lot of good jobs because I missed too many Mondays or showed up hung over. Marguerite tried to get me to join the musician's union and get better gigs, but even then I couldn't make ends meet without working, and I just wasn't good at keeping jobs. We'd had our third baby, Barbara Jean, by then, and with three kids she needed more than I could give her at that time. We got separated, and after that I moved to Chicago to follow the blues."

* * *

Since before the Civil War when it was known by southern whites as a "nigger-loving town," the city of Chicago, Illinois, has meant freedom for the American black. From its antislavery campaigns and liberal policies towards segregation to its role as a thriving industrial metropolis, the Windy City offered an enticing alternative to the sunbaked cotton fields and pestilent swamps of Georgia, Louisiana, and Mississippi.

Following the abolition of slavery in 1865, the city's pioneer black newspaper, *The Chicago Defender*, called for a "Great Northern Drive," inducing thousands of southern blacks to abandon their plows for a chance at a new life far from the painful reminders of whips and servitude. Before long, observes Francis Davis in *The History of the Blues*, "There were stretches of the South Side that resembled Mississippi, with chickens raised in backyard pens and hand-lettered signs on grocery stores advertising fresh fish."

For the most part, however, Chicago was a city of brick walls and concrete streets with the southern willow trees and cattails replaced by buildings and signposts: a place where the mystique of the mighty Mississippi was completely lost in the frigid depths of Lake Michigan, and where the fresh country air, long taken for granted, was now just a sweet memory, rudely swapped for the choking smog belched from the smokestacks and factories.

Thus, it was no surprise that, despite the negativity associated with the South, many blacks soon found themselves longing for familiar southern amenities, namely the food, the weather, and the countryside, none of which could be accurately reproduced in a city environment. Nothing was as good as fresh vegetables grown in the rich southern soil or the guaranteed quality of one's own livestock. The Chicago winter would always be harsh and bitterly cold. And the only thing a man had to fall asleep to at night were the dissonant sounds of a restless city.

In the end, the only part of their past they could really bring with them was the music. The music, like the souls of the people, lived within. And as long as grandfathers kept picking their guitars for their grandsons in the evenings after work, and as long as granddaughters harmonized while their grandmothers peeled potatoes and sang the old songs, the music would never die, but would continue to thrive in the fertile soil of youthful exuberance.

* * *

The tradition of the Delta blues can be tracked to the first boatload of slaves to arrive in America and the heavy-hearted "work songs" they sang in the fields to take their minds off the grueling labor. Its musical roots can be similarly traced from the single-stringed diddley-bows and banjos (based on the West African konting) which led to the first guitars, and subsequently to the men like Son House and Blind Lemon Jefferson who learned through trial and error to make them speak. To most blacks living in Chicago during the twentieth century, the blues represented tradition, and where there was tradition, there was home.

One of the key figures in making Chicago more liveable for the black transplant was a Georgian named Hudson Whitaker, who because of his fiery red hair and the fact that he was raised in Tampa, Florida, carried the moniker "Tampa Red."

A wicked slide guitarist, Red brought his southern stylings to Chicago in the mid-1920s. By the 1930s, the small apartment he shared with his wife over a pawnshop on 35th and State had become the waystation for bluesmen and the centerpiece of the developing Chicago blues scene. Artists such as Big Bill Broonzy, Lonnie Johnson, and Washboard Sam practically lived in Red's living room as did producer Larry Melrose, the man whose Bluebird beat became the standard for how a pre-WWII blues record should sound. Later, Muddy Waters and Willie Dixon would be seen regularly at Red's place as well, strumming along with the master in the traditional Delta style. Tampa Red would remain the godfather of Chicago blues until his death in 1981.

Needless to say, by the time Johnnie Johnson arrived in 1949, the Chicago style of blues was well established. Players like Waters and Dixon began defining the genre for a new generation of blacks to whom the South was known only as a heritage and not a remembered reality. Chess Records, a family owned company controlled by two brothers, Leonard and Phil Chess, had been recording blues artists for two years, and for the first time, black America was recognized as an important and profitable buying market. Chess, in fact, often gauged the potential success of their records by the favorable or unfavorable reaction of the old black women waiting at the bus stop in front of their Cottage Grove studio.

"In the summertime we'd have the door open and we had the turntable," Phil Chess says in the PBS documentary *Rock and Roll*. "We'd cut a session the night before and we'd test record it, play it over and over. You'd see these old women waiting for the bus with the Muddy Waters record and they'd say 'What is that? Man, that sure sound good!' Well hey, we got a record!"

As an aspiring blues pianist, Johnnie Johnson could not have arrived at a better time, although as he says, "It wasn't easy on the heart." His experience on the lines at Ford provided him with a good job at the company's Chicago plant. But coming home to an empty apartment made him miss the comforts of the family he had taken for granted and lost. Lonely and frustrated, he turned to the clubs for support, spending his evenings on State Street, where he drank the night away, immersed in the sounds of some of the greatest blues players of all time.

In the late forties and early fifties, Chicago was known as the Mecca of the Blues. In one night, and for a small price, a young student of the blues like Johnnie Johnson could attend master classes in the style with professor Muddy Waters and his unparalleled band, sit in on an extensive lecture by Memphis Slim, or perhaps catch Big Joe Williams, a genuine Delta legend with his famous nine-string guitar, picking out history on his worn fretboard.

With such a slew of talent available for review, it is little wonder that Johnnie could not stay away from the clubs, and before long he came into contact with several kindred spirits who shared his love and enthusiasm for the blues. One of these enthusiasts, an outgoing veteran of the club scene named Milton Rektor, took Johnnie under his wing and began introducing him to the men who would become known as the fathers of post-WWII blues.

"Milton and I hit it off one night and after that he got me into the scene right away," Johnnie recalls. "He was a friendly kind of fella and he knew everybody in town, all the big players like Muddy Waters, Little Walter, Memphis Slim. Milton Rektor knew all these people and he'd take me around and introduce me to them. 'This is Johnnie Johnson, he's a good piano player, you should let him set in with you.' Fool hadn't even heard me yet and he was tellin' people like Muddy Waters I could play! They was liable to laugh me off the stage, but he convinced 'em and, sure enough, they would. Muddy Waters was real good about that and he didn't mind lettin' me set in once and a while.

"I liked Muddy and for the most part we got along real well. There was only one time I can remember that I got on his bad side. This was years later in St. Louis. We were all hangin' around backstage one night after a show just talkin' and whatever, when Muddy handed me some money and asked me to go out and get him a bottle of this whiskey that he liked—I can't remember what it was called right now, but whatever it was it was good whiskey, better than I could afford.

"Anyway, since I was no stranger to the bottle, I couldn't help openin' it up on the way back and takin' a little sip. I didn't think nothin' of it, I was just tastin'. Well, when I gave him the whiskey he took one look at it and handed it back. 'Why's this bottle open?'

"I told him I had taken a little taste of it and he gave me this stare. When I tried to give him the whiskey he wouldn't take it. 'It's yours now,' he said. I felt awful because there was no way I could afford to buy him a new bottle. I tried and I tried to get him to take it, but he just shook his head and wouldn't touch it. I always thought it was because of superstition or not wanting germs, until I found out about what had happened to Robert Johnson getting poisoned by a club owner for foolin' around with the man's wife. Muddy heard about that, and from then on he wouldn't take an open bottle from anybody—friends, family, it didn't matter.

"Muddy and Chuck were on the same label, and a lot of times he came in the studio right after us. In fact, it was Muddy who sent Chuck over to see Chess before we did 'Maybellene.' Muddy was the big man around there so I got to see him a lot through the years, even after I'd moved to St. Louis.

"Another good friend from those days was Memphis Slim. He was a piano player too, and he and I became pretty tight with each other. He'd call me up to play sometimes and was always real encouragin' to me. Slim was another guy I saw a lot, even after I'd moved to St. Louis, since he recorded for Chess, too, every now and then. I remember him tryin' to convince me to go to Paris with him in 1962. But I wasn't gonna leave the states and I wasn't gonna fly. "Years later, when Chuck and I went to Paris, he was the openin' act, and man, you talk about a followin'! Slim had built himself an empire over there with mansions and cars and everything you could want. I don't think there were any other blues players in France, so Slim had the whole place to himself. That man pulled up to the show in a Rolls. He was a king over there; they gave him all kinds of titles and awards. I think he was still tourin' when he died. What a character!"

In 1951, Rektor, a part-time bass player, asked Johnnie about forming a group to cash in on the live music scene. "It was me, Milton Rektor on bass, some guy named Curtis on sax, and Andrew 'Boots' Thomas on drums," Johnnie recalls. "After we played together, the fellas agreed to call the band the Johnnie Johnson Quartet, after my name, which was somethin' Milton came up with. I guess 'cause my name sounded the best out of all of them. We all loved the blues, but at that time the blues was still considered 'old man's music' and all the youngsters, people under forty, wanted to hear jazz. So jazz was what we played. Sometimes, when we thought we could get away with it or when we was practicing, we'd do some blues, which was kind of like a break for us.

"See, technically, the blues is not hard to play at all. With jazz you can have up to sixty-four bars with all kinds of tempo and key changes. But in blues you got twelve or eight bars with changes every eight or four, so you just pick a key and ride it out. After jazz it ain't no big thing."

While this generalization may have held true for Johnnie Johnson, it is not always necessarily so. According to Francis Davis, one of the biggest myths in music is that any "jazz improviser worth his salt is also a superlative blues player." He cites several examples of great jazz improvisers like Art Tatum, Coleman Hawkins, and Bud Powell, who were only average or even subpar blues players.

In Davis' view, this discrepancy derives from a difference in definition. "When jazz musicians speak of 'playing the blues,'" he says, "they mean using a tune twelve bars long and in the key of B-flat as a springboard for harmonic improvisation. This is quite different from what Robert Johnson took the phrase to mean, and different from what John Lee Hooker still takes it to mean close to sixty years after [Louis] Armstrong more or less set the guidelines for jazz improvisation with his solo on 'West End Blues.' And for what it's worth, blues musicians have long favored the keys of A and E, not B-flat."

Johnnie Johnson developed his blues style by capturing the feel of a piece, then elaborating with his own ideas. Although he was surrounded at the time by great blues pianists, including his friend Memphis Slim, Johnnie chose not to imitate, but instead developed his own interpretation of blues piano.

"When people ask me about what's the best way to play this or how they should play that, I tell them just relax and play what they feel," Johnnie says. "Do what you think is right for you. I have all kinds of jazz heroes like Oscar Peterson, Count Basie, and Earl Hines, but I've never had any blues piano heroes. What I learned about blues I taught myself. People have said to me many times that they can tell my playin' as soon as they hear it, even if it's just for a second or two. They say I have a style all my own. This is because of the way that I learned. It don't mean that I am any better blues player than anybody else. If you've ever heard Oscar Peterson sit down and play straight blues, then you know that's true! It's just because it's different. What I play is what I hear in my head, and a lot of what I hear in my head has a swing feel to it that is different from how most blues pianists play. When this band I had with Milton got together, there wasn't nobody tellin' you, 'Don't do this' or 'You have to play like that.' You played what you felt was right to you. I think that's what makes the blues special. In jazz you got a conversation with all kinds of people sayin' different things. In blues you got a bunch of folks sayin' pretty much the same thing but in different ways. It's how you say it that matters."

The Johnnie Johnson Quartet remained together for Johnson's entire stay in Chicago. Through Rektor's connections, the group was able to land regular gigs, and though they never became big by any stretch, Johnson was doing better than he ever had. He felt good, and more importantly, he was doing what he loved.

"I was livin' fine at first. I finally joined the musicians union—local 208—and Milton started gettin' us gigs at places like the Subway Lounge, Ada's Lounge, Smitty's Corner, little clubs. Most of them have been torn down and replaced by highways. I had a good day job workin' at the motor plant and plenty of time for music on the weekends. I felt so good and I was hopin' to get Marguerite and the kids—you know, to get another chance and try to start over. Well, this was in 1950 and it wasn't but a few months until Marguerite's brother was killed in Korea. Her family was real close and havin' a real hard time of it, so Marguerite took the kids back to Fairmont to help out. Her daddy was glad to see her home. He didn't like me much—said I was a bad provider or whatever. Anyways, what happened was, while she was there she met another man and ended up stayin' in Fairmont for good. I didn't see her again for seven years."

His family gone, Johnson began a dramatic downward spiral. Although he was able to hold onto the band, the rest of his life crumbled, and before long he was out on the street with nowhere to go and only the bottle to keep him company.

"After Marguerite left, things went pretty much downhill. I was drinkin' a lot by then and losin' every day job I had because of it. After a while I quit tryin' to find jobs and started tryin' to make a livin' off the gigs. I thought I could do all right, but it just didn't pay the bills. Back then you could make anywhere from eight to ten dollars per show and you'd be lucky to get three shows a week. Well, what seemed like a lot of money when you had a full-time job wasn't much when it was all you had to go on. I usually cleared about twenty dollars a week and my rent was twelve dollars a week. That didn't leave much for anything else and my money was runnin' out. Pretty soon I couldn't make the rent anymore and I was out on the street.

"This was in the wintertime and it was cold—lots of snow. If you stayed outside you'd freeze to death, and I had to learn quick where to go to keep warm. Most nights I spent goin' back and forth between the bus station and the train station tryin' to catch some sleep. When one kicked me out I'd go to the other until they kicked me out, and on and on until mornin'. Sometimes I'd get a hold of a quarter and then I could sleep in the movie theater where it was warm. The ushers would let you stay inside as long as you wanted if they didn't catch you sleepin'. The way I got around this was by waddin' up newspaper length-wise and stuffin' one end in my shirt and the other under my chin. That way I could keep my head up and the ushers couldn't tell if I was asleep.

"I lived this way for quite a while until I got so desperate that I called my mother and asked her to wire me a loan. The only problem with this was that I didn't have no address where she could send the money, and I didn't want to tell her the truth. I was embarrassed enough that I had to ask her. I finally just decided to starve rather than let her think I was on the street and worry her. I had really hit the bottom.

"Finally, I called my oldest brother Pless, and he told me to come out to East St. Louis 'cause he could get me a job at Penn Railroad.

I arrived in the middle of the night on March 31, 1952. I remember 'cause it was the evenin' before April Fools, and when I went out the next morning and saw the city, I said right then and there that I was never gonna leave. I've been in St. Louis ever since."

Johnnie chuckles at the memory and takes a cigar out of his breast pocket, lighting it with practiced precision. The room fills with the sweet brown smell of tobacco.

"I stayed with my brother for a little while 'til I got on my feet. First thing I did was get a job. Turned out Penn wasn't able to give me full-time work, so I found a higher payin' job at the Swiss Meat Packin' Plant, workin' on the line slittin' pigs' throats. That ended up being a bad decision 'cause I almost lost my career over it.

"We were real busy and I was workin' faster than usual, grabbin' the pig, slicin' the throat with this big 'ol knife they give you...when I just happened to look down to see my left thumb hangin' by a thread. I had almost cut it off and didn't even feel it. It had gone numb right away, and there was so much blood on my hands anyway, I just figured it was pig's blood.

"I left work and went up to Barnes Hospital where this little Oriental doctor sewed my thumb back on. He said if my thumb hadn't been as thick I probably would have sliced it clean off. I guess I can thank him as much as anyone for my career, and I wish I could remember his name. He did a real good job, 'cause there ain't hardly any scar left and I can move my thumb without any problem. After that day, I never went back to the meat packin' plant. Next job I got was at the American Steel Foundry, and I stayed there 'til we started goin' out on the road."

A year after he arrived, Johnnie's life was once again marred by tragedy. Pless, who had all but rescued him from a life on the streets, was killed by a self-inflicted gunshot wound. Johnnie was devastated.

"Pless died not too long after I got to St. Louis," he says somberly. The memory still bothers him. "He shot himself accidently. He and I loved to fish together, and Pless loved bein' out in the country, 'cause that's where we was from. Only one thing he hated 'bout being out in the woods, and that was snakes. He used to carry a .25 with him for when he went fishin' to kill snakes. Well, .25s have a hair trigger on them—it don't take too much to set them off. Pless had bought himself a washing machine and the bell was broke on it. So he went back to the store to get it repaired and while he was takin' the gun out of his pants pocket and puttin' it in his jacket pocket so he could get his money out, the gun went off and shot him in the stomach. Pless had ulcers and that bullet tore him all up—he walked outside, fell down on the sidewalk and died."

To combat the grief in the aftermath of his brother's death, Johnnie delved into his music. The clubs in East St. Louis weren't as plentiful as those in Chicago or even Detroit, but there was one benefit—they stayed open twenty-four hours a day.

Once again, Johnnie began to explore the idea of forming his own band. Within two weeks, he had hooked up with a local jazz drummer named Ebby Hardy. After a couple shows with just piano and drums, Johnnie hired a saxophonist named Alvin Bennett to fill out the sound. Within a month, the Johnnie Johnson Trio, or Sir John's Trio, was born.

"Back then, the way to get regular gigs was by gettin' a trio together, so I hired Alvin and Ebby," Johnnie remembers. "We played mostly popular standards like 'Stardust' and 'Satin Doll' with some boogie and blues mixed in. Both Ebby and Alvin were great musicians and good people, so we got along real well and enjoyed playin' together.

"Wasn't too long, couple months maybe, we started to make a name for ourselves around East St. Louis, and Joe Lewis offered us a job playin' Friday, Saturday and Sunday at his Cosmopolitan Club for twenty-six dollars a night plus tips. I got ten dollars and the other fellas split the other sixteen dollars, which was a high payin' gig at that time. I guess we had a good thing goin' compared to a lot of the musicians in town."

By the summer of 1952, Johnnie Johnson was twenty-eight years old. He had played with some of the best jazz and blues musicians and was now a seasoned professional. More importantly, in a matter of just four months, he had won a regular gig at one of the biggest clubs in East St. Louis and established himself as a top-rate pianist in a city where piano playing was more than just a form of entertainment. It was a tradition.

* * *

According to pianist James "Stump" Johnson, a legend in his own right, boogie-woogie piano was invented in St. Louis by an aging and unrecorded barrelhouse player named Son Long. Although this is a highly controversial theory, since boogie-woogie roots can be traced back to a number of areas including Chicago and New Orleans, the very fact that Johnson would make such a claim points to a very proud and rich musical heritage. Scott Joplin wrote his "Maple Leaf Rag" in St. Louis, and Charles Thompson and Louis Chauvin, both masterful ragtime pianists, also operated in the city.

In *A Left Hand Like God,* Peter J. Silvester notes that the St. Louis style "has an underlying sense of urgency and disquiet to its music which is some way removed from the relaxed playing of pianists from the southern states." Taking into account the city's troubled history, it is no surprise that the music of St. Louis might have a tinge of disconcert.

Originally a French trading post, St. Louis developed quickly into a commercial port town worked primarily by black immigrants from the South. By the early 1900s, it had become one of the toughest cities in America. Gambling, prostitution, police corruption, and poverty were rampant and citizens were discouraged from traversing the downtown area whenever possible.

In 1917, racial tensions between longtime white residents and newly arrived blacks erupted into one of the worst race riots in American history. Thirty-nine blacks and nine whites were brutally murdered in East St. Louis over race-related issues, most of which involved job competition. Outnumbered and outgunned, the black citizens came out on the losing end and as a consequence, life became harder than ever.

Forced to reside in overcrowded slums for exorbitant prices, most blacks found the monthly task of making rent payments a weary struggle and barely worth the effort. In order to survive, some enterprising members of the community began teaming together. Thus "rent parties," a tradition originated in Chicago, became a regular part of the St. Louis lifestyle in the early to mid-1900s. These gatherings were most often held in the unfortunate resident's flat, where bootleg liquor was consumed and dancers performed to the music of a pianist. Local brothels and gambling joints soon caught on to the popularity of these "buffet flats" and began hiring their own pianists to draw in the crowds that would normally frequent these shindigs for the liquor and the music.

Out of the demand for dance music, a new style of piano playing began developing to complement the wild and rowdy nature of the patrons. This style, called "boogie-woogie," was built around an ostinato "eight-to-the-bar" bass pattern and a right hand that either followed or played off the bass. Perhaps the most essential element of the style was the irrevocable need for complete independence— the ability to play two different and separate patterns often in different time signatures, without one hand impeding the other. From this vein sprang a number of talented individuals, each well-versed in the boogie style. Among them, Walter Davis, Henry Brown, Rufus "Speckled Red" Perryman, and the great Roosevelt Sykes, became legends on the rent-party circuit and in the local saloons. When Johnnie Johnson came to town in 1952, each of the four were still active in the music community.

Unlike Chicago, East St. Louis had no curfew, and a person could party all night if he was so inclined. For Johnnie, this rule or lack thereof provided an endless array of playing possibilities. Drinking and carousing at all hours, Johnson would sometimes stay up two or three nights in a row, bouncing back and forth between East-side clubs, sitting in with the bands, or just listening to the music. The long hours took their toll, but as Johnson says, "I was young enough that it didn't bother me much."

"In them days I never got tired of playin' piano," he recalls. "Didn't matter how I felt before I got up, once I was behind them keys, everything was fine. I'd sit in with a group from four to eight, then run over and do my show at the Cosmo until two. After that I'd go sit in around town until nine or so the next mornin', play a breakfast show until noon or so, catch a little nap, and then play again from two until six in the evenin'. Then it was back at the Cosmo again, and so on. This was my typical weekend activity. Now, lots of folks have told me that I would have had to be on drugs to keep up that pace, but I never touched no dope or speed or nothin' like that. Alcohol was my one and only drug—not sayin' that drinkin' is any better than drugs, they both bad for you. But like I tell them: When you love something that much, the way I loved playin' piano, the way I still love playin' piano, there wasn't no such thing as tired. Any chance you got to play, you took. No questions asked. Playin' the piano was everything to me, and I wasn't about to let sleep get in the way of that. I guess you could say I needed the piano more than I needed to sleep."

A true lover of music, Johnnie did not discriminate based on the size or reputation of a club. Throughout the course of an evening, he may have stopped by the Manhattan Club, which was one of the hottest spots in town, or ended up at the smaller clubs where up-and-comers tried to make their mark and down-and-out musicians continued to play for the sake of playing plus a little pocket change to buy beer.

Of these "hole in the wall clubs," Johnnie frequently visited a place called Huff's Garden, located just a few blocks from the Cosmopolitan Club. The club was dim and tiny, with a stage so cramped it was impossible to fit an upright piano and still have room for the band. It was in that little club that Johnnie Johnson first met a fledgling guitarist named Chuck Berry.

"I used to drop by this place called Huff's Garden, which was quite a bit smaller than the Cosmo," says Johnnie. "The feature act on most nights was the Tommy Stevens Band, which was basically a blues band that played some of the popular jazz as well. They were an okay group, and I would have liked to sit in, 'cept they didn't have a piano on stage. The reason I liked watchin' Tommy's band was 'cause they had this fella' playin' guitar and singin' that could make me laugh more than anybody I ever saw. They would be playin' a regular blues set when all the sudden this man would break into a country song—what I called hillbilly music—which was a music I knew and liked 'cause I'd grown up around it in West Virginia. The funny thing about it was that this man was black and his audience was black and they wanted Muddy Waters—the blues. And I was surprised 'cause the people seemed to really get a kick out of it when Tommy would have him do his little songs. They'd be hollerin' and dancin' havin' a good 'ol' time. The singer's name was Chuck Berry."

* * *

Suddenly we are interrupted by a knock on the door. A beautiful young woman, John Lee's singer, sticks her head in. "Do you mind if I warm up in the bathroom?" she asks. Johnnie nods. "Go right ahead. You won't bother me." We smile as she leaves. Within a few moments she begins to sing, slow and sultry at first, rising into a powerful crescendo that resonates throughout the structure. Johnnie seems to appreciate the distraction.

"They're gonna ask me to sit in with John Lee, so I better get up to the stage," he says. He rises slowly, putting out the cigar in an ashtray by the door.

"Do you ever get nervous about playing, Johnnie?" I ask.

"No. I used to be real nervous about singin', but never about playin'. John Lee sings out of time, so if you with him you got to keep straight time 'til he gets back in. That's about it."

"The blues in general?" I ask.

Johnnie has a way of carrying himself that lets you know when he thinks you've asked too many questions. Or maybe too many dumb questions. He looks at me wearily.

"I suspect I know the blues pretty well."

And with that he turns and walks out, headed towards the stage.

III

BROWN EYED HANDSOME MAN

> In effect, Berry's blend of blues and country eventually turned the Sir John's Trio into a prototype rock & roll band, though history has not accorded it that honor.
> —Robert Santelli, *The Big Book of Blues*

In East St. Louis, Illinois, on the corner of 17th and Bond, sits an abandoned building. Weathered red bricks, mottled brown with age, line the barren walls. Doors and windows, long since boarded up, hide behind iron bars burned orange with rust and scarred by shattered glass. The years have shifted the foundation, leaving gaping rifts through which derelict weeds grow thick and unkempt, pushing desperately against piles of rain-washed refuse. From the gutter above, a steady drip of water bleeds, tapping out the seconds as a puddle gathers underneath and rolls away. There's history in this building; it whispers with the wind, murmurs to those passing by of times long gone.

Far above, near the flattened roof, a sign juts out precariously, sickly yellow and sagging wearily under its own weight. It has been painted over many times; this place has had many names. On the surface is a skeleton of broken neon and wire—the remnants of letters. The last three are barely there at all, flecks of a vague white. But squinting into the sun, one can still make out the name—COSMO. The Cosmopolitan Club, the pride of East St. Louis and the birthplace of rock and roll. This is where we have come.

"There it is," Johnnie Johnson says as we pull up next to the curb. "Where it all began."

We get out of the car and walk toward the front. A few people have come out on their porches to stare. We are in a bad part of town; angry faces peer from behind tinted windows, huge speakers pounding out exaggerated bass and profane lyrics. Menace is the goal—and they succeed.

"Here comes trouble," Johnnie says as a gang of about a dozen youths approaches from across the street. They're dressed in basketball jerseys, hats turned sideways, pants hung low around the waist exposing faded boxer shorts. They don't so much walk as bounce erratically toward us like a brakeless car careening down an expressway tunnel. I brace myself for conflict, but they simply pass over us in a wave of disdain, pointing and laughing in defiance of all social etiquette. No respect, no conscience. The comments are mostly imperceptible, but I catch the last one as they step into the street.

"You the F.B.I., man?"

I choose to ignore them, and out of the corner of my eye I see the smallest of them looking back, daring us to stare as they disappear into the fringe. Johnnie shakes his head.

"Terrible. Just terrible," he says. "Things have gone down hill around here. Even in my neighborhood, you can't walk the streets at night. It just ain't safe no more." He points at the building.

"Back in the fifties, though, when I first started playin' here with

Ebby Hardy and Alvin Bennett, there wasn't no such problems. Joe Lewis ran the Cosmo and he worked as a state trooper—didn't take shit from nobody. You caused a problem, you was gone. He'd walk out in the middle of a crowd and fire his service revolver in the air to break up a fight. You could stumble outside here drunk, fall asleep right on the sidewalk with a pocketful of money and nobody bothered you 'less they was wakin' you up to go home. Everybody knew each other. Not like now."

We make our way to the back, a fenced in area full of garbage and wet rot. Thick black mold grows on the walls. "Back here they used to have barbecues—ribs, burgers, you name it. Had the whole place smellin' good. Over across the street where them kids went, that's the park. If you were a fella back then, that's where you'd take your lady friends for a 'walk.' 'Course, you always had to be careful not to trip over all the couples laid out on the grass 'walkin'.'"

He laughs and fixes me with a sly grin. "'Course, I'd be lyin' if I said I wasn't out there myself once or twice trippin' people. You know, my second wife stabbed me in that park one night?"

"Say what?" I had no idea that this had happened.

"Oh, she thought I was foolin' around with this woman named Frieda 'cause she saw me talkin' to her once or twice. This was my wife, Rose. Anyway, she comes up to me before we were about to go on—Chuck was with us at that time, so it was either right before 'Maybellene' or a little after, 'cause I married her in 1955—and asks for some money to go see Fats Domino. Fats was pretty popular at that time and she really liked him so I didn't think nothin' of it. I told Chuck to sit tight and went and got an advance on my pay for the night so I could send her on her way. Instead of leavin' though, she asks me to walk her to a cab over across the park.

"Right then I should have known somethin' was up, 'cause you could catch a cab right in front of the club. But I was probably drinkin' and not thinkin' right. We was halfway across the park when she pulls out a blade, slashes me right under the lip and starts screamin' about Frieda. Well, I'm bleedin' like a stuck pig, so I take off to her mother's house which was just a couple blocks away and she fixed me up, all the time cussin' her daughter for doin' such a thing. Meanwhile, Chuck and Ebby are left without a piano player and Joe Lewis is tellin' them to go on anyway. Chuck doesn't know what to do, so he starts into 'Mary Jo,' which was a hillbilly tune he played all the time, and tried to make it last as long as he could, wonderin' the whole time where I was.

"'Bout halfway through the set, I showed up all covered in blood with a big old bandage on my lip and Chuck's eyes got real wide.

"'What happened to you?'

"When I told him, he 'bout had a heart attack. Chuck was real nervous in them days. 'She's gonna come back in here and start shootin' up the place, Johnnie! She's gonna shoot us!'

"I tried to relax Chuck the best I could and we went out for the second show. 'Course, she didn't ever come back that night, but Chuck was real skittish until it was over. To this day I still have a scar under my lip from where she cut me up. That's why I always wear a goatee."

Johnnie breaks off and goes around the corner to relieve himself, obviously knowing where to go and not be seen. While he's gone I try to imagine the Cosmopolitan Club as it was back in the fifties. It's difficult. The building just looks too small to have held so much. Director Taylor Hackford opened the building and tried to recreate the original Cosmopolitan again for his 1986 concert/documentary, *Hail! Hail! Rock 'n' Roll*, a celebration of the life and times of Chuck Berry. But there is nothing left to remind one of the film. I am struck by its meek, broken-down appearance. They ought to make a museum out of it, I decide—take care of the place. The East St. Louis homeboys cruising by need to know what it's all about. They need to know who the man in the baseball cap is, the significance of it all. This is where their rap came from, their R&B. But in the end, they just walk by, cussing and spitting, oblivious to history. They smirk at the old black man, they smirk at the old building, just a pile of bones and a pile of bricks.

"So this is where the famous New Year's Eve gig happened?" I ask as Johnnie returns.

"Mmmhmm. This is the place, right here. My saxophone player, Alvin Bennett couldn't make it, so I hired Chuck to fill in for the night. That one night lasted thirty years!" He chuckles and leans back against the car.

He has told the story too many times. Answered too many questions. They all want to know how and why. Why did he hire Chuck Berry? Did he know? Could he have known? He answers them quietly with practiced indifference. He is old and tired. He doesn't want to play rock and roll anymore, doesn't want to think about it. Hell, he doesn't even like it. He wants to talk about blues and jazz. Sometimes he'd like to forget it ever happened at all. Go back to the way things were before. The questions dredge up things he'd rather not think about, things that embarrass him, things that happened because he didn't know any better. Because he was drinking.

But today it is different. Today we are actually here. We have come to the home of rock and roll—where it all started some forty-five years before—in a little club called the Cosmopolitan. Johnnie seems at ease here despite the dangers of the inner city. He is home. When he speaks, it is directed toward the building itself—his eyes never leave it. It's almost as if he is reminding the old place of what it once was—cleaning it up, repainting it in his mind, until the Cosmopolitan Club is before him once again in all her splendor. He speaks like the ghost of rock and roll past, his heart sonorous with mysteries.

* * *

"New Year's Eve was the biggest night of the year for musicians. Always has been—still is today. Everybody was workin' and every place was booked up solid. Pay was almost double. Anyways, we was all set up with the Cosmo to play that New Year's Eve in 1952.

Then Alvin got sick a day or two before the show and I had to find someone to replace him for the night."

Alvin Bennett: A man known only as the nameless 'sick band mate' by rock historians was a saxophonist whose inability to show up for a New Year's Eve gig in 1952 holds the distinction as being perhaps the most important absence in the history of popular music. Bennett's illness was not merely a cold or stubborn hangover, he had suffered a stroke. Paralyzed, he would never play again.

"Alvin's sickness was a great loss to the musical community," Johnnie says. "We didn't know how sick he was at the time, and I tell you there was a lot of folks, including me, who was sorry to see that man put down his horn. When they talk about Chuck and me, they never talk about Alvin. They just say he was one of my musicians who couldn't make the show. Alvin was a good man, fun to be around and he could play, boy. I guess if he had made the show, I wouldn't have gotten together with Chuck, and I guess that was pretty important. But I tell you what, if Alvin could still play, he'd be first on my list anytime. People forget how good a saxman he really was."

With Bennett out of commission, Johnson was left with little time to find a replacement. All the competent musicians he knew were working, and as he had been booked as a trio, he stood a chance of losing his own job as well.

"I knew Alvin wasn't gonna to make it," recalls Johnnie of that fateful evening. "So I started callin' around tryin' to find someone to sit in. I was about to give up when I thought about Chuck. He wasn't too experienced, but I figured with his personality he could carry off a one-night gig and keep the folks entertained. I also knew he hadn't had much luck findin' jobs 'sides Tommy Stevens's group, so I was glad to help him out with some work. Sure enough, when I called him up he said he wasn't playin' anywhere and that he'd be glad to sit in with Ebby and me."

Chuck Berry had only been playing professionally for six months when he got the call from Johnnie Johnson. Yet, what Berry lacked in experience, he made up for with confident enthusiasm, and a cutthroat intensity. Vibrant and handsome with an intrinsic instinct for the stage, Berry bore a striking contrast to the subdued and unassuming Johnson.

"He was a go-getter," Johnnie says. "Real ambitious right from the start. He wanted to make that money any way he could. He was different from me. All I knew about was makin' music. Chuck wasn't satisfied with that, though, just makin' music. It wasn't enough for him. Never was."

* * *

Charles Edward Anderson Berry was born in St. Louis on October 18, 1926. Although he grew up in a musical home where both parents were active in the church choir and required their children to join as well, the young Berry was more interested in science and photography than music.

That all changed after the his first non-secular musical performance. At fourteen, Berry sang Jay McShann's "Confessin' the Blues" in the Sumner High School All Men's Review. Not an instrumentalist himself, the teenaged Berry was accompanied on the piece by fellow student and part-time blues guitarist Tommy Stevens. In his 1987 autobiography, Berry recounts, "the sheer audacity of singing a blues song on a school program, where classics like 'Danny Boy' and 'Old Man River' were usually rendered, was less than the least of my concerns."

Nevertheless, the song went over big, and the previously shy Berry discovered that he both enjoyed and felt completely at home in the spotlight.

"I realized as I was performing," Berry wrote, "that the audience will respond if you give them what they want to hear and that regardless of your ability (meaning texture of voice) to deliver a song, they will enjoy the feeling that you put into it. At the completion of my selection I was complimented again with a tremendous ovation. As I remembered my dad doing in his play, I bowed away and exited the stage backwards, watching my pathway through my legs. I feel satisfied that stage fright, if it ever lived within me, was murdered during that applause."

In addition to eliminating his stage fright, the performance at the All Men's Review provided Berry his first lesson in audience manipulation—a craft in which he later became an undisputed master. Nearly every performance mentioned in his autobiography has some passage or observation concerning the crowd's response and how he learned to tailor his stage persona in order to elicit the most favorable response from each and every type of audience encountered. Be they white, black, northern, southern, hostile, friendly, or a mixture of all—Chuck Berry had their number.

Reading the audience is a skill taught in any performance art, but few master it to Berry's level and even fewer by way of self-education. Like Johnnie Johnson's piano, Chuck Berry's stage ability was a gift from God.

Had Berry rested on his laurels, his music career might have ended then and there on that Sumner High School stage. But destiny was calling. The blues picking of his accompanyist Tommy Stevens inspired the teenager; so much so that he borrowed an abandoned four-string tenor guitar from a classmate's father and began teaching himself the rudiments of the instrument through *Nick Manaloft's Book of Guitar Chords*. He also procured the occasional lesson from a local jazz guitarist named Ira Harris, whose brother Pat was the neighborhood barber. When he went for a haircut, Berry would jam with Ira and attempt to strum along while the older man soloed.

Soon he was taking his guitar along on dates and discovered like many musicians that crooning love songs in the front seat often got you in the back seat. Thus, his motivation to play grew even stronger. How far he would have progressed as a musician in this way, however, we'll never know.

By his sophomore year, Berry had become a full-fledged juvenile delinquent, shoplifting and siphoning gasoline with his drop-out pals Lawrence "Skip" Hutchinson and James Williams. After accidently setting fire to a coal yard while stealing gas from trucks, the teens settled down into ripping off hubcaps and what Berry calls "parked car creeping and window peeping." The three boys appeared to be headed for serious trouble, but according to Berry they were just kindred spirits looking for adventure.

"They [Hutchinson and Williams] were rebellious and lazy but they were otherwise my kind of guys," he recalls in his autobiography. "We were all fairly no good but we were together, bound by a common aim to get somewhere in the world — maybe California!"

They never made it. In the summer of 1944, after a weekend excursion gone awry, Berry was arrested along with Williams and Hutchinson and charged with armed robbery. Then seventeen, he was sentenced to ten years in the Algoa State Reformatory. While his future partner was serving his country in WWII as one of the first black Marines, Berry spent the same three years serving in a different capacity–as a convict. He was released on October 18, 1947, the day of his twenty-first birthday.

Following his release, Berry returned home and began working carpentry jobs with his father and sweeping floors at the Fisher Body auto assembly plant. He married Themetta Suggs in 1948, and soon after began trying to make some extra cash by way of music, playing his acoustic four-string and singing. Evidently it had been a number of years since he'd touched a guitar for while he claims to have formed a vocal quartet during his stay at Algoa, Berry makes no mention in his book of having played guitar in prison. Needless to say, if this was the case, he had a lot of catching up to do technically.

Based on his lack of experience, it is not at all surprising that although he joined the Local 197 musician's union, he was unable to get any gigs other than small parties and the occasional sit-in with some of the local groups in need of a rhythm guitarist or singer.

It was two years later, while working as a janitor at radio station WEW, that Berry's career took a turn for the better. Recognizing the outmoded state of his four-string tenor guitar, he approached Joe Sherman, a popular St. Louis guitarist, who sold him his used electric guitar for thirty dollars. As most guitarists had gone electric by then, Berry's new instrument greatly enhanced his chances of finding jobs, and by the following year he was back with Ira Harris, who began to teach him some basic fingering techniques for solos. Although still rough around the edges, Berry was becoming more and more technically proficient and his confidence began to rise.

Finally, in the summer of 1952, the twenty-five-year-old got his first real shot.

"On June 13, 1952," Berry recalls, "Tommy Stevens phoned me to ask if I could sing with his three-piece combo at Huff's Garden. It was to be our first time to play together since the All Men's Review yet we had seen each other at many intervals. My heart leaped as I answered, 'When?' We squared away the address, agreed on the finances, and I showed up shouting that Saturday and every Saturday thereafter on through to December; earning six dollars a night. It was my first paid nightclub appearance."

Once Berry had gained his footing, he began to add the occasional country-western song to Stevens's blues sets. Working with his father in the white neighborhoods, Berry had been exposed to this "hillbilly" music quite frequently. The cut-time tunes were easy to play, the words simple, and he was able to learn them quickly. Berry recalls that Stevens, like Johnnie Johnson, both enjoyed and encouraged his experimentation and that the songs received quite a positive response from the surprised audience.

"I would suddenly break out with a hillbilly selection that had no business in the repertoire of a soul-music-loving audience," he remembers, "and the simple audacity of playing such a foreign number was enough to trigger the program into becoming sensational entertainment."

Six months and twenty-four shows later, he got the call from Johnnie Johnson, who had remembered him as the "black hillbilly from Huff's Garden." Berry's country-western style was nothing new to Johnnie. Growing up at the foot of the Blue Ridge mountains, Johnnie Johnson knew hillbilly music even better than Berry. Yet in all those years, he had never seen nor heard a black man perform in this genre. Consequently, he was just as intrigued by Berry as the rest of the East St. Louis blues fans and often stopped by after his own shows to watch Berry sing with the Stevens Combo. Johnnie realized even then that Chuck Berry, regardless of his eccentricities and technical limitations, had a certain charisma that "made folks want to listen to what he was saying."

"Chuck brought something to the group that was missin'," Johnnie says, "that dancin' and playin' to the crowd. Ebby and me, Alvin, we was quiet, didn't none of us sing or dance around. We'd been playin' music for a long time and we were good at it. We played for the love of playin' and we figured our music would do the talkin'. That's the mistake a lot of musicians make, and 'cause of that, a lot of the best ones never get out of the small clubs. It don't matter who's better at playin', although that matters some. It's who can hold the crowd. People want to be entertained. When Chuck started with me, he didn't know but twelve songs all the way through and he couldn't play guitar all that well. But Chuck was special in his own way. I've seen Little Richard, Jerry Lee Lewis, the Rolling Stones...ain't none of 'em can hold a crowd like Chuck. That's his talent. Chuck Berry is an entertainer. He shot out right to the front."

The Johnnie Johnson (or Sir John's) Trio took the stage at nine in the evening just as the club began to fill. Berry had been prompted on the keys and changes and was told to just strum along and stay in tune. This was nothing new to Berry. In Tommy Stevens's group, he played rhythm guitar and sang occasionally. But this was the big time, in a much larger club, and Johnson and Hardy were on an entirely different level.

Nevertheless, Chuck Berry's sense of showmanship would not allow him to remain in the background for long. Unlike Johnson, Berry was an opportunist, and he realized that the heavily attended Cosmo gig provided the perfect setting for him to make a name for himself. Johnson remembers the fateful moment when Berry broke free and began to try out his own material on the seasoned Cosmo crowd.

"We started out at nine and went until one playin' the usual set. I took all the solos 'cause Chuck was pretty much a rhythm guitarist, and that meant I had to do twice as much 'cause I had to play Alvin's solos, too. Things were going all right. But that wasn't enough for Chuck— he didn't like just being part of the band. I guess it was the size of the audience and the excitement he felt bein' up on stage, but he got the confidence to try one of them hillbilly songs he'd been doin' over at Huff's Garden. That took a lot of guts for Chuck to do. Huff's Garden was a little bitty club and the folks at the Cosmo were straight blues fans. He couldn't know for sure whether or not they'd throw him out of the place. He knew me well enough by then that he wasn't worried 'bout me gettin' angry. I'd seen him do his thing at Huff's and I thought it was fun. But he didn't know these people, and half of 'em was drunk 'cause it was New Year's Eve and all.

"That didn't stop Chuck, though. After a couple standards he broke into this old country shuffle, 'Mary Jo'. I think Ebby was a little surprised, but I didn't mind at all. I've never been one to hold someone back from tryin', and I knew Chuck was just gettin' his feet as a musician. 'Sides, I liked the way he'd mess around with the words. Chuck didn't just sing, he told a story with all the faces and gestures. He could've been a comedian. Since he'd been playin' mostly rhythm with Tommy, I had to come up with some melodies on the spot to put behind what he was singin'. Luckily, it wasn't no trouble puttin' piano behind it since I'd grown up around country music.

"Well, let me tell you, the people loved him. They just ate it up.

And I felt really happy for Chuck, 'cause like I said, that was real brave of him. I guess I should have known. The public was always lookin' for somethin' new and a group of black men playin' hillbilly songs was definitely new."

The dawning of 1953 signified not only the beginning of a new year, but a new phase in the life of Johnnie Johnson. Based on the tremendous ovations gleaned from the unlikely combination of jazz, blues, and country, Joe Lewis asked Johnnie to hire Chuck Berry as a permanent part of the Sir John's Trio. Johnnie didn't hesitate.

"The audience loved what Chuck was doin' 'cause it was so different from what you'd expect a black man to be doin'. His singin' and carryin' on really got the audience into the show, and people were dancin' all 'round the stage and whatever. When Joe Lewis asked me could I make Chuck part of the band, I didn't think twice 'cause I felt comfortable playin' with Chuck and the people seemed to really enjoy him. Sometimes in music you just click with another musician just like you would a person you meet at a party. The conversation just fits. They know what you sayin' and you know what they sayin'. You understand where the other one is comin' from. That's what happened with me and Chuck."

Despite the popular addition of Berry to the group, the Johnnie Johnson Trio continued on as before, rolling out jazz standards, rhythm and blues, and boogie woogie, with Berry performing the occasional country-western song as a novelty. These excursions, though well-received, were not as numerous in the first year as Berry seems to indicate in his autobiography. In fact, as Johnnie remembers, Berry did not know very many songs at all.

"Chuck was still young musically," he recalls. "He hadn't been playin' very long and like I said, he only knew twelve songs that he could perform. I'll never forget that. We still played mostly standards over that first year until Chuck started to learn more hillbilly tunes. Then we'd work with them until they sounded good enough to play on stage. We hadn't come up with anything original yet, though. I had some things I did on the piano like 'Johnnie's Boogie' and some different blues things that I had made up on my own. But none of these had any words to 'em.

"Then Chuck started on writin' these poems, and I'll tell you what, them little poems he was comin' up with were somethin' else. The first one I think he did, he made up while we was all sittin' around one night. Called it 'Beer Drinkin' Woman.' We started doin' it on stage. Wasn't no singin' though, just recitin'. Chuck would tell this story 'bout tryin' to get with this woman, and all she did was keep orderin' up beer. He'd say a line and then I'd put somethin' behind him on the piano.

"Another thing he did was a pantomime called 'The Buggy Ride' that had no talkin' or singin' at all. Chuck pretended he was takin' this imaginary girl on a buggy ride and he'd be makin' faces, actin' like he was tryin' to get this girl to fool around with him. The whole time, Ebby and me would be puttin' some music in the background, just comin' up with some things on the spot, like the music on a TV show—improvisin'. Then when he finally got tired of waitin', he'd jump on the girl and Ebby would go crazy on the drums like there was a big struggle. Then I was the cop, so I'd break into a fast shuffle, actin' like I was chasin' him. I even went to a five and dime and bought a police siren to put on top of the piano. This was the kind of things we did, and the people loved it."

With Berry beginning to take center stage, Johnnie found himself pushed into the background. Although he still controlled the band if only in name, the repertoire was becoming all Berry's, and as the guitarist picked up more and more "hillbilly songs," the blues and jazz standards were all but eliminated from the Johnnie Johnson Trio's performances. Johnnie saw what was happening, but said nothing.

"I could see Chuck takin' over," says Johnnie, "but that's his personality type. Chuck has to be in control. Besides, we was becomin' one of the most popular bands in East St. Louis, and everybody, includin' the whites, were wantin' to check us out. At first you'd see the occasional white lookin' all scared and out of place, and then every weekend you'd see more and more white faces in the crowd 'til it was almost equal. We never got that kind of response 'fore Chuck come along, and I knew the people were comin' out to see the new stuff. This was perfectly fine with me. I was just happy to play the piano and this was what the people wanted to hear. Like I said, Chuck was an entertainer and a singer. We didn't never have a singer 'til Chuck joined and I was much too shy to try myself. 'Sides, Chuck was no ordinary singer: He made up his own words, talked to the audience, made faces, and whatever. People liked this and the fact that we was doin' somethin' different musically."

Despite Johnnie's accepting and easygoing nature, Berry's notorious ego, present even in those early days, began to take its toll. As adulation rained down upon him, he grew more and more assertive, flaunting his star status in front of his bandmates, and showing anger if he did not get his way on stage. Johnnie didn't mind: The boisterous behavior drew the crowds. But then one night in 1954, Berry pushed too hard and Johnnie was forced to draw the line. It was a lesson the guitarist would never forget.

As part-time musicians, The Johnnie Johnson Trio depended heavily on the tips received from customers. Normally at the end of a gig, the group would immediately sit down and Johnnie would split the tips up equally among the group. But that particular evening, for whatever reason, Berry had decided to take the initiative and collected the tips himself. "He was tryin' to see what he could get away with," Johnnie recounts. "Testin' the water."

It should have come as no surprise. Johnnie Johnson knew the piano inside and out, but when it came to the business, recording, and publishing end of music, he was completely oblivious. "I didn't know nothin' about nothin' 'cept playin' the piano," he says. "Nothin' 'bout the business end of things. Chuck figured that out real quick and I guess he thought he could take advantage 'cause I didn't know no better."

What Berry failed to realize at the time was that, despite his limitations in several crucial areas, Johnnie Johnson was well-versed in the code of the nightclub: When you played you got paid, and if there was any left over—meaning bonuses or tips—you split it up equally. It was simple and straightforward. When Berry violated that rule, he was fooling with tradition, not to mention robbing his bandmates of their hard earned pay. It was a slight that could not be ignored, not even by Johnnie.

"Chuck and I only had one problem and it was after a gig at the Cosmo," Johnnie remembers. "It had to do with the tips. We got paid twenty-six dollars per gig back then which we split between the three of us and sometimes them tips would be thirty-dollars or more, which means we'd be makin' twice as much as we'd regularly get. I knew Chuck had collected the money, I saw him do it, so I figured I'd wait and see if he was gonna split it up.

"We got in his car and pulled out into the street. I didn't say nothin' 'bout it the whole ride home. I thought maybe he was just waitin' 'til he stopped to let us out. When he dropped Ebby off without a dime, I knew we was gonna have a problem. Ebby just looked at him but Chuck stared straight ahead, didn't say a word. Ebby wasn't no fighter, and I think he was a little scared of Chuck. He got out and didn't make no deal of it. Chuck thought he had it then. Sure enough, he pulls up to my place and sits there lookin' at me like I was just supposed to get out like Ebby did and not say nothin' 'bout the tips. Well, he was wrong. I said, 'Don't you have some money for me?' He said, 'I don't know what you're talkin' 'bout.' That's when I told him, 'I know you got that tip money.'

"He got real mad then. He got this look on his face, cold as ice. 'They came to see me, not you. Nobody cares 'bout you.' I kept my cool and said, 'Well, I know you're new to this scene, but we are a trio and we're gonna split the tips three ways.' He just sat there tryin' to stare me down and I stared him right back. Next thing I know, Chuck jumps out of the car and says, 'You want the money come and take it!'

"I guess he had me figured soft 'cause I was so quiet, but I got out the car and went after him. He took a swing at me but I just dodged it and threw him up against a fence and held him there by the throat. Chuck was used to intimidatin' people, but I'd run into tougher guys than him in the ring, and I was bigger than him and a lot stronger. He looked real surprised when I got inside on him. 'We fightin'!' he said. 'Damn right we fightin',' I said. 'Give me my money.'

"I figure he knew he wasn't gonna win, so he said, 'Fightin's not for us, Johnnie.' I let him go and he gave me the money he owed me and Ebby. That was the end of that, and Chuck never tried to threaten me again. That was the only problem we ever had. From then on everything was cool."

Chuck Berry had made a mistake in judgment when he tried to bully his bandmates out of their share of the money. But to him, mistakes were part of the music business–a business he was becoming better and better acquainted with over time. In *Hail! Hail! Rock 'n' Roll*, he talks about his philosophy on mistakes and how that wisdom shaped his career.

"You feel your way when you don't know," he says. "Sometimes you step on rocks, sometimes you get your head bumped. But not twice. That's a smart man. Don't let the same dog bite you twice."

Berry would never be "bitten" by Johnnie Johnson again. He was foolish to take a bone from a dog's mouth while he was awake. That was the dangerous way. The wise man waits until the dog is asleep then takes all his bones.

And as Berry would soon learn, the naive and heavy-drinking Johnson was almost always asleep.

IV
MAYBELLENE

"Maybellene" is to rock and roll what Adam and Eve are to the Bible. Sure, rock-and-roll-style songs predate it, but they were all hybrids. What "Maybellene" says, essentially, is "accept no imitations, it all starts here."
—Thomas Ryan, *American Hit Radio*

"We'd been together about two-and-a-half years when Chuck went up to Chicago to see about makin' a record," Johnnie says as we circle the block around the Cosmopolitan. "Back in them days you didn't have too many people recordin'. I guess 'cause most of us who had been playin' in the clubs didn't know nothin' 'bout the record business. Now you got all these bands, the only reason they get together is to make a record. But back then you just wanted a regular gig at a big club, to play your music and make money—nobody even thought about makin' records. But Chuck got hung up on the idea. I told him I didn't know nothin' 'bout the record business myself, but if he wanted to make a record, I wouldn't stand in his way. See, at that time, it was still my band even though he was the singer and the star of the show."

We continue to walk. Near the front of the building, I spot a breach in one of the windows where the boards fail to meet the frame. The exposed glass has been broken, leaving a gaping hole. Peering into the darkness, I can faintly make out the insides of the building—the crumbling walls, and a number of misshapen lumps on the floor. I push my flash camera into the opening and snap a couple of pictures that will later reveal the lumps to be a pile of dirty clothes and meager supplies where some unfortunate had set up residence. Perhaps that poor soul was hiding in the shadows, watching as Johnnie and I took turns gazing inside.

"I can't see a thing in there," Johnnie says, pulling away and shaking his head. "'Course, my eyes ain't what they used to be. But right in there is where we used to play every weekend, and it's also where we made the tape Chuck took to Chicago."

Johnnie tries the barred front door, but the rusty lock holds true and we resign ourselves to leaning against the doorway, two patient patrons waiting in vain for an opening that will never come.

"Now by that time, when Chuck made the tape, we was playin' a lot more of the hillbilly music, 'cause that's what the audience wanted," Johnnie continues. "Chuck was bringin' in all these hillbilly songs like 'Jambalaya,' 'Mountain Dew,' and 'Ida Red.' Stuff he had heard on the country stations. 'Ida Red' turned out to be one of the songs people liked best, so Chuck recorded us doin' that song and took the tape up to Chicago with him. First place he went was Vee Jay, but they turned him down flat. Wasn't no surprise; they was strict blues. Later that night, Chuck went to see Muddy Waters play at the Palladium. After the show he asked Muddy where he needed to go to make a record, and Muddy told him to go see Leonard Chess up at Chess Records. That's where Muddy recorded. Anyway, the next day Chuck went up there with the tape of 'Ida Red,' and Chess liked what he heard. Told him to get me and Ebby and come back up to Chicago to record it. That's how the whole thing started with the Chess brothers, Leonard and Phil."

* * *

On Columbus Day, 1928, two wide-eyed little boys stood huddled together on Ellis Island staring up at the Statue of Liberty, the symbol of opportunity. Nine-year-old Leonard Chez and his younger brother Phil had just arrived with their mother from Motol, a small town on the Russian-Polish border. Following immigration procedures, the family joined their father in Chicago and began making a life for themselves in a brand new country. Before long, they would abandon their native "Chez" for the more Americanized name, "Chess."

Growing up in a Jewish ghetto near the South Side, the Chess brothers learned to survive early. "You got smart quick," Phil Chess says today. "Or you didn't make it."

As young men, Leonard and Phil were overtaken by the American entrepreneurial spirit and left their father's junkyard to capitalize on the prospering post-Prohibition liquor business. World War II called Phil in 1942, but not Leonard, who was exempt from the draft due to a childhood polio condition that left him with a permanent limp. With his brother overseas, Leonard continued to dabble in various business ventures including liquor stores and nightclubs, until finally succeeding with the Macomba Lounge, a South Side nightclub catering to the burgeoning blues and jazz scenes. It was there that Leonard Chess first recognized how popular black music was at the time, and how little exposure the artists received from the recording industry. "They didn't have anyplace to record, these black musicians," recalls Phil. "Here was all this great music...blues, jazz...and no one was making records. Leonard saw the potential right away."

Two years after Phil returned from the war, the Chess brothers bought in to the small Aristocrat label and set up shop in a rented studio owned by Bennie Clapper's Universal Recording Services. Their first records were mostly jazz and R&B, featuring local groups like the Five Blazes, Jump Jackson's Orchestra, and Macomba Lounge house vocalist Andrew Tibbs. And while neither Chess brother was especially musical—Leonard was widely known to be unable to keep a beat—they were both intelligent and aggressive businessmen with a knack for pushing merchandise.

Leaving his brother home to manage day-to-day affairs, Leonard periodically set off with a car full of records, shopping them to radio stations within a thousand-mile radius, trying to get his music played, and more often than not, paying a pretty penny for his efforts. Leonard was keen to the game. This was during the days of payola, when disc jockeys expected a little extra for the airplay, and while most labels of the time made use of payola, only the Chess brothers deducted the payments as legitimate expenses. "Payola was a standard practice," Leonard Chess told the *Chicago Tribune* shortly before his death. "At least I was doing it honestly."

While Aristocrat's first records were far from chartbusters, the Chesses were encouraged enough by the results to explore the possibilities of mainstream blues. For their first blues recording, Leonard brought in Delta-style pianist Sunnyland Slim and a small group of musicians to record two songs for the blues market. The resulting "Johnson Machine Gun" and "Fly Right Little Girl" were released as a single in 1947 to a lukewarm reception. Although Leonard was disappointed with the mediocre response, he was nonetheless intrigued. Not by the raucous Slim, but rather his borrowed guitarist, a deep-throated bottleneck player with a stage name that seemed the very essence of the Mississippi Delta blues and the river that is her bloodline: Muddy Waters.

On the basis of an almost uncanny intuition that would consistently prove fruitful in the coming years, Leonard Chess invited Waters and bass player Big Crawford to record alone in their traditional Delta style. Aristocrat single number 1305, "I Can't

Be Satisfied," and its flipside, "Feel Like Going Home," was released in 1948. The record sold out in twenty-four hours.

By 1950, Leonard and Phil had bought out their partner in Aristocrat and Chess Records was born. Besides Waters, who would become the father of post-WWII blues, Chess had also recruited Waters' former harmonica player, Little Walter Jacobs, newcomer Jackie Brenston, and blues giants (in stature as well as reputation) Chester "Howlin' Wolf" Burnett and Willie Dixon.

Brenston and Burnett had been sent to Chess via Memphis, Tennessee, by Sam Phillips. Although enthusiastically recording blues artists, Phillips was still a year away from starting his legendary Sun Records label. Brenston's 1951 classic "Rocket 88," a horn-driven song about the 1950 V-8 Oldsmobile 88—"the lowest-priced car with 'rocket' engine"—was Chess Record's first No. 1 hit and arguably the first rock and roll-style record, although some consider the song more along the jump-blues vein. Recorded by Ike Turner and His Rhythm Kings, for whom Brenston was a singer and alto saxophonist, "Rocket 88" was mistakenly credited to Jackie Brenston and His Delta Cats when released by Chess. The blatant omission of his name left Turner embittered and caused a rift between he and Brenston that would eventually lead to a parting of the ways. Turner, however, would get his revenge nine years later, hiring the then broke and destitute Breston as a session sax player on his first No.1 hit, "A Fool In Love."

Ironically, while "A Fool in Love" meant redemption for Turner, it also marked the beginning of a tumultuous partnership with the woman who would become a pop music icon. When Turner's lead vocalist failed to make the session, Ike replaced her with his pet project, a shy, raspy-voiced singer from Nutbush, Tennessee, named Anna Mae Bullock. Bullock, whom Turner eventually married, burst onto the national scene as Tina Turner, giving voice to her husband's material, and like Jackie Brenston before her, pushing Ike Turner into the background before leaving him behind. This time, however, Ike would not be redeemed with another hit record, although, to his credit, he never gave up trying. Ike Turner's contributions to rock and roll were officially recognized when he was inducted into the Rock and Roll Hall of Fame in 1991.

In the end, Jackie Breston proved undisciplined. Without Turner to guide him, he burned out quickly, a classic one-hit wonder, sinking into alcohol and the excesses of sudden stardom. Meanwhile Phillips's other transfer, discovered playing in a juke joint by Ike Turner, became a legend. In Howlin' Wolf, Chess not only had an electrifying performer, but a legitimate rival to the throne held by Waters as "King of the Blues." Both shared the songs of bassist/lyricist Willie Dixon, whose "Little Red Rooster" and "Hoochie Coochie Man" became hits for Burnett and Waters, respectively, and both possessed the sort of down home authenticity that both legitimized them to the public and earned the respect of their peers as well.

In contrast to the stoic Waters, Burnett was a huge, powerful, and dangerously paranoid man, prone to violent outbursts when agitated. Supposedly, the only person able to control the Wolf was the formidable Dixon, who was not only bigger than Burnett, but a former heavyweight boxer as well. In his autobiography, Dixon recalls having "to get Wolf off stage and take him back in the alley and talk to him."

"I've threatened him and I even had him in the collar a couple times but I don't remember actually coming to blows with Wolf," writes Dixon. "Sometimes, guys can be so illiterate by inexperience and all like that you have to take them off to the side and talk to them. If they won't act right, you threaten to send them home or something like that."

Dixon would stay with Chess for most of his career. A natural leader, he served many functions including studio musician, lyricist, uncredited producer, and arranger for several of the label's biggest stars, including Muddy Waters and Bo Diddley.

Diddley, born Otha Ellas Bates McDaniels, had released his first single, the Dixon-penned "I'm a Man" on the Chess subsidiary label, Checker, in March of 1955. Although "I'm a Man" would reach No.1 on the R&B charts, it was the self-titled flipside, "Bo Diddley," with its unique hambone rhythm, that secured the bespectacled former street tough (his name means "bully" in street parlance) a place in rock history. Diddley's beat would influence countless rockers including Buddy Holly, Johnny Otis, the Rolling Stones, and even bluesman Jimmy Rogers, who would record a version of "Bo Diddley" in 1959.

Nevertheless, despite their success and experience with the styles of both Brenston and Diddley, the Chess brothers had yet to hear anything like the music Chuck Berry brought to their office at 4750 Cottage Grove in May of 1955.*

"Different. Different from Bo, different from everybody. Like nothing we'd heard before," recalls Phil Chess upon first hearing 'Ida Red.' "We figured if we could get that sound down on a record, we'd have a hit. There was just something about the rhythm—the beat. The song had a whole new kind of feel to it. Leonard knew we had something."

And Leonard, of course, always did.

* * *

Johnnie is trying to sing "Ida Red" as best as he can remember it. "Ida Red, Ida Red, I'm a fool 'bout Ida Red." He slaps his hand in time on the brick wall.

"That's pretty much how it went and we'd put a little cut-time shuffle beat behind it—umpah-umpah-umpah-umpah. Put it in the key of B-flat. Most of the hillbilly songs—fact, all of 'em—had

---

* The reader may notice a discrepancy between the recording dates listed in this book and those catalogued by Chess. Upon interviewing Johnnie, I found that his memory coincided more with the dates reported by Chuck Berry in *Chuck Berry: The Autobiography*. Regarding the Chess listings, I have found numerous errors in terms of personnel, spelling, etc., to be conducive to the list being termed unreliable. Phil Chess, himself, conceded in my interview with him, the existence of several mistakes in the listings. As a result, I saw no point in following the "historical records" but instead, based my timeline on those dates reported by Johnson and Berry.

that same music. Chuck just put different words to 'em. 'Ida Red' was just one of the songs we did.

"I guess I have to say I was real surprised that Leonard and Phil liked 'Ida Red.' I'd always figured people liked the hillbilly stuff at the Cosmo 'cause it was a novelty. But Chess was a serious blues label. I knew a little about Chess 'cause some of the blues artists I sat in with in Chicago recorded there. I didn't think hillbilly songs was what they was lookin' for. No way. But Chess thought we was on to somethin' new. That's why they called us up there. I remember Leonard Chess real well. He was the first person we saw when we drove up there the next Friday after Chuck got back. Me, Chuck, and Ebby. He showed us in the studio and right away he started in on the song. Leonard wasn't the type that wasted time. 'You got to change the title,' was what he said. ''Ida Red' sounds too rural, and there's already another song out with that name. You can't just do someone else's song.'

"So the five of us—Phil was there, too—we started puttin' our heads together tryin' to come up with a title. See, it had to be somethin' with the same number of syllables so Chuck could fit it into what we was already doin'. Well, we were sittin' there thinkin', when all of a sudden Leonard looked over in the corner and saw a bottle of Maybelline mascara. Leonard got a big ol' smile on his face and said 'Why don't we call the damn thing Maybelline?' We had to change the spellin', 'cause Chess said he didn't want to get in trouble with the company, but that's where the name 'Maybellene' came from—from the makeup."

Johnnie chuckles and takes off his hat to scratch an itch on his balding pate.

"After that, Chuck had to come up with some new lyrics which wasn't no problem for him," Johnnie remembers. "He was a genius with words. He'd make 'em up as he went along sometimes, even on stage, and they'd always work."

In *Hail! Hail! Rock 'n' Roll*, Berry claims his loquacious gift for verbosity assured the facile creation of his early songs despite the fact that he did not write his own music. "It wasn't too hard to write," Berry admits, "because I had been making up songs—verses that is—on the bandstand to other people's songs. So I take my verses and put them to the same rhythm and I was on my way. You know poetry is my blood-flow."

Johnnie agrees.

"For 'Maybellene,' all Chuck had to do was come up with some words to fit the music we'd been doin' at the Cosmo," he says. "That was the easy part for him. The hard part was gettin' the song exactly where Leonard and Phil wanted it, 'cause they didn't even know themselves what it was supposed to sound like. I guess that was what made the whole thing kind of excitin'. The fact that we was kind of makin' up this new kind of music right on the spot."

For over nine hours they labored, breaking only shortly for sandwiches and drinks. Willie Dixon came in to supervise the session, and at his suggestion, standup bass was added to give the song more bottom. It was also Dixon's job, Johnnie remembers, to make sure that each take was completed in three minutes or under—the standard length of a single. Surprisingly, although Dixon would later claim to have known all along that "Maybellene" could be a "crackshot hit," Chuck Berry remembers in his autobiography that Dixon seemed to have doubts about the tune.

"Electric bass instruments were yet to come," Berry recalls, "and Willie, stout as he was, was a sight to behold slapping his ax to the tempo of a country-western song he really seemed to have little confidence in."

Johnnie has similar recollections.

"First thing you noticed about Willie was how big that man was," he says. "That bass fiddle looked like a violin in his hands, and in all the years I knew him, I never saw him with a shirt that he could button the sleeves on. Second thing you noticed was that he was just doin' his job. He never gave us no encouragement. He just played his bass and made sure we stayed under three minutes."

Perhaps he was stoic at the time, but in his 1989 autobiography,

I Am The Blues, Dixon contradicts the memories of both Chuck Berry and Johnnie Johnson, going so far as to claim someone other than Johnson was the pianist and that he and the Chess studio band were Berry's first road band–not Johnson and Hardy.

"Me and Lafayette Leake, Harold Ashby and Al Duncan were the first road band Chuck Berry had," claims Dixon. "Chuck was a fast driver—I always thought he was trying to prove something to 'Maybellene' when he was out there. Just about every time we went to eat, he would order chili. I guess that was about the best thing we'd get for the money we had.

"It was me and Phil Chess, Chuck and a bunch of other people who went down to Universal Studios to record [Maybellene]," Dixon writes. "I had a studio band that was doing most everything for Chess and we recorded most of the first stuff with him. Chuck had a guy named Johnny (sic) Johnson who was a hell-of-a good piano player but he didn't play on the first sessions—it was Lafayette Leake."

In the world of blues, Lafayette Leake is an enigma. An intensely private man, little is known of his early life other than that he was born in Winona, Mississippi, in 1919 and that he was introduced to Willie Dixon in 1952. An excellent pianist, Leake was called in by Dixon to play on several of Chess's blues hits including those by Muddy Waters, Howlin' Wolf, and later, Bo Diddley. According to Phil Chess, however, he did not play on Chuck Berry's early records, despite Dixon's claim to the contrary.

"Lafayette Leake was a house pianist and a good friend of Willie's," Chess remembers. "Real good piano player. But Johnnie Johnson was Chuck's pianist, and I can't remember a single song that Johnnie didn't play on with him. I don't know what Willie was thinking. The only reason Leake would have come in is if Johnnie couldn't make it or if we had to redo the recording for some reason. But even if he did...see Johnnie was so important to Chuck's sound. Leake was a good pianist, real good, but he wasn't Johnnie Johnson, and Chuck didn't want to play with anyone else."

When asked about Leake's subsequent credits as the pianist on such Berry milestones as "Sweet Little Sixteen" and "Reelin' and Rockin'," Chess responds with a surreptitious grin. "They were real good friends, Willie and Lafayette Leake. We didn't really pay too much attention to who got credit for what in them days, it was the star whose name was on the record. Let's just leave it at that."

In the section labeled Appendix 3 of Dixon's autobiography, co-author Don Snowden acknowledges that such disparities were commonplace in the bluesman's recollections and not limited solely to the Berry sessions.

> Willie Dixon's studio contributions for Chess and other labels extended beyond just writing blues songs. He was a musician hustling to make ends meet and session work was one avenue that offered the prospect of steady income. Dixon wound up playing bass on a label's blues sessions—and he was landing a fair amount of studio work from other labels and producers before then.
>
> But it was a time when documenting backing musicians was a haphazard process at best and hence discrepancies creep in. For instance, Dixon claims to have played on the sessions which produced the first Sonny Boy (John Lee) Williamson's 'Elevate Me, Mama,' but according to the discographies, it was Ransom Knowling playing on the track. Similarly, Dixon said his first recording session with Muddy Waters came at the same time—probably November 10, 1948—that he cut four songs with Robert Nighthawk and Ethel Mae for Aristocrat. There was a Water's session that weekend—which yielded 'Train Fare Home,' 'Down South Blues,' 'Kind-Hearted Woman' and 'Sittin' Here and Drinkin"—but the credited bassist is Big Crawford. And the second Nighthawk session Dixon played on followed a Waters session—but Big Crawford is again listed as the bass player.

Based on this information, it comes as no surprise that Dixon's memories of Berry's first sessions contradict both Berry's and Johnson's memories as well as Phil Chess's, whom Dixon claims was there with he and the other band during the first session. Chess adamantly denies the session ever took place and cannot remember Dixon ever touring with Berry. Johnson and Hardy were the musicians on his first recordings assures Chess. Still, Dixon made claims to the contrary, a fact which is more bewildering than vexatious to the soft-spoken Johnson.

"Willie and me seemed to get along real well and I don't understand why he would say them things," Johnnie says. "He knew I was there in the beginning. Maybe he did go out on the road with Chuck later on, after Ebby and I were back in St. Louis. But he didn't go with us on the first tour, and Chuck never mentioned any of them fellas when he talked to me. Not that I'm callin' Willie a liar, now. People get old and forget. And with them records, it never occurred to me to check who got credit for playin' on them. Back then they didn't put sidemen on the record like they do now. Like I said, maybe Chuck recorded them songs again after we had already did 'em, but I was with him when he first did 'em all, 'cause I helped him come up with the music for 'em. The only recordin' I didn't play on was 'Johnny B. Goode.' Chuck did that as a surprise for me."

In regards to the modern liner notes now included in Berry collections, both Johnnie Johnson and Chuck Berry and even Phil Chess himself have acknowledged the existence of several miscredits (and misspellings–Ebby is called "Eddie" and Johnnie is written as "Johnny") on Berry's albums—mistakes that have gone unchanged and unchallenged for years. In several different interviews, Berry has had to correct journalists in regards to who played on his records. Besides the Leake mixup, Otis Spann, a great pianist known for his work with Muddy Waters, is mistakenly credited for "Downbound Train," "No Money Down," and "You Can't Catch Me." Berry drummers Jaspar Thomas and Ebby Hardy have frequently been confused for each other (Thomas who joined Berry's group after Hardy quit in 1956 was listed as the drummer on "Maybellene") or even with other drummers such as Odie Payne or Fred Below. Johnnie Johnson does remember other drummers besides Thomas playing on later recordings, so it is highly possible that both Payne and Below might have worked with Berry. But for the most part, according to Johnnie, "it was me, Chuck, and Ebby on the first records. Jaspar Thomas joined up later. Willie Dixon played bass most of the time and there was another fella named Van Arsdale who played bass, too. That's it. We had some different drummers later on, but these were the musicians who played on all of Chuck's records. At least the first time he did them."

* * *

The first session rolled on into the night. "Maybellene" was played over and over again by the weary musicians, who soon grew frustrated with the constant repetition. "We struggled through the song," says Berry in his autobiography, "taking thirty-five tries before completing a track that proved satisfactory to Leonard. Several of the completions, in my opinion were perfectly played."

"I couldn't tell no difference between most of them," Johnnie accedes. "They just had us keep doin' it over and over and we was all gettin' tired, especially Chuck, 'cause he was doin' all the singin'."

"You have to remember, we didn't have anything to compare it to," says Phil Chess when asked about the numerous takes. "This was an entirely new kind of music. Maybe some of them were fine as they were, but we just kept playing with it, trying to get the sound down on record that we heard in the studio. My brother came out with a phone book and a drum stick and started beating on it. We even had Chuck doing his vocals in the bathroom, so when his voice went through the pipes, we'd get an echo. Stuff like that. We were just trying to get it right."

After take thirty-six was finished, Leonard Chess asked Berry for another song in case they decided to press a record. But as Johnnie remembers, the Trio was ill-prepared for such a request.

"Chuck didn't have no other original song that we could play," he says. "Like I said, we was playing standards and hillbilly songs at the Cosmo, stuff other people had done already."

The answer came, says Johnnie, during one of the breaks. Bored with playing the same cut-time pattern over and over again, Johnson broke into a slow blues to pass the time. "Nothin' complicated," he remembers. "I was just foolin' around with a regular old blues in G. Kind of thing I did all the time at the Cosmo. Later on, when Chess asked us for another song, Chuck had me play that blues again and he started puttin' words to it. Wasn't but fifteen minutes later we had 'Wee Wee Hours,' which was the first song we did, Chuck and I, that was all our own—music and everything. I figured if they did end up makin' a record, then that would be the side people listened to, 'cause it was straight blues. 'Course, I was wrong 'bout that."

As Berry recalls in his autobiography, the lyrics to 'Wee Wee Hours' were hardly difficult to write and inspired for the most part by the sorrows of first love gone wrong.

"'Wee Wee Hours,' Berry writes, "was based on the memorable tears that Joe Turner's 'Wee Baby Blue' brought from me when I was a teenager and so much in love with Margie. Blues are simple anyway and only seem to need the lyrics of a lonely confession to be put to music. It took the memory of one of the evenings that I didn't get to see Margie at her window to put the words together and the tune is anybody's cry for companionship. With the exception of a couple ten minute repair changes, I think it took all of an hour to complete the writing of 'Wee Wee Hours.'"

With the songs finished and their session fee paid, the Johnnie Johnson Trio piled into the car and headed back down Interstate 55 to St. Louis to wait on the release of their record. Perhaps the biggest myth concerning the first recording session was that Berry had already taken over the band when he and Johnson and Hardy put the first two songs on tape. In Berry's book, he mentions changing the name of the group shortly after the first Cosmo gigs to the Chuck Berryn Combo (the n supposedly added so as not to embarrass his Baptist minister father), yet the poster advertising this combo, printed in Berry's book, names three other musicians:

Erskine Rodgers on piano, Richard Culph on sax, and Bill Erskine on drums. Johnnie says he knows nothing of this Chuck Berryn Combo and the other musicians mentioned on the poster, but insists that the group consisting of himself, Berry, and Hardy remained under his name for two months following the first Chess sessions.

"The band that recorded 'Maybellene' and 'Wee Wee Hours' was still called the Johnnie Johnson Trio," he states. "The record came out under Chuck's name, but we didn't think nothin' of it—that was somethin' he wanted to do. Me and Ebby didn't care nothin' 'bout no records. We didn't know any better—none of us club musicians did. We had full bellies, good whiskey, and money in our pocket, and that's all we cared about. We did a job, we got paid, we went home.

"Anyway, we stayed the Johnnie Johnson Trio until August, when 'Maybellene' started gettin' popular. In the meantime, we was back at the Cosmo, which was like our home base, doin' what we'd been doin' before we recorded. Except now Chuck was gettin' worried 'cause we hadn't heard nothin' from Chess 'bout his record comin' out and people was askin' questions.

"Then about the beginning of August, Chuck gets this telegram tellin' him to join up with Alan Freed's rock and roll tour. 'Maybellene' was gettin' popular on the radio and Chess wanted us to go out on the road. That's when Chuck comes up to me and asks me about changin' the name from the Johnnie Johnson Trio to the Chuck Berry Trio. When I asked him why, he told me about the record makin' it big and the Alan Freed deal, and how he could get us more gigs if he was the leader. I knew Chuck had a car, a Ford Station Wagon, and he could get around further than I could. Rubber wheels beat rubber heels any day. 'Sides, I knew Chuck was a hustler and knew more about the business than I did. He proved that real quick. All I knew was music—I didn't have that go-getter instinct that Chuck did. I figured we'd keep on gettin' gigs with Chuck in charge and that maybe I'd be able to work full time as a musician if I stayed on his payroll and did what he said. So I told him that I didn't have no problem with him bein' in charge. And that's how we became the Chuck Berry Trio."

What followed for the newly named group was an exciting whirlwind tour in the midst of an exploding rock and roll scene. Taking a leave of absence from his job at the American Steel Foundry, Johnnie Johnson joined Hardy and Berry with the promise of living a dream. Loading Berry's station wagon with Hardy's drums and a few meager supplies, the trio began the long trek eastward to catch up with the Alan Freed Rock and Roll Jubilee, currently in the middle of its first anniversary tour.

"We played a few little gigs before we started the big tour," Johnnie remembers. "Places like Cleveland and Atlanta. Then we joined up with the tour bus in New York, after a show at the Apollo Theater. The Gale Agency who was in charge of bookin' us, sent this guy Teddy Reed to kind of manage us, and he went with us to the gigs, makin' sure we got paid. But Chuck didn't like what he was doin', so he got rid of him. He wanted to be in charge of the money. He didn't want nobody in control but him."

The tour itself was exhausting, and doubly so for the black performers once they passed beneath the Mason-Dixon line. Not only were they lacking the luxury of modern touring facilities—the drafty bus was a far cry from today's comfort coaches—the black performers often times could not find lodging or a decent meal due to segregation laws in the Jim Crow South.

"One hundred and one one-nighters, workin' our way down south and back," recalls Johnnie. "That's what the first tour was like. A lot of times we couldn't find no place to sleep or eat, 'cause most of the places down south didn't let black people in the hotels and restaurants. We'd sleep in the bus a lot of times. When the bus stopped for dinner, we'd go 'round back of the restaurants to get food from the black cooks, and sometimes they could get us in with some folks who would take us in for the night. They kept things separate down there. A lot of times we had to play two shows for the price of one—one show for the blacks and one show for the whites. I remember being in Texas and playin' in a barn with cows mooin' all around us, smellin' up the place. That kind of stuff just don't happen nowadays."

The first major booking for the Chuck Berry Trio was at the Brooklyn Paramount, where they played alongside such artists as Tony Bennett, Lillian Briggs, and the Four Fellas. The Trio had been scheduled as the opening act with orders to play "Maybellene" and "Wee Wee Hours," then get off the stage so as not to run the show overtime. A consumate businessman, Alan Freed ran a tight ship. This was his second rock and roll tour and he understood the value of a promptly choreographed show for keeping a long tour schedule. It was a lesson he'd learned the hard way.

In 1952, Freed had held a dance for listeners of his *Rock'n'Roll House Party* radio show in which he unknowingly sold seventeen thousand tickets for a ten thousand capacity arena. The huge ticket sales had been unexpected and the resulting melee almost landed Freed in jail. From then on he was in complete control. And because he felt some of the problem was caused by the nearly all-black crowd, he made sure future audiences were no less than one-third white before the artists took the stage.

The day of the Paramount show, Chuck Berry was a nervous wreck. His popularity now spread beyond the safe confines of East St. Louis, and with his reputation on the line, he began to feel the pressure. He writes in his autobiography: "The day of the first show we dressed and waited. They had us booked as the opening act, and while Johnnie and Ebby seemed quite relaxed I was scared out of my wits. The show was about to start, and I was the newest act on the show with the hottest tune on the charts."

"Chuck was real nervous before the show," recalls Johnnie. "But you got to remember, he'd only been playin' on stage for three years, and the audience was mostly white. A lot of times we'd come out on stage and the people would 'ooh' and 'aah' 'cause they thought Chuck was a white man from how he sounded on 'Maybellene.' Like I said, there wasn't no other black men doin' this type of music—the hillbilly music."

But as Johnson remembers, "The show went pretty well. We didn't have but two songs to do and we played them both and got off the stage for the next band. I think we did shows for about a week at the Paramount. After that, Chuck went and got us some green and tan rayon suits and some shoes so we'd look more professional."

Back on the bus, the Chuck Berry Trio learned the rules of the road from veterans like Laverne Baker, Clyde McPhatter, and the Cleftones, who had been among the inaugural rockers on the first Alan Freed's Rock and Roll Jubilee in 1954. The countless hours in cramped quarters forced the artists to come up with diversions to pass the time. One of the most popular pursuits of the restless travelers was gambling—namely shooting craps. The games were hard-fought, competitive, and could go on for hours, often lasting all night and into the next morning.

"I saw things going on among [the other musicians] that I had never known about a month before," says Chuck Berry in his autobiography. "I saw my first live gambling, a bold and blazing crap game in the aisle of the bus that carried on until dawn. When I woke up at the announcement of a breakfast stop, only three were left in the game and maybe twenty thousand dollars had changed hands in the aisle."

For Johnnie, the cross-country trip was a musician's paradise. In almost every town he could find a jazz or blues club to suit his needs, and more often than not, he spent the post-gig layovers in these establishments, getting drunk and sitting in with the local talent. According to Johnnie, his drinking and carousing inspired Berry to pen the lyrics to perhaps his most famous work.

"The song 'Johnny B. Goode' was a surprise for me, and Chuck told me it came from when we used to tour," Johnnie says. "See, back then we didn't play nothin' but 'Maybellene,' 'cause that's what the hit was. If we had an encore or a little extra time, we'd play 'Wee Wee Hours.' Well you get tired of playin' that same damn song over and over again. Chuck didn't seem to mind, but I was 'bout to go crazy. I missed playin' my jazz and blues like I was doin' before. So a lot of times after we'd get finished with a show, I'd go out to the clubs and sit in with the local groups. This was my first time goin' 'round the country, so I was real excited about gettin' a chance to play with so many different musicians. The problem was, we had a schedule to keep, and I'd get caught up playin' and drinkin'. By the time I finally dragged on in, the rest of the bands would be gone! A couple of times I had to call Chess and have them wire me some money so I could get on a bus and catch up with them. I'd get there just in time for the show and Chuck would be shakin' his head askin' me, 'Why can't you just be good, Johnnie? Stay with us.' That's how he got the idea for the song."

The Alan Freed Rock and Roll Jubilee continued down the coast, picking up the hottest acts and losing others to the wear of the road or a drop in the charts. Every night for over three months, Johnnie Johnson cranked out the cut-time boogie of 'Maybellene' behind Berry's twanging guitar and Hardy's shuffle beat.

"I could do it dead drunk or half-asleep. Hell, I could have played it while I was asleep," Johnnie laughs. "You play a song enough and it gets to where your hands could be busy, and the whole time you're thinkin' 'bout what you was gonna eat for dinner or where you was gonna go after the show. You're just like a robot."

The highlights of the tour, according to Johnnie, came not during, but after the show, when he could escape and go off on his own to explore or relax on the bus or in his hotel room. Keeping company with rock stars was not as attractive a proposition as it would later become. The blossoming genre was still in its infancy. Instead, Johnnie preferred the low-key atmosphere of the after-hours club where he could smoke his cigars, drink, and listen to good old-fashioned blues or jazz. He found solace under the blue lights in the smokey din. He didn't want to be a star—he just wanted to play music.

"It just wasn't no big deal to me," Johnnie says. "Rock and roll was new and there wasn't nobody like Elvis or Little Richard on that tour we was on. This was before they was famous and rock and roll was a household name. Freed was always on to whatever was happenin' and he knew 'fore anyone else who was popular and who was sellin' records. He'd call people up along the way, like Della Reese and Screamin' Jay Hawkins, who had made big records. I guess Alan Freed more than anybody was the one who made Chuck and Elvis and Little Richard famous. He invented the name rock and roll. I even remember the first time I ever heard him call it by that name. We were backstage and the Spaniels was doin' one of their songs and the kids was just going crazy in the aisles. Alan Freed looks out from behind the curtain and says 'Look at them kids rockin' and rollin'. He knew what was goin' on before any of us."

Looking back on his early touring experiences, Johnnie Johnson is amazed at the vast differences between then and present-day rock stars who travel in private jets and coaches and stay in only the finest hotels under assumed names. Having experienced both the hardships of the first rock and roll tours and the luxury of life on the road with stadium-fillers like the Grateful Dead-sponsored Furthur Festival Tour, Johnson has a unique perspective with regard to the evolution of the traveling rock and roll show.

"It was a lot different back when me and Chuck and Ebby first started," he says. "Now you have the Rollin' Stones and RatDog...all them Grateful Dead folks. When I was with RatDog on that Furthur tour, we had our own beds and TV's in the tour bus. You talk about nice—that bus was better than most people's homes. If we stayed in a hotel, it was always a nice hotel with room service and everything you could want. Wasn't nothin' like that back in the old days.

"There's all kinds of security now like we didn't have back then, either. You try to call Keith Richards up at a hotel you know he's stayin' at and the deskman will tell you he's not there. 'I don't know what you're talkin' 'bout,' they say. Keith and Mick and them, they just usin' another name. Bob Weir does the same thing.

"On those first tours, no one was makin' up names 'cause we weren't anything but musicians. Look at those folks that follow Bobby and the Grateful Dead. There weren't nobody followin' us around and campin' out in front of where we was playin'. We did have fans though. A lot of times we had to go in and out the back entrance to wherever we was playin', 'cause if the fans saw you they'd mob you. We had one instance when some girl stole Chuck's hat and Chuck had to take off after her to get it back. Another time some girls had wrote "We love you, Chuck!!!" in lipstick all over the car we was drivin'. But this wasn't no big deal and nothin' we couldn't handle ourselves. We were just looked at as musicians. We didn't stop bein' regular people."

With "Maybellene" riding at No.5 on the white-dominated pop chart and holding on to the No.1 spot on the R&B chart for eleven weeks, the Chess brothers knew they had a moneymaker in Chuck Berry. Of course, before they could reap the rewards they had to "pay for the play"—grease the wheel. In order to ensure that "Maybellene" was played and distributed to the buying public, Chess had, without Berry's knowledge, listed Freed and record distributor Russ Fratto as co-writers of "Maybellene."

This was not the first time that Chess had played politics with songwriter's royalties. Relatively few musicians were aware that the money existed, and an even smaller number knew anything regarding the rules and regulations of royalty payments. Chess had added Freed as co-composer on the Moonglows's "Sincerely" and "Most of All" in 1954. Both songs were hits.

"In those days that's how it was done," says Phil Chess. "You had to play the game if you wanted to have your records played. It was business."

Arc Music, an in-house publishing company which the Chesses

co-owned with Gene and Harry Goodman, brothers of big-band leader Benny Goodman, owned the publishing rights to Berry's songs for years. The method used to secure these rights was quite interesting.

The Library of Congress copyright files on Berry's songs reveal a constant pattern of addendums. The original copyright for "Maybellene" was dated July 5, 1955. On August 2 of that same year, the song is copyrighted again with the addition of a Ben Kendall as the piano accompaniment. Kendall also appears as accompaniment on "Roll Over Beethoven," "Sweet Little Sixteen," "Too Much Monkey Business," "School Day (Ring, Ring Goes the Bell)," "Rock 'n' Roll Music," "Reelin and Rockin'" (in which he supposedly added chords and harmony), "Sweet Little Rock and Roller," and "Oh Baby Doll," which was re-filed only sixteen days after the original, on July 25, 1957.

Another man, Chris Langdon supposedly improved both "Brown Eyed Handsome Man" and "Bye Bye Johnny" with his added riffs, while Al Cohen was named as the guitar and piano soloist on the reissue of "Memphis," four years after its original copyright in July of 1963.

The reason for these addendums is unclear and according to Johnnie Johnson, the men listed as contributors were not known to either Berry or himself. "I don't have a clue who they talkin' 'bout," he shrugs.

When Chuck Berry found out about Freed and Fratto appearing as co-writers on his record, he was outraged. He had arranged to receive full benefits himself, or so he thought. Much chagrined by the loss of two-thirds of the potential profits, Berry eventually sued for and won sole rights to "Maybellene." In later years, he would also sue Brian Wilson of the Beach Boys for borrowing the tune to "Sweet Little Sixteen" in their 1963 hit "Surfin' U.S.A." The copyrights to his songs, however, remained the property of Arc Music until the 1980s when Berry filed for renewal under his own name.

"I just recovered the full rights to 'Maybellene' some thirty years later," says Berry in his book. "That loss was two-thirds of the total, or twice as much as the royalties that I received from 'Maybellene' for years. I was told that registering their names was a compliment of the record business that was generally practiced to promote a song that would likely not be a success without the push. With the first royalty check I received being right at ten thousand dollars, over twice as much money as the cost of the home I'd purchased a few years prior, I wasn't about to question the trends of the trade. Yet, blind as I was, I wondered.

"Back in the studio, things were so harmonious and friendly that there did not seem to be any room for distrusting the integrity of the Chess brothers with the paperwork that followed a recording session. I was just learning about much of the paperwork because back then I had no idea how big the business of writing and publishing was in itself. I had thought publishing was only promoting or advertising a product. But as time went by I learned that a publisher held the fate and direction of a tune and had a great equity in its sale. Nevertheless, I continued to write my songs, knowing at least of copyrights and recording royalties.

"Had I known the music business better, or for that matter, at all, I would have known I was not receiving due fairness. Then there's another saying my mother dwelt on, 'Don't let the same dog bite you twice' and, believing it also, I learned from my mistakes. Woe be unto him whose wrongs are revealed."

* * *

By September of 1955, "Maybellene" was starting to lose steam and Chess decided to pull the band off the road for another recording session. Johnnie remembers the second session as a much more leisurely affair.

"'Maybellene' had done so well that Chess wanted us to do more records to keep up the popularity," he recalls. "Chuck had written out the lyrics for some new songs on the road and we went back into the studio. That's when we did 'Thirty Days' and 'You Can't Catch Me.' Then 'round Christmastime we did 'Downbound Train' and 'No Money Down.' We knocked both those records off in no time flat. I don't think it took more than an hour for each one."

With 101 nights on the road and three recording sessions under their belt, the Chuck Berry Trio returned home to St. Louis and a regal reception at the Cosmopolitan Club. At the start of the new year, they played a week-long engagement in Buffalo, New York, at a club called Mandy's Lounge, where blacks mixed freely with whites in a liberal atmosphere. This was a turning point for the three men who had spent their entire lives in a state of segregation. Rock and roll had become the great unifier, the barrier breaker, the wall smasher. For the first time, whites and blacks had something to share and enjoy together. While Johnnie appreciated the freedom, he was still guarded and hesitant to exploit it. Berry, on the other hand, found the lack of restriction irresistible. "Once I learned that there were places in the United States with such harmony in racial rapport," he says, "I started keeping a mental tabulation of them."

In many ways, Berry had become popular enough that he transcended racial boundaries. But just as the fighter Jack Johnson had done in the early part of the century, Berry began to push his luck, flaunting his taste for white women in the face of a racist nation. He would pay dearly for his predilections.

After the refreshing experience at Mandy's Lounge, the trio followed with a gig at home in the segregated Casa Loma Ballroom, where in order to impress the audience and fill out the sound, Berry recruited bassist Albert Moseby and tenor saxophonist Leroy "L.C." Davis. Both Moseby and Davis would tour with the trio, and Berry made use of Davis's sax on several recordings.

"Picking up Leroy was one of Chuck's best ideas," remembers Johnnie. "He had the whole rock and roll sound down. Leroy was the perfect sax player for the kind of music we was doin'. He didn't do a whole lot with us but he came out when we needed a sax player for a gig or to play on a record."

* * *

It was the Spring of 1956, and Chuck Berry had ruled as top dog for almost a year. But since the release of "Maybellene," he had done little to secure his position. His name was completely absent from the pop charts, and he seemed uncertain as to where he should go with his style, dabbling in blues and ballads. In the meantime, three new talents, each with their own distinct style, emerged on the scene to challenge Berry's dominance: Little Richard, Carl Perkins, and Elvis Presley.

Growing up gay in a deeply religious Georgia family, Richard Wayne Penniman hit the road when he was just sixteen. Upon leaving home, the boy joined the carnival circuit, hawking snake oil and singing in minstrel shows before graduating to nightclubs where he learned the rudiments of boogie piano from Eskew "Esquerita" Reeder, a popular gay performer.

By the time he arrived at Art Rupe's Specialty Records studio in New Orleans, Richard had long since cultivated the bawdy, somewhat hysterical, and flagrantly androgynous image that would become his trademark—complete with stacked pompadour and makeup. Yet when he sat down to record the first day, backed by a tight studio band led by drummer Earl Palmer, Richard's sound was anything but rock and roll.

"I knew I had to go back to Los Angeles with at least two good songs that Rupe could put out on record," remembers Specialty A&R man and future Little Richard manager, Robert "Bumps" Blackwell. "But I didn't think [Richard's] prepared stuff had any hit quality, and it disturbed me. Then during a break—things had gotten tight so we needed to relax—I heard Richard playing around with 'Tutti Frutti.' It was a nightclub song. But it was risque, none of the words were useable."

With the aid of songwriter Dorothy LaBostrie, who happened to be in the studio that day, Richard transformed 'Tutti Frutti,' a song about anal intercourse ("Tutti Frutti, tight booty...went the original words") into a wild rock and roll record that kids purchased covertly and danced to behind closed doors. For unlike Berry, whose clear diction led many to mistake him for a white man, Little Richard's sound was undeniably black—a trait that still threatened much of white America in 1955.

The solution would come, and not surprisingly so, from the heart of the South, in Sam Phillips's Sun Records Studio in Memphis, Tennessee, where over a year before, a shy young man named Elvis Presley recorded a version of Arthur "Big Boy" Crudup's "That's Alright Mama." After years of filtering rhythm and blues acts to Chess Records, Phillips had finally established his own headquarters at 706 Union Avenue. Now he set about on his own personal quest to find a white boy with a black sound to drive the teenagers crazy and keep their parents relaxed enough to let them buy records. "I had always thought," said Phillips in the PBS documentary *Rock and Roll*, "at that particular time in history, and that's exactly what it is and was, that if I could find a white southern boy, we just might be able to do at least a few of the things that I knew it would take a long time to do."

Elvis Presley was the answer. Although his remake of "That's Alright Mama" never made the national charts, it caused enough of a stir to attract the attention of RCA Victor who bought out the singer's contract in November of 1955 for thirty-five thousand dollars. To this day, Phillips' claims he never regretted the decision to sell off the future "King of Rock & Roll." "I needed the money so bad," he says. "And people have asked me repeatedly, 'Do you regret selling Elvis Presley?' I do not, and I did not, and I will not. It gave me the financing when I sold his contract to RCA to merchandise 'Blue Suede Shoes.' I mean, you know what that is don't ya? It's an anthem."

Carl Perkins, who had until then been recording straight country for Sun, wrote "Blue Suede Shoes" based on a story he heard from fellow country artist Johnny Cash. As Perkins remembered, Cash was laughing backstage before a show about a black soldier he had known in the Air Force who jokingly warned the other G.I.'s not to step on his spit-shined government issue footwear. "He called them," Cash told Perkins, "his blue suede shoes."

Perkins' "Blue Suede Shoes" and "Honey Don't" were released in January of 1956, the same month as Elvis Presley's "Heartbreak Hotel." "Blue Suede Shoes" peaked at No.2 on the R&B charts, but could not surpass "Heartbreak Hotel," which rode the No.1 spot three straight months. Ironically, despite the success of his first release, it was not "Heartbreak Hotel," but his rendition of "Blue Suede Shoes" that scored Presley national fame on TV's *The Milton Berle Show*. Two months after the release of "Shoes," while on a national tour, Perkins was seriously injured in a car accident, destroying his chance to take full advantage of the "Blue Suede Shoes" phenomenon. Following his recovery, Perkins made several good records, but never again hit it big on the pop charts. As Sam Phillips has said, "There's no way Carl could hide that pure country in him." Nevertheless, Perkins left his mark.

Rock and roll was changing, expanding to include a multitude of styles and forms. In a period of just six months, Little Richard had introduced the world to the wild side of rock, Carl Perkins had invented the style known as "rockabilly," and a white boy from Tupelo, Mississippi, who did not write his own songs and could barely play guitar, became the King of Rock &Roll.

And so when Chuck Berry walked into the studio that spring day in 1956, he was at a professional crossroads. He needed to produce a song that would push the rock movement forward, or risk disappearing from the scene altogether, drowned in the rising tide of incoming talent. He had the lyrics in his pocket, literally, but that wasn't enough. He needed a sound—something new to set the rock world on it's ear and reaffirm his status as the spokesman for the nascent genre. With Ebby Hardy, L.C. Davis, and Johnnie Johnson,

Chuck Berry entered Chess Studios for what would be his most important recording session. One of the songs, based on Berry's childhood frustrations over his sister Lucy's monopolization of the family piano, would become the anthem of a new generation, and redefine rock and roll music for the next forty years. "Roll over Beethoven," sang Berry. "Tell Tchaikovsky to move."

And while parents everywhere shook their heads in disgust, their children embraced rock and roll and its heroes with the passion of a backseat rendevous at Lover's Lane. The days of Mitch Miller and Tennessee Ernie Ford were gone, crew cuts gave way to ducktails and leather jackets, and girls wore their skirts just a little bit shorter.

The rock and roll era had begun.

V

ROLL OVER BEETHOVEN

"Without somebody to give [Berry] them riffs...Voila! No song. Just a lot of words on paper."
—Keith Richards, *Hail! Hail! Rock 'n' Roll*.

The radio is on in Chuck Tillman's house. Gospel music spills out from a back room in his quaint St. Louis home and overtop the far away melody, a soulful voice preaches fervently for Jesus. Tillman sits alone, exuding warmth and grandfatherly kindness like the sweet ethereal perfume of an autumn wind. He is almost seventy years old. His thinning hair is peppered with gray, and the years have carved deep lines in his round, mahogany face. But when he speaks of his lifelong passion for music, a seraphic smile washes over that venerable visage, alighting in it a spark of youthful vigor.

"Music," he declares, "keeps me young. Keeps that passion in my life. There have been times when I finished playin' my sax, whether

I was alone or with a band, and I wanted to cry. Other times I wanted to laugh, or sing. Music takes you out of reality, it's euphoric, you walk in clouds. It's a beautiful place to visit. But you don't want to stay there all the time 'cause you'll flip out, lose your sense of reality. I've known cats who were not all there 'cause they never wanted to come back down off that high. Not me. I always liked to return home with my feet on the ground–to my family."

Cornelius "Chuck" Tillman has blown his saxophone professionally for over fifty years. He has played jazz, blues, classical, and rock and roll. During the fifties and early sixties, Tillman was one of the hottest young saxmen in St. Louis, working with the Tommy Dean band and doing sessions at Chicago's Vee Jay Records behind the Spaniels, the El Dorados, and bluesman Jimmy Reed. "I was on my way," he remembers. "I went to New York to try for the big time. Then my wife got sick. She had a stroke and was completely paralyzed. Couldn't move. Couldn't even talk. The doctor said, 'Here's your wife. Take her. We can't do anything for her.' We had five kids. I said to myself, 'Say man, you gonna shoot for that star or are you gonna come home and take care of your family and raise your kids?' There wasn't no question. I came home to St. Louis and got a job working the four a.m. shift at the auto plant and seein' to my wife. I was just a musician, I wasn't no doctor. I had to figure it all out on my own. I fed her, bathed her, saw the kids through school. When I retired twenty-five years later, she still hadn't spoke a word or moved a muscle in all that time. She stayed that way until she died."

His eyes mist over as he speaks and I know he is fighting for composure. I look away in deference. He is a prideful man, strong and disciplined, a veteran of the Korean War–the kind of man who doesn't cry in front of strangers. Swallowing hard against the pain, he wills himself not to break. He coughs twice, a rattling and manufactured diversion, then clears his throat and continues.

"It's still hard to talk about even after all these years," he admits, his voice thick with emotion. "But I have no regrets. Everyone can't wear the same shoes. We all got different paths to take, and fortune and fame is not my game. The thing is, through it all, I never stopped playin' music. Never stopped visiting that beautiful place, man. Never."

He laughs self-consciously and glances towards the ceiling, wiping his left eye. I pretend not to notice.

"'Course, you didn't come here to talk about me and my music," he says with a smile. "You want to know about Johnnie Johnson and Chuck Berry's music, and I guess I know that just about as well as I know my own. At least I used to. See, I've been a BMI writer since 1955. I can read music, and more importantly, I can write it out. I can write out my own compositions note for note or I can listen to someone else's music and do the same thing—what you would call transcribing. I'd known Chuck and Johnnie since before 'Maybellene' came out, and we had all worked together before. That's how Chuck knew about what I did—transcribing on the side for extra bread.

"Well, it wasn't but a couple years after 'Maybellene' that Chuck started bringing me tapes of his songs. He said he wanted me to write lead sheets so he could submit them to the Library of Congress for copyright. I think the first one I did was 'Too Much Monkey Business,' and it went from there on into the sixties. Chuck would call me up and say, 'I got somethin' for you.' And he'd bring copies of what he had done in the studio. I had to listen to them quite a bit because they were different than what I was used to. In fact, I had quite a hard time.

"Now you say why would I have a hard time? Well, this music they were doing, Chuck and Johnnie, was mostly ad-lib. Meaning they played off of each other, one inspiring the other to do things, you know, without any written music to guide them. And what they were playing, they were playing it emotionally, and that's not the easiest thing to write down. In fact, it's very difficult. See, they just did what they wanted to do, and whether it was musically correct or not, they just did it. As a transcriber, I had to ask myself,

'Should this music be contained and given boundaries?' It's like throwing a cat and a dog in a cage and letting them go at it. You can't script it all out and say, 'Okay, the dog's gonna do this and the cat's gonna do that, and neither one is going to get hurt.' You let them loose and they are gonna go at it, and whatever happens, happens. All you know for sure is that you're gonna see a good fight. That's how their music was. You throw musicians together and let them do what they feel. Next thing you know, you got a hit record."

He shrugs his shoulders and smiles. In his hand is a copy of *Chuck Berry: The Autobiography* which I have brought for him to look at. He opens it up and begins thumbing through the list of songs at the back of the book.

"Chuck Berry had his name on a lot of hit records, man. Whole lot of hit records. 'Wee Wee Hours'...'Monkey Business'...'School Days'...there's 'Nadine', I remember that one real well...'Promised Land'...There's over two-hundred songs in here. Duke Ellington didn't have that many songs in him. Nobody does." He closes the book firmly and stares at me intently.

"Now this is the something those rock and roll history books won't tell you—something I got from listening to those songs over and over and writing them out. Well, I shouldn't say just from listening—I knew it anyway from playing with them both and knowing their styles. One man did not write these songs by himself like the records will tell you. Now, a few times Chuck had a complete idea of what he wanted to do right from the beginning. But most of them, and especially the ones that were hits, they weren't done that way. Chuck and Johnnie would get together up in Wentzville where Chuck lived, or somewhere else, and without the aid of a band they'd put whole songs together, just the two of 'em. Remember the thing about the dog and the cat fighting? Now you say if two people were putting these songs together, adding their piece to the whole, why was only one of them getting paid for the song? Personalities.

"Chuck Berry and Johnnie Johnson—they were buddies. This wasn't just hire me and I'll hire you. These were friends, partners. But you can't get anything if you don't ask. I think if Johnnie had insisted...but then again, I don't know. See, Johnnie came from a different era than Chuck. Chuck was only a couple years younger than Johnnie, but he hadn't been playin' near as long as Johnnie had. Johnnie was the elder musician, the experienced musician on stage. But he came from a scene where nobody knew about recording. Most of them cats didn't even know that money was out there. I daresay, had Chuck ever told Johnnie about the money he got, not just from the gigs, but from his songs being played all over the world...That's money, man. And Johnnie deserved his fair share. But like, I say, you can't get anything if you don't ask, and so many musicians didn't know that money existed. Even today, you get together with some of the old timers: 'What's that you got, here? A recorder! No. Turn that thing off!' They play music for that moment and they don't care about anything but that moment. I know I've had times where I'll be playing, really feeling the music, and after I'm done people say, 'Hey, do that again.' I'll say, 'What?' 'What you just played.' I'll say, 'I don't know what I just played.' And it's true! I won't have any idea.

"That's where Johnnie was comin' from. He didn't know nothin' about recording. He'd go out and do a session, help write a song, get paid $100 and feel happy 'cause he thought he made out. Meanwhile, the cat he helped is making thousands and Johnnie ain't gonna see a dime of that money. It all comes down to the bossman. Who's the bossman? That's what matters. After he did 'Maybellene', Chuck took over that band and he became the bossman. What the bossman says, goes. You see what I'm saying? The bossman, if he knows what's happenin', can bring you to a session, pay you, then steal all your stuff, and there ain't a damn thing you can do about it. You can say, 'Well he paid me to exploit me!' That was your choice. You didn't have to take the gig. Ignorance will hurt you in the music business. A lot of old cats won't have nothin to do with makin' records because they were exploited and don't trust nobody no more.

"That kind of thing happened a lot back then and it still does 'cause people just don't know the system. When you get to talkin' about Chuck Berry and Johnnie Johnson...well that's a sad story 'cause like I said, they were friends. 'I get a piece of bread, you get a piece of bread.' This was the kind of friends they were. And they made most of those hit songs together, meaning they should have shared the profits from those songs. Now I say 'should' because I look at it from the point of being fair. I am a fair person and that's how I look at the world. But dollar bills and fairness don't go together. If it did, we wouldn't be having this conversation. Chuck would have said a long time ago to Johnnie, 'Hey man, me and you brother. Wherever you want your name.' But that's not Chuck Berry. Remember the personalities. You can't expect Chuck Berry to be fair in the sense we are speaking of. Listen to him play. You can tell a lot about a person, a musician at least, by the way he plays his instrument. A person can only play what is inside of them. Look at Chuck Berry. Take his music and convert it to personality. Now, show me the compassion in his playing–the fairness. Now look at Johnnie Johnson. Would he be fair to Johnnie? No way. They were a team. But one person's ego is not going to allow him to admit that. You talk about Chuck's book. I've never read it, but I know it's an 'I' book because Chuck Berry is an 'I' person. I know the individuals. 'I' people are not 'we.' They never contend that 'we' did anything—'I' did a lot."

Tillman falls silent for a moment, allowing his point to sink in. Then he leans towards me.

"Now take Johnnie Johnson. Johnnie Johnson would take his last dollar and try to feed somebody. I don't know if he's ever done that, but I've observed him and know that he would. You can say that kind of personality kept him from getting his due. Sure. But at least he can look in the mirror and not think about cutting his own throat. At least he's not looking over his shoulder. That's a good feeling to have when you get to be our age. You can look back at your life and still sleep at night."

Chuck Tillman smiles.

Somewhere in the house, a preacher shouts for Jesus.

* * *

At ten o'clock they wandered in, road-worn and weary, a pack of restless marauders, intently focused on the task at hand. Chuck as usual, led the way, exchanging greetings with the Chess brothers, carrying his guitar and a stack of lyrics. Johnnie, Ebby, and L.C. Davis followed behind him, smiling as they entered the studio. They shot the breeze for half-an-hour or so, munching on sandwiches, talking about anything but music.

Then, as if responding to a signal heard only by them, the four musicians stood up and began preparing for the session. Ebby found the drum kit and began shifting it around, raising cymbals, moving the hi-hat, testing each drum head for tuning. The sound of his meticulous thudding filled the studio. Leonard Chess manned the control room. Willie Dixon and Phil Chess busied themselves with setting up microphones. L.C. Davis sat in the corner, fingering his horn valves and blowing plaintively into the mouthpiece.

Johnnie Johnson was becoming used to the prerecording routine. He brought out the cigar Phil Chess had given him, eyed it lovingly for a moment, then lit it up, savoring the rich taste. Finally, he stood and began making his way towards the piano. Chuck Berry followed behind with his guitar at the ready. There was a moment of exquisite tension. Berry brought his guitar up to chest level and began picking out runs while Johnnie settled in behind the keys. Someone counted off softly. And then they began to play, slipping comfortably into the groove; two veteran fighters sparring each other for the thousandth time. Only this time it would be different. Berry's words required something faster, but not the cut-time hillbilly beat he'd used so many times before. This wasn't hillbilly,

Berry told Johnson, this was rock and roll. And Leonard Chess had told him directly, as was his custom, that the music world didn't need two Little Richards or two Elvises. Chuck needed to come up with his own style of rock and roll, and he needed to do it quickly. Johnnie took a long puff on his cigar, the tip glowing orange, and exhaled a cloud of smoke which hung around the piano like the thick mist on a Louisiana swamp.

"Just start singin'," he said cooly. "And I'll start playin'."

* * *

The hands are restless again. We have left the shell of the Cosmopolitan Club behind; Johnnie stares straight ahead as we drive away; he doesn't look back.

A half-hour later, we sit together in his tiny house by the Wonder Bread Factory, a two-family flat in North St. Louis he shares with his wife, her mother, and her mother's husband. Johnnie is playing a ballad for me on his electric piano—a gift from a friend. For years he didn't have the money nor the room to keep a piano in his home. In fact, there really isn't enough room for this one in the cramped living room. But somehow Johnnie has made the bulky instrument fit, defying spacial limitations in the face of desire, willing it to conform.

He is playing "Georgia On My Mind." Softly. Slowly. The hands caress the keys with a practiced and graceful touch that borders on daintiness—an almost comical trait in a man so large. Bent down in concentration like a child at his first recital, he sees only the keys—and the hands. The face is blank, void of expression. Where once I have seen joy and wonder, there is only impassivity now, tranquility . He is immersed in the utter beauty of the piece and nothing else exists in his world but the notes floating in the air around him and the hands engaged in a deliberate, languid courtship dance on an ivory stage.

He finishes with a cross-hand flourish reminiscent of Liberace and settles back, chuckling softly to himself as he always does when the music satisfies him. I chuckle as well.

"That was great, Johnnie," I say.

"Awww, ain't nothin' to it," he replies. But he is secretly pleased.

"Play something else," I ask. His response defines him in a nutshell.

"Okay. That'll work."

Suddenly the hands leap upon the keys, side by side, spread wide like two tarantulas on an egg carton. Their very breadth seems to fill the entire middle of the keyboard, devouring it whole. Then they attack. Violently. The sound is like a symphonic thunder, filling the room, as if every key on every piano in the entire world were struck hard and simultaneously.

Then just as fast as they attack, they separate. The right hand shoots to the higher octaves, where it runs a lightning quick pattern towards the middle and back. The left plants itself firmly, small finger on G, index on D, thumb E and begins to rock, alternating a fifth and sixth on every beat. *Dun-de-duh-duh-Dun-de-duh-duh-Dun-de-duh-duh....*

"Johnnie's Boogie." It's his signature song, inspired by Meade Lux Lewis's "Honky Tonk Train," and he has been playing it since he was sixteen. The intro is, in fact, the very same one used in Lewis's song—and in a song called "School Days" by a certain Chuck Berry, who used a guitar to mimic the sound of Johnnie's piano.

The train keeps a rollin', and I try to hold on as Johnnie's right hand scrapes, rakes, pushes, drags, and pounds the keys with blinding speed and mind-blowing intricacy. Just as I start to catch on to a pattern he has changed it, inverted it, moved it up an octave, or down another. All the while, the left keeps chugging away—a G-chord, down to C, back to G, then D—a completely separate entity unimpeded by the movements of the right hand. *Dun-de-duh-duh-Dun-de-duh-duh.* The tempo is perfect, flawless, better than most drummers could ever hope to achieve. The foot begins to tap.

Solo time. Now he changes the bass. A rolling bass. Rocking his hand, boogie-woogie style, playing two octaves at once *GG BB DD EE FF EE DD BB*. The right hand never hesitates, never falters. Doesn't seem to care at all that the left is leaping seven keys at a time backwards and forwards, forwards and backwards.

Then like a flash he is back in the familiar rhythm, in the pocket, that steady bass rollicking along like a locomotive. *Dun-de-duh-duh-Dun-de-duh-duh.* And then, because it is his signature song, and because he knows I love it when he does it, he pulls his signature lick.

The right hand expands an entire octave—from G to G—what is known as a G7—and while the left hand rocks, the right begins to roll—the thick brown fingers whirling sixteenth note triplets, blurring to my astonished eyes until they resemble five Mars bars in a blender on high speed. The sound is a waterfall, a rushing cascade of notes, dropping from high onto my head and washing me in music. There is nothing better, I think.

And just when I start to lose myself, it is done, and Johnnie is laughing. I have been dancing in his living room.

"Now that," says Johnnie, fixing me with a wry grin, "Is where rock and roll started."

I stare at him gape-mouthed. It hits me all at once. Years spent listening to Chuck Berry records—and it all comes together in a moment of flash revelation. *The left hand.*

"Pull up a chair," he says motioning to the powder blue recliner beside the piano. "If you're gonna do this book on me, I guess it's about time I start talkin'."

* * *

The living room is dark. We are alone. Johnnie switches on the television, bathing the room in a pale blue incandescence and casting playful shadows in the folds of his old brown face. "You gonna put your movie in?" he asks.

"Sure," I answer. "If you don't mind."

"No, I don't mind," he chuckles. "I said I was gonna talk so you can go ahead and ask me about whatever you want."

"All right."

I get up and turn on the VCR. In my hand is a copy of *Hail! Hail! Rock 'n' Roll*—already cued up in case the chance to play it would arise. I put in the tape and Johnnie pushes play on the remote control beside the chair.

"There's Keith," he says, smiling as I sit back down. He adjusts the volume just as the Rolling Stone finishes his speech.

"...He ain't copying Chuck's riffs on piano," Richards rasps. "Chuck adapted them to guitar and put those great lyrics behind them. But without somebody to give 'em them riffs—Voila! No song. Just a lot of words on paper."

As soon as the last word is spoken, Johnnie himself appears on screen ten years younger, but looking ten years older than he is now. His face is bloated, his teeth a discombobulated collection of yellowed nubs.

"No I didn't write the music with him," the old Johnnie says "I'd just be in the room sometimes when he was writing."

"That's it; he and I would get together and we'd play some kind of music that he could put the lyrics into and it would all come out just right, you know. Some of it would be fast, some of it would be slow, like this piece 'Havana Moon,' for instance. That was a slow, subtle calypso thing, so we had to find some kind of calypso music to go with the lyrics to 'Havana Moon.' And then pieces like 'Baby Doll' and 'Roll Over Beethoven,' all these were fast stuff, so we had to come up with some fast music that would blend in with the words he was writin' so he could get all of his sentence out and still come out on time. That's how we did it."

I get up and switch the tape off, and sit back down. Two contradicting answers. The whole thing didn't make any sense. Johnnie turns the channel to the local news.

"Johnnie," I say. "I don't understand. First you say you didn't write the music with Chuck, but then you describe how you did write the music with him."

He considers this for a moment. Then he sighs heavily and folds his hands.

"I've never wrote a single note of music in my life," he says without even taking his eyes from the screen. It is not a confession. Just a cold hard fact. But I feel the sharp stab of bitter disappointment nonetheless. The great rock and roll mystery, solved with one sentence. All rumors put to bed.

"'Course neither has Chuck Berry."

"I don't understand." It comes out before I can stop it. But it's true—I don't. He stares at the screen. I want to shout at him. Tell him that this is all just a big mess and it doesn't make sense. And then, just when my patience has reached the limit, he explains it all. And the funny thing is, he does so without missing a single second of the weather report. Not one.

"Me and Chuck didn't write music," he says. "That's 'cause neither one of us can. Can't read music and can't write it. You throw a lead sheet in front of me and it might as well be Chinese. I can't read it and there ain't no way I could write it. I knew a lot of fellas who could write music; Jimmy Vaughan from Albert King's band, Chuck Tillman, lot of 'em that could put music down on paper for other folks to read and play. That's what I call writin' music. What me and Chuck did wasn't writin' music. What me and Chuck did was make up songs. We'd get together and come up with music, and some of it would be new, but it wasn't nothin' we could write down. We'd just remember what we had did.

"The only one doin' any writin' on them songs was Chuck 'cause he wrote the words. I wasn't there all the time when he was writin', but I'd be in the room sometime with him, or in the car with him. That's where he wrote a lot of them songs. And he did all that writin' on his own. He never needed anybody's help with words. Think I could come up with words like, Chuck? Ain't nobody could. He'd write out the song, kinda like a poem, and then I'd help him find some music to put with the words.

"Now, at first I didn't have to help Chuck out with the music much. He knew exactly what he wanted to do—which was the hillbilly music. He'd get on his guitar with this *umpah-umpah-umpah* and I'd stay right with him, and if he wanted to stop playin', like if he was dancin' around, I'd just keep up that beat—me and Ebby—that *umpah-umpah-umpah*. That's how it was with them hillbilly songs. Blues, boogie, that was my department. But Chuck had those hillbilly songs down.

"Course when Chuck started with me, he wasn't no T-Bone Walker. Never was. But he could play pretty good in the major keys and he could do the flats. When he was with Tommy Stevens, he had to play in different keys than when he was with me—keys like A-natural and E-natural. That's cause Tommy was a guitar player. When Chuck joined my group he knew which keys I liked to play in which was the major keys—C, F, G, some D, and B flat and E flat. So since he was joinin' my band—those were the keys he had to play in. And he did. So I guess if I had anything to do with the hillbilly songs, 'Maybellene' or whatever, besides puttin' some boogie feel into it, it was that he got used to playin' it with a piano player, and playin' in keys that were easy for a piano player. That's it. 'Maybellene' and 'Thirty Days,' songs like that, with the cut-time beat—those were all hillbilly. That was the style. I just helped him with the arrangement and put a little boogie in 'em to change the feel a little bit.

"Now 'Wee Wee Hours,'" I made up all the music to that one. Chuck only did the words. He'll tell you that hisself. 'Maybellene' might've been Chuck Berry, but 'Wee Wee Hours' was the Trio. 'Cause that's the kind of stuff me and Ebby was playin' way before Chuck ever came along. We were all real proud of that one. Then songs like 'Downbound Train' and 'No Money Down' we just used standard types of blues, wasn't nothin' new. Fact, I'd call those songs blues 'fore I'd call 'em rock and roll.

"See, Chuck was tryin' to find his sound. He got the hillbilly thing down, and he could play the blues all right. But Chuck wanted to be Nat King Cole. He loved Nat King Cole. And after 'Maybellene,' seemed like everything he wanted to do was Nat King Cole. That was where 'Havana Moon' came from. He'd been havin' me try and teach him this song Nat did called 'Just A Shy Guy.' He worked and worked at it, but he never did get it under his fingers. The tune that came out of it though, from Chuck trying to learn, we turned that into the music he used for 'Havana Moon.' When we went to record it, Leonard Chess killed the piano 'cause he thought that it sounded more calypso with just guitar and drums. But that's how we did it. Fact, those songs we did that day, that was when I really started helpin' Chuck out, 'cause like I said, we was playin' around with all kinds of different music. We did another slow song that day called 'Driftin' Heart.' That was the same thing. Nat King Cole. Leroy Davis played sax on that one. Fact, he played on just about everything we did that day.

"Funny thing is, that same day we did them slow ballads was when we came up with that rock and roll style that he used from then on out. Chuck had wrote out the words to these three songs: 'Too Much Monkey Business,' 'Roll Over Beethoven,' and 'Brown Eyed Handsome Man.' We talked about it and decided that we was gonna have to come up with some kinda fast music to go with them. We just didn't know what. 'Monkey Business' had a whole bunch of words strung together, so the music we put together had a lot of stops and starts, 'cause the rhythm depended on him gettin' them long sentences out. That was different style, too, than what we had been doin'.

"But as far as me and Chuck comin' up with rock and roll together, 'Roll Over Beethoven' and 'Brown Eyed Handsome Man' was where that all started. There's a left-hand style I use when I do boogie's, what you call a choppin' bass. It's my favorite bass— I've just always felt comfortable with it. The good thing about the choppin' bass is you can speed it up or slow it down and you still get a swing feel to whatever you playin'. I call it my lazy bass 'cause it don't take no effort for me. I even use it on some of the slow blues I play. It fits with anything. When we started puttin' music together for 'Beethoven,' the way he had written out them lyrics, it just had a boogie feel to me, so it was just natural for me to start that choppin' bass. Chuck knew that bass from when I'd play 'Johnnie's Boogie' at the Cosmo, so when I started, he caught on to the rhythm right off. All we did was take the choppin' bass, the left hand from 'Johnnie's Boogie' and speed it up a little bit so it had more of a drive instead of that bounce. Once you got that rhythm, then you on your way.

"We just built everything on top of that bass. Willie Dixon, I remember, didn't try to copy what I was doin' on his upright. He'd just put a regular old walkin' bass behind Chuck's songs and I borrowed that idea sometimes when I was playing 'Maybellene' on the road. Ebby would play a shuffle. I'd fill in some with my right hand and Chuck, he had got to where he could play that same rhythm on his guitar. He wanted to have a steady rhythm so he could sing and duckwalk and use his hands without worryin' 'bout the music stoppin'. When Chuck went back to rhythm, he just got back in with my bass line and maybe I'd solo or whatever. When we got comfortable with each other, Chuck could start out with a solo and fall right into the rhythm, and then it was just blendin' and playin' off each other. Chuck's solos was all his. I gave him some change-ups, turnarounds, and of course I gave him that boogie rhythm style. But I never taught Chuck any solos. That 'Johnny B. Goode' solo, how he started the song, how he started 'Roll Over Beethoven,' Chuck did all those on his own. 'Cause he was listenin' to a lot of jazz guitarists like Carl Hogan and Charlie Christian, and T-Bone Walker. Chuck had his own guitar style that was different from everyone else. I didn't teach him how to play the guitar, I just gave him some ideas and a rhythm style to lay his guitar over.

"The way we came up with that song, 'Beethoven,' was the way we came up with most of the songs. Chuck was always the one with the ideas for what the songs was gonna be about. He'd say somethin' like, 'I got this song about going to school.' Then he'd read me what he had written. Most of the times he'd write two or three paragraphs of lyrics riding in the car from St. Louis to Chicago or just when we was on the road. When we would get to the studio, he'd read off what he'd written kind of like a poem and we'd try to find some music that would fit. I'd say, 'Well you want it fast or slow?' He might say to try somethin' fast. Sometimes it wouldn't work out that way, so we'd play around 'til we found somethin' that fit. I'd tell him if I liked somethin' and he'd tell me if he liked somethin'. If he came up with a little tune on his guitar, I'd help him put it together. Sometimes on the road he'd call me up to his room when we got to the hotel and play me somethin' he was workin' on. I'd say, 'That don't fit.' or 'Try puttin' this here,' and Chuck usually listened to what I had to say. If he heard me playin' something that he liked, then he might say, 'Play that again, man.' or 'What you got there? Let's see if it will fit with these words.' Then Chuck would get his guitar and I'd play it over and over until he could get what I was doin' under his fingers. Same as if he had somethin' worked up, I'd play along with what he had and add my stuff to it. Like 'Maybellene': He had that already put together when he met me. I added my own little things to it, but he already had the idea. 'Wee Wee Hours'—that tune was somethin' I worked up and he just added some words to it and kind of strummed along.

"But songs like 'Roll Over Beethoven,' those were things we did together from the start. The words were all his, but can't one of us say we did the music all by ourself. We did that music together."

"So you never got any credit all these years?" I ask.

Johnnie shakes his head.

"They told me they didn't put sidemen on the records. I didn't know nothin' 'bout the record business."

"You didn't ask?"

"I got paid."

He flips the channel.

"Yeah, but..."

"You ever drink?"

The question catches me off guard.

"No. No...I guess...I mean not really."

"Mmmmhmmm. That's good," he nods. "Don't ever start. Life will run right by you when you drinkin'. Or I should say, when you let drinkin' run your life."

And with that he is silent. And so am I.

* * *

"Whites like actually a lot of boogie woogie with the twangin' singin' on top of it," observes Ike Turner in the documentary *Rock and Roll*. "It's actually nothin' but boogie. That's what it really is."

Turner's thinly veiled reference to his St. Louis rival, Chuck Berry, and Berry's appeal to the white teenage market was not entirely off the mark. In fact, rock transcriber Fred Soklow reached the very same conclusion during the 1990s, when he provided stylistic analysis and sheet music for seventeen Berry hits in a Goodman Group publication called *Recorded Versions*. Upon setting to work on the notes and tablature, Soklow noticed in a vast majority of Berry's music a distinct "tension between the boogie-woogie shuffle and the modern straight-four rock beat."

As Soklow saw it, Berry and his sidemen (Johnnie Johnson and Ebby Hardy) were "inventing the new rock beat" using a boogie-woogie pattern. This pattern, he found, was used interchangeably on both shuffle-beat tunes like "Almost Grown" and straight-time tunes like "Roll Over Beethoven."

"Berry took his cue from players like Big Bill Broonzy, Lightnin' Hopkins and John Lee Hooker, who imitated the boogie-woogie pianist's left hand by playing two-string patterns over the first position E and A chords," asserts Soklow. "Each variation alternates the root of the chord with the fifth and sixth (and sometimes flat seventh), creating a boogie-woogie bass pattern.

Soklow's stylistic analysis, while thoroughly detailed, fails to mention the most obvious source of Berry's rhythm-guitar style. A style that, as he says, "imitated the boogie-woogie pianist's left hand." Johnnie Johnson's left hand. The alternating fifth and sixth on every beat was an exact description of his "chopping bass."

* * *

Chess single number 1626, "Roll Over Beethoven" and "Drifting Heart," was released in May of 1956. At its peak, the record hit No.7 on the R&B chart and No.29 on the Billboard Hot 100. Boosted by the success of the record, the band hit the road for another summer tour. Things were looking up again for the Chuck Berry Trio and for Chess which sold his records by the truckload all over the country. Rock and roll was taking off.

And so it was that Berry, standing on the brink of anonymity after his first hit, had called on his faithful pianist. And the solution Johnnie Johnson provided him was the sound that would set the rock world on its ear, solidifying Chuck Berry's status as the genre's most inventive and influential performer. He would never surpass Elvis in popularity; he was simply the wrong color. But within the music community, Berry's status as the uncrowned King of Rock & Roll was secured by the results of that February 1956 session. Together, in one eight-hour period, two club musicians from St. Louis redefined rock and roll for the next fifteen years. Charles Edward Anderson Berry became a star, and eventually a millionaire many, many times over. Johnnie Clyde Johnson got a Cuban cigar, several shots of good whiskey, and $100.

"And that," as Johnnie says, "Was good money back then."

* * *

In the end, it was the drinking that destroyed them. That and Berry's unchecked ambition. Chuck Berry, Johnnie Johnson, and

Ebby Hardy were three different people bound together by the fact that they had stumbled into a new style of music that just happened to set the world on fire. Admittedly, the first tour had been a carnival, a flurry of fascination that had bonded the three men inexorably. But the excitement had worn off. Now looking around at each other—different faces, different beliefs, different values—they realized that they actually had little in common.

"The three of us were so different," Johnnie says. "Chuck was always up to his own thing, and Ebby and I went out, but not a whole lot 'cause he liked to stay in his room. Actually, it got to where we didn't socialize much off stage. One reason was that Ebby and I drank a lot and Chuck didn't. I always had my whiskey and Ebby liked his highballs. It got on Chuck's nerves because he never drank at all. Never. I saw him pour some rum in his Coke recently and I'd have liked to pass out from shock. I'd never seen him drink before. He'd buy you all kinds of drinks, and he knew how to make 'em from when he had his club, but Chuck never touched alcohol hisself. I guess that's why we had some of the problems that we did."

The assumption that many of the group's problems derived from alcohol abuse is grounded in fact; Chuck Berry's distaste for the substance is legendary. In his autobiography, he speaks candidly about his feelings towards drinking and the difficulties of life on the road with alcoholic bandmates. "While the fun of traveling increased," says Berry of the Trio's post-"Maybellene" touring, "so did the problems."

> Johnnie and Ebby were vividly showing increasing deficiencies in their performances due to their drinking*. Johnnie would become quiet and clumsy when intoxicated, while Ebby would become loud and silly. This annoyed me to the point where I began to try to set drinking rules for them. I tried to reason with my band that if they were drinking to bring pleasure to themselves it was a fact that they would not feel the wanted effects as much when the mind and senses were dulled from the liquor. And if it was meant to dull agony or sorrow, the fact of the feeling would return once intoxication subsided, plus a hangover. They

didn't understand. This drinking pattern continued throughout a tour that worked us on out to a dozen cities in California. My restrictions against drinking in the station wagon was followed—Ebby and the bass player who rode in the rear seats would hold the jug of wine outside the window and swallow. When I would protest, Ebby would confidently reply, 'Not in the car, boss—just as you said,' and take another swallow.

"That wasn't Ebby Hardy," says Johnnie upon hearing Berry's version of the backseat story. "Both me and Ebby were quiet when we was drinkin'. Chuck's talkin' about another piano player he took with him once named Floyd Nallum. Not too long after the Alan Freed tour, I took sick with the gout and couldn't even put a shoe on. We was about to go back on the road for a couple dates, so Joe Lewis introduced Chuck to Floyd, who was his nephew. Floyd was a pretty good jazz piano player, but he didn't quite know how to play rock and roll. That didn't matter 'cause the Gayle Agency had booked the gigs for a trio with piano and drums, so Chuck took him out anyway. That's when all the stuff happened with Floyd holdin' the bottle out the window. Chuck and Ebby told me all about it when they got back. I'm sure Chuck would have liked to bust that man in the head, but he was Joe Lewis's nephew, so he couldn't really do nothin'. He was glad to have the group back together after I got well, I tell you that much."

Johnson and Hardy may not have been the true culprits in Berry's tale, but Johnnie admits that both his and Hardy's drinking caused many a problem and frustrated Berry to no end off stage. And while Berry confesses a grudging appreciation for Johnson's tolerance in his book, the guitarist had little patience or pity for those who drank.

One of the most telling points in Berry's autobiography involves a disturbing episode he witnessed in the back alley of a burlesque club when he was still just a boy.

---

* "It seemed at first [Alan Freed] could hold his take as well as Johnnie Johnson could, without it affecting his ability to perform his professional obligations." —*Chuck Berry: The Autobiography*

Around the same age [fifteen] I rode downtown on the streetcar to a burlesque theater in the skid-row area where they had women dancing on stage in what now are mere swimsuits. As I turned into the alley on my way to the stage door where I would enjoy peeping at the women coming on and off the stage, I saw a man bending over a fairly well dressed drunk lying against the alley wall. The man standing reached stealthily into the pocket of the one in a stupor and lifted his wallet. What molded most to my memory was that the drunk man awakened during the lift but still did not have enough control of his movements to defend himself or resist against the robber completing the lift. I heard the drunk pleading pitifully, 'Don't take my money.' Witnessing that scene was the most touching and fruitful of my past in molding my determination never to fall into a condition where I would not have control of my senses at the highest level achievable.

My feelings about the incident is that the drunk, though within his rights to indulge in alcohol, was stupid and careless to place himself in so vulnerable a situation. In view of the situation the drunk was in, which in the first place could have been prevented, I had no sympathy for him. Whereas the thief, soberly taking a thoughtful chance to engage in a gainful wrong, was to me clever and ingenious to find an opportunity so likely of gain.

Thoughtful. Clever. Ingenious. In Berry's words, it is more than okay to exploit a drunk. Especially, when there is something to gain.

* * *

In the fall of 1956, Ebby Hardy decided to leave the Chuck Berry Trio. He had held court behind the trap kit for three years, watching as the quiet little weekend jazz-blues combo became a country-western novelty band, and then a full-fledged traveling rock and roll act. Hardy was older than his bandmates; in 1956 he was already well into his thirties. Also, he came from a school of drummers more akin to Gene Krupa than Freddy Below. But through it all Hardy held steady, adapting to whatever came his way–just like a drummer should.

In the end, it was just a matter of the sacrifices not paying off. In order to keep up with the rigorous touring schedule assigned by the Gayle Agency, Berry had left his job at his sister's hair salon, Hardy had left work, and Johnson had taken a leave of absence from his day job at the American Steel Foundry. For Berry, the life of a traveling musician was a sweet deal, as he pocketed $750 out of every $1000, plus tips. But for Ebby Hardy, the measly $250 he split with Johnnie was not enough to support his wife and six children. In short, he could no longer afford to travel with Berry. Johnnie Johnson was not surprised when his friend left the group.

"Ebby's wife begged him to quit after the 101 nights and he eventually gave in to her," Johnnie remembers. "They had six kids, and he wasn't makin' enough to support that big of a family. We weren't gettin' paid but union scale; Chuck was pretty tight with that wallet, and Ebby just couldn't afford it anymore. He loved to play, but it just wasn't worth his family starvin', so he quit."

After leaving Berry, Hardy searched haplessly for work until, out of necessity, he began hustling for money, shooting craps and such on the streets of East St. Louis. In 1958, he joined up with the newly formed Albert King band, but his drinking did not sit well with the demanding King, who fired him soon after. As a result, Hardy returned to playing club gigs in and around the St. Louis area. Johnnie never forgot his old friend, and the two continued to play off and on around town for years, just as they had done before Berry joined them. Sadly, at the time of his death from a heart attack in the mid-1980s, Hardy was on relief and living in poverty. "Ebby...he was my friend," says Johnnie. "I wish like anything he was still around today. I wasn't much better off than he was when he passed. But things are goin' a little better for me now, and I could have helped him out. I wish he hadn't of gone so soon. I miss him dearly."

By the fall of 1956, Johnnie Johnson had married again. After divorcing Marguerite, he had met Rose Hill at a nightclub in East St. Louis. Attracted by her beauty and fiery charm, Johnson was smitten and they began to date heavily. After a whirlwind courtship, during which time Rose became pregnant with his child, Johnson and Hill exchanged vows "before she started to show" on the first day of the 1955 World Series. Shortly afterwards, Rose gave birth to a son, Peter.

Unlike Hardy's wife, Rose Johnson supported her husband's musical career, and Johnnie felt no pressure from the home front. "She could get downright nasty about some things," Johnnie recalls. "But when it came to music, Rose was behind me one-hundred percent."

Johnnie stayed on the road with Berry steadily for the next year. His original drummer gone, Berry began taking Jaspar Thomas, a local jazz drummer, on the road with him and Johnson. Although highly skilled, Thomas was the prototypical rock and roll drummer—a wildman who was hard to control once he'd been drinking. His impetuous antics did not sit well with Johnson and Berry.

"Jaspar was real good, better than Ebby," Johnnie admits. "But Ebby held his liquor. You never knew what was gonna happen with Jaspar on the road. When he was sober, you couldn't find a better person. But when he was drunk—watch out! He did some crazy things."

Needless to say, Thomas was not always invited to go along with Johnson and Berry and thus the trio became more or less a duo. Driving cross-country in the little red station wagon, they played gigs all around the nation, joining up with Alan Freed's caravan for a few shows, then moving on to wherever the Gale Agency sent them.

"We put a lot of miles on that car," Johnnie says. "For a year or two after Ebby quit, it was mostly just me and Chuck. Jaspar and Leroy Davis usually only came along to record, or for special engagements, 'cause they were both in other bands in St. Louis. I did most of the drivin', but we switched off now and then, sometimes without even stoppin' the car. There'd be times we'd be runnin' late for a show and one of us would be tired, so instead of pullin' over, we'd just change seats while we was drivin'. Chuck would climb under me and for a minute we'd be all tangled up, then he'd get around me and I'd hop over to the passenger seat without the car ever stoppin' or even losin' speed. We had some close calls at first, but it wasn't long 'fore we was changin' seats goin' eighty miles an hour and not even worryin' 'bout it!"

As the shows became more and more frequent, Berry began to pull in a larger take. Yet despite their growing prosperity, Johnnie saw no appreciable difference in his paycheck. "I got paid union scale," he remembers. "But Chuck started buying Cadillacs about then."

"We were doin' a lot of shows all over the country and the money was gettin' better," says Johnnie of the tours following Ebby's departure. "I remember one time we was in California and the club we was workin' at had paid Chuck all in one dollar bills. Don't ask me why, but they did. Naturally, Chuck wanted to change them out for bigger bills, so we stuffed the money in a bag and went walkin' around tryin' to find a place to cash it.

"Of course, when you're gonna go walkin' around in a strange city with a bag full of money, you don't want nobody to know you have a bag full of money. So Chuck came up with the idea of tossin' the bag back and forth like a football, like we didn't even care what was inside, so nobody would rob us. We ended up at this hotel and when Chuck went up to the desk with a bag full of money, the manager got suspicious and called the cops.

"Next thing we know, here comes a bunch of men in suits lookin' like the C.I.A into the lobby. They got me and Chuck and took us into separate rooms then they started askin' us all these questions. 'Do you have any I.D.? Where did you get all this money? Why is it all in one dollar bills?' Things like that. Chuck showed them the receipt from the club and told them who he was, but they didn't believe any of it. To them we was just two black men with a bag full of money. Finally, they called Gale and everything got cleared up. Soon as they found out he was a rock star, they started apologizin' and askin' for autographs. One of 'em says, 'I don't know who the hell you are, but I bet my kid does.' Chuck hadn't even done nothin' on that one and them cops were on him. Scared me to death."

Traveling the country as a two-man group, Johnson and Berry were forced to deal with a different backup band every night. The task could be daunting, and Johnnie found the years of experience paying off as he guided unfamiliar, unenthused, and often subpar house bands through Berry's repertoire.

"When we'd show up at a gig with just the house band backin' us, it was always my job to explain the music to 'em," recalls Johnnie. "The drummer had to know when to swing or shuffle and when to play straight 4/4. The horn and bass players had to get used to the keys we was playin' in, and the fact that they was gonna be followin' me more than Chuck, since I held the rhythm constant so Chuck could play around for the audience and solo. We would have little problems now and then, and if someone got off, I'd have to get 'em on track 'cause Chuck was entertainin' and you can't entertain and have to worry about the band at the same time. That's what I did...keepin' everybody where they was supposed to be."

Johnson's presence certainly made Berry's life easier, if only on the bandstand. But before long, the lure of fly-by-night gigs (Johnson was reluctant to fly) and the prospect of pocketing all the pay, led Berry to a decision that would in many ways tarnish his reputation within musical circles. As Keith Richards observes in *Hail! Hail! Rock 'n' Roll*, "Even when it's going great, [Berry] won't leave it at that. He'll come in with a potential 'screw it up'." And so it was that Berry began doing shows alone, without Johnson to lead his band. Berry wrote:

> A major decision I reached after my first couple years of touring was to stop carrying the two other musicians of my

trio with me to performances. My contacts at the Gale Booking Agency explained that they could book me more easily as a single, which would also clear more revenue for me. Plus, they enlightened me that most local bands were playing a lot of my hits on their gigs anyway. I didn't consider myself any better than any other musician out there. In fact, half the time I knew I wasn't as good. I asked them about the responsibility for securing a backup band and about the pay. They informed me that the respective promoters would be responsible for the backup bands' cost, character, and traveling. The first thing I thought of was no more botheration of drinking or being late on the gig. Since I had started flying on airplanes I could work in Miami one night and Seattle the next. The advice soon turned into arrangements and I acquired the capability of flying cross-country if necessary to make consecutive engagements. The agency drew up my contracts with the provisions for the promoters to supply amplifiers for my use as well as a backup group. It seemed logical. I could brief the different guys about the progression of my songs, those they didn't know, during rehearsals.

But Berry didn't have rehearsals. And the plan, though logical in practice, failed miserably. Studio players unfamiliar with Berry's unique sound and strange keys, and lacking Johnnie Johnson's guidance, found the music bothersome—too much trouble for too little money. Chuck Conner, Little Richard's tour drummer, recognized Berry's problem even then.

"Chuck Berry was a powerful act when he wasn't on a bill with Richard," declares Conner. "We met Chuck a lot of times on the road. He was down there and Richard was up here, though. Chuck would have been bigger if he'd had a regular band. See, he'd have the house band backing him. They'd be good musicians, studio musicians, but they'd actually be downing the guy they were playing for. They'd say, 'Chuck Berry? It's a drag. Just play anything.''

"They were good musicians but they couldn't do what Chuck wanted them to do," says Johnnie. "They could have played the music, but they didn't care nothin' 'bout learnin'. Rock and roll was just startin', so most of the backup bands would be jazz musicians and they didn't care about no rock and roll. They thought it was a bunch of noise. To them, Chuck wasn't even a musician, and since he couldn't give em no lead sheets or nothin', he didn't seem too professional."

But Berry's records continued to sell, despite increasingly mediocre live performances, and by the end of 1956, he was a full-blown star. *Billboard* named him Most Promising R&B Artist in their annual DJ Poll, and he had two singles chart in less than a year. In December, he made his first film appearance, singing "You Can't Catch Me" in the movie *Rock, Rock, Rock*.

By Christmas, Chess was calling for more records, and Berry was ready. Returning to St. Louis, he found Johnnie Johnson and Jaspar Thomas, and went back in the studio on January 21, 1957. Over the next two years, their prodigious output would set the standard by which all were measured. Between 1957 and 1959, fifteen chart-topping singles were released to hungry fans who devoured the sound with adolescent ardor. "Most of the best stuff," says Johnnie, "was done durin' that time. We got the system down real good."

As the first writing/performing team in rock and roll history, Chuck Berry and Johnnie Johnson would not only influence musicians of their own generation, like Little Richard, Elvis, and Carl Perkins, but those second-generation rockers like the Beatles, the Kinks, the Animals, and the Rolling Stones, through whom the genre would continue to evolve into its present-day form.

Yet despite their tandem efforts, only one would thrive. By relegating Johnnie Johnson to the role of silent partner, Chuck Berry placed himself in a highly profitable but equally precarious position. For he alone bore the full weight of the rock and roll mantle on his shoulders. And while he would reap all the benefits—the money, the cars, the women, the fame—he would suffer significant consequences as well. Consequences that in a few short years, would nearly destroy him.

VI

JOHNNIE B. GOODE

"Playing with Johnnie today is about as close to rock and roll heaven as you can get. Just when you think it can't get any better, Johnnie will start to roll those triplets against the 4/4 beat. Then the triplets start to swirl like the world is upending and dumping sweet little sixteen right in your lap. At that moment you know deep down...it isn't that this guy plays rock and roll...he *is* rock and roll...Thanks, Johnnie."

—John Sebastian 1995

The primary motivation behind every Chuck Berry song was money. He admits this freely, without shame and without coercion. In 1969, he told an audience at Berkley that he "wouldn't have had the time" to write had he not been paid. "The commercial value of songs," Berry told the crowd, "is a great instigator."

Indeed, Johnnie Johnson recalls, Berry never seemed to be in it for the love of music. Rather, Johnnie suspects, he saw the music business as a wide-open market for someone with a quick wit and ruthless nature.

"I don't know about what Chuck was like before I met him," says Johnnie. "But from the very start, after he joined my group, he was a hustler. A lot of musicians, they so into what they doin' and they love playin', but once they get off the stage and start talkin' to the club owners and the promoters and the record companies, they're lost. Lot of 'em so doped up they can't even make a sentence. Not Chuck. He was always on the ball. He wanted that money and he went after it. Wanted to get them records out as fast as he could. Chuck loved playin' Nat King Cole, and Muddy Waters, and Harry Belafonte, but once we came up with that rock and roll formula and he saw how them kids were eatin' it up, Muddy and them was gone, and every record started soundin' the same."

In a sense, Chuck Berry was and is a businessman first and a musician second; and it was because of his mindset that he was so successful in the music industry. He wrote his songs not to impress, only to sell. Yet by combining hip, unthreatening lyrics with Johnnie Johnson's boogie rhythm and a few catchy jazz licks a' la T-Bone Walker and Carl Hogan, he was able to do both effectively.

"I was trying to shoot for the entire population instead of ,shall we say, 'the neighborhood,'" explains Berry in *Hail! Hail! Rock 'n' Roll*. "Muddy Waters, I knew he was dynamite in our neighborhood. He was dynamite with me. One of the best-loved artists that I liked. But working for my father in the white neighborhoods, I never heard Muddy Waters, I never heard Elmore James, Howlin Wolf—never heard him. I heard Frank Sinatra, I heard Pat Boone—Pat Boone doing Muddy Waters or whoever's number/selection. I said, 'Why can't I do as Pat Boone does and play good music for the white people, and sell as well there as I did in the neighborhood.' And that's what I shot for writing 'School Days'—nice, nice music and it...uh...caught on."

"School Days," Berry's debut recording of 1957, was his first stab at cataloging the teenage experience. While "Roll Over Beethoven" and "Too Much Monkey Business" had made reference to them, "School Days" was all about the teenager, the student, who spent his or her days trapped in a classroom yearning for the end of the day when they could flock to the "juke joint," "drop the coin right into the slot," and dance to the beat of the newest rock and roll song.

At the time of the January 21 session, Chuck Berry was thirty years old and the father of a six-year-old daughter. Yet his gift for expression allowed him to relate to the average American teenager.

> 'School Days, was born from the memories of my own experiences in high school. The lyrics depict the way it was in my time. I had no idea what was going on in the classes during the time I composed it, much less what's happening today. The phrases came to me spontaneously, and rhyming took up most of the time that was spent on the song. I remember leaving it twice to go get coffee and while out having some major lines come to me that would enhance the story in the song, causing me to rush back to my room to get them down. Recording the song with breaks in the rhythm was intended to emphasize the jumps and changes I found in classes in high school compared to the one room and one teacher I had in elementary school. That's ninety percent of the song; I suppose the remainder could have been talent.

Johnnie Johnson remembers the moment he and Berry sat down to prepare music for the song. "Chuck came to me with this thing he called 'School Days' which I really liked a lot," he says. "We decided right away to put a shuffle behind it. I guess that was becomin' our sound. Chuck had to speed the words up a little bit to keep on time, but we were both real happy with how it was comin'. The only problem was how to start it out. You can't just go right into a shuffle, it don't sound right. You need an intro. Chuck had that Carl Hogan intro he liked to use, but it didn't seem to fit what we was doin'. We played around and played around, finally I said since we was doin' it in G, we could use the intro from 'Johnnie's Boogie,' which I got from 'Honky Tonk Train.' That was supposed to sound like a train whistle. Well, when Chuck played it on his guitar, we thought it sounded like a school bell ringin', and that was perfect for a song called 'School Days.' After we had that intro down, Jasper came up with a little drum thing where he'd roll from the snare to the tom and then we went right into the shuffle in G. It really came out soundin' good and I'd have to say it was one of my favorites."

Released in March of 1957, "School Days" blasted to the top of the charts. By the time Chess single 1653 had run its course, the record had claimed the No.1 spot on the *Billboard* Rhythm & Blues chart, No.3 on the *Cashbox* Top 100, and No.5 on the *Billboard* Hot 100. Altogether, it sold a million copies.

On the lesser-played B-side of "School Days," was another experiment—a steel guitar/piano instrumental called "Deep Feeling." While Johnnie pounds out a slow, chopping bass, Berry plays on the two-week old Gibson Electraharp steel console he had purchased for what he described as a "never-you-mind $585," laying mournful licks over Johnnie's left-hand rhythm and right-hand accents. With Johnnie's support, Berry is freed to improvise while still keeping in touch with the basic feel of the piece. In other words, "Deep Feeling" captures perfectly the essence of Johnson and Berry's musical relationship, although the song itself received little in the way of accolades.

With the cash garnered from the success of his chart-topping singles, Berry purchased thirty acres of land west of St. Louis in the community of Wentzville, Missouri. His idea was to build a country club/amusement park where he could charge visitors to camp, fish, and swim. In addition, the star also intended to build a mansion for himself on the grounds, complete with a recording studio and stage where he hoped to have the major acts of the era visit and perform. The last dream would be fulfilled eventually, but not for some three decades.

The following month, his first album, *After School Session*, was released. To Berry's surprise, the EP sported two previously unreleased instrumental tracks, "Roly Poly" and "Berry Pickin'," which were not legitimate compositions, but rather warmup jam sessions recorded two years before unbeknownst to both Berry and Johnson, and named by the Chess brothers. Berry was not amused, but nonetheless accepted the transgression as a matter of course.

To celebrate the compilation of his two years worth of hit singles, Berry, Johnson, and Jaspar Thomas returned to the studio the following May. In the course of the session, the trio recorded three songs: "Oh Baby Doll," "Reelin' and Rockin'" and "Rock and Roll Music."

"Chuck wrote the words to most of them songs while we was travelin' on the road," Johnnie says. "'Sides havin' more of a honky-tonk feel to it, 'Baby Doll' was pretty much the same as any other we did. Same with 'Rock and Roll Music.' We was so used to playin' them shuffles that all we had to do was make it a fast tempo or a slow tempo and decide where we wanted the changes. It didn't take more than an hour to get those two songs on tape. "The other song, 'Reelin' and Rockin',' was a little bit different. We borrowed a lot of that song from that Bill Haley fella, who did 'Rock Around the Clock,' and we just did it our own way. A lot of folks call 'Rock Around the Clock' a rock and roll song, but it really wasn't nothin' but swing music. Jaspar came up with some more little drum riffs for that one, too. He'd been a big-band drummer with the Eddie Johnson Band and he had a lot of beats that he could put in that me and Chuck would approve of. That was also the first song where Leonard Chess asked me to rip the keys. What rippin' the keys meant was you dragged your hand up the keys while you was playin', like Jerry Lee Lewis does. I didn't usually do that 'cause I felt it was all flash and no technique, but Leonard said it made the piano sound more excitin', and I figured he was the expert 'cause he'd been into recordin' a lot longer than me. While we was rehearsin', he'd come out of the booth and rip the keys himself while I was playin'. Then he'd give me this big ol' smile. It was kinda like he was sayin', 'That's right, I did it.' Leonard was a character, boy. Thing was, he was right most of the time, too. He knew what he was doin' when it came to makin' records. They did a lot of business at Chess."

As a whole, the three new songs did extremely well. Although "Oh Baby Doll" peaked at No.57 on the Billboard chart, "Rock and Roll Music" hit No.10 and "Reelin and Rockin'," when it was released the following year, would climb all the way to No. 2, Berry's best placing as of yet. In September, he appeared in his second film, the Paramount release *Mr. Rock and Roll*, for which he performed "Oh Baby Doll."

Riding his growing popularity, Berry tapped Johnson again in early September to join him on tour with Irving Field's Biggest Show of Stars. Field's 1957 lineup featured a variety of acts including Buddy Holly, Paul Anka, the Drifters, the Everly Brothers, and Clyde McPhatter.

Sadly, little had changed in the way of racial relations in the two years since Johnson, Berry, and Hardy traversed the country on Alan Freed's second rock and roll tour. Due to segregation laws, the white and black acts were often not permitted to play on the same stage and could not stay in the same hotels. Nevertheless, despite the various indignities and inconveniences suffered in the name of segregation, Johnnie recalls an encompassing feeling of racial harmony amongst the artists themselves.

"They were all cool," he says. "Color didn't matter. White, black, we all got along like it was nothin'. The only thing that separated us was the laws down South. That's when you had to worry about what restaurants you ate at and whatever. Sometimes the white groups couldn't play the show 'cause blacks and whites couldn't be on the same bill. But most of the time we was together. We mostly all rode in the buses, except for the kid Paul Anka; he had his own car, I think it was a 1955 Chevy convertible, and he'd follow behind on his own. When the tour hit St. Louis, me and Chuck took an idea from Paul, and followed the rest of the way in Chuck's pink Cadillac."

For Johnnie, the tour would have been perfect except for one minor inconvenience. In order to meet deadlines, the performers were sometimes required to fly from gig to gig. And Johnnie Johnson was scared to death of flying.

"I'd had to fly in the service, only from island to island, but even then I got real nervous, and if there was any way to get around it I did," he confesses. "Once I got out, the only way I'd get on a plane was if I was drunk. Some of the groups didn't mind at all. Buddy Holly didn't mind, which I guess was too bad seein' what happened to him and all. He and I sat together on the plane and talked about music and whatever. He knew I was nervous and he calmed me down some. I really liked Buddy a lot. I sat in with his band a couple times on the tour and he really had something goin' with his music. I wish I'd got to know him better. Anyway, when it came to flyin', and especially later on when Chuck started flyin' to Europe, I had to say no. It took me years before I could get on a plane without gettin' the shakes. Now I fly more than I walk!"

The Irving Field tour ended on November 24, and Johnnie returned to work at the American Steel Foundry where his comings and goings had been accepted as routine. Following the Christmas holidays, Berry again asked Johnnie to record and the pianist was happy to oblige. Christmas had drained him financially, and although he'd been able to secure some club dates around town with Hardy, he had little money left over.

On January 6, 1958, the trio met in Chicago where they recorded "Guitar Boogie," "Rockin' at the Philharmonic," and the seminal hit "Sweet Little Sixteen."

"I'd have to say, of all the songs we did, I liked 'Sweet Little Sixteen' best of all," recalls Johnnie. "'Course, I 'bout tore my thumbnail off tryin' to get the piano part where Leonard Chess wanted it. He'd have me rippin' the keys up and down and up and down on the solo 'cause he said that's what folks wanted to hear. Anyway, I just liked how the song felt and I was pretty proud of it when we'd finished. One thing about that song, I've heard people tell me they thought it was done in E-flat. That's not true. The original was done in C.

"Another song I remember from that day was 'Rockin' at the Philharmonic' which was Chuck tryin' to play jazz with me and Jaspar. See, Chuck had some bits of jazz solos he used in songs, but he could never quite get his fingers to really play jazz. It wasn't his fault. One problem was the size of his hands, 'cause you know Chuck has some big hands. My oldest son was seven feet tall and Chuck's hands are as big as his ever got. They look like baseball gloves hanging off his arms. His fingers were so big that his notes was always blarin' instead of soundin' clear. I remember he used to try and play piano once and a while, but he had such a hard time playin' 'cause he'd go to hit a key and he'd be hittin' two at a time with one finger.

"Naturally, guitar was a little easier for him and he'd work at gettin' down pieces of things he'd heard on records. Jazz stuff. We were playin' around, jammin' or whatever, and Leonard said, 'Hell, let's put this down on record.' 'Guitar Boogie' was the same thing; ain't nothin' but us jammin'. I don't know if it was ever released or not."

Soon after the "Sweet Little Sixteen" session, the Chess brothers approached Johnson about the idea of making his own record. Phil Chess remembers distinctly that both he and his brother spoke to him several times about making a solo album, but each time the humble pianist refused. For whatever reason, Johnnie seemed reluctant to be the focus of attention, favoring instead the anonymity and perhaps the safety allowed in the humble role of a sideman.

"We were after Johnnie for years to do something on his own," recalls Phil Chess. "'Cause he was so good at the blues and he had all the jazz licks down, and we figured he could do something that would sell a few records and get him out from under Chuck. But it never worked out. I don't know if it was the drinking or what. He just seemed to want to be a sideman. After a while, the idea just kind of faded away."

Johnnie remembers being asked several times to lay down some solo tracks for a potential album, but balked because, as he says "I wasn't ready to be a frontman."

"Phil Chess was the first one that started askin' me 'bout doin' a solo album playin' jazz and blues, but I was too scared," he admits. "It's one thing to help somebody come up with their music, but it's another thing to be in the spotlight. I wasn't ready for it. Even though he asked me a few more times over the years, I just never did it. Then they just stopped askin'."

On February 28, Berry fresh from a stint of solo traveling, visited Chess studios for the first time without Johnnie Johnson and Jaspar Thomas. He'd been working up a song intended as a tribute to his faithful pianist, but true to character, the finished product had ended up more of a self-portrait.

Released in March of 1958, "Johnny B. Goode" wasn't Berry's most successful song, peaking at No.5 on the R&B chart and No.8 on the Hot 100, but it would become his most famous. Recording with a band that included bass stalwart Willie Dixon, drummer Fred Below, and Dixon's favorite pianist, Lafayette Leake, Berry was simply rehashing a tried-and-true formula developed with Johnnie Johnson; yet he makes no mention of this fact in his book. As is common with Berry, when discussing his most celebrated work, he is more apt to explore the lyrical development of the song as opposed to the musical. Of the character "Johnny B. Goode," he writes:

> 'Johnny' in the song is more or less myself although I wrote it intending it to be a song for Johnnie Johnson. I altered the predictions that my mother made of me and created a story that paralleled. It seems easy, now that it's been around so long, that it took only a period of about two weeks of periodic application to put the lyrics together when I worked on 'Drifting Heart' almost four months and it sold scarcely twenty copies.

It is obvious that a story that brings a subject from out of the boondocks to fame and fortune is more dramatic than one out of midtown to somewhere crosstown. 'Rags to riches' even sounds more attractive than 'fortune to fame.' It was with this in mind that I wrote of a boy with an ambition to become a guitar player, who came from the least of luxury to be seen by many, practicing until the listener believes he has all but made it to the top as the chorus prompts him like his mother's encouraging voice, 'Go Johnny Go.'"

Berry ends his explanation with a word of advice to the up and coming. "Chances are you have talent," Berry writes. "But will the name and the light come to you? No! You have to 'GO!'"

In his book, Berry claims to have recorded five other songs during the February 28 session, the first being the flipside of "Johnny B. Goode," "Around and Around," followed by "It Don't Take But a Few Minutes," "Ingo," "Surfin' Steel," and "Blues For Hawaiians." The session seemed stressful for Berry. On the 1986 album *Rock 'n' Roll Rarities*, a collection of unreleased versions and studio outtakes from Berry's Chess sessions, the frustrated guitarist can be heard yelling at Lafayette Leake during the first recording of "Johnny B. Goode": "You were making 'Roll Over Beethoven' on the piano solo that time. Stay away from that!" Berry ordered. Before Leake could make a retort, Berry was already counting down the next take.

"Chuck could be real hard on musicians in the studio," remembers Phil Chess. "A lot of times, if he made a mistake, he would yell at somebody in the band. But Chuck never yelled at Johnnie. He was always very respectful of him. In fact, whenever Chuck would start getting difficult, my brother or I would ask Johnnie to talk to him and try to calm him down. As far as we knew, Johnnie was the only guy Chuck would listen to."

Johnnie remembers, "Chuck was always yellin' at folks, but he never gave me no problems. I guess he got so used to playin' with me that he didn't want to be worryin' 'bout some other piano player. By the time Chuck did 'Johnny B. Goode,' he had that formula down. Even though we kept makin' up music together on most of the records after that, Chuck didn't need me like he used to. He never did tell me who he recorded 'Johnny B. Goode' with, but I'd say it was probably that Leake fella. The first time I ever heard the song was at a gig and Chuck looked back and said, 'This is one I did for you.' I had no idea that he'd recorded it."

That same year, Berry expanded his enterprises. Based on the growing popularity of the Chuck Berry Fan Club and inspired by television's "American Bandstand," Berry and his secretary Francine Gillum created Club Bandstand, a sort of Chuck Berry headquarters in St. Louis, where they hosted fan club meetings and worked towards procuring a liquor license for a night club they hoped to open.

Meanwhile, Johnnie Johnson, who had become a father once again when Syble was born in 1957, continued working at the American Steel Foundry, although his habit of taking off on long tours began to tax his credibility with the company.

"Anytime I went on the road, the company would let me off for a while and let me have my job back when I came home," Johnnie recalls. "They were real understandin', and I think they was proud of what I was doin', but you can only take so much."

In June of 1958, despite being extremely busy with his numerous projects, including two corporations, a nightclub, a fan club, and the construction of Berry Park in Wentzville, Chuck Berry scheduled another recording session and invited both Johnson and Thomas to join him.

Two songs made the *Billboard* chart that August. "Carol," about a friend of Clyde McPhatter, whom Berry and Johnson often toured with, hit No.10, while "Beautiful Delilah," a revision of the cut-time pattern used in "Maybellene" and "Thirty Days," stalled at No. 81.

Following the release of "Carol," Berry and Johnson went back on the road for a brief east coast summer tour that ended in September with a ten day run at the Brooklyn Fox Theater. Days later they returned to Chicago only to discover that things had changed considerably since their last recording session.

September of 1958 was the beginning of a new era for Chess Records. Due to their growing enterprise, the company moved its headquarters to a larger, more modern studio on 2120 South Michigan. The Chess brothers were seldom in the studio anymore, relegating the recording operations to staff engineers and employees. Nevertheless, Leonard Chess still popped in from time to time in order to supervise his top money maker. Says Berry in his book: "It seemed the sessions were becoming cold and foreign but we managed to have our tunes run down enough to be ready for tape."

> I got Johnnie Johnson and Jaspar Thomas, who was my main drummer along about then, and wheeled in to the Chess studios, where we ran through a bunch of cover tunes and galloped over a few lyrics I had scribbled on the long Show of Stars tours. At this time I let many distractions hinder me from really writing as I had in the beginning of my career, until my attention to women practically prevented me from giving any time to improvisations at all. Although Leonard and I both knew the recording session was inferior to the past ones, he congratulated me on coming up with something that kept the burner glowing with different sounds.

Despite Berry's misgivings, each of the four songs recorded that day reached the charts. "Sweet Little Rock 'n' Roller," and it's flipside, "Jo Jo Gunne," reached No. 47 while both "Anthony Boy" and "Memphis" hit the following year. Three more albums had been released—*Sweet Little Sixteen*, *One Dozen Berrys*, and *Pickin' Berries*—and the guitarist topped off the year with yet another film appearance, this time with a speaking role in Hal Roach's *Go, Johnny, Go*, about a young rocker named Johnny Melody and his rise to stardom under the guidance of Alan Freed.

Finally, to capitalize on the Christmas market, the three rushed back into the studio and recorded "Run Rudolph Run" and "Merry Christmas Baby" before relaxing until February of the following year. In total, the Chuck Berry Trio had recorded together six times in two years, an average of one session every four months.

According to Berry's records, thirty-one songs were recorded during this period, of which twenty-two were released with half of them making the charts, the highest topping at No. 2.

Needless to say, the years 1957 and 1958 had been extremely busy for both Johnnie Johnson and Chuck Berry. They continued to tour together, bringing Jaspar Thomas along occasionally. But these trips were declining in frequency. Johnnie had his family and a job with American Steel that kept him home, and Berry did not pay him enough to survive as a full-time musician. On top of everything else, the guitarist had begun phasing out car trips in favor of the expediency of air travel and now, more often than not, chose to fly rather than drive from gig to gig. In 1957 alone, Berry had endured 240 one-night concerts. Johnnie simply could not keep up.

"It got to where I just couldn't go with Chuck every time he wanted," he says. "If I did I would lose my job, and that's the only thing that kept me payin' the rent. Music just didn't do it."

By 1959, they'd become more or less recording partners, their interactions limited almost entirely to the studio. With his constant touring, Berry was seldom in St. Louis anymore and Johnson couldn't travel with him. When they met again, it was February in Chicago at Chess Studios for another session. Three songs, "Almost Grown," "Little Queenie," and "Back in the U.S.A.," were produced that day.

As was often the case, Berry and Johnson opened up the session with a few warmup instrumental jams. Fifteen years later, Chess would release a compilation album titled *Chuck Berry's Golden Decade Volume 3*, which included one of the jams recorded during this session. "Blue on Blue," an instrumental in much the same vein as "Wee Wee Hours," features Johnnie's blazing piano work, but unlike most Berry records, the piano is not mixed down in favor of the guitar. This is Johnnie Johnson's show. At one point during the song, an excited onlooker, one of the Chess brothers perhaps, can be heard calling to Johnnie from the side, encouraging him to "Play it!" as his fingers dance intensely on the keyboard. It was the closest he ever came during his years with Berry to filling the solo album the Chess brothers had dreamed about. Johnnie remembers recording the number, but never heard "Blue on Blue" until I played it for him.

"That was a good song," he says. "I remember that session pretty well, 'cause that was the first time we ever had a backup group singin' behind us. They brought in Harvey and the Moonglows, Etta James was part of that band, and they sang all the 'doo-wop' stuff in the background. I thought it was a good idea. We had been usin' the same music so long that I was gettin' tired of it. At least when they came in, we had something new. I liked 'Almost Grown' and I did the little rip up and down the keys on the solo for Leonard Chess, without him even havin' to ask. Just to keep him happy. Otherwise, it just wasn't much different from what we'd been doin'. I got to admit, I was gettin' tired of rock and roll."

* * *

The Beechcraft Bonanza should have never been cleared for takeoff that February night in 1959. Visibility was going to be poor due to snow and fog in Iowa, and it wasn't any better in North Dakota. They were heading straight into a band of snow there. Then, too, the twenty-one-year-old pilot was not as familiar with the plane's instruments as he might need to be, given the poor weather that night. He had failed his latest instrument flight-check test in 1958 and his Airman's Certificate stated unequivocally, "Holder does not meet night-flight requirements."

But the plane did take off, and by the time the twisted wreckage was found in a cornfield near Mason City, Iowa, Buddy Holly, Ritchie Valens, J.P. "The Big Bopper" Richardson, and pilot Roger Peterson were dead. Rock and roll had its first full-fledged tragedy. It would not be the last.

The three musicians had been the feature acts in a twenty four date "Winter Dance Party" tour set to end on the fifteenth of February in Springfield, Illinois. Due to the fact that their tour bus had broken down on the way to the last show, forcing the performers to wait it out in the bitter Wisconsin cold (Holly's drummer Carl Bunch was hospitalized for frostbite afterwards and had to be replaced), Holly and the others decided not to chance having to freeze again and resolved to charter a plane. Two members of Holly's touring band, Tommy Alsup and future country star Waylon Jennings, were originally scheduled to fly but gave up their seats to Valens and Richardson—Alsup as the result of losing a coin-toss to Valens. According to Alan Freed who witnessed the toss, Alsup said to Valens "You won the toss." To which Valens gruesomely replied "What do you know? This is the first time I've ever won."

A nation of teenagers fell into mourning over the loss of their rock and roll heroes. Don MacLean, then a fourteen-year-old paper boy, was shocked to find upon delivering the February 4, 1959, morning edition, that his idol had been killed. "Buddy Holly was the first and last person I ever really idolized as a kid," MacLean told *Life* magazine after his 1972 tribute to Holly, "American Pie," hit the top of the charts. In his song, MacLean designates February 3, 1959, as the "day the music died," meaning that the magic of the early years of rock and roll had died with Holly and the others in that frozen Iowa cornfield. Yet in retrospect, Holly's death was only the lowest point of a two-year curse fate seemed to have laid upon rock and roll as, one by one, the very pillars of the rock community were sent tumbling by a variety of circumstances.

The course of extirpation began on Columbus Day, 1957, when Little Richard, after dreaming of his own damnation, renounced rock and roll as the devil's music, and left the stage to begin studying for the ministry.

Shortly after Richard's announcement, Sun Records' fireball Jerry Lee Lewis married his own thirteen-year-old cousin Myra Brown, and set off a blaze of a scandal that would nearly incinerate his career.

In March, the monarch was lost. Elvis "the Pelvis" Presley, the King of Rock & Roll, idol to boys and girls alike, was drafted into the U.S Army.

And then the most savage blow, the tragedy of 1959. Just when it was their turn to grasp the spotlight, three of the brightest young stars Holly, Richardson, and seventeen-year-old Ritchie Valens were silenced forever. The music had not died, as McLean claimed in his song, but it was certainly on its way to an early grave.

Nevertheless, the show must go on, and the rock community picked up the pieces and continued producing records. Several Buddy Holly singles were released posthumously including the aptly titled "It Doesn't Matter Anymore," which reached No.13 a month after his death. Around the same time, Eddie Cochran burst onto the scene with "Summertime Blues" and Frankie Ford hit No. 14 with "Sea Cruise."

As of yet, the only first-generation rocker unaffected by "the curse" was Chuck Berry, who held fast to his claim as the uncrowned King of Rock & Roll. Near the end of 1959, New Yorker Films released a concert documentary, *Jazz On a Hot Summer's Day*, featuring the first live motion picture recording of a Chuck Berry performance. Unfortunately, Johnnie Johnson and Jaspar Thomas had not made the gig and Chuck was backed by a house band. Dave Davies, later of the Kinks, remembers seeing the film soon after its release in Britain.

"Chuck Berry was fantastic," Davies recalls in his autobiography, *Kink*. "He was in at the beginning of something that was going to change the face of popular music and it seemed as if he knew it. His back-up musicians were old jazzers, and it seemed like they were taking the piss out of him behind his back. They didn't understand what was really going on, looking smug and almost condescending in the background. They just didn't get it. But Ray [Davies] and I did."

After recording "Let it Rock" in July, the Chuck Berry Trio began touring again. This time they brought along L.C. Davis who had played on both "Let it Rock" and a song called "Too Pooped to Pop," the story of a man too old to rock and roll. Having just turned thirty-five, Johnnie Johnson began to feel like the character in the song. He was old enough to be the father of most of Berry's fans and he often found himself wishing privately that he could finish with rock and roll completely. The music bored him. At the same time, however, he was loyal to Berry and would not leave him. Little did he know that fate would grant his wish sooner than he could have ever imagined.

On December 1, 1959, the trio with L.C. Davis arrived for a gig in El Paso, Texas, and decided to cross the border into Juarez for a little rest and relaxation. While in a cantina, the band struck up a conversation with two young women. One of the girls was reclaimed quickly by a reproachful husband who seemed more angry with her than with the band. The other, a young, quiet Apache Indian from Yuma, Arizona, named Janice Escalanti claimed she was game for anything. Berry asked her to come along for the rest of the tour and she enthusiastically agreed.

Escalanti traveled with the band for the remaining dates, selling pictures of Berry before gigs and riding with the band in Berry's Cadillac. With Johnnie Johnson at the wheel, the band continued on from Tucson to Phoenix and on to Santa Fe. Things seemed to be heating up between Berry and Escalanti. In Denver, the group stayed at the Drexel Hotel, where Berry registered Janice and himself in a room with a single bed under the names 'Mr. and Mrs. Janet Johnson.'

The last stop on the tour was Kansas City, Missouri, after which Berry flew back to St. Louis. Johnnie Johnson, Jaspar Thomas, L.C. Davis, and Janice Escalanti drove home in the Cadillac, arriving hours later. The following evening, Escalanti began work at Club Bandstand as a hat-check girl. The arrangement did not last, however. Within days Berry had sent her on her way. According to Johnnie, her promiscuous behavior soured the jealous Berry who had taken a liking to her and wanted her all to himself. "Chuck didn't want her foolin' around with other men, and he told her so right from the start," Johnnie says. "When she didn't stop, that was all she wrote."

On December 18, Berry drove Escalanti to the bus depot and, although she asked for a ticket to Yuma, Arizona, Berry instead bought a ticket to El Paso, Texas, and gave her some cash. Hours later, Escalanti showed up once more at Club Bandstand. Enraged at her presence, Berry confiscated the unused bus ticket and kicked her out once again, this time with only a paper bag full of her worldly possessions and no place to go. As Johnnie remembers, such cruelty was not at all unusual for Berry.

"Chuck could be nasty to women sometimes," Johnnie says. "He gets in these moods and you have to know when to stay out of his way and let him be. I don't know how many times some half-dressed girl would come bangin' on my door on the road talkin' 'bout, 'What's your boss's problem? He's crazy!' I just told them to get dressed and get on back home. It wasn't like he was beatin' them or anything. Chuck just had some different ideas about things...about sexual things. He liked to take pictures and all that...none of my business. With Janice, Chuck brought her back, gave her some rules, and she broke them. That was the end of that."

Unfortunately for Berry, it was not the end. In fact, his troubles with the little girl from Arizona had only just begun. On December 21, 1959, Charles Edward Anderson Berry was arrested at Club Bandstand by two black plainclothes policemen and indicted on charges of violating the Mann Act.

Enacted in 1910, The White Slave Traffic Act, named after Congressman James R. Mann, who put the statute in the books, made it illegal to transport females across state lines "for the purpose of prostitution or debauchery, or for any other immoral purposes." Escalanti claimed that she had had sex numerous times with Berry, including twice in the back of the Cadillac while Johnson was driving across state lines. She was also a known prostitute. But the worst news was yet to come. When police examined her history, Escalanti was found to be only fourteen years old.

In order to seal Berry's doom, the prosecution brought to light an earlier arrest for transporting a white woman, Joan Mathis, across state lines from June of 1958. Although Berry was only cited for possession of an illegal firearm at the time, the case was dug up again and Berry was faced with two separate charges. Naturally, Johnnie Johnson was called to testify as a witness and did so obligingly.

"They asked me if I saw what was going on in the car and I said that I was mindin' my own business," remembers Johnson. "That was true. I knew what Chuck and Janice were doin' back there when we'd be drivin', but I was mindin' my own business and it was dark. I didn't look or nothin'. It wasn't nothin' new. When it came time to drive her back to St. Louis, she rode with me and Jaspar and Leroy while Chuck flew home. I told them what I knew and that was all. They was askin' all kinds of crazy questions. Finally, they let me off the stand and I went home.

"That whole trial was real tough for Chuck. His wife was sittin' beside him the whole time tryin' to relax him, tellin' him, 'It's gonna be alright, baby,' and things like that. She was real good to him. But Chuck was scared, smokin' a lot of cigarettes, real nervous, and I don't blame him one bit."

At the close of the Escalanti trial, Berry was found guilty, sentenced to five years in prison and fined $5000. But because of the obvious racial bias of the eighty-year-old Judge George H. Moore, Jr., who demonstrated his belief throughout the trial that blacks were not equal citizens, Berry was able to secure a new trial.

During the break between trials, Berry returned to Chicago with Johnson and Thomas and recorded "Bye Bye Johnny," "Worried Life Blues," and "Down the Road Apiece." Of the three, only "Bye Bye Johnny," the sequel to "Johnny B. Goode" charted—topping off at a mediocre No.64 in April.

The following month, Berry's second trial began and then ended suddenly in a dismissal when Joan Mathis pledged her love for the star. The result was a break for Berry, but only a temporary one.

More frustrations were yet to come. In his autobiography, he discusses the anxieties that plagued him during his legal wrangles.

> Things were close to good but far from over. I had rocky reservations about the way the Indian affairs would roll. It would be an unlikely miracle for a black to be in the lead on the road in a race that was that white. I had but little faith in my attorney, seeing many opportunities in the course of the trials where he had missed in rebuttal or could have intervened with a pertinent point, challenging the prosecution.
>
> Meanwhile, Francine was getting a backlash trying to maintain the operation of Club Bandstand. The city came down with all sorts of ordinances about fire protection orders, and complaints were said to be coming from businesses a half block away about the noise and prowling late at night. When the liquor license was threatened because of an owner being involved in criminal activities, I decided to pull stakes and split.

Back in Chicago, Leonard Chess watched the papers carefully. He knew by the tone of the commentary that Berry more likely than not faced a prison sentence and he was eager to build up a storehouse of singles to be released during the rocker's incarceration. A realistic man, Chess did not mince words. Berry remembers:

> The course of the Indian trial was not promising and Leonard Chess was anticipating a negative result for the appeal. He wanted to get as many songs on tape as he could before I should have to go off to prison so he could keep some product on the market. He advised me to immediately write some more songs and come up and record. That suggestion brought about a recording session that compiled some eleven run-through tunes done in a couple days. Most of the songs were cover tunes that I had always done at the Cosmopolitan Club and, with the condition my head was in regarding the trials, it shows I was less concerned in the results of what was going down then than in what was coming up.

On the basis of Chess's suggestion, ten songs were recorded during two sessions in 1961. Only three of the tracks were made into singles—"I'm Talking About You," "Go, Go, Go," and "Come On" featuring Berry's sister Martha on backing vocals. All and all, it was an unusually slack effort for Berry and the group, but understandably so. The pressures of the trial were wearing on the guitarist and music was forced to take a temporary back seat as he struggled to clear his name.

When the retrial of the Escalanti case began on October 28, 1961, both Chess and Berry's fears were realized. The media had a field day with the story of the young innocent taken advantage of by the Negro. Berry's attorneys put up a weak defense, and Escalanti's testimony elicited pity from the jury. By the end of the trial, Berry's attorney was, as he says, "begging for leniency" and things looked highly in favor of the prosecution. When all was said and done, Berry was convicted of a violation of the Mann Act and sentenced to three years in prison and a $5000 fine.

The last pillar had fallen.

Johnnie Johnson was a free agent. But not for long. Upon learning of Berry's fate, he quickly succumbed to the urgings of another St. Louis bandleader, a left-handed guitarist from Mississippi named Albert King, who'd been begging Johnnie to join his group for three years. King played blues and jazz, all the things Johnnie loved to play. For the next three-years, rock and roll was only a distant memory for the pianist. When Chuck Berry went to prison, Johnnie Johnson went home.

VII

DYNA FLOW

"We stole the show from everybody we played with. I know for a fact that Albert loved that band better than any band he ever had and that includes the guys down at Stax. They copied the sound we came up with—three horns and a rhythm section."
—Kenny Rice, drummer for Albert King

He was born in Indianola, Mississippi, on April 25, 1923, the son of a preacher. When his father left home five years later, his mother remarried, and that man had a guitar.

Little Albert King was not a bright boy, but he knew what he wanted. So a year later he built his first instrument, a diddley bow, out of a wire and two nails. He played on this diddley bow for a few years until he was older and more capable. Then he made his own crude guitar out of an old cigar box and string.

By 1940, Albert was no longer little. He stood six-four, and years of farm work had left him a two-hundred fifty pound body that was more muscle than fat. Perhaps he could have been a boxer, or maybe a football player, but Albert knew what he wanted. So he bought his first real guitar, a Guild hollow-body, and then he went out to play.

For the next ten years, Albert led a double life. In the daytime he worked construction and drove a bulldozer. In the evening he played music. First with a family gospel group called the Harmony Kings and then with a roadhouse band called the In the Groove Boys. It was not a creative name by any means, but it didn't need to be. Albert was in charge.

When he moved to Gary, Indiana, in 1950, he took a day job at a service station and at night he roamed the clubs looking for gigs. One night he sat in with Jimmy Reed, an up-and-coming bluesman. Albert wanted to join Reed's band, but Jimmy already had two guitarists, himself and Eddie Taylor. Reed told Albert he didn't have any room for him and besides, Albert was left-handed and played upside-down which was highly unconventional. Jimmy explained all this to Albert. Albert quietly asked to speak to Jimmy alone. No one knows what passed between them, but when they came back inside, Albert King was Jimmy Reed's new drummer.

In 1953, he went to Chicago and recorded five songs for the Parrot label. Of these five, two were released on a single, "Be on Your Merry Way" and "Bad Luck Blues." The record didn't sell, and so a frustrated Albert moved to St. Louis, where he hoped to have better luck. It was there, in a downtown club, that he met Harold White for the first time.

As a young man, Harold White played tenor sax with his brother-in-law, Jimmy Forest, the man behind "Night Train." By the time Albert King came to town in 1955, White was an established jazz/blues player on the St. Louis club circuit. A musician's musician, the cream of the crop, White recognized talent when he heard it, and he heard it in Albert.

"The first time I saw Albert, he had an amplifier made out of a

Chuck Berry and Johnnie Johnson circa 1957.

The Sir John's Trio
Johnnie Johnson, Chuck Berry, and Ebby Hardy.

"The Beast Within": Berry and Johnson at the Bluenote Club in the early nineties.

A blues fan's dream come true. Johnnie Johnson sharing a piano with the late great Charles Brown in 1993.

Johnnie with Billy Peek at the St. Louis Music Awards in 1996.

"Where it all began..." Johnnie, Gus Thornton, and Tom Maloney in front of the shuttered Cosmopolitan Club in East St. Louis.

Backstage with the "N.Y. band." (L to R) Michael Merritt, James Wormworth, Johnnie, and Jimmy Vivino.

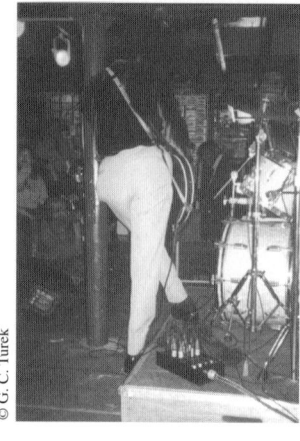

"Please Mr. Johnson, don't play them blues so sad...." Berry and Johnson at Blueberry Hill in 1996.

With Frances and "Number-one Johnnie Johnson Fan" Michael Williams.

The man with the mission. Johnnie and good friend Don Abrams backstage at the *Vicky Lawrence Show*.

Johnnie with good friend and agent Margo Lewis.

Doing what Johnnie loves to do best. Goin' fishin' in Key West with George Turek, Sr.

Johnnie with Texas guitar legend Bert Wills.

Johnnie jamming in 1992 with the Kentucky Headhunters in their practice room during rehearsals for *That'll Work*. (L to R) Greg Martin, Mark Orr, Fred Young, Anthony Kenney, and Richard Young.

"The Leader of the Band." Johnnie controlling the action on stage during a tribute concert for friend Tommy Bankhead in 1997. Tom Maloney is behind him.

Johnnie poses with George and Linda Turek following their 1993 wedding bash.

With Frances and Linda Turek at Sheldon Hall in St. Louis.

Struggling to make a living with Tom Maloney and Gus Thornton during a gig in the mid-eighties.

At the newly renovated historic Sheldon Hall with a seven-piece band in 1998. Oliver Sain blows sax, with Kenny Rice on drums, Tom Maloney on guitar, and Frank Dunbar on bass.

Johnnie shaking hands with President Clinton at the latter's 1997 Inaugural Ball.

Johnnie rocks the '97 Presidential Inaugural Ball with RatDog. Rob Wasserman is in the foreground, Bob Weir in the back.

At the Kennedy Center with Buddy Guy before the 1997 Muddy Waters Tribute.

Slowhand meets Bluehand. Johnnie with Eric Clapton in 1996.

Johnnie with good buddy Keith Richards at the latter's surprise 50th birthday party in 1993. Jane Rose, Richards's manager asked that Johnnie and a piano be the only live music at the event.

Johnnie and pal Jim Marsala at a recording studio in Houston, Texas.

© G. C. Turek

FATHER OF ROCK & ROLL

Familiar faces in the crowd during Johnnie's 1998 induction into the St. Louis Walk of Fame. Chuck & Themetta Berry.

Johnnie's acceptance speech.

Blueberry Hill owner Joe Edwards congratulating Johnnie.

"Hail! Hail! Rock 'n' Roll!" The first and most influential writing/performing team in the history of rock and roll show a mid-nineties Blueberry Hill crowd how it's done.

"Deep down in Lousiana cross the New Orleans..." Johnnie "B. Goode" Johnson and Chuck Berry perform at the 1995 New Orleans Heritage and Jazz Festival.

Turek's first full page ad as it appeared in *Billboard* magazine on July 12th 1997. Designed by Spike Longoria, the ad featured the first publication of the Johnnie Johnson Hall of Fame nomination letter.

The second ad appeared on January 10th, 1998, and featured Chuck Berry's personal letter to the Hall of Fame, in which he called Johnnie "my friend and musical collaborator for over fourty years."

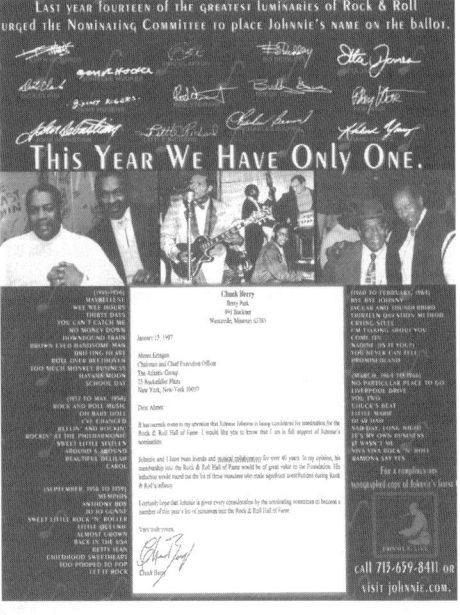

The Johnnie Johnson Nominating Committee: Keith Richards, Eric Clapton, Bo Diddley, Etta James, John Lee Hooker, Dick Clark, Jimmy Rogers, Rod Stewart, Buddy Guy, Bob Weir, John Sebastian, Little Richard, Charles Brown, & Richard Young

TRAVIS FITZPATRICK

CERTIFICATE OF REGISTRATION
PRINCIPAL REGISTER

United States Patent and Trademark Office

Reg. No. 2,131,397
Registered Jan. 20, 1998

SERVICE MARK
PRINCIPAL REGISTER

FATHER OF ROCK & ROLL

JOHNSON, JOHNNIE (UNITED STATES CITIZEN)

EXAMINING ATTORNEY

FOR: ENTERTAINMENT SERVICES IN THE NATURE OF A MUSICAL ACT BY AN INDIVIDUAL PERFORMER OR A MUSICAL GROUP, IN CLASS 41 (U.S. CLS. 100, 101 AND 107).

The Mark shown in this certificate has been registered in the United States Patent and Trademark Office to the named registrant.

The records of the United States Patent and Trademark Office show that an application for registration of the Mark shown in this Certificate was filed in the Office, that the application was examined and determined to be in compliance with the requirements of the law and with the regulations prescribed by the Commissioner of Patents and Trademarks, and that the Applicant is entitled to registration of the Mark under the Trademark Act of 1946, as Amended.

A copy of the Mark and pertinent data from the application are a part of this certificate.

This registration shall remain in force for TEN (10) years, unless terminated earlier as provided by law, and subject to compliance with the provisions of Section 8 of the Trademark Act of 1946, as Amended.

Bruce Lehman

Commissioner of Patents and Trademarks

FATHER OF ROCK & ROLL

"They were a team...yes, they were a team."
--Chuck Tillman

soda case and a guitar that looked like it was made of wet plywood," White recalls. "But he could play that thing like you wouldn't believe. There was potential there for something big, so I helped him get a band together right away. First a three-piece and then a full six-piece group."

With White and the band behind him, King quickly began making a name for himself in the St. Louis club scene. Chuck Berry notes in his autobiography that around the time "Maybellene" hit the airwaves, "Albert King, another artist from the St. Louis area who sported a left-hand guitar, began climbing to the Ike [Turner] and Chuck level."

Says White, "We started getting pretty good and we'd go around checking out the competition on off nights, and I have to say honestly that there wasn't anyone, even in them early days, who could hang with us. We saw Little Milton and Ike Turner over at the Manhattan Club and then Albert said he wanted to go check out Chuck Berry's act at the Cosmopolitan Club. So we get to the Cosmopolitan Club and Chuck's doing his thing, the whole country-western bit. Then he gets into doing some blues, you know. So I turn to ask him about what he thinks, but he isn't even watching Chuck—doesn't even see Chuck. He's watching Johnnie. 'I got to get that man in my band,' he says. 'That's the baddest piano player I ever heard.'

"So after the gig he starts talking to Johnnie about joining the group, right in front of Chuck. I'm sure Chuck was mad, 'fact I know he was, but he wasn't gonna say a word to Albert. Nobody messed with Albert. He asks Johnnie if he wanted to join up, but of course Johnnie says he can't quit Chuck, but that he'd be glad to sit in sometime. I'll never forget the first night he came and played with us. Let me tell you, it was something. The man was incredible. I don't care about what they say about this jazz player or that blues player—Johnnie was the man. He could play anything and he was better than all of them put together."

Johnnie Johnson was determined to stay with Chuck Berry. But

Albert knew what he wanted. So for the next five years, despite the fact that he had two fine pianists of his own, Jimmy Vaughan and Sam Wallace, Albert continued to pursue Johnnie, approaching him whenever possible about joining his band. Finally, with Berry facing a likely prison sentence for violating the Mann Act, Albert had his chance. He asked Johnnie again, and this time, the pianist accepted.

"Albert never gave up chasing Johnnie," remembers White. "When Chuck got in trouble, Johnnie was pretty much on his own. So when Albert asked him again about joining the band, he said okay. We were all excited 'cause we figured now we had the missing piece to the puzzle, you know. Before Johnnie we had a pianist named Sam Wallace who was pretty good. But he didn't have the push we wanted. With Johnnie, he played what we call 'a full piano,' meaning he just filled it up—his playing wasn't choppy like a lot of pianists. He filled in the gaps and there was no empty intervals. He had what we call soul in his playing. He just filled it up."

For Johnnie, the chance to play with Albert King's band couldn't have come at a better time. Rock and roll held no more challenges for him. In the King band, he saw the opportunity to grow as a musician and expand his knowledge of the blues.

"Albert King was askin' me about joinin' his band way back when Chuck and I were just gettin' started," Johnnie says. "I liked what he was doin' 'cause I had seen them play before, but at that time, Chuck and I stuck together and I had to tell him no. But then after Chuck started havin' his problems, I figured I didn't have no reason to keep tellin' Albert no and I went ahead and joined up with him in 1960.

"Now I was still doing some recordin' with Chuck, 'cause this was before he went to jail, but I also started recordin' with Albert. The first song I did with Albert and them was called 'I Walked All Night Long.' After that we did a song called 'I've Made Nights By Myself.' This was real blues like I'd always wanted to play and it was fun.

And the band—the band was the best I'd ever played with."

The group that came to be known as the original Albert King Band, was built up over a period of five years. Under White's guidance and with a dogged tenacity, Albert recruited the best of the best from the St. Louis jazz and blues scene. He did not bother with false pretense. When he walked into a club to see a band, he wasn't there to enjoy the show. If he liked someone's sound, he would try to take them for his own and rival bandleaders dared not stand in his way; they could only hope that the chosen bandmate remained loyal. Oftentimes, as in the case of Johnnie Johnson, Albert would not quit until he had secured the man for his own group. His persistence paid off. By the time of it's completion in 1960, his stellar seven-piece band was arguably the most talented group in the city.

"We had an amazing collection of musicians," White says. "Albert on guitar and vocals, Wilbur "Buttercup" Thompson on trumpet, Lee Otis Wright on bass, little Freddie Robinette on baritone sax. Then there was me on tenor sax, Johnnie Johnson on piano, and the "mascot," Kenny Rice on drums. We called Kenny the mascot 'cause he wasn't but seventeen or eighteen when he joined the band. He wasn't nothin' but a kid, but he could sure play."

Like Johnnie Johnson, Kenny Rice was a prodigy. He'd begun playing drums in the school band and had progressed so rapidly that he was soon being sought after by major nightclub acts around the city. For Rice, the invitation from Albert King was a dream come true. "I've always known what I wanted to do from a very young age," he says. "I wanted to be a jazz drummer."

"I was seventeen-years old when I started with Albert," Rice remembers. "He'd seen me play with Billy 'Tore Up' Gales' band, and after that he came after me. I was still in high school at the time and Albert had to ask my father to give me permission to go out on the road with him. Like I said, it was a dream come true for me. My older friend David Hines and I used to sneak in and watch all those bands like Albert, Ike Turner, and Chuck, so it was a big honor to be playing with one of my heroes at such a young age. I couldn't believe it."

With the band in place, King and White began discussing how to develop a sound based on the talents of the respective members. At first, Albert wanted to mimic the sound of B.B. King, who was selling big at the time, but White convinced him that they had the talent and the potential to be more than just a cover band.

"I said, 'Look, Albert. Look at the talent we have,'" White remembers. "We can be better than B.B. King. We don't need to be copying someone else's style. Let's do our own thing.'"

And so the Albert King band set about the task of coming up with a distinct sound they could call their own. In the manner of a well-polished team, each section of the band elected a "coach" to keep the members on track. White became the leader of the horn section and Johnnie Johnson was appointed the head of the rhythm section.

"Best thing we ever did was let Johnnie run the rhythm section," says White. "He was a quiet man and he led the only way he could, which was by example—no bossing around or nothing. The guys just loved him. We got such a great sound out of that rhythm section, Johnnie, Lee Otis, and Kenny. See before Johnnie, we sounded just like what we were, a seven-piece band. But after we got Johnnie, we started soundin' like a twelve or fourteen-piece band, 'cause he could do so much. He just filled it up. And the power. You hear a lot of piano players today that need an amplifier and electric piano to be heard. But not Johnnie. He had those big hands and wrists and he was strong. Other guys would have to pound as hard as they could to get the sound that Johnnie got when he was just playin' regularly."

* * *

If things appeared to be looking up for Johnnie, it was merely on the surface. Offstage, his personal life was a shambles. Rose had given birth to two more children, Althea and Johnnie Jr., but by

1960, the couple had separated. "All I cared about back then was the bottle," Johnnie laments. "And me and Rose just didn't mix. She had a violent side to her and my drinkin' brought it out of her. She'd just go crazy sometimes."

One hot September evening in 1960, Johnnie showed up at the house he had shared with Rose before the separation, and asked if he could see his children. Rose invited him inside and Johnnie stumbled in half-drunk and walked upstairs to the children's rooms where he kissed them as they slept. On his way out, Rose called to him from her bedroom and he went in to see her. That's when all hell broke loose.

"All I wanted was to see the kids," remembers Johnnie. "I didn't feel like arguin' or talkin' 'bout our relationship. I figured we were through. Anyways, she started in talkin' 'bout her new boyfriend and how he was 'puttin' the meat in her deepfreeze' and all that kind of stuff. So I told her that I was glad she was happy and that I wished her nothin' but the best. I really wasn't interested in gettin' back together with her 'cause I knew it wasn't gonna work out between us. She started talkin' 'bout her new man and whatever and I knew she was tryin' to make me jealous so I just figured I'd play it cool so she'd know it was okay with me if she wanted to be with somebody else. That was the wrong move. She got mad 'cause I didn't react how she wanted, and next thing I know, she pulled out a gun and started shootin' at me. Right there in the bedroom.

"The first shot hit the plaster right by my head, and if it had been an inch closer, I wouldn't be talkin' to you right now. The second one hit me in the elbow and stuck in my arm—it's still in there and you can feel it in my forearm, like a little knot, or a bump. After that, I started runnin' down the stairs tryin' to get out the house, and here she came right after me firin' that gun. I got hit a couple more times and went crashin' through the screen door tryin' to run away. But then she got me good, right through the back. That put me down 'cause it had hit my lung. I just laid there in the yard, bleedin' everywhere, and hardly able to breathe. Next thing I know she's standin' over me with that gun and I'm thinkin' this is the end. She's gonna kill me. I was numb all over and I saw my whole life flash before my eyes. But she just throws the gun down and starts cryin'. 'The ambulance is comin', baby! Don't worry, baby!' I just closed my eyes after that.

"They fixed me up in the hospital and the doctor said I was lucky to be alive the way that bullet had tore up my lung. Then not too long after, these two cops come in my hospital room and said they was gonna put Rose in jail. She had confessed to them that the reason she had shot me was 'cause I didn't react to her tryin' to make me jealous and she got mad. She didn't even try to make up no excuse. The cops heard that and they came in and said, 'She's goin' to jail for a long time.' Well, I got to thinkin', and I knew that if she went to jail, ain't no one gonna be there to take care of my kids. I knew I couldn't do it with all my drinkin' and late hours. The kids needed their mother. I told the police that I wasn't gonna press charges. They thought I was crazy. But I just told 'em, 'That's the mother of my children.'

"Well, the funny thing was that since I didn't press charges and I needed somebody to take care of me for a month while I recovered—I ended up stayin' with Rose in that house for thirty days. We stayed out of each other's way for most of the time, but then it came up and she started talkin' 'bout us gettin' back together. I said 'No way. We through. You done already cut me once, now you shot me. The only reason you ain't in jail is 'cause I want my children to have their momma with 'em.' That was it. I got better and got out of there as fast as I could."

Johnnie rejoined the Albert King Band in November of 1960. At the same time, Chuck Berry was in the middle of his legal troubles and had hoped to get Johnnie in the studio during the fall months to lay down some more tracks. Burdened by his problems, Berry was more or less tied down and had limited himself to the occasional recording session, the purpose of which was to build up a store of songs to be released during the course of his inevitable prison stay.

Since Berry didn't need him on the road for any extended amount of time, Johnnie still found time to record with his old partner, without it affecting his status within the Albert King Band. As it was, with Johnnie recovering and Berry preparing for the second of his two trials, they would not get to Chicago until January of the following year. Johnnie remembers that Berry got the news about the shooting second-hand. "Chuck was in trial, or jail or something when I got shot," he recalls, "and he told me afterwards that people had been talkin' 'bout it right in front of him and didn't know that he knew me. That's how he found out."

While Berry wrangled away in the courtroom, the Albert King Band was playing the local clubs and honing their skills. Harold White remembers that it wasn't long before they had established themselves as the best band St. Louis.

"We were getting better and better, but how could we not with all the practicing we did?" says White. "Back in those days we used to have what was called the 'Battle of the Bands,' where the best groups in town would get together and let the audience decide by way of applause who was the king of them all. These contests were usually held at places like the Manhattan Club where Ike Turner played a lot. Three times we went up against Little Milton and three times we went up against Ike Turner and His Rhythm Kings. We never lost. Not once. We wiped up the stage with them. I had told Ike beforehand that we were the best band in town, but he didn't believe me. He thought he had the best band. So did Milton. Let me tell you, they were both crying after them shows. And you know what else? Milton's band busted up shortly afterwards and Ike tried to steal us away from Albert! The whole band! We weren't going nowhere, though. We had something too good to fool with and we all knew it. Nobody was leaving."

Before long, the Albert King Band took their show on the road. And like a barnstorming team of blue-chip all-stars, they came into town with the sole purpose of winning over the local crowds and outplaying any other bands that happened to be in the area.

According to White, it wasn't just the regional talent that went down, but some of the legends as well.

"Wherever we played, we stole the show, and whether it be Howlin' Wolf or Muddy Waters, it didn't matter. I remember playing on a bill with both Howlin' Wolf and B.B. King. Albert was the opening act and after we were finished, Wolf went on and hardly got any reaction at all. He was just fuming backstage. 'Next time I come through St. Louis, I'm tearing the house down,' he said. Now of course, B.B. King had all the women cheering with 'Sweet Sixteen.' But I can definitely say we were the best band that night. We had the horns, the solid rhythm section, and Albert doing things with a guitar that no man is supposed to do—bending the strings and making it cry. We had those people going crazy.

"Another night we were playing the top deck on a boat called the Admiral, and Count Basie was in the main venue, down in the ballroom. Not for long. We stole his whole audience! Everyone was running up to the top deck to see us! One thing I remember from that night was Johnnie doing 'After Hours' and the people going crazy jumping up on tables and whatnot. Johnnie made 'After Hours' his song. He played it better than the cat who wrote it!"

Kenny Rice remembers the Albert King Band as a well-rehearsed, eclectic group of musicians who could play almost anything from big-band jazz to rhythm and blues.

"We were a tight, versatile band," says Rice. "We played jazz and blues with a kind of Max Roach/Art Blakey influence. I use them as examples because they are drummers and I'm a drummer, but that's a good way to explain it. Every show we'd open up with two or three straight-jazz tunes before Albert came up on stage. One of these numbers was 'Cookin' at the Continental,' which was originally done by a jazz pianist named Horace Silver. When Albert came on stage we'd change right into 'Let's Have a Natural Ball,' right out of 'Cookin' at the Continental,' and from then on we'd do blues songs. People just loved it."

Yet through it all, Albert was King. Overshadowing the immense talent of his backing musicians, literally towering in the forefront with his trademark Flying-V Gibson guitar, Albert remained, as always, the focal point of the band. His guitar style, as powerful as it was unorthodox, would influence countless blues and rock stars including Stevie Ray Vaughn, Eric Clapton, Mike Bloomfield, and Jimi Hendrix.

As Chuck Tillman said, a musician can only play what is inside them, and by the accounts of his former bandmates, Albert King's leadership style was as simple and nasty as his guitar style. Some bandleaders put on airs, affect a facade of kindheartedness, or worse, feign honesty while stabbing you in the back. Not Albert. He didn't pretend to be anything other than what he was—a big man with a mean streak and hellish temper who would tolerate no dissension. An absolute dictator on the bandstand, he was known to fire musicians on stage in the middle of a gig and did so once on a television show later in his career. Off the stage he was brooding and surly. Once when a young, substitute bass player dared mouth off to him on the tour bus, Albert ordered the driver to stop and bodily removed the offender from the bus, leaving him alone on a desolate stretch of highway in the middle of the night. He was not a man to be crossed. Johnnie believes that much of his anger had to do with insecurities over his illiteracy.

"Albert could be hard to get along with 'cause he thought everyone was lookin' down on him," remembers Johnnie. "That's 'cause he couldn't read or write. Not a word. You could pass a billboard with his name on it and poor Albert wouldn't know any difference. He had a lot of superstitions, too. He wouldn't allow anyone on the bus who had peanuts 'cause it was supposed to be bad luck. He'd fire you right on the spot. Tell you how serious he was 'bout them superstitions of his. He had a bass player in the seventies named Gus Thornton who is a real good friend of mine. Gus is just about the nicest fella you'd ever want to meet. Great bass player, too. Albert loved Gus as much as he loved anybody. But when Gus brought his pregnant wife on the bus, he kicked her off and Gus, too. Wouldn't let 'em on the bus. Albert thought pregnant women brought bad luck. It was the middle of winter, but Albert didn't care. If he said you was gone you was gone. Period. He didn't care who you were."

Naturally, King's gruff demeanor made for a lot of turmoil within the band. On any given night he could explode or attack without reason. "Some nights," Johnnie remembers, "he'd be mean just to be mean."

Kenny Rice recalls the evening he learned just how cold Albert could be. "Albert was a perfectionist, and he was always real hard on me because I was young," Rice says. "He didn't tolerate mistakes. Of course, if he made a mistake he'd blame it on one of us. You know what I mean? We played just about every night of the week and we did two shows a night. Real busy, you know. One night we'd finished a show and were in the car on our way to the second show when I realized that I had left my tom-tom drum in the parking lot. Naturally, I panicked. I was just a kid and my family didn't have much money, you know, and tom-toms were expensive. I begged Albert to turn the car around, but he refused. Nothing I could do or say would make him turn around. He just stared out the window. I started to cry, and that's when Johnnie Johnson spoke up and told Albert to turn around and get my drum. He told Johnnie no at first, but the fact that Johnnie said something—he was usually so quiet—I think Albert respected that he meant business. Johnnie kept on him and finally he turned around. I couldn't believe it. The whole ride I was worrying because I figured it was too late and someone must have stolen it, but when we got there my drum was still sitting in the parking lot! That's when I fell in love with Johnnie Johnson. From then on he was like a father to me."

Johnnie, it seemed, had finally found his niche. And while King could be difficult, the band was of a sort that provided a nurturing environment for musical growth and exploration regardless of each other's technical limitations. In Johnnie's case, it was his inability to read music.

"I was the only one in the band who couldn't read or write music," Johnnie admits. "So I had to pay extra close attention to what we was doin'. I couldn't forget 'cause I didn't have no paper to look at. Playin' with the Albert King Band, I learned a lot. I learned to solo in all the keys you could play in, even C-sharp which is very difficult for a pianist. I learned F-sharp, A-minor, E-natural, B-natural. Albert wanted us to be the best, and we tried as hard as we could to do it."

During his eight years with Chuck Berry, Johnnie Johnson rarely needed to rehearse. The music he and Berry developed together had become automatic and they simply did not need to hold a formalized practice before taking the stage. With the Albert King Band, however, rehearsals were held daily, and sometimes lasted all night.

"We'd go all night long sometimes," White remembers. "Most of the time it was just the band. Albert was the boss on stage, but he wasn't there a lot of times when we were working on the music. Albert would be out shooting craps and we'd have to go get him so he could practice getting his part down. He couldn't read or write so we had to write it all down, read it to him, and then have him repeat what we'd done over and over till he could remember it. A lot of times his voice would get hoarse trying to master whatever we had given him.

"As far as the music was concerned, we all contributed our parts. It was a team effort and everybody played their part. Perfection was the goal. I was always real impressed with Johnnie because he couldn't read music, but he was right on the ball and knew all the arrangements backwards and forwards. He was always coming up with ideas for new arrangements and he could tell you right away if something didn't fit right. He had a gift for understanding music."

Sadly, as was common in the day, Albert King took sole benefit from the efforts of his band, copyrighting the songs in his own name and collecting the royalties for himself though he had little to do with the creation of the songs themselves.

"We should have gotten royalties," says Kenny Rice. "Sure. Every single one of us had something to do with each and every song. Johnnie and Harold White contributed a lot. Half the time Albert wasn't even there when we were coming up with new material, but he got it all. That's the way they did it in those days, though. The headliner got all the credit. Albert wasn't no different."

Indeed. As opposed to being seen as "one of the guys," Albert instead chose a regal role, seeming to care little for the resentment his luxurious habits stirred within the rest of the band. On the road, when not traveling by bus, the six bandmates rode together in a '55 Ford Station Wagon similar to Chuck Berry's while King led the way, riding alone in his brand new Cadilllac. In hotels he always reserved his own room, leaving the band to fend for themselves. Often all six slept together in one room on pallets to save money, and stayed up half the night bonding, talking about women and music.

"We were a family," says White. "I say that with all my heart. I love each one of those fellas like a brother and I'd do anything for them. Those times brought us together."

Yet regardless of the family atmosphere, or perhaps because of it, indiscretions against proper conduct were not tolerated. Of particular concern was the band's aversion to Johnnie Johnson's heavy drinking. Although, as Harold White remembers, his playing was never affected, he could sometimes be sloppy and irresponsible off stage. His bandmates begged him to quit.

"We all drank," White confesses, "and most of the time we took a case or two of beer on the road with us. But Johnnie...Johnnie took it to extremes. I used to get angry at Johnnie because he wouldn't stop drinking. 'If you could just get that drinking under control, everything would work out,' I used to tell him. He wasn't a sloppy drunk, although he had trouble keeping his uniform clean, and he wasn't a mean drunk either. He used to take a fifth of whiskey on stage with him every show. Every show. And remember this was two shows a night sometimes, so he was doing two fifths in an evening! I'm not joking. And it would be gone by the last song! He'd buy anybody a drink, but nobody was allowed to touch his fifth. I remember one night he bought so many people drinks that he ran out of money and couldn't afford a room to sleep in. He ended up coming in my room and sleeping on the foot of the bed! The amazing thing was that the drinking never messed with his playing and he never had hangovers. That man had the highest tolerance that I've ever seen in my life."

Over the span of his career, which stretched four decades, Albert King would release a vast number of albums. However, during his years in St. Louis, King's band was recognized more as a touring band than as a studio group. This was because at the time, Albert believed that the real money was in traveling the country and playing as many shows as possible. Nonetheless, the Albert King Band cut some excellent singles for both the Bobbin and King (no relation) labels between 1959 and 1963.

On the suggestion of Ike Turner, the band recorded at the Technosonic studios, which at the time housed the most state-of-the-art recording equipment in St. Louis. On September 20, 1961, Albert and the boys rolled into the studio with some new material they had worked up over the past year during rehearsals. The first track, a slow blues called "Goin' To California" featured strong drumming by Kenny Rice, who demonstrated his dynamic control by matching the intensity of the swelling horns with his snare roll on the changes while keeping perfect time throughout. The real interplay however, was between Johnnie Johnson and Albert King. King was obviously out front, but Johnson echoed his solos, filling in and giving them body and substance. Seven years later, the innovative Jimi Hendrix would adopt "Goin' To California" into his repertoire based on the powerful arrangement heard in the original recording.

While "Goin' to California" exemplified Johnnie Johnson's ability to blend in with a band, the instrumental "Dyna Flow," named after a St. Louis bar in which the band often performed, showed what happened when he was allowed to cut loose.

In the past he had not been so lucky. Excepting "Wee Wee Hours" and the virtually unknown "Blue on Blue," Johnnie Johnson was forced to play with restraint during his Chess recording sessions. Berry was the star and it was Johnnie's job to make him sound good without outshining his boss. For that reason he was recorded at low levels while Berry's guitar was pushed up in volume to draw the focus on to him. The consequence of this type of preferential recording is that much of Johnson's best piano work with Berry is lost in the background, a feint tinkling that demonstrates only a fraction of what he actually added to the song. Johnnie remembers that King had heard the Berry records and disliked them for that very reason.

"Albert used to request that the recordin' engineer turn up the piano on the record to make sure that it was heard," Johnnie remembers. "At Chess I played a little ol' Spinet piano and they put the microphone in the bottom panel. So, all you could hear on record was the treble. I had to pound real hard, and even though you could hear the bass in the studio, it didn't come out too well on the record. Albert King didn't like the way I sounded on Chuck's records 'cause they had me turned down so low. He thought it took away from the music."

In contrast, "Dyna Flow" features Johnson at his full, undiluted volume and captures many of the subtle nuances missed on the average Berry record. In a sense, this is Johnnie Johnson in his musical prime. At thirty-seven, he had been playing with the best in the business for nearly twenty years. His style was fully formed and he performed with the confidence of the mature musician. The right hand swirls and sixteenth note triplets, which were to become his trademark in the coming years, are present throughout, and he seems unafraid to take the reins from King from time to time and stretch out on the keys.

Says Johnnie, "Albert never held anybody back from doin' well. He'd tell you if you was doin' bad, believe me, but he never held you back. He liked the way I played and he always told me to just play what I felt."

The next sessions were held two days later on September 22, 1961, and although he cannot remember the reason, Johnnie Johnson did not show up to the studio. Kenny Rice remembers the session well and the void that Johnson's conspicuous absence left in the finished product.

"I was in and out of Albert's band for years, but I made both of those sessions," he says. "We cut some good tracks that first day like 'Dyna Flow' and I think 'Goin' to California.' Johnnie was on fire with that 'Dyna Flow' which we named after this club we used to play at. We spread it out over a weekend and did the next session a couple days after the first. Now for some reason...I don't know if he was up recording with Chuck or what...Johnnie didn't make the next session. That was really too bad because the song we did called 'Don't Throw Your Love on Me So Strong' was Johnnie's baby. He'd done almost all the arranging and writing on that one. Ike Turner was in the studio that day, so we got him to play and he did a great job. Of course, Johnnie could just kill Ike...I mean Ike's good, but we're talking about Johnnie Johnson, the best blues pianist in the world. He was back then, too. I don't care what they say about Otis Spann and Pinetop whoever. Johnnie was and is the best. But like I said, Ike was a solid musician and he did a good enough job that it came out pretty good. In fact, that song turned out to be Albert's first hit record. Imagine how good it would have been if Johnnie had played on it, though."

"Don't Throw Your Love on Me So Strong" hit No. 14 on the R&B chart in 1961 and brought Albert King into the national spotlight. Five years later he would be in Memphis recording with Booker T. and the MG's on the Stax label and becoming a certified blues legend. For the time being however, he was content staying in St. Louis and swinging with his band, although the success did inspire him. It was about that time that he and Johnnie began to have problems.

"Albert had strict rules," recalls White. "You had to be on time, you had to be clean, you couldn't smoke or drink on stage, and you had to be sober. Johnnie broke every single one of them. We used to call him 'Fats Waller' 'cause he was always fat and wore a cap on stage just like the real Fats Waller did. Johnnie also liked to smoke cigars on stage and I already told you about the fifths he took up there. I was in charge of monitoring most of this stuff so I kind of let it pass when Johnnie would be late, or show up in a dirty suit with alcohol on his breath. But Albert couldn't stand it if he caught sight of anyone breaking rules. Funny thing is, it wasn't like Albert was an innocent. He was as addicted to gambling as Johnnie was to drinking and we'd have to go pull him away from the crap games all the time. But Albert couldn't see himself in perspective. He would turn around and give him this look but there was nothing he could do about it because Johnnie was so important to us. Johnnie had a serious drinking problem, but it never affected his playing and, above all else, he was our friend. Albert didn't care about the friend part, though. He fired Johnnie twice for drinking. Once in Chicago and once in Arkansas. But both times I went to Albert and said, 'Hey man, the band don't sound right without Johnnie.' He knew it was true. Nobody could replace him. Albert would call him right back the next day and everything would be back in order."

Johnnie remembers that Albert was both quick to fire and just as quick to rehire once his temper had cooled. "Albert was the kind of guy who would lay you off one day and call you back the next," he says. "He gave me a bus ticket back to St. Louis once then met me at the bus station 'fore I even got there and asked me back. I said, 'You can't be doin' this to me.' He never apologized, but he let it be known that he was wrong. He fired just about every single one of us at one time or another. One thing he used to do was, if he liked a girl, he might ask you, 'Say, you mind if her cousin sits in for you just for tonight?' He did that to us a few times. Once he was after this drummer, when Kenny was gone and the only way the drummer would play is if Albert let his brother play piano. So Albert comes up to me and 'fore he could even ask I said, 'Just tell me when you need me to meet back up with you and I'll be there.' I never had to go nowhere, though. It never lasted more than a night 'fore he was askin' me back."

Albert King liked to give off the air that his bandmates were expendable and could be hired or fired on a whim. But as Kenny Rice remembers, Johnnie Johnson was more than just a sideman to the miserly guitarist.

"Albert loved Johnnie," says Rice, "Not just because he outplayed every other pianist around, but because he came up with the sound that made Albert a star. See, Albert liked a hard-driving band with horns because he played such a powerful guitar. He liked our band because it swung and Johnnie Johnson's driving boogie-woogie piano was the catalyst of the sound of that band. It was that sound that helped Albert and made him popular enough to launch his career. You better believe he loved Johnnie Johnson. Every check he cashed he owed to Johnnie Johnson and he ain't the only musician in that situation, if you catch my drift."

Harold White elaborates, "We all knew the story about Johnnie and Chuck Berry. Ebby Hardy told us everything before Johnnie even joined the band. He said Johnnie would come up with all this music and Chuck would wait until he was drunk and take advantage of Johnnie—steal it for his own. He said Johnnie didn't know any better. This was true. Johnnie used to make us so angry because he had so much talent and he never pursued it because of drinking. He was always letting people take advantage of him."

* * *

As a member of the Chuck Berry Trio, Johnnie Johnson had been forced to juggle a day job between frenetic touring and numerous recording sessions. With the Albert King Band, he was making enough money from the nightly gigs to become a full-time musician for the first time in his twenty-year professional career.

"We made two more records with Albert King," recalls Johnnie. "In 1962, I believe. One was called 'I Get Evil' and 'What Can I Do To Change Your Mind' which we did in the springtime, and then we did one more in the summer called 'I'll Do Anything You Say' and 'Got To Be Some Changes Made.' That was it. We stayed together for a while afterwards but as far as recordin' goes, we was finished. All we did was tour around from then on."

The band continued to play the St. Louis area and toured the country frequently for the next year. King was spreading his name and his unique guitar style, and the band was becoming more and more cohesive as a unit. Then at the start of 1963, Kenny Rice left the band over a salary dispute. A number of drummers came and went in his place but none could replace him in the hearts of the band members. He was the "mascot," and his youthful charm and exuberance had brought many a smile to the road-weary faces of his companions.

"Kenny was a character, boy," Johnnie laughs. "He was always sayin' crazy things and crackin' us up. That band wasn't the same without him. I still see him quite a bit and we play together which is always a treat no matter how many times we do it. Kenny Rice has always been my favorite drummer. Ain't no question 'bout that."

By 1963, the Albert King Band was falling apart. The disputes and altercations with King were becoming more and more frequent and even the patient Harold White was beginning to show his temper. A quiet man, Johnnie Johnson could not exist in an atmosphere so full of turmoil and heated emotion. Much to the surprise of his bandmates and King himself, Johnnie turned in his stained and rumpled suit and promptly quit the band.

"I can't stand fussin' and fightin' around me," explains Johnnie. "Never could. I like things relaxed and Albert was gettin' so hard to be around that I knew it was time for me to go. I couldn't see no other choice."

Johnson's departure decimated the band. As Albert watched despondently, Harold White packed up his horn and walked out followed by Freddie Robinette, Wilbur Thompson, and Lee Otis Wright. There was no question of their leaving with him. Even Albert knew that. They had spent many a day and night together, hunched over their instruments, perfecting arrangements and developing a sound for Albert, while the latter was out gallivanting and gambling. They had traveled together, six men cramped in a Ford Station Wagon, while Albert cruised along in front in his new Cadillac. They had slept in the same room, shared laughter and tears, stood up for one another during Albert's tirades. Like a good drill instructor, Albert had instilled in his band a fear and resentment towards himself, that in turn had bound them together as a unit. Albert knew what he wanted. But this time, he would not have it. The original Albert King band was no more.

"When Johnnie quit, that was the end of the band," Harold White says. "We were tired of the road, tired of the arguments, and tired of Albert. We just all up and left right then. We knew it was over. Things could never be the same."

Indeed they would not. Soon after the split, Albert formed a new band consisting of friends and relations from Memphis and recorded another side for King Records called "Had You Told It Like It Was (It Wouldn't Be Like It Is)." But it was a subpar effort with a subpar band and Albert would soon leave for Memphis where Stax was calling and a new group of top-notch studio musicians sat waiting. Before he left, however, he took his first loss in the Battle of the Bands competition. The victors were a tight cohesive unit with an all too familiar horn-driven sound: Johnnie Johnson, Harold White, Kenny Rice, Wilbur Thompson, Freddie

Robinette, and Lee Otis Wright—formerly The Albert King Band, now known as The Magnificent Six.

"We all teamed up together after we left Albert and formed the Magnificent Six with Lee Otis doin' all the singin'," Johnnie recalls. "Most of what we did was jazz, blues, Bobby "Blue" Bland stuff, nothin' original. We didn't record either; the whole thing was just for fun. It was all 'bout playin' music 'cause you loved to play music. We kept that band together for ten years, and even though we had people comin' in and out, the main group stayed the same for all that time."

In 1966, Albert King officially signed with Stax Records. A year later he released his debut album, *Born Under a Bad Sign*, with producer/drummer Al Jackson, guitarist Steve Cropper, bassist Donald "Duck" Dunn, keyboardist Booker T. Jones, and the Memphis Horns.

Thanks to the soulful undertones provided by this eclectic group of musicians, and the backing of a powerful label, Albert became an immediate crossover success. By the time he died of a heart attack in 1992, Albert King had released eighteen albums, become the first blues artist to play at the legendary Filmore West in San Francisco, and was the first bluesman ever to record with a symphony orchestra when he performed with the St. Louis Symphony in 1969. When all was said and done, Albert had gotten what he wanted.

"I remember when Albert died," says Johnnie. "Me and Harold White and Kenny Rice drove to Memphis for the funeral. It was the biggest funeral I ever saw—you wouldn't believe the flowers. I was sad when Albert died. We'd all stayed friends over the years and Albert had kind of mellowed out in his old age. He used to come by and visit sometimes when he was in town and we always had a good time. People always ask me if I disliked Albert for the way he was and 'cause he took all the music we'd made up as a band. But I never held no bad feelings towards Albert. You have to learn to forgive people. It ain't good to walk around with a grudge."

In the end, it is the friendships that matter. At least that's what Harold White believes. "Playing in the original Albert King band caused all of us to become better musicians," he says. "But more importantly, it made us all into a family. I have friends for life—brothers—because of that band. When Johnnie Johnson told me he'd stopped drinking...I'm a grown man, but I got tears in my eyes. I cried, cause I was so happy for him. That's how close we were...all of us...Lee Otis, Freddie, Wilbur...we were a family. That's worth it all right there."

Johnnie Johnson is uncharacteristically sentimental when he talks of his former bandmates. "They are all my brothers. All them fellas from that band. Best friends and best musicians anyone could have. That's the truth. I learned more in playin' with those fellas than in the whole rest of my career put together."

Johnson's brief stint as a full-time musician had ended. He continued to play with the Magnificent Six on the weekends but took a day job at the St. Louis Steel Foundry. Reality had come calling again and Johnnie accepted it in stride. He had lived his life like a kite, soaring high or plummeting down, floating wherever the wind willed him, depending on someone else to launch him, to the hold the string while he flew. But the string had become tangled in knots of his own making, and with each bound knot, the string grew shorter. Before long, he would not be able to fly at all. Meanwhile, hundreds of miles away, on a crisp October day in 1963, Chuck Berry emerged from prison, a different man from before. Bitter. Angry. And for the second time in his career, he would face those winds of change threatening to blow him over. Only this time the winds were a hurricane, a typhoon, raging across the Atlantic. And as he would soon realize, those easterly winds that threatened to smash him whispered to him as well.

And the name they whispered was his own.

VIII

NO PARTICULAR PLACE TO GO

"Go. I'll see you in three years."
—Leonard Chess to Chuck Berry upon learning of the latter's deal with Mercury Records.

The Minneapolis airport is already crowded at eight a.m. on this bitterly cold November morning. Johnnie, dressed in a jacket and a heavy gray sweatshirt, his ever-present ballcap pulled firmly atop his head, checks his bags out front and hurries inside to the welcoming warmth of the main terminal.

"It's cold out there," he says, more to himself than me. "Well, I guess we better hurry and find this gate."

Ten minutes later, we have made it approximately halfway. Johnnie plods in front, coffee in one hand, his silver, sticker-covered briefcase in the other. I walk behind him, trying not to step on his heels, shouldering my carry-on dufflebag, and balancing a box of donut holes Johnnie purchased on the ride to the airport. His version of a continental breakfast.

Before long I feel obtrusive, like a dumptruck chugging up the center lane of a freeway at rush hour. Johnnie and I cause quite a diversion moving along at such a dragging pace. People stream by us on both sides, carts swerve to miss us, but through it all Johnnie seems oblivious and treks on like a stubborn tortoise. Finally we reach the gate and find a pair of seats near the window.

As a rule, Johnnie prefers to arrive early for his flights, so we still have a half-hour until check-in time. He arranges himself neatly, briefcase on his lap, coffee at his side. I hand him the donut holes and he places them on top of the briefcase, fashioning sort of a lap table upon which he begins to munch the miniature pastry balls one after the other, the crumbs collecting in his goatee and spilling onto his sweatshirt.

Adjacent to us, the pre-boarding for another flight has begun. As the announcement is made, a harried young woman, eyes still swollen from sleep, rushes towards the ticket taker. In her arms is a small boy, three, maybe four years old, and she balances him awkwardly on her hip as she rummages for her boarding card. The child is certainly old enough to walk himself, but he clings desperately to his mother with white knuckles and eyes wild with fear. As they pass through the door, the child begins to scream, a shrill and terrible sound that carries down the corridor and into the terminal. Johnnie stops eating momentarily and watches curiously.

"He's scared to fly," he states flatly.

"You think so?"

"Mmmmhmmmm. I know that look. Last place that boy wants to be is on an airplane."

"You know what that's like, I bet."

"Uh-huh. That's for sure. I was scared to death of flyin'. That's one of the reasons I stopped tourin' around as much with Chuck, 'cause he was wantin' to fly over to Europe and I just couldn't do it."

"When was that?"

"Around '64, right after he got out of prison. See, 'cause he had gotten out in '63, but he had to get permission from his parole officer to leave the city. He'd called me in '63 about going up to Chess do some recordin', but he wasn't allowed to go nowhere 'til January in '64."

"So he had written some songs in prison, then?"

"That's it. Four or five of 'em, just like the other ones. He had put together some words and he wanted me and him to get together and put some music behind 'em."

"He'd been pretty busy then?"

"I guess so. Chuck was always busy."

* * *

On October 18, 1963, Chuck Berry drove his Cadillac up Interstate 66 from Springfield to St. Louis, a free man. He had achieved a great deal during his incarceration. Besides the normal chores such as dishwashing and mopping the mess hall, he also had found time to earn his high school diploma, study business, law, and accounting, and write lyrics to six songs: "Brenda Lee," "No Particular Place to Go," "Nadine," "Tulane," "You Never Can Tell," and "Promised Land."

Berry certainly made the best of his time in prison, but the time that had helped to better him had hardened him as well. The Chuck Berry that emerged from prison was a different man than the one who had entered it twenty months before. Once engaging off stage, he was now brooding and private, aloof to the point of being introverted. Carl Perkins, with whom Berry had often conversed prior to his arrest, noted that the guitarist scarcely spoke a word to him after 1963. Others recall a shrewder more business-minded Berry with little time for personal interaction.

"Chuck changed," Johnnie says. "He wasn't too much different with me, we always got along good. But I could see him, how he acted with other people, and I knew he had a chip on his shoulder.

He was angry at how the law had treated him and he thought everybody wanted to cheat him. He calmed down a little bit over the next couple years, but he was definitely a different person after he got out of prison."

Much of Berry's frustration with the system following his release stemmed from the difficulties posed by his St. Louis parole officer, a by-the-rules stickler who required the performer to formally request permission to travel outside of the area, and strictly forbade any commuting to Chicago for recording purposes. The restrictions severely hampered Berry's career, and Leonard Chess suggested that he transfer to Chicago where the parole officers had a more "sympathetic" attitude towards professional artists. Berry agreed, and for the next fourteen months, he officially resided in Chicago, although the time spent on the road during this period hardly lent itself to qualify the Windy City as his home.

At the start of the year, before he left on his travels, the Chess brothers requested he put some of his new material on record so that they could market his return to music. The date was set for January 14, 1964. Before they could begin, however, Berry had some phone calls to make.

* * *

"I forgot to fix the phone," Johnnie Johnson thought upon awaking to the sound of bells ringing in his apartment. Even when he was drunk, he always remembered to fix the phone. Especially the night of a gig. All you did was open it up, put a little wad of paper between the hammer and the bell. Silence. The person calling would hear the ringing from their end, think he hadn't gotten home yet, and hang up without ever disturbing him. Not this time. He'd forgotten.

He rolled over and sat up, his head throbbing. The woman beside him (Who the hell is she? He couldn't remember picking her up, much less her name) continued to snore blissfully, a fine line of drool stringing from her lip and pooling nicely on his yellowed sheets. Mistake number two, he thought to himself. Then he rose and made his way to the telephone, the whole time rehearsing what he was going to say to whichever one of his six girlfriends was on the other end. He'd told each of them that he was not interested in a serious relationship and they had agreed to see him on those terms. But jealousy was jealousy and he knew he'd better have an excuse handy. He ran the conversation through his mind: "Sure I knew you were there. Yeah, I was looking for you afterwards. You were looking for me too? Well, there you go. We must have just missed each other. With somebody? Me? No, I just came home and went straight to bed."

It was the usual line of bullshit, but who cared? His head was killing him. He had to make the ringing stop. He reached down and picked up the receiver.

"Hello?" He could smell his own breath on the mouthpiece and it nearly gagged him.

"Johnnie. This is Chuck."

"Hey now." He was genuinely surprised. He'd heard Chuck was out of prison but didn't expect to hear from him so soon.

"I just got out of the joint and I'm up in Chicago. You interested in doing some recording?"

"When you talkin' 'bout?"

"January 14."

"All right, then."

"How you doing, Jack?"

"Fine."

"Good...I'll have Fran call you later to set everything up."

"Okay, then."

"All right, Jack. See you later."

"Bye."

He hung up the receiver and quietly removed the back of the phone, silencing the noisome ringer with a piece of paper found on the floor. Then settling on a chair by the door, he grabbed a half-empty bottle of Tanqueray, one of many lying around his apartment, and took a long pull, feeling the liquid warm his stomach. "Hair of the dog," he thought smiling. Then as soon as it had come, the smile was gone. Johnnie folded his great hands in his lap and drifted off to sleep.

* * *

"The first session after Chuck got out of prison?" Johnnie is racking his brain. "Well, we went in the studio that first time and did about four songs. 'Nadine' was one of 'em and 'You Never Can Tell,' was one of 'em. The other two I can't remember, right off. I remember Jaspar Thomas and Leroy Davis both made that session with me. We worked on 'Nadine' first, I believe. Chuck had wrote the words out to sound like 'Maybellene,' but when it came to the music we decided to do 'Nadine' a little bit slower with more of a boogie feel to it. We kept the same key, though, as 'Maybellene,' which was B-flat. After that we did 'You Never Can Tell.' Chuck wanted to come up with some New Orleans-soundin' music 'cause it was about New Orleans and Pierre and 'c'est la vie' and all that business. We all worked on that one. Jaspar came up with the idea for that stagger-beat rhythm and both me and Leroy came up with our own parts. In fact, the little piano thing I did...well, you can hear it on the record. It's a little bit different than most of the other stuff I did with Chuck. 'Course, 'You Never Can Tell' was different altogether. That really was a song we all came up with together from the start. Me and Chuck, and Jaspar and Leroy."

* * *

The plane has arrived. Johnnie drains his coffee and watches the stream of disembarking passengers spill out of the door. On our left, a prunefaced woman in a wheelchair is barking trite orders to the flight attendant rolling her towards an embarrassed-looking heavyset man who seems none too pleased to take the reins. Probably her son, I think. Johnnie takes it all in with rheumy eyes.

"He probably want to send her back where she came from," he says under his breath as the woman gesticulates impatiently. We share a laugh and watch them roll out of sight down the walkway. Before long they have become just another part of the crowd.

"Say Johnnie?" I ask then.

"Mmmmhmmm?"

"When you were talking about that first recording session after Chuck got back, how many more did you do?"

"Well I think that was the only one we did in '64. Chuck and I took about a year off from recordin' together. He was up in Chicago a lot and then he went out on some tours to Europe and whatever. I wasn't gonna have none of that flyin' all them hours over the ocean, no way. I stayed in St. Louis."

"So that was the first time he went to Europe?"

"That's it. See, Chuck was goin' through this popular streak. Right after he got out of jail, he found out about all these kids in England likin' our music. We didn't know 'bout any of what was goin' on over there, at least I didn't. But once he found out what them folks over there thought about him—thought he was a god or something—he wanted to get right over there and make some money. I'm sure he made a lot, too. 'Course, that wouldn't have meant anything to me or Jaspar, 'cause we got paid the same no matter where we played. But Chuck was a big star over there. And it all started 'cause of the Beatles. That's how we knew. They was doin' our songs on their albums—I think the first one they did was 'Roll Over Beethoven.' The Beatles. I remember when they first came over. The Beatles changed everything in rock and roll."

* * *

On February 7, 1964, at approximately 1:20 p.m., Pan Am flight number 101 touched down at John F. Kennedy International

Airport in New York City. Capitol Records had done quite a good job hyping the event—perhaps too good. For when moments later, the four smiling young lads stepped off the plane and attempted to move towards their waiting cars, they were nearly crushed by the mob of screaming girls who had come just to see them, to touch them, or better yet, take home a shirt sleeve, a trouser leg, or if luck would have it, a nice souvenir fistful of mop-top.

Two days later, the Beatles made their live U.S. debut on CBS-TV's *Ed Sullivan Show*. It was estimated that seventy-three million viewers tuned in that evening to watch them perform "All My Loving," "Till There Was You," "She Loves You," "I Saw Her Standing There," and their first American release, "I Want To Hold Your Hand."

The effect was enormous. Unbeknownst to most American fans, rock and roll had been stewing in the Isles ever since the first bootleg Elvis Presley and Chuck Berry records found their way into the fret-calloused hands of rebellious British schoolboys like John Lennon and Keith Richards. Now the Beatles had opened the door, and before long a number of bands from across the Atlantic would flock to the United States in the hope of unseating them. The American dominance of rock and roll was over. The British Invasion had begun.

Bob Dylan remembers being in his car soon after the Beatles' 1964 *Ed Sullivan Show* debut and hearing the group all over the dial. "Their chords were outrageous, just outrageous," recalls Dylan. "And their harmonies made it all valid. You could only do that with other musicians...I knew they were pointing the direction where music had to go."

Not everyone agreed with Dylan's assessment. Since Chuck Berry had been in prison, rock and roll music had evolved far beyond the simple three-chord guitar/bass/drum/piano format. Super-producers like Phil Spector and the Beach Boys' Brian Wilson were attempting to take the music to a higher plane of complexity. In a 22 x 31 ft. studio jam-packed with musicians, Spector had taken the concept of the black girl group and added a vast array of sounds and harmonies from jazz to classical orchestration. Spector called the results "little symphonies for kids." By mid-1963, the music world had renamed it the "Wall of Sound."

Spector wasn't the only one expanding rock's horizons. The same month that Spector debuted his new sound, Brian Wilson took over the role of producer of the Beach Boys. Combining many of Spector's advanced production techniques with his own love of harmony, Wilson essentially created his own wall of sound by way of his bandmates' voices, which he wove and wound together into a joyous blend of corporal music far beyond what any doo-wop group had yet to even conceive.

Therefore, it was highly discouraging for both Wilson and Spector when the Beatles arrived in the middle of what was essentially a race for supremacy, and led the fans back to an archaic uncompounded style of rock and roll. Said Wilson in the PBS documentary *Rock and Roll*: "I couldn't understand how a group could just be...you know...screamed at...and it doesn't really make...the music that they made... 'I Wanna Hold Your Hand', for example, wasn't even that great a record. But they got screamed at. I couldn't understand that. I couldn't understand how something like that could happen—the Beatles."

Wilson and Spector were not the only ones threatened by the British Invasion. For black musicians like Ben E. King and the Shirelles, who were just starting to gain acceptance in a white-dominated market, the sudden popularity of groups like the Beatles signified a return to the racial boundaries they had worked hard to overcome. The old black rock and rollers were revered, but the new black rock and rollers could not get played; the R & B songs once recorded only by black artists were now sucked up by the British Invasion groups who took them to the top of the charts leaving the often superior black versions to fall into obscurity.

"There was a bit of jealousy because we were cut off at a time when we were just getting ready to become stronger than strong ourselves," recalls Ben E. King in *Rock and Roll*. "All the signs were there. The music that was being created right here at home was gonna be tremendously big. And then all of a sudden these kids come along and stopped all that. It was a strong pill to swallow."

Perhaps so. But the Beatles made it as easy a task as could be expected. They were cute, inoffensive, and generally well-liked, or at the very least accepted by the older generation, even if they couldn't quite understand their music or their strange hair cuts. Rock and roll was becoming a safe option for the children; a harmless diversion. The Beatles and others like them—Herman's Hermits, the Dave Clark Five, Freddy and the Dreamers—were clowns. You could laugh at their long hair or scoff at their music, but you didn't have to fear them.

That all changed in 1965 when a rag tag collection of miscreants calling themselves the Rolling Stones slunk in from the dingy bowels of the London R&B clubs. Sneering and rebellious, they were the antithesis of the Beatles. Where the Beatles were relatively clean cut, the Stones were worn and dirty; where the Beatles were good looking, the Stones were skeletal and homely. The Beatles were well-mannered— the Stones were arrested for urinating in public.

Suddenly the tide had turned. The bubble-gum simplicity of "I Want to Hold Your Hand" and "I Saw Her Standing There" was now being challenged by the blatant sexuality of "I Can't Get No Satisfaction," and the biting satire of "Mother's Little Helper" and "Stupid Girl." As fast as it had become safe, rock and roll was dangerous again.

* * *

"Those English groups, like the Beatles and the Rolling Stones, they wasn't doin' anything different at first," Johnnie says as we board the plane. "Just doin' a lot of the music me and Chuck did. Lot of Little Richard and Elvis. Some of 'em was even doin' Muddy

Waters. That was another thing—they especially seemed to like the blues, which was funny to me, 'cause at that time in America, only black people seemed to be into the blues. You couldn't hear no blues where the white folks lived. But I guess over there in England it was different. I remember Keith Richards tellin' me how he used to get all Chuck's records from Chess back in the fifties. How they was listening to Muddy Waters and Howlin' Wolf. Bunch of white boys. That really surprised me."

* * *

"The English discovered Chess," Marshall Chess says in *Rock and Roll*. The son of Leonard, Marshall is the former vice-president of Chess records, and now heads Arc Music with his cousin Kevin, who is Phil's son. "The real fanatics always knew it, but the mainstream English music lovers discovered it."

And so it was that, much to the dismay of artists like Brian Wilson and Phil Spector, rock and roll was taking a huge jump forward by taking a huge jump backward. Thanks to groups like the Rolling Stones, who carefully credited each remake to it's rightful owner, blues and rock and roll legends like Muddy Waters, Howlin' Wolf, Willie Dixon, and even Berry himself, were being "rediscovered," as it were, by a new generation of afficionados. Muddy Waters was especially appreciative of the Stones for opening the ears of the mainstream public. "When I started out," Waters said, "they called my music 'nigger music.' People wouldn't let that kind of music into the house. The Beatles started, but the Rolling Stones really made my kind of music acceptable. I really respect them for opening the doors for black music. I'll tell ya, the guitar player ain't bad either."

The realization that so few white Americans appreciated the blues came as a great shock to many of the British groups, but especially so to the Stones, who all but worshiped the music and it's legendary practitioners. Said Rolling Stone bassist Bill Wyman in his autobiography, *Stone Alone*, "We really thought that when we went to America and played them that music that it wouldn't work because it was their music. We didn't realize the white kids had never heard that music."

Yet before long, the American white kids had heard the music, the Stones saw to that, and soon suburban record stores were selling Muddy Waters and Howlin' Wolf to mop-topped teenagers. But no good deed goes unpunished. The Stones had opened white America's ears to the blues, a product of their own country, and in doing so, inadvertently harmed their own chances at success. Donald Clarke talks about the problem in his book *The Rise and Fall of Popular Music*

> 'Can you imagine a British-composed R&B song? It just wouldn't make it,' said [Mick] Jagger in 1963, before somebody told him how much money the Beatles were making with their own songs. Jagger was right; British R&B was and is a contradiction in terms. The first Stones album included songs by Rufus Thomas, Willie Dixon, Chuck Berry, Slim Harpo, and even Motown artists (Holland-Dozier-Holland). They had their first U.K. chart entry in mid 1963; an American edition of their first album reached number eleven in the Billboard album chart in 1964, but many Americans could not figure out why they should listen to white English kids singing Chuck Berry when they already had Chuck Berry records.

But the English kids had to sing Chuck Berry. To them he was more than a hero—he was the embodiment of rock and roll. John Lennon expressed it best when he said, "If you had to try and give rock and roll another name, you might call it Chuck Berry." Both the Beatles and the Stones idolized him—and both recorded versions of his songs as an homage to him: the Beatles with "Roll Over Beethoven" and "Rock 'n' Roll Music" and the Stones with "Carol," "Down the Road Apiece," and "Around and Around."

Berry recalls in his autobiography that the coming of the Beatles boosted his career considerably. "The Beatles were then in the stratosphere of popularity and soaring higher as my 'Nadine' and

'No Particular Place to Go' hit the market. The media quoted their mentions of some of my songs that they had recorded, which naturally was a great help to my then-sleeping repertoire."

For the first time in nearly five years, the public was screaming for new Chuck Berry records. Recognizing their chance, both Berry and Chess did their best to answer the call and take advantage of the market.

Before Berry had even been released from prison, Chess put together a compilation album of prime Berry studio cuts and dubbed in audience noise behind them. Billed as a live album, *Chuck Berry on Stage* would rise all the way to No. 29 and become his first charted album, an achievement due almost entirely to the British artists's revival of his music.

The following May, Berry traveled alone to London and began his first U.K. tour at the Astoria Theater in Finsbury Park. Among the groups performing on the bill with Berry were the Animals, who like the Stones, lived and breathed American R&B. They were, in fact, a rougher lot than even the Stones, for while the Stones gave off the air of being street-toughs, they were all from middle class homes. This was not the case with the Animals. Singer Eric Burdon had grown up poor and tough in Walker, Northumberland, and fell in love with the blues early on due to the relevance it had to his own life.

"I heard John Lee Hooker singing things like 'I've been workin' in a steel mill, truckin' steel like a slave all day, and I woke up this mornin' and my baby's gone away,'" recalls Burdon. "And I related to that directly because that was happening to grown men on my block."

At thirteen, Burdon slashed his arm and wrote "blues forever" in his own blood. Nine years later, he was the gravel-throated lead singer for the premier R&B band in Newcastle—a group considered proficient enough to back up such notables as John Lee Hooker, Memphis Slim, and Sonny Boy Williamson. But the legend of Chuck Berry presented an even more intriguing challenge. "We're going on the Chuck Berry tour," remembers Burdon of the American legend's first U.K. visit, "and everybody's gonna try and out-rock Chuck Berry."

In their hearts, The Animals knew this was not feasible. As the British saw it, Chuck Berry invented rock and roll. Trying to "out-rock" him, even with superior musicianship, was like trying to out-pious the Pope. They had to do something different. It was as a result of this necessity that the band performed the song that made them famous.

The Animals went on stage early. After working their native crowd into a frenzy with their usual grinding R&B, the band closed their set with an unexpected treat—a brilliant reworking of an old folk-blues song "House of the Rising Sun." The haunting ballad electrified the audience, and the Animals succeeded in overshadowing Chuck Berry, if only temporarily, becoming the talk of the tour. Not long afterwards, they came to America. Johnnie Johnson remembers recording with the group sometime in the mid-sixties.

"I remember the Animals real well," he says. "In fact, I played on one of their songs, only one. I think it was called 'Club Go Go.' They had heard me playin' with Chuck and asked would I come in and play on their record. This was at Chess, so it must have been 'round 1965. I was real impressed with them. You hear a name like the Animals you think they was gonna come in and tear up the place, but they were real cool, nice fellas. They did a lot of old stuff but they were doin' their own thing too. Like that song 'Risin' Sun.' I think Chuck really liked them a lot, too."

In essence, what the Animals were conveying by this foray into new territory was what people like Phil Spector and Brian Wilson had been trying to communicate before the British Invasion—the formula is established, the rules are set, you cannot improve on what Chuck Berry and Johnnie Johnson created—but you can expound on it, embellish it, and in the spirit of those who came before, find your own angle, your own interpretation and contribute to the growth of the music.

The trend towards innovation was spreading. Around the same time as the Animals' enlightenment, Beatle producer George Martin, bored and uninspired by the group's lack of originality and simplistic style, had challenged the Fab Four to write something new. The lads were understandably perturbed by the implications of the challenge, but took it on nonetheless. The result—eleven No.1 hits in a row written almost exclusively by John Lennon and Paul McCartney. The dynamic duo would continue producing hit records for six years, including an album that has been called the highest achievement ever by a rock and roll band, *Sergeant Pepper's Lonely Hearts Club Band* in 1967.

"The greatness about Paul and John being songwriters was that they had a style but the style was continuously changing," George Martin recalls in *Rock and Roll*. "I give them four marks for not saying, 'We're gonna do this song again.' They never did the same song again—they did something different. And they weren't sitting down and saying we'll design this like a formal piece of architecture—this stuff just came at them by this time."

Rock and roll had experienced a changing of the guard. Elvis was no longer the King, and neither Chuck Berry nor Little Richard could claim the throne. The mantle had been passed to another generation. Now two bands, both British, held an unquestioned dominion over the rock world—the Beatles and the Rolling Stones.

* * *

Following the London tour, Berry traveled alone to Santa Monica, California, where he met up for the first time on stage with the Rolling Stones. It was their second meeting altogether. The band had run into Berry once before during a two-day recording session at Chess Records in June of 1964.

For the Stones, recording in the same place as their heroes was a dream come true; but actually getting to meet one of their heroes was the icing on the cake. Phil Chess said of the Stones and other British groups begging to be let in during the British Invasion, "The world loves a winner and Chess studios was hotter than hell. Everybody wanted to come to Chess."

The Stones' introduction to Berry occurred immediately after their recording of "Down the Road Apiece," which Berry himself had recorded in 1960 with Johnnie Johnson and Jaspar Thomas. When they had finished, Berry walked in to congratulate the band. "I stood outside there for a while when you were doing the last number," Berry supposedly told them. "It was great. You got a real great sound going. Swing on, gentlemen."

Despite these reported pleasantries, subsequent meetings with Berry would not find the icon so affable. Bassist Bill Wyman recalls in *Stone Alone* that Berry's "attitude towards [the Rolling Stones] was weird, uncommunicative."

> Our relationships with the originators of blues and rock 'n' roll music should have been excellent. As genuine lovers of their art, we had substantially helped its recognition. Mick said as our popularity zoomed: 'I believe that the acceptance of music like ours, the Yardbirds and other R&B groups, has done tremendous good for people like Bo Diddley, Muddy Waters, and others like them. It seemed odd to us, therefore, that Chuck Berry continued to treat us with such disdain. As his great record 'No Particular Place to Go,' raced up the British charts and he toured the U.K., Mick and Charlie [Watts] had a strange encounter with him—or, rather, a non-encounter. They were in a hotel elevator; the door opened and there stood Chuck Berry. He stepped in, saw the two Stones, turned his back and, when the doors opened again walked out without saying a word.

Things began to go downhill for Berry shortly afterwards. In the fall, the sequel to "Memphis," "Little Marie" faltered at No.54 while "Promised Land" did slightly better reaching No.41. His London album, *St. Louis to Liverpool*, the first ever recorded without Johnnie Johnson's input, scored at a disappointing No. 124 on the album charts and the single "Dear Dad" barely squeaked into the top 100, peaking at No. 95. Berry would not have a song on the charts again for over seven years.

In June of 1966, Chuck Berry made one of the worst business decisions of his career. Frustrated by his slump and hungry for more cash, the guitarist left Chess Records for a guaranteed $150,000 advance on future royalties offered by Mercury Records. Leonard Chess let him go without protest, knowing full well that his star would return once his three year contract with Mercury had expired.

Meeting in a Mercury studio in the fall of 1966, Berry and an all new studio band recorded updated versions of eighteen of his hit singles plus a new composition "Club Nitty Gritty" for his first Mercury album, *Chuck Berry's Golden Hits*. The album failed miserably and Berry soon regretted his decision to leave Chess. When asked in a 1987 *Guitar* magazine interview about the substandard sound of his Mercury albums, Berry was contrite.

"For the first time I didn't really have an A&R [artists & repertoire] man telling me how to play for a certain market*," he told Tom Wheeler, "and also I now had a whole band. I hired Billy Peek's band as sidemen. Mercury just wanted me to re-record my hits so they could have masters of their own, about eighteen tunes."

When asked by Wheeler if he felt the Mercury records were as good as the originals, Berry revealed in one sentence the crucial role Johnnie Johnson played in the development of his music. "They were not as good," Berry admitted, "because I couldn't get them to play like Johnnie."

* * *

"I've never heard what Chuck did at Mercury, but from what I've

---

* Berry contradicts this statement directly in his autobiography stating, "I'd always A&Red my own recording sessions, even during the three years I recorded with Mercury. Artists and Repertoire? What was that?"

been told, they ain't too good," Johnnie says on the airplane. "I don't know why he didn't want me to play on them albums, and I wasn't 'bout to ask him his reasons. That's one thing 'bout Chuck— he don't like to be asked a lot of questions 'bout his business. I just figured he had his own thing happenin' and I had mine, so that was that.

"I was playin' a lot of blues and jazz at the time. No rock and roll. The closest I came to that was when I'd be in Chicago and stop by Chess to visit. There was always someone recordin' in there: Muddy Waters, Little Walter, and I'd stop in and listen. Phil Chess was there, and he knew how much I liked cigars, so every time I walked in the studio he had a cigar for me. That's the kind of guy Phil Chess was. With the bigger studio and all the new people workin', Leonard and Phil weren't always there. But it was a big treat to see them and catch up on what was goin' on every now and then."

Johnnie Johnson was out of rock and roll indefinitely. Buried in obscurity, overshadowed by Berry, the world seemed destined to never hear his name. Only a handful of musicians recognized the importance of his achievements, fewer still knew who he was. Nevertheless, the music he helped create continued to blossom in the innovative hands of a new generation of artists.

In 1965, keyboardist Ray Manzarek and his pal, poet/vocalist Jim Morrison, formed the Doors, ushering in a new era of music that would come to be known as "psychedelic." The music demanded a change in attitude. Two years earlier, Bob Dylan had turned the youth of America on to what was going on around them. Now the Doors urged them to look inward and explore the boundaries of their minds. A masterful musician adept in a variety of styles, Manzarek more or less filled the same role in the Doors, and specifically with Jim Morrison, that Johnnie Johnson had with Chuck Berry—creating music for a frontman's poetry. Jim Morrison may have voiced the genre, but it was Ray Manzarek with the help of guitarist Robby Krieger and drummer John Densmore, who created the actual sound of psychedelic rock. In many ways, the music of psychedelia was an expostulation of the base rock and roll formula. Yet despite its often complex key structures, use of sound effects, and metaphorical lyricism, the music itself was strongly rooted in the rhythm and blues piano stylings that Manzarek garnered while growing up in Chicago listening to his predecessors—Otis Spann and Johnnie Johnson. In his autobiography, *Light My Fire: My Life With The Doors*, Manzarek explains how these two artists influenced his approach to the keyboard and its subsequent role in a band format.

> Spann was the man. He and Johnny (sic) Johnson with Chuck Berry taught me how to play blues/rock piano. They were the masters of the craft. Listening to them gave me the way into the labyrinth. And the way was in silence. The space. Here's what you do: You leave space for the guitar player to make his statement; maybe you comp a little behind him, play a simple little repetitive pattern as a foundation for him to float over. Allow him to make his musical statement...and then you answer him. You follow the same procedure with the singer. But when it comes time to do your own solo then you become the lead. The psychic energy is all yours. When I solo, I am the lord and master. I control the destiny of the song. All must obey me. I have a paroxysm, I go manic...and then I acquiesce. I harmonize again with the energy of the group. The collective energy. I become a cog in the gear again.

The Doors were on to something. For the next five years, groups such as Jefferson Airplane, Cream, and the Jimi Hendrix Experience would continue to develop psychedelic music while at the same time managing to remain in touch with their roots. Jimi Hendrix was known to perform such Berry hits as "Carol" and "Johnny B. Goode" on stage, and both the Airplane and Cream could break into old-fashioned rock and roll when desired. It is no coincidence that out of these three, Hendrix and Cream guitarist Eric Clapton have been cited by many rock historians as the two greatest rock and roll guitarists of our time. Clapton, in fact, used the music of Berry and Johnson as a springboard into a deeper study of rhythm and blues, tracing it all the way back to the acoustic wizardry of Robert Johnson.

"It was almost like I'd been prepared each step to receive him," said Clapton, "like a religious experience that started out by hearing Chuck Berry, and then at each stage I was going further and further back, and deeper and deeper into the source of the music, until I was ready for Robert Johnson."

Ironically, while Clapton was exploring the influences of the past, his hero was attempting to bond with the present generation. Chuck Berry was forty years old and the father of two teenage daughters during the Summer of Love. He had slowed down his touring schedule and now spent much of his time holding court at Berry Park, which had recently opened up to the public. The property covered a vast area and for a small fee, visitors could hang out on the grounds and swim in the guitar-shaped swimming pool, or even stay overnight at the park's motel. Before long, Berry would begin hosting full-blown rock and roll festivals where he could be seen amongst the visitors dressed in full hippy regalia including vest, bell-bottoms, lovebeads, and a headband. "It's beginning to be what I might call a 'swing city' with groovy people," said Berry of his park in 1969, "and I hope it grows."

Johnnie Johnson turned forty-three that July. And he would not be found at Berry Park. He'd married singer Maudell Powell, a friend since the Cosmopolitan days, in 1968 and had more or less resigned himself to a domestic lifestyle, playing music on the weekends with the Magnificent Six, and working a day job. He rarely saw Berry, if at all, and the two men seemed unlikely to work together again.

"Chuck was off in his own world," Johnnie says. "I never saw him, never heard from him. That was perfectly okay with me. I had my own life. Me and Maudell never had no kids, but I had other responsibilities. My momma had got remarried while I was in Chicago and now her second husband, fella named Tom Wright, had died from a heart attack. I didn't want her livin' by herself, so me and Maudell drove down to Fairmont and got her. By that time she was gettin' sick herself and needed somebody to take care of her. She stayed with us for quite a while. It was nice havin' momma livin' with me again. Kinda like bein' at home. Then after a while she started gettin' real sick and I had to take her to the nursin' home or hospital, whatever you want to call it. That was the hardest thing I ever did. I used to visit her every single day and bring her little presents or whatever, to make her happy. She lived for a few months in there before she died. She was eighty-two years old. That woman took care of me my whole life. It was sure hard to see her go. Tore me up real good for a while."

Following the death of his mother, Johnnie fell into a depression and began to drink heavily again, staying out all hours of the night, passing out on the street. He lost one job, then another, then another. Finally, Maudell had enough. In 1969, she packed up her belongings and moved out. Johnnie Johnson was alone again.

* * *

Leonard Chess had been right again. By 1969, Chuck Berry had seen the error of his ways and yearned to return to Chess. But Chess Records was no longer the "family" company it had been when the Johnnie Johnson Trio first walked in the studio in 1955. Since Berry had left for Mercury, the Chess brothers had moved their studios to its final location at 320 E. 21st Street. Meanwhile, Leonard's son Marshall, who had become vice-president of the company, started marketing towards the white college students who were quickly becoming the most voracious blues consumers. With the psychedelic era in full swing, Marshall Chess attempted to capitalize on this market by signing such groups as Status Quo and the comically named Atilla & the Huns of Time. In a futile attempt to bridge the generations, Chess released two psychedelic albums near the end of the year: Muddy Waters's *Electric Mud* and Howlin' Wolf's *Howlin' Wolf Album*. Neither album fared well in the marketplace. Waters claimed he was not happy with the result, and the cantankerous Wolf reportedly called his voyage into the psychedelic realm "birdshit."

In January of 1969, a dejected Leonard Chess sold the family company to the GRT corporation for $10 million and quietly phased himself out of the business. Nine months later, while driving home from work, Leonard suffered a massive heart attack and died. He was only fifty-two years old.

Leonard Chess's passing marked the end of an important age in American music. Regardless of the accusations of exploitation and dishonest business practices by some former Chess artists, he will go down in history as a great visionary. Through his efforts, rhythm and blues and rock and roll became part of the vernacular of America's, indeed the world's culture. He had given artists such as Muddy Waters, Howlin' Wolf, and Willie Dixon a haven to work their magic—a place to produce records that may have never been recorded otherwise; records that in turn dictated the course popular music would take in the future.

"Leonard Chess gave us a chance when no one else was interested in what we was doin'," Johnnie says. "Vee Jay turned Chuck down flat. 'Who wants to hear a black man doin' hillbilly music?' Leonard did. He knew it was more than that and that somethin' could be made of it. He knew the same thing about Muddy Waters and Bo Diddley—all them folks at Chess. Leonard Chess made rock and roll. Alan Freed might have named it, but Leonard saw it first. Chuck and I would have still been playin' weekends at the Cosmopolitan Club if it wasn't for that man."

Berry's first sessions after his return to Chess took place in November of 1969, three months before he officially resigned. Obviously unaware of Leonard's passing at that time, he complains in his autobiography that "Leonard was never there anymore and his brother Phil was not a man who could replace Leonard's authority or humor."

Berry goes on to mention how the sessions were becoming "more foreign than ever, full of red tape and requirements for permission from other departments of the company for any changes, as opposed to the family-type, small-business settings of the earlier sessions." Former Chess session man, Phil Upchurch, expressed similar sentiments in *I Am The Blues: The Willie Dixon Story*.

> The only time the feeling it was over started setting in was after Leonard died because they were basically a one-man operation. When Leonard passed, everybody kind of felt, 'Well, there goes the company,' because he wasn't going to let his baby go down while he was on his feet. It started going downhill right after he passed.

Chess wan't the only thing going downhill. An interesting decision that Berry made upon returning to Chess was not inviting Johnnie Johnson to record on his comeback album. For some reason, Berry seemed determined to seperate himself from his partner, to the point that he all but denied Johnnie's existence. In an 1969 interview at Berkeley that appeared in *Rolling Stone* magazine, Berry reffered to Johnnie and Ebby as "jive musicians" and claimed that he didn't even remember their names. When someone in the crowd asked him specifically about Johnnie, Berry responded as if he'd just been reminded that Johnnie had played with him. "Ah yes," he said, "Johnnie Johnson."

It was perhaps the lowest point in the Johnson/Berry relationship. Berry seemed consumed with his own ego. During the interview, he also claimed that he'd sat in with Muddy Waters the night the legend had steered him toward Chess—an assertion Berry vehemently denied in his autobiography. "Somewhere, somebody wrote in their column that on the occasion when I met Muddy he allowed me to play with his band," Berry writes." It has always hurt me when a writer replaces the truth with fictitious dramatic statements to increase interest in his story." Regardless of the inconsistencies, one fact remained undeniably clear: Berry had been given a chance to acknowledge his friend and partner and he had forsaken him.

Released in early 1970, Berry's *Back Home*, featuring seven new songs, failed to dent the charts, although one of the numbers, "Tulane," would become a U.K. hit for the Steve Gibbons band. In reality, the album's failure was hardly unexpected. Chuck Berry was old news to the new generation of rock and rollers mourning the breakup of their beloved Beatles and reveling in the wild sounds of Led Zeppelin and Black Sabbath, two British bands who were busy ushering in a new type of music that would come to be known as heavy metal.

Suddenly obsolete, Berry was desperate for a hit record. He called Johnnie Johnson.

* * *

The eyes are closing. The hum of the plane engine has lulled him to sleep. I know if I let him go, I won't hear from him again until we land.

"Johnnie?"

"Mmmmmhmmm."

"Tell me about that last record you did with Chuck. The one in '71."

Silence.

"Johnnie?"

He sighs heavily.

"Ain't too much to tell. I hadn't seen him for a while. I think we'd played a couple times around town, but that was it. Chuck was just livin' in a different world. He didn't have time for any of us from the old days. All of a sudden he calls me up out of the blue 'round Christmas time. Says he's thinkin' 'bout doin' another record and would I like to join him. I said sure, as long as it was after New Year's Eve, 'cause I needed the money from that gig. He said that wouldn't be no problem. That's all there was to it. I went up there and helped him figure out some music to put behind his songs, same as always."

"Do you remember any of them?"
"Not really. Nothin' to remember."
"Same old thing, huh?"
"Same old thing."

* * *

San Francisco Dues, the first Berry/Johnson project in six years was released to a quiet reception in September of '71. Some critics contend that, technically, *San Francisco Dues* may have been Berry's best album overall. But technical details meant little in the buying market. The Berry style had gone virtually unchanged since he and Johnson had developed it some fifteen years before, and while the drive remained intact, the freshness was gone. Berry seemed destined to remain a non-charting artist for the rest of his career.

Then in 1972, Berry traveled to London where he cut some tracks with members of the Faces, a British band that had produced both Rod Stewart and Ron Wood. Released in tandem with a recording of a live show at Lanchester with the Average White Band, *The London Chuck Berry Sessions* would become Berry's most successful album, reaching No. 8 on the U.S. charts—an achievement based on the phenomenal success of a novelty audience-participation number titled "My Ding-A-Ling."

By the time of the recording, Berry had been performing the song on stage for over a decade. However, contrary to popular belief, it was not his own. "My Ding-A-Ling" was actually called "Toy Bell," and had been written and produced by New Orleans bandleader Dave Bartholomew—the man behind both Fats Domino and Lloyd Price. A group called the Bees released the song sometime in the mid-fifties and it was this version that Berry heard and subsequently copyrighted in his own name. Somehow he got away with this blatant transgression, as he had to a lesser degree in 1955, when he changed the words to Bob Wills' "Ida Red" in order to produce "Maybellene." Why Bartholomew never challenged

Berry's copyright incursion is unknown. Perhaps the fact that "Toy Bell" was just one of the countless songs he created lent to a tolerance of the younger man's encroachment. Maybe he simply forgot. Whatever the case, after 1972, the world knew Bartholomew's "Toy Bell" as Chuck Berry's "My Ding-A-Ling."

By August 5, 1972, "My Ding-A-Ling" was the hottest song in America and Chuck Berry had his first No.1 hit single. It had been nearly twenty years since Chuck Berry and Johnnie Johnson sowed the seeds of rock and roll. Now in what could only be called a great irony, Berry's first No.1 hit held no trace of their influential style. Johnnie Johnson's boogie rhythm was absent in the mix as were any of the trademark guitar solos. In fact "My Ding-A-Ling" could not be called a rock and roll song at all.

"It is strange when I realize the magnitude that came from ["My Ding-A-Ling]," says Berry in his book. "I had been singing it for four years prior where audiences were appropriate and suddenly after recording it, it came to be No.1 on the record charts. What's more strange, at least to me, is that I had not registered a hit in seven years. In fact, after having two surges of popularity, I never expected to reach near the top of the charts again."

For a short while afterwards, Berry was back in the spotlight. A 1967 greatest hits collection *Chuck Berry's Golden Decade* rode to No. 72 on the charts, five years after its initial release, while the brand new *St. Louis to Frisco to Memphis*, featuring a live recording at the Fillmore with the Steve Miller Band, checked in at No.185. A year later, the live single "Reelin' and Rockin'" hit No.27 on the U.S. single charts and the second volume of his *Golden Decade* album peaked at No.110.

Near the end of 1973, the inevitable became official. Over the past decade, Johnnie Johnson and Chuck Berry had grown further and further apart. The music they created together years before in a little club in East St. Louis, had grown in scope beyond either man's imagination. For one it had brought fame, fortune, and success— for the other a few hazy memories and a solemn resignation. Keith

Richards said it best when he observed in *Hail! Hail! Rock 'n' Roll* that the two men "have a strange relationship." They do. And the lines of that union run deeper and stranger than we will ever know. In almost every way they are opposites. Personality-wise, temperament-wise, even physically. But together they created the sound that rocked the world and it was this alone that united them in the face of convention. Off the stage they lived in two different worlds—but on the stage, in the studio, they were a team. They were rock and roll.

But nothing lasts forever. And the gulf that separated them off the stage was now too vast to bridge. Johnnie knew he had no choice. It was time to leave.

* * *

Touching down in St. Louis, the old man stirs awake. He was dreaming he tells me as he stretches his arms. When I ask him what he was dreaming about he is silent. *The secrets I think, "You have so many secrets inside you, Johnnie. And I will never get them out of you. You'll go to your grave with secrets. So will Chuck Berry. But not as many as he planned. Not now.*

"Can I ask you a question Johnnie?"

"You know you don't have to ask me that."

"When did you finally leave Chuck Berry?"

"About 1973. That's when I officially left his payroll. Didn't want to mess with flyin' all over the place."

"Is that the only reason?"

He gives me a look then that lets me know I have overstepped my bounds. Johnnie does not like to be pressed. He seems to mull the question over in his mind. Then he answers.

"They say birds of a feather flock together, and I didn't want to be part of that flock. So I guess you could say I pulled a Houdini. Got out of there 'fore any trouble started. That what you mean?"

"I guess so. Yeah."
"All right, then."
"One more thing."
"Mmmmhmmm."
"After you quit...where were you for all those years?"
 He stares at his hands and swallows hard.
"I guess I just disappeared."

IX

BYE BYE JOHNNIE

" Never forget; Johnnie Johnson is still alive and playing."
— Rolling Stones pianist Ian Stewart

Don Abrams was on a mission. In the summer of 1974, he left everything behind. He packed his bags, hopped in his car, and drove from New York to St. Louis to find the man he considered the father of rock and roll music. Friends regarded his behavior as extreme, but Abrams was certain he was on to something that most of the world had missed.

"I was always looking for what was hot," he remembers. "When I first heard Johnnie Johnson, it was an indelible flame in my mind. Everybody was into Chuck Berry, into the guitar and the cute words, but Johnnie Johnson was the powerhouse of that band. When I first heard him play on those records, way back in the early sixties when I was playing drums for a group called the Delvons, right then I said this is the man—this is the man behind the music.

It took a while to find out his name because they didn't put the band's names on records back then. But I eventually found out who he was and where I might find him. I don't know what possessed me to seek him out after all those years, but something told me I had to do it. I think it was fate, and I'll tell you why. My old car was on its last legs; she could have broken down anywhere during that trip. In fact, I expected it. But, you know, I made it all the way across country before she died. And she died right under the St. Louis Arch."

Homeless and jobless and without a car, Abrams went immediately to the downtown Y.M.C.A., where he settled in a room and began his search for Johnnie Johnson. Over the next month, Abrams spent his days looking for work and his nights hunting for the elusive pianist. At the end of thirty days, he had found nothing. Then, while showering in the communal bathroom one morning, he approached a fellow resident, a man whom he had a nodding acquaintance with, and asked him if he had ever heard of the "greatest rock and roll pianist of all time, Johnnie Johnson."

"He just looked at me kind of stunned for a minute and then he said in this deep voice, 'You're looking at him,'" remembers Abrams. "Of course, I didn't believe him at first—who would? I mean, here's the man who sparked rock and roll, and he's living in the Y.M.C.A. in downtown St. Louis? Give me a break. But I started asking him questions, detailed stuff only he would know...and when he started talking and I realized he was legitimate...I just went crazy."

Johnnie Johnson laughs when he recalls the morning Don Abrams came into his life. "He asked me if I knew who Johnnie Johnson was and I told him that I was the man he was lookin' for," says Johnnie. "Well, he starts jumpin' 'round the bathroom screamin', 'I found him! I found him!' I thought he was nuts for a minute. Here I was shavin' in the bathroom, hung over from the night before, and this little white man is dancin' all around the bathroom–'I found him! I found him!' Then when he finally calms down enough to talk, he tells me that he's come all the way across the country just to find me. That I am his hero or whatever. I tell you what, that's a lot to take in at seven in the mornin'."

Despite the unusual conditions of their introduction, the two men became fast friends. Knowing Abrams's travel money had all but run out, Johnnie used his position as a foreman at St. Louis Steel to secure his young friend a much-needed day job at the plant. On the weekends, they hung around East St. Louis, hopping from club to club and party to party, often staying out to the wee hours of the morning. As Abrams remembers, Johnnie opened the door and allowed him into his world as easily as if they had been brothers.

"Johnnie had this old, rusted-out, copper-colored Cadillac," recalls Abrams, "with two stick-on J's on the side. I'll never forget that. Since I didn't have a car anymore, that's the car we drove around town in. And Johnnie took me everywhere. He took me to the jazz clubs where he liked to jam, all kinds of blues clubs, he showed me the Cosmopolitan where he and Chuck started. We even went out to see Billy Peek, who was Chuck Berry's guitarist, do a gig that was just dynamite. We went to all kinds of parties around town. He even took me out to eat soul food with him. I remember I tried chitterlings for the first time with Johnnie and I'd like to have died!

"But the most meaningful time, the moment that truly made it all worthwhile, was when Johnnie and I drove up to Wentzville, to Berry Park, and he and I went up on that little stage...the same stage where they rehearsed for *Hail! Hail! Rock 'n' Roll.* That very one. I don't know where Chuck was at the time...maybe on the road..because it was just Johnnie and I sitting behind the piano. I asked him then if he could teach me the solo from 'Wee Wee Hours,' and before I know it, he's playing it, right there beside me. It was magical, man—indescribable. To be so close to that power...and I'm not just talking spiritually—although Johnnie's talent is certainly God-given—I'm talking about Johnnie's physicality. He is a big man with big hands, thick fingers, powerful forearms—his physicality affects his ability to play so well. Just like Jimi Hendrix, Johnnie is a messenger of how sound can be utilized to present power and subtlety at the same time. When he finished, I was just like 'Wow!' Then it was my turn. I teach piano now, and at the time I was familiar with the instrument, but I had to laugh when Johnnie told me not to rake the keys. I was so nervous playing in front of him that my hands were flying in the air."

Eventually, Don Abrams moved on to chase other dreams, ending up in California where he lives to this day, running a successful food-truck business and teaching piano and drum lessons to children. In Abrams's words, the time spent with Johnnie Johnson was a "wonderful experience that changed my life completely."

"I can't tell you how important that time was both in my development as a musician and a man," recalls Abrams. "It was something I'll cherish forever."

Johnnie Johnson and Don Abrams remain close friends to this day, and although they do not see each other as often as they would like, the two talk often on the phone and visit occasionally. Abrams remembers fondly when Johnnie's first CD was issued and he brought a copy to St. Louis for his friend to autograph.

"I remember it was morning and I was over at his house," he says. "We were having pancakes in the little kitchen, just the two of us. I watched him sign, but I couldn't see what he was writing. When he finished, he gave it to me and when I saw what he had written I had to fight back the tears. I've never been so touched. He wrote, 'To Don, the best friend a person could have. Love, Johnnie Johnson.' One sentence, man. But as far as I'm concerned, they can put that on my gravestone, because I have met no better friend, no better man, or no better human being, than Johnnie Johnson."

Abrams's departure in 1974 marked the beginning of an extremely rough period for Johnson. Shortly afterwards, his estranged wife, Maudell Powell succumbed suddenly to cancer.

They had been in the midst of a separation at the time of her death, but Maudell had been planning to join her husband's band when she passed away. Johnson felt the pain of her loss.

"Maudell and I weren't livin' together at the time she died but that didn't make it any less hard on me," recalls Johnnie. "The feelings you have for people don't just go away 'cause you're separated. All my marriages ended over the same thing—we just realized that we weren't right for each other and that was that. There wasn't no fightin' or arguin' or bad feelings—even with my second wife Rose. We just knew it was time. But when you care for someone, you care for them, and I was pretty shook up over her death. She was in a full body cast at the end and she couldn't do nothin' for herself. That's not something you want to see for somebody you care about."

After the funeral, Johnson received more bad news—Lee Otis Wright was moving to California and Harold White had decided to move on to other projects. After fourteen years together, the Magnificent Six, the original Albert King band, was splitting up. The sadness brought about by the band's demise was compounded by the fact that Johnnie had also lost his job at St. Louis Steel because of drinking and was now entirely without income. "I was in a mess," he recalls. "Nothin' seemed to be goin' my way. First my momma died, then Maudell, then the band splittin' up, and me losin' my job all in a short time. But I had made it through tougher times and I knew I would make it through again."

Meanwhile, Johnnie's old partner Chuck Berry, was going through his own difficult time. His 1973 taxes were under investigation by the I.R.S. based on his admission that he had received cash under the table for gigs at New York City's Madison Square Garden and the fact that his reports of income received for a European tour did not match the report of the now bankrupt promoter. Before long, government agents were crawling around Berry Park examining every document and record they could find and requesting those they could not. For the third time in his life, Berry began to feel the heat from the law.

"Back home from a concert," writes Berry in his book, "my mail informed me that an indictment was likely to be issued for underpayment on my 1973 and 1974 taxes. Even to me there were some mysterious amounts, which enlarged the cloud of guilt that hovered over me. I intensified the search for the amounts missing and the bits that were insignificant began to fall more into line, but two large quantities still remained lost from the source of where or just when they were earned. My philosophy of 'as long as you know you have it why bother where it is' was proving to be incompatible with reality."

During the time of this investigation, Berry once again contacted Johnnie Johnson—not for an invitation to record or perform together— but to offer him the position of handyman at one of the apartment buildings he owned on Delmar Street in the west end of St. Louis.

"He said I could live there if I wanted and all I had to do was take care of the place for him," Johnnie remembers. "Since I was livin' at the Y.M.C.A. at the time, it was an offer I couldn't refuse. Also, I needed a job. So I moved into one of the rooms and started workin' for Chuck."

Johnnie was in the building a short time when he acquired a roommate, a mutual friend of his and Berry's named John Crosby. An older gentleman, Mr. Crosby was alone and unable to take care of himself, so Johnnie offered to let him stay in his room so he could keep an eye on him. The task was not an easy one. As Johnnie soon discovered, Mr. Crosby had slipped further and further into senility since the death of his wife and was now quite mad.

"Mr. Crosby hadn't been with me too long...just a few weeks I think," Johnnie remembers. "I was in the kitchen makin' supper and he was in the other room watchin' TV. All of a sudden he starts screamin' and carryin' on like he was about to die. Well, I ran in to see what was happenin' and he's standin' up hollerin', and wavin' his cane at the TV. I tried to calm him down but he was half crazy. Then I looked over and saw what he was carryin' on about. He was watchin' the movie *The Jungle Book*, and you know how they have that big snake in the movie? Well every time that snake came on the screen, Mr. Crosby would jump up and try to kill it 'cause he thought it was gonna come out of the screen and get him. Wasn't too long 'fore we had to send him to the home."

A few months later, Berry sold the property and the new buyers politely informed Johnnie that they had no need for his services. At fifty years of age, Johnnie Johnson was homeless once again. He had given twenty years of his life to rock and roll and had nothing to show for it. His former partner lived in a mansion, he now lived on the street. Johnnie took a hard look at himself— the life he had chosen. Then without a word, he gathered his belongings together and went looking for a job.

* * *

Otis Woodard was hoping to hire a dependable truck driver for his church's charity organization. When Johnnie Johnson walked into his office, he knew he had his man. "He was a nice, soft, quiet, and gentle man," recalls Woodard on first meeting Johnnie. "I felt completely at ease with him. I knew he could be trusted."

Woodard ran the Lutheran Outreach program providing food and shelter for poor and homeless families in the city of St. Louis. A former civil rights activist in Alabama and once on the street himself, Woodard campaigned tirelessly to improve the lives of the city's downtrodden. As the Outreach truck driver, Johnnie's job required him to visit the nicer homes in the area and pick up donated clothing and furniture for delivery to the needy. His affable nature helped him greatly in this position. Before long, Johnnie became a favorite of the donors, who spoke often to Woodard about the kind and trustworthy Brother Johnson.

"They loved Johnnie and so did I," Woodard says. "How could you not love someone so kind? He was and is a beautiful person. For all the problems he had with drinking, Johnnie Johnson was always easygoing, never said a cross word to anyone. I'd get calls all the time from people who just went on and on about how much they liked him. I felt bad for Johnnie because I knew he was going through just as much misfortune as the people he was delivering clothes and furniture to. Maybe more. He lived in a rundown little apartment in the poor area of town and he didn't have any money. I know I couldn't afford to pay him much. But he never complained and he never asked for anything for himself. Johnnie Johnson was all about giving."

For three years, Johnnie worked daily with Otis Woodard. Not once in all that time did he ever mention his music. "I had no idea Johnnie Johnson was a musician," Woodard says. "I used to play my ukelele around the office all the time, which is embarrassing to think about now. But he never said anything about who he was that whole time—not a single word."

Still, Johnnie was not completely able to hide his identity. Woodard remembers the time he walked in from visiting the church and was met with a surprise. Piano music coming from the storage room.

"I heard this lovely music coming from inside, piano music, and I didn't know what was going on," he recalls. "Johnnie was supposed to be there sweeping up, so I figured maybe he had the radio on or something. I remember we had a piano sitting in there waiting to be delivered, one of those old-fashioned uprights. I didn't think anything about it. When I walked in the door, Johnnie was sitting behind the piano, right in the middle of all the boxes and things. And he was playing it.

"When he saw me watching, he looked embarrassed and turned away. I was amazed. 'Was that you Johnnie?' I asked. 'No,' he said and closed the piano case. Then he just picked up his broom and went back to sweeping. We never mentioned it again. But naturally, I was curious. It wasn't until about a year later that my questions were answered.

"I was in the library that day, looking for books for the children, when I happened to pass this display they had set up on St. Louis music and musicians. Just a city-pride sort of thing, you know. Well I was about to walk on by when something caught my eye and I looked closer. One of the books was open and there on the open page, before my very eyes, was Johnnie Johnson! In a sailor's hat! 'That's my truck driver!' I screamed it right out loud. People looked, but I didn't care. Under the picture it said something about 'Johnny B. Goode.' Well that was it. I marched right back to the office and confronted him about what I had found. I said 'Okay, Johnnie...who are you?' He kind of looked away for a moment and when he looked back I could tell he was trying to keep from crying. 'I played the piano once upon a time, but I got burned out,' was all he said. The way he said it, the pain in his voice, I fell into tears myself. I said, 'Johnnie, you have to get out of here. What will it take?' 'I don't know,' he said. 'I guess I need to get me a piano.'"

With Woodard's help and encouragement, Johnnie bought himself a portable keyboard and amplifier and began to play gigs around the area. Before long, he was back in the swing of things. But his personal demon—alcohol—continued to drag him down, pushing him into the same rut which had repeatedly impeded his progress. Many a morning found Johnnie Johnson passed out on the sidewalk with his pay in his pocket and his keyboard and amplifier by his side. The locals all knew him, and out of respect no one bothered him or took his keyboard. In fact, many times Johnnie returned home to find his keyboard and amplifier propped neatly against his door where some anonymous friend placed it after its owner had lost consciousness. "There'd be times we'd check to see if he was still breathin'," remembers friend and fellow musician Tommy Bankhead. "We didn't know if he was gonna make it or not." Life looked rather hopeless for the old pianist by all accounts. Then in 1977, just when things seemed at their worst, Johnnie Johnson got a second chance.

* * *

Leading me down the steps to the basement of his spacious St. Louis home, Billy Peek reminds me of a jolly leprechaun—diminutive in size, his bearded face, the mischievous twinkle in his eye—as we enter his fully furnished rec room. And like a leprechaun, he has gold, lots of it, in the form of records lining the walls of the room, the remnants of a long and distinguished career in rock and roll. "Well," he says, "This is where I live most of the time. I guess you could call it my shrine to the music."

Music has been a vital and integral part of Billy Peek's life. Growing up in St. Louis where his parents owned the landmark Peek-a-boo Inn, Peek fell in love with black rhythm and blues at a young age. Many a night found him sneaking off to East St. Louis to watch Albert King, Ike Turner, and Chuck Berry work their magic for the local fans. "I was very fortunate," he says, "to be growing up at the time that all them cats were playing here."

Needless to say, it was no surprise when young Billy showed an aptitude for the guitar. He'd heard so much of the instrument. And it was while practicing the licks he'd heard from King, Turner, and Berry that he made the discovery that would define his career. For some odd reason, perhaps due to his unusually double-jointed fingers, Billy Peek had quite a knack for playing Chuck Berry-style guitar—a knack that in the next few years, caught the attention of the man himself. Before long, Peek was playing shows at Berry Park for hundreds of fans who also found his mimicry of Berry remarkable. After a number of shows with just himself and a backing band, Berry finally invited the youngster to join him for a paying gig. It was on that evening, at Park High School, that Billy Peek met for the first time the other half of the most influential writing/performing team in the history of rock and roll music: Johnnie Johnson.

"I first met Johnnie at a gig I did with Chuck Berry in the late sixties at Park High School," Peek recalls. "In fact, that was the first gig I'd ever played with Chuck. We'd been acquainted and he'd asked me to play at his park in Wentzville when I was just a kid in the early sixties, but this was the first time I'd ever played with him. I guess he was just waiting until he felt I was ready to do a major gig. In '69, I think this was, and that was the first time I met Johnnie Johnson because he had come up to play piano.

"Now of course, anyone who'd ever heard a Chuck Berry record...even though Chuck was my idol and since I'm a guitarist, I leaned more towards him than I would Johnnie...I couldn't deny the fact...that piano was amazing! I mean, Johnnie was a phenomenon. He's just too much. Rock and roll, boogie-woogie piano, you really can't beat him. To me he's even better than the guys who came before him...Fats Waller, Roosevelt Sykes, Fats Domino...Johnnie picked up what they were doing and embellished it—made it better.

"Anyway, this was my first time playing with Chuck and with Johnnie, too. So I'm over on the side near where Johnnie is, you know, 'cause Chuck is up front doing his thing. And I'm playing Chuck's rhythm, you know, and I happen to look over at the piano...and then I look down at my own hands...and then back at the piano...and that's when I notice that Johnnie is playing the exact same thing with his left hand. That boogie rhythm that Chuck plays is exactly what Johnnie plays on his left hand. And some of the fills and things....I mean 'Rock and Roll Music' was in E-flat, 'Nadine' was in B-flat—a guitar player would do it in B, but it's in B-flat—which in music lends itself more to the piano than it does the guitar. That's because on a piano, the natural keys are spread out more...even on the black keys...the octaves are still that much further apart. But when you're playing in a flat, the voicing of your fingers are much closer and you can do that much more with it. You know what I'm saying? Like on a guitar, the difference between open strings and closed chords—in some keys to roll your fingers...make it sound good...you just can't do it.

"So I guess what I'm saying is when you start looking at the keys and that left hand...It just gives you something to think about. It did me."

Peek is standing behind the bar. He offers me a drink. A Jack and Coke, very strong. I take one swig and wince. Peek laughs. "Pretty good, huh?"

"Definitely so."

He continues.

"I hooked up with Johnnie again in 1972 at the Hilton in Vegas with Chuck. I don't know how Chuck would work it, but sometimes Johnnie would be there and sometimes he wouldn't. I don't know if it had anything to do with his drinking or not. He never seemed to have any problems playing his gigs with Chuck. Chuck kinda kept his eye on him though. In a way he kind of looked up to Johnnie...but then again, how can you play down to him? If you're in his ballpark; if you're into blues or rock and roll, you can't play down to him. He was the greatest.

"After that I didn't see him much. I think he and Chuck just stopped playing together. And then I went off with Rod Stewart. That's another story, man. A great story."

Peek laughs and points to his walls. Most of them are Rod Stewart albums: *A Night On The Town, Blondes Have More Fun*, they wrap all the way around the room. Near the bar is a photo of a young, beardless Peek on stage with Stewart. They appear to be sharing a microphone.

"Frankly, the reason I got the job with Rod Stewart was because I could play like Chuck Berry," he shrugs. "In *Rolling Stone* magazine, Rod told the story about how they found me. I guess he and Ron Wood were in a Denver hotel room before a show and Ron had the *Midnight Special* on, which was a rock and roll concert show that used to come on in the seventies. So Ron turns it on and right away Rod was like, 'Oh, that's too loud! I don't want to hear a rock concert right now!' So Ron's about to shut off the TV, when the announcer comes on and says, 'Stay tuned for Chuck Berry.' So then they were like, 'Yeah, Chuck Berry! Let's watch this before we go to the concert!' Well it turns out that on this particular show, for whatever reason, Chuck let me do a lot of the playing and he even let me sing a couple songs. Now I heard about this later, I'm not making this up. Ronny is watching me play and he tells Rod right then, 'This guy can outdo Chuck Berry, man. You oughta hire him for your band.' 'Cause Ron wasn't worried, he was going to the Rolling Stones, why should he care?

"So anyway, nip comes to tuck and about three months later I get this call. They'd been looking for me and found me through the musician's union. I had a gig here in town playing a joint called the Rainbow and that was my living, man. I wasn't making much, but that was it. I couldn't just go running off with Rod Stewart and leave my job. So what they did was fly me to L.A. on Sunday and fly me back on Tuesday so I could keep my Wednesday-thru-Saturday gig. We did this for a month and the first album I made with them was *A Night On The Town*, which had all of these other great guitarists—heavyweights like Steve Cropper, Joe Walsh, Jesse Davis...top guys, you know.

"Anyway, what happened was, even though they were flying me out to L.A., it was still sort of like an audition, you know, a try out. The way they became sure I was right for the job...we were at Cherokee Studios and they decide to pull a fast one on me. Rod and Tom Dowd, who was the producer, they were behind the glass watching me and all these other guitarists—Walsh and Cropper, you know. Well, all of a sudden it was just like a signal had gone off, and everyone gets up and starts to go back towards the control room. I don't know what's going on, so I start to go, too. Then Tom Dowd comes over the speaker: 'Uh no, Billy...you stay there.'

"So here's Joe Walsh, Jesse Davis, Steve Cropper, the drummer, the bass player, Rod Stewart, and Tom Dowd, and they're all in that booth looking at me. I'm starting to sweat a little. Tom gets on the speaker again and says, 'Billy, we're gonna play this track now and I want you to listen to it. We've already recorded it but Rod isn't satisfied with the rhythm. So I want you to listen to the track a couple times and then we'll play it again and you just play what you feel.' So I'm listening to this record and as luck would have it, it was a song my dad used to play all the time, a country song called 'The Wild Side of Life': (sings) 'I didn't know God made Honky Tonk Angels...' Anyway, Rod did a cover of that in rock and roll. So Tom Dowd asks me, 'Are you familiar with this song?' And I said, 'No, I don't believe so!' (laughs) 'Cause I'm thinking if I screw it up I can say I wasn't familiar with it, you know. But I really knew the song forwards and backwards.

"Anyways, I ask them if they want me to blow some lead guitar or what and he says, 'No, just play a rhythm.' 'Chords?' I ask him. 'Don't ask me, Billy—you're the boss. Just play what you feel.' So they put it on and I start doing that Chuck Berry rhythm...and I ain't lying to you—Rod was standing in the booth and he jumps up in the air. Just starts jumping. I'm thinking to myself, 'What's wrong? What did I do?' But he comes running into the studio shouting 'That's it! That's it! That's the sound I want! That's it!' So all he really wanted was that Chuck Berry rhythm, which, like I said, was Johnnie Johnson's left hand.

"Well that leads me on to the next part of the story. I got the gig and it's a year or two later. Rod and I are talking and he asks me about Johnnie. 'Hey man, Johnnie Johnson, is that the guy who plays piano on all the Chuck Berry records?' I said, 'Yeah, that's him.' 'Well is he still alive?' I said, 'Yeah, he's alive and in St. Louis. I know him pretty well.' Rod thinks for a second then he asks, 'Well, how old is he?' Back then Johnnie was in his fifties, so I told him the truth. He says, 'Well...I don't know...' And that's when I said, 'Look man, let me tell you something. Twenty years, fifty years, 100 years old—this is Johnnie Johnson! The one and only! I mean the man can play the piano!' Back in 1956, if you wanted to learn how to play rock and roll piano, you didn't listen to Little Richard, you didn't listen to Jerry Lee Lewis, you listened to Johnnie Johnson, right? He invented the art!

"So Rod says, 'Let's bring him out here and do some recording.' So I got a hold of Johnnie back in St. Louis and, as usual, he says he would do the job, no problem. We flew out to L.A., which was an experience in itself. I didn't realize that Johnnie was scared to death of flying—I figured he had been flying all over with Chuck. But he was from that old school of musicians. In the old days, those guys didn't fly. They rode buses and cars. Johnnie wasn't used to flying first class and all that. I mean, it took me a while to get used to, but when I was doing that touring with Rod, you were in a plane every single day, and when that becomes your lifestyle, you don't think anything about stepping on an airplane. So I wasn't really thinking about what effect it would have on Johnnie. I'll never forget it, man. He was grabbing that seat!"

Johnnie remembers flying to Los Angeles in 1977. "Billy called me and asked me to do the record with Rod Stewart. I said yes right away. I knew I was gonna have to fly and I didn't want to do it, but I couldn't afford to turn down the kind of money they was offerin'. Now I fly all over the place, but then it was something I had to get ready for. I used to start drinkin' the day before so that by the time I had to get on the plane I'd be good and drunk. That way I could just fall asleep and wake up when we was on the ground. I'll never forget the way Rod treated us when we got there—the best of everything. He had a car for you, best hotels, best restaurants—you name it. I was real excited to get in there and start makin' music."

Sadly, it was not to be. Since Johnnie had first recorded with Chuck Berry at Chess, the concept of a recording session, and of rock stars, for that matter, had changed dramatically. Gone was the thrifty, business-minded attitude of producers like Leonard Chess. The executives were no longer in charge. The rock stars ruled the seventies, they were worshiped like gods in many cases. Johnnie was shocked by the change.

"When Chuck and I started out it was all about business," he remembers. "Chuck didn't fool around and neither did Leonard Chess. You had three minutes a song and there was always someone waitin' to get in the studio after you was done. I don't need to tell you that people like Howlin' Wolf and Little Walter weren't gonna wait for you any longer than they had to. Wolf was bad. He would walk in and throw you out—I never knew him to do this but you better believe he would if you was just sittin' 'round shootin' the breeze. When you came in to do a record, you had a certain amount of time to get it done and you worked until you had a track. A lot of times we'd have a 45 done in an hour, recorded and everything. Ready to go."

The work ethic of the fifties was based on the fact that music, especially for black performers, was a shaky business. Even the most popular acts lived with the constant threat of falling into obscurity. Therefore, the predominant mindset of most early blues and rock and rollers in America was to make as many good records as you could—as fast as you could—without ever quitting your day job. Already considered rock and roll royalty by the time they arrived to record at Chess in 1964, the Rolling Stones were taught a hard lesson in the precarious nature of fame by a man they considered their godfather.

In Victor Bockris's biography of Keith Richards, Richards and bassist Bill Wyman recall the astonishment of seeing one of their heroes, the great Muddy Waters, working as a studio aid at Chess.

"Muddy Waters was in Chess Studios in 1964," recalls Richards, "and he was painting the goddamn ceiling—'cause he wasn't selling records at that time. That throws you a curve, 'ere's the king of the blues painting a wall."

Says Wyman, "We were unloading our van and taking the equipment in, amps, guitars, mike stands, et cetera, when this big black guy comes up and says, 'Want some help here?' And we look around and it's Muddy Waters. He starts helping us carry in the guitars and all that. It was unbelievable. The awe we all had for something like that. As kids we would have given our right arms just to say hello to them—and here's the great Muddy Waters helping to carry my guitar into the studio. I mean, it was unreal."

In contrast, Stewart's session was a far cry from the hungry days of early rock and roll. As both Peek and Johnson remember, the time in L.A. was spent partying and lounging around, coming and going, based on the singer's mercurial whims.

"Well, the first day we get to the studio, Rod is sittin' in this chair and he's doin' all these exercises, like Yoga, or something," recalls Johnnie. "Then he yawns and kinda stretches out like a big cat and says, 'I don't feel like recordin' today, you can all go home.' Now what am I supposed to do in L.A.? I just went back to the hotel and watched TV. We had a few days like that. But the good thing was Rod paid you just like you had been in the studio, so I wasn't complainin'."

Billy Peek was not as easily abated. He was both angered and embarrassed by the situation and he felt sickened that Johnnie's time had been wasted.

"It was a shame, you know. A damn shame. Because at that time...years ago...Johnnie had a problem with alcohol. Anyway, we get to the session and everyone's acting goofy. Andy Johnson was the engineer and everyone's fooling around and not doing the session. Half of them were probably high. So, anyway, as it turned out, it was a big waste because Johnnie was out there trying to cut the tracks and someone asks Johnnie if he wants a drink and before you know it, everyone's screwed up and nothing ever came of the tracks.

"Well, I thought that was rotten. Rod thought Johnnie was great..but it's like I told Rod, I mean you can't bring a guy like Johnnie Johnson out...it was obvious we weren't going to do a record. It pissed me off. Actually it probably hurt more than it pissed me off. Johnnie at that time wasn't doing too well. He was living in these subsidized apartments and he wasn't very healthy. He could have really used the publicity and the money from an album. Then everyone starts acting foolish and it all got pissed away. But I don't think Rod meant anything by it, that's just how the business is—some days people just goof off. I mean, we'd cut records with Rod where we'd start out in a studio in L.A., have half an album done, and he'd come in one day and say, 'I don't like this studio, I think we can do better somewhere else.' And we'd all fly to Toronto or someplace and start recording the album all over again. When we did *Blondes Have More Fun*, we spent $750,000 going from one studio to another six times! Of course, by then Rod was doing six million worldwide, so he wasn't losing anything."

But neither was Johnnie Johnson. That's because he had nothing left to lose. By 1978, his drinking was completely out of control. He consumed Crown Royal and Tanqueray by the bottle and at such a rate that many a horse would have fallen dead had it tried to keep up. His coordination deteriorated noticeably. For the first time in nearly fifty years, his playing began to suffer, and he found himself hitting the wrong keys on standard tunes that he'd been playing flawlessly for decades.

"I'd be so drunk on stage sometimes that the keys would look like elephant tusks," says Johnnie. "I don't know how I made it through, especially on the jazz tunes. I might as well have been playin' blind, or in my sleep, 'cause I couldn't remember a damn thing after I got off stage."

In the mornings, he awoke with tremors so intense that he needed a drink "just to stop my hands from shakin'." In turn, most of his days were spent trying to piece together the previous night's events. Where was all his money? Where did this bill come from? Who is this woman? Where is my car? Johnnie admits he should have died many times over in car accidents. "God watches over drunkards and fools," he says. He shakes his head in shame.

"I woke up one mornin' and there was all these little spots of color all over my car—looked like it had been rainin' paint," recalls Johnnie. "I looked at it for a minute then I started seein' the little dents and scratches. That's when I figured out what happened. The night before I'd been swipin' parked cars on my way home. I couldn't even remember comin' home at all, so God knows how I was drivin'. I checked around my street but I didn't see no dents in anybody else's cars, so it must have happened along the way on some side street. That was usual. I was always wreckin' cars. Soon as I got it, I'd smash it up. One time I was sittin' at a long light, drunk as a skunk, and I fell asleep with a whole line of cars behind me. Just passed right out. Next thing I know, I wake up with all these horns honkin' and it startled me so bad, 'cause I didn't know where I was, I slammed on the gas and caused a big ol' wreck. Nobody got hurt, but I had to go to court on that one. Then there was the time I was on a date with this woman, drunk of course, and all I can remember is her screamin', 'Turn around! Turn around, fool! You gonna kill us! Turn around!' What happened was, I was goin' down the highway the wrong way. The whole time I was cussin' at the other drivers 'cause I figured they was the ones goin' the wrong way! People were swervin' to get out of the way and yellin' all kinds of things, but I just kept on. Naturally that was the last time we ever went out. I was a real mess back then. A real mess."

* * *

In February of 1979, Johnnie picked up the phone and heard a familiar voice with an all-too-familiar request; one he hadn't heard in over seven years. Chuck Berry called Johnnie from his mansion on the grounds of Berry Park in Wentzville to ask about doing another record together. But this time it was different. For the first time in the history of their partnership, Johnson and Berry would record outside of Chess Records.

Atlantic Records, who had been courting Berry for some time, had finally gotten him to sign for a new deal with their subsidiary, Atco. Berry planned to record the album at his own home studio built within the park and asked to handpick his own musicians for the album. Needless to say, he called Johnnie Johnson immediately.

"I was surprised to hear from Chuck and even more surprised to hear that he wanted to do another record," recalls Johnnie. "I'd figured he was long done with makin' records and that he was just tourin' on his name. But I was wrong. When he asked me if I was interested I said yes, I'd play anytime anywhere, and so I went up to

Wentzville and we did some more songs together."

Over a two-day session, Berry, Johnson, and Berry's touring bass player Jim Marsala (whom he had recruited from Billy Peek's band), joined a group of session men at Berry Park to record *Rockit*, the first all-new Chuck Berry album in four years. Of the ten songs recorded (one was a poem entitled "Pass Away"), two were released as singles—"Oh What a Thrill" and "California." As an added precaution, Atco sent down an executive producer to supervise the session, a move which seemed to make Berry uncomfortable. "And what was an executive producer anyway?" he asks in his book. "I wrote a song, went somewhere with the band and recorded it, and the record company processed and released it. That was that. All these titles and execs were 'new wave' to me."

Berry claims in his book that the album took only two days to record, but according to Jim Marsala, it took much longer–at least two weeks. The studio brought in other musicians, including their own bass player, and Marsala suggested two local drummers whom he thought could handle the chore. Unlike the Chess recordings which were basically mixed on the spot, *Rockit*, Marsala remembers, was pieced together bit by bit after he, Berry, and the drummer laid down the first track. Many times, he says, Johnson was present and played live. Other times he was dubbed in afterward.

"I just did what they told me to and that was that," Johnnie remembers of the *Rockit* session. " It wasn't like it was at Chess. Chuck knew a lot more about how he wanted to do things on that last album—where he wanted the changes and all that. You know how I don't like to dub in, so if I could play with 'em while they was layin' it down, I felt better about it. To be honest, I don't really remember a whole lot from that session 'cause that was at a time when I was drinkin' pretty heavily. I don't think Chuck liked the way they were doin' things in the studio, though. He got pretty riled up a few times."

Berry needn't have worried too much about the "new wave"

recording fads he claims to have had no knowledge of. *Rockit*, released in October of 1979, would be his last studio album. While some critics lauded the albums technical attributes, Marsala, who had been touring with Berry since 1973, thought it sounded "much too clean" to be a true representation of Chuck Berry and Johnnie Johnson.

"It wasn't mixed right—it was kind of canned," says Marsala. "It might have been technically superior to the old Chess stuff, but it didn't have the same feeling. The great thing about Chuck and Johnnie was that neither one of them read music at all, so everything they did together was spontaneous. That's what they needed to get. They really needed to capture the live sound because that is closer to what Chuck Berry is all about. He's not a studio musician and neither, I think, is Johnnie. They like to be on stage. So no, I'd have to say I didn't like the album very much."

If indeed *Rockit* had its faults, then considering the timing of the recording, there is little wonder why. As in 1961, when he and Johnson rushed in to Chess to lay down some hurried tracks before he left for prison, *Rockit* was cut during a time when Berry faced losing his freedom once again. The evidence of tax evasion gathered by the I.R.S. over a five year period was condemning to say the least and Berry had little hope of escaping sentence. His attorneys negotiated heavily and were able to arrange to have the trial moved to Los Angeles and out of St. Louis where Berry felt unjustly persecuted by the populous.

"I was determined not to go to trial in my dear hometown," he states in his book. "Ironically, I feel there are some certain few, of (no doubt) influencing authority, who love me none too much. Perhaps the same wheels that rolled themselves to get rid of Club Bandstand would once again roll over me."

Berry would be granted his request of a trial in California, but he would not fare well. Ironically, in what could be called an extreme example of American publicity paradox, just one month after performing per special request of Jimmy Carter at the White House in June, after pleading guilty, Berry was sentenced to five months in prison for income tax evasion. He had battled furiously for five years, but the game was up and he left for Lompoc, California, where he would serve his sentence. In the end, Berry felt betrayed.

> It had been eighteen and a half years since I'd stood before a judge and all the thoughts of what I could say to summarize the information for a truly fair judgement took wings, leaving the cosmic question—why was I even being judged? Patriotism, religion, liberty, and crime all pounded at my statement to intervene for acclamation, but none achieved precedence. The simple thought of what my eighty-four year old mother was feeling from my behavior instantly brought visions of her face in sadness. Though a twenty year sentence could not have buckled my knees, the mere vision of her thoughts of my being arrested for anything did. Only some five or six times in the last twenty years have occasions arisen that have brought tears to my eyes. This was one of those times.

Berry emerged from prison in November and headed back on the road, touring all over the world and enjoying his riches, his fame, and most of all—his freedom. But for Johnnie Johnson, the man who helped him achieve those riches and fame by first hiring him, then providing him with the rhythm and music behind many of his hit songs, life kept rolling on one day after another, morning to night; a blurred and undeviating pattern of drinking into unconsciousness. His body began to show the effects of long-term alcohol abuse. His face bloated, his eyes dimmed, his teeth rotted. He suffered from diabetes and gout. His hands shook constantly and his speech began to slur. In a lonely rundown apartment in East St. Louis, amongst a pile of garbage and debris, Johnnie Johnson, co-founder of rock and roll music, the anonymous inspiration to an entire generation, was slowly and surely drinking himself to death.

X

I'M GOIN' FISHIN'

"He lived a lonely life. Staying up in that little apartment, driving around town in a beat-up Oldsmobile with a bunch of fishing poles and tackle in the back and his piano and amplifier on the front seat. Just going from gig to gig with nothing but alcohol to fill the in-between times. It hurt me to see a legend living in that kind of state, man. It hurt a lot."
—Johnson's best friend, Tom Maloney.

They say the Lemp Mansion is full of ghosts. Or at least that's what Johnnie tells me as we walk up to the front door of the grand old manor. And sure enough, the brochure I pick up inside states proudly under the authentic nineteenth-century ink rendering of the house (complete with horse-drawn carriages and top-hat dandies) "Rated by *Life* magazine as one of the Ten Most Haunted Houses in America." Johnnie notices me reading. "You read that, you might run on out of here," he laughs. "Them Lemps was cursed."

The lamentable saga of the Lemps began in 1838, when John Adam Lemp emmigrated from Germany and opened up a small grocery store in downtown St. Louis. Two years later, after noticing the popularity of the homemade lager beer he sold from his grocery, Lemp decided to pursue the beer business full time—a novel venture, as America had no large-scale lager beer producers.

Thus, with a wide open market and little or no competition, success came quickly for John Adam Lemp. By 1864, he was a millionaire with a production plant large enough to cover five city blocks. That same year, his son William, the heir to the business, purchased the newly built mansion as a residence. The house became an heirloom. And for the next eighty-five years, Lemp Mansion was tenanted by John Adam Lemp's immediate descendants—a custom that ended in 1949, when great-grandson Charles became the fifth member of the occupant family to put a bullet in his brain. Suicide seemed a tragic tradition for the Lemps. And it was the family's predilection for untimely and self-inflicted demise that propagated the mansion's spectral infamy. Excepting William Lemp III, who died of a massive heart attack in 1943, six members of the family perished violently within the walls of the mansion. As we wait to be seated, Johnnie points to the room on our immediate left. "That's where one of them shot hisself in the head," he says. I scan the room warily, half expecting to see William Lemp, Jr. (who committed suicide after Prohibition forced him to sell the brewery in 1922) floating eerily about the room like a grey-faced Jacob Marley. But summer sunlight pours through the shuttered windows, casting a warm glow throughout the room. Any ominous night creeper would certainly be driven out by the brilliance, I decide. The only motion is the tiny dust particles dancing in the sunbeams. I see no ghosts.

"So this is one of the most haunted places in America," I say aloud.

"Mmmhmmm," Johnnie says. "They got all kind of ghosts up in here."

Naturally, I have only one question.

"Well?"

"Well, what?" he answers with a smile knowing full well what I want to know, but making me ask just the same.

"Did you ever see anything? Any ghosts?"

"No. No ghosts. I even played on Halloween here one year when they said the ghosts might come out, but they never did. Not a single one. Which I guess is good 'cause I probably would've fell on the floor dead if I seen a ghost." He laughs.

"Nothing strange happened at all?" I ask.

He thinks for a moment. "Well, I guess there was one thing. I've been playin' piano for years, and I've probably played on more pianos than anybody. The worst beat-up uprights with the ivory worn out, top-of-the-line baby grands, electric keyboards, all of them. I've played standin' up, sittin' down on benches and chairs all different heights. I've also played all night long and into the mornin' without ever gettin' up from the piano. But I'll tell you what, there was times I came home from playin' at Lemp's, my arms would be so sore I could hardly lift 'em. That never happened any other place."

"Maybe the ghosts don't like blues?" I joke.

"Maybe they don't," he laughs. "Most of the time I wasn't playin' blues, though. I'd play standards like "Stardust"—old jazz stuff. See, it was my job to play music, so I kept it nice—dinner music. They made this place a restaurant after the Pointers bought it."

When the last of the Lemps, Edwin, died of natural causes at age ninety in 1970, the mansion was purchased by the Pointer family and remodeled into a restaurant/bed and breakfast. The Pointers were a large brood, nine children altogether, and in the tradition of the Lemps, who as the brochure says, "seemed to have an almost morbid attachment for the family mansion," the restaurant became a family-run business. The patriarch of the family, the late Dick Pointer Sr., was a diehard rhythm and blues fan, and it was his idea to build a piano bar in order to fill the house with his favorite music.

"Dad loved rhythm and blues. I grew up stomping my feet to Ray Charles and Little Milton," recalls Paul Pointer, who joins us as we finish our lunch. He is a friendly man, full of exuberance, and seems genuinely glad to see Johnnie. They have been friends for years, ever since Dick Pointer, Paul's father, hired Johnnie to replace their regular pianist, a man called Silvercloud.

As usual with Johnnie, the Lemp Mansion job came about solely by chance. At the time of his hiring, he had a regular night gig playing with balladeer Lee Barnes at another piano bar in town. During intermission, he remembers, a patron approached him about the need for a one-night replacement at the mansion. One night was all it took. "My father knew who he was the moment he walked through the door," recalls Pointer. "There was no question of him having the job—we just couldn't believe we had him."

The Pointers saw the acquisition of Johnnie as a chance to further both their careers. They could draw business into the restaurant and drum up notoriety for the forgotten pianist at the same time. Says Pointer, "We knew we had a gem back in the early eighties when Johnnie started playing here. We just didn't know how to capitalize on it. Our partner, Bert Couch, was always saying we needed to make a big deal of Johnnie. So we had a few parties, cocktail parties—you know, very classy events—and we'd bring Johnnie up in a limousine and treat him like a star. See, we were trying to get him exposure. Johnnie had fallen into an almost reclusive state—an unappreciated reclusive state—to the point where we had Johnnie 'B.Goode' Johnson playing for thirty people in our piano bar and he should have been out in front of thirty thousand in some stadium somewhere. At least that's how we looked at it. We wanted so bad for people to recognize him for what he had done. Unfortunately, we just didn't have the means or know how to do it on a large scale."

For Johnnie, the pomp and celebration were not necessary. He enjoyed the restaurant, found the Pointers amiable employers, and most importantly, cherished the chance to play music for the patrons who lauded him with constant praise. In turn, these regular guests were treated to a mélange of musical styles. Manning the keys in the dining area, Johnnie stuck to the mellow standards in order to blend in with the dinner atmosphere. But after midnight, when the dinner guests would move into the piano bar for a cocktail or three, Johnnie would treat them to the rollicking boogie-woogie barrelhouse blues stylings that made him a legend.

"Dad was the kind of guy who loved to have fun," says Pointer. "He'd purposely make mistakes behind the bar so he'd have to drink them himself. You know what I mean? Well, Johnnie was a drinker, too and he'd get Johnnie back there around midnight—two in the morning—and they'd start drinking, and before we know it he's got Johnnie playing that driving rock and roll and the blues and people are just loving it. It was great. My dad and my brother, who is also named Dick, would be back there having the best time. They realized what was happening. We all did. Those thirty people back there in that piano bar were being treated to something they should have had to buy tickets for. This was Johnnie 'B. Goode' Johnson. This was a living legend playing in our piano bar. We were glad to have him. I mean who wouldn't be? But honestly, there was something not right about that. Johnnie deserved more."

* * *

In the fall of 1982, Johnnie 'B. Goode' Johnson was fifty-eight years old and living in a one-bedroom apartment at the James Senior Citizen Apartments. During the evenings he played at Lemp Mansion. During the day he drove a bus for Area Citywide Transportation Company, picking up senior citizens and taking them on outings to the store, to the doctor's office, wherever they needed to go that required vehicular transport. He had found the job through Title 5, a program developed to provide work for underprivileged citizens fifty-five or over. Laura Harris, who was working for A.C.T., at the time Johnnie was hired, remembers him well.

"He was excellent, a good driver, and everyone loved him," says Harris. "He really got along well with the passengers. He didn't talk a whole lot, so nobody knew much about who he was or what he had accomplished. He just came to work, exchanged hellos with everyone and did his job."

But as he found out working with Otis Woodard, Johnnie Johnson could not keep his identity hidden for long—especially in a city so keen to its musical history. It wasn't long before his fellow drivers and dispatchers began to put two and two together.

"As I said," Harris continues, "Johnnie never mentioned anything about his music. But after a while, some people around the office who were into the local music scene realized who he was and started asking him about playing with Chuck Berry. He answered questions whenever we asked and we found out a lot about those times and how he had helped Chuck Berry with writing his music but never received credit for it. Most people would have been upset, bitter even. But not Johnnie Johnson. He never showed any ego, or bad feelings, never bad-mouthed Chuck Berry. He was just Johnnie. In fact, one of our dispatchers, Gary, asked Johnnie to play at his wedding in 1985 and Johnnie did it for him. That's the kind of guy he was."

One person who knew Johnnie Johnson's history very well was blues artist Larry Davis. While he would never become a household name as a performer, Davis's "Texas Flood," recorded for the Duke label in the mid-1960s would become a huge hit for Stevie Ray Vaughan, who used the song as the title track for his 1983 debut album. Davis had met Johnson during his tenure with the Albert King Band and at that time, Johnnie remembers, Davis sang often but did not play guitar on stage.

"I knew Larry pretty well, he was a real easygoing fella. Later on he would become a pretty good guitar player, but when I met him he was just a singer. If he played guitar, I didn't know nothin' 'bout it."

Davis's career took a serious turn for the worse in 1972, when he injured his hand in a motorcycle accident. Then came a crushing blow. While still recovering from the wreck, Davis suffered a stroke. The back-to-back misfortunes put him into an early retirement, and for nine years he was completely absent from the music scene.

Then in 1981, Davis fan and Rooster Blues Records owner Jim O'Neal offered the bluesman a chance to return to the recording studio. When it came time to build a studio band, Davis had only two requests: former Ike Turner band member Billy Gales on drums, and his old friend Johnnie Johnson on piano.

Johnnie remembers, "I was working for the bus company when Larry called me up out of the blue and asked me to play on his comeback record. I was real honored. It was nice to see Larry back out playin' and singin' again after his illness. Naturally, I hadn't been in the studio since the last album with Chuck—and things had changed a little bit as far as equipment and all that. But Larry and I went way back, almost twenty years, so we had a real good time makin' the record."

The album, *Funny Stuff* released in 1982, would propel Davis into national prominence and a dramatic comeback seemed imminent. That year Davis would walk away with four W.C. Handy awards including the Artist of the Year and Best Contemporary Blues Album. But time was not on his side. As his style and instrumental technique were not flashy enough for the early eighties pop crowd, Larry Davis quickly faded away once more, never to be in the spotlight again. He and Johnnie would continue to be close friends and Johnson would visit Davis whenever he was in Los Angeles. Following Davis's 1991 album *Sooner or Later*, the two joined up for a short, but well-received, national tour. The album would be his last. Three years later, Larry Davis was stricken with terminal cancer and began the slow painful descent toward death. Johnnie recalls that, despite the hopelessness of his situation, Davis held steadfast to the end.

"Larry was such a strong man inside. Even when he got sick. He didn't try to pretend that everything was fine, like some folks do. He was real honest. I was gettin' ready to go out to California back when he first got sick and Larry called me up and says, 'Hey, Johnnie, when you get out here I'd really like you to come see me 'cause I got cancer and I don't know how long I have.'

"Well, I visited him and we had a great time talkin' 'bout music and old times, playin' with Albert and all. I tried to act like nothin' was wrong 'cause I didn't want him to feel bad. But like I said, Larry didn't try to hide from what was happenin'. He talked about what was goin' on with his treatments or whatever, and I told him that I hoped he would get through it. But he said no, he was pretty sure that this was it. Sure enough, it wasn't too long after I came back to St. Louis that he passed."

Larry Davis died in 1994, four years after Stevie Ray Vaughan, the man who'd made his song "Texas Flood" famous, perished in a helicopter crash in East Troy, Wisconsin. While Vaughan's death dominated the airwaves, Davis's barely made a ripple. As Johnnie sees it, Larry Davis was just another talented performer who had never been given his proper due.

"I've played in a lot of cities and in a lot of clubs," Johnnie says. "And I've seen a lot of great players who nobody will ever hear 'cause they never made no records. Back in the early days when nobody even thought 'bout makin' records, you had guys in St. Louis who could've played with anybody...Muddy Waters, Howlin' Wolf, Roosevelt Sykes, anybody...guys who could have filled up clubs out the door, but they never got the chance. There was guys I sat in with on the road, back when I was travelin' with Chuck who would have just drove you crazy. I can't remember their names or anything, but I remember them. How they sounded. I know they was good—some of the best I ever played with. Larry Davis was just one of them—one of them singers who never became famous for whatever reason. I guess he just didn't have no luck."

* * *

It's early when Tom Maloney knocks on the door of my hotel room. I have showered, shaved, and dressed, but when I pass the bathroom mirror, my eyes are still swollen from sleep and I cannot resist the impulse to yawn. Maloney smiles when he sees me.

"You look tired, man," he observes with a laugh. His perpetually cheery brown eyes crinkling in mirth.

"I suppose so," I answer.

"Well only one thing to do," he says.

"What's that?"

"Breakfast."

"I'm with you," I say immediately. And the two of us head down to the car.

Tom Maloney met Johnnie Johnson in 1983, a year after he'd made the album with Larry Davis, and for the last fifteen years he has been Johnson's lead guitarist and best friend. It is a job, he says, that has required him to be both disciplinarian and protector, confidant and conspirator—especially during the drinking years. Listening to him talk about the old pianist, I note that Maloney has all the qualities that make a good friend—loyal, deferential even, but with enough self-respect not to take any crap. It is the latter quality, he says, that has kept them close for so many years.

"The Johnnie Johnson you know today is different from the Johnnie Johnson I met fifteen years ago," he says frankly. "We have to get that straight first because some of the things I tell you will be hard to believe knowing how the man is today. He was drinking a lot when I knew him and that can change a person as you probably well know. Seeing him now, I sometimes have to rub my eyes and say, 'Johnnie, is that you?'

"I first met Johnnie in Houston, Texas back around '83. I was playing with the Soulard Blues Band at a place called Rockefeller's, opening up for Roomfull of Blues, and Johnnie was playing a gig with Albert King and Paul Butterfield over in another club. The drummer that was with us, Kirk Grice, knew some guys that were in Albert's band, so after our gig we went over to check them out. I'll never forget it. They were playing in this place that looked like an old schoolhouse. It was a big white-framed place. Looked like it was built back in the twenties. So I walk in, and Johnnie Johnson is playing piano, and there's Albert King yelling at him on stage which is something Albert was famous for doing. I felt really embarrassed for him, mainly because I hadn't heard him make any mistakes, and my ear would have picked it up if he had. Albert was the type of guy, if he got insecure about something he did himself, he'd yell at someone in the band. You know what I mean? I guess it must have been Johnnie's turn.

"So after the gig I walked up to Johnnie and introduced myself, told him that I was from St. Louis and that his music had been really important to my life. That was true. The first song I ever learned on guitar was 'Wee Wee Hours,' which I think is one of the greatest blues records of all time. Just the first four measures alone, the way it was recorded— that sound—it made you think of a smoky old club at three in the morning with a bare light bulb glaring down. And here's the guy who did it. I told Johnnie, 'I'm from St. Louis. Screw Albert King, you're great!' He just smiled and thanked me then he walked out and that was that."

The two would meet again very soon. Upon returning to St. Louis, Maloney met up with Albert King's young bass player, Gus Thornton, at a club in St. Louis. Thornton, who was off the road and gigging around town, informed Maloney that he was playing with Johnnie Johnson at Lemp Mansion the following weekend and invited Maloney out to see the show. Maloney went, anticipating a night of raw, rock-rollin' rhythm and blues. What he got, however, was a lesson in musical diversity.

"The wife and I went down to Lemp's," recalls Maloney, "and there's Johnnie, and you know, I'm expecting to hear blues and boogie. Well, Johnnie's up there playing 'Stardust' and 'Moonlight in Vermont.' So I'm going, 'Man, this is weird.' I didn't know about that side of him. It wasn't at all what I expected."

A year later, Thornton quit the Albert King Band and joined Maloney, who was playing with Thurston Lawrence and the Sounds of the City. Lawrence, whose real name was Larry Thurston, was a soul singer and the Sounds of the City played roots R&B and blues. One evening, Johnnie happened to catch their act and afterwards approached the band about the possibility of joining the group.

"So Johnnie Johnson comes up to us and says, 'If you fellas are looking for a piano player, I'd like to play with you,' Maloney remembers. "So we huddle together in the corner—have a little band meeting—'yep, yep, yep...Johnnie you're in!' (laughs) I mean, would you turn down Johnnie Johnson if he asked to be in your band? You'd have to be insane."

The band continued on for the next few months, but with Johnson now in the group, Thornton and Maloney became restless. Dissatisfied by the direction the band was taking, the two men began to talk about leaving and starting their own band. "Gus and I were like, 'we ain't making any money and we're going nowhere. Now we have Johnnie Johnson, we need to get out there.' So what happens? Larry all of a sudden quits *us* and joins up with Matt 'Guitar' Murphy's band. Next thing we know, he ends up singing with the Blues Brothers! Gus and I had to look at each other afterwards and say, 'Well, we missed the boat on that one!' But how were we supposed to know? If anything, that gives you an idea of how deep the talent is here in St. Louis. We couldn't believe it."

Now more or less a trio with interchanging drummers, Thornton, Maloney, and Johnson began playing together almost every evening. As a connoisseur of blues, rock, and R&B, Maloney in turn felt obligated to help Johnnie acquire recognition for his role as one of the founding fathers of rock and roll. He decided that the group would only play the best gigs for the best prices, and at the same time he made every effort to trumpet Johnnie's name around town and in the music community. The intentions were all good. But as

Maloney soon learned, you can't help someone who won't help themselves, and Johnnie's alcoholism made it nearly impossible for him to make responsible decisions concerning his or anyone else's best interest.

"Johnnie was always borrowing money against jobs and getting into these rent-to-own type deals with terrible interest," remembers Maloney. "He couldn't hold on to his money very well. He was just a loveable drunk who screwed things up. He'd borrow half the money for a job then get drunk and not show up when he was supposed to. It happened all the time. I remember one night I was just sitting down to watch a television program...it had to be about nine...and the phone rings. So I pick it up and there's this club owner on the other end screaming at me. 'Where is he?' I was just like, 'Whoa! Calm down, man! What's the problem?' And he's screaming, 'Where is he? Where is Johnnie Johnson? He's supposed to play here tonight with his band! I gave him half the money I was gonna pay you guys!'

"So I'm saying to myself, 'Oh shit'...you know, 'cause Johnnie never told us about a gig. He'd probably told the guy we would play over a drink, you know, and didn't even remember what he had said. So I had to tell the guy, you know, and he's cussing at me and everything. Meanwhile Johnnie was probably out drinking and having a good time somewhere and not even thinking about what he was supposed to be doing.

"Those were the kinds of things that got him in trouble. But at the same time he was such a loveable guy...I mean you had to love him. He was like a little kid. But that was the alcohol in him. Johnnie was a fun drunk. The first forty-five minutes you couldn't be around a better guy than Johnnie Johnson. He'd spend all his money trying to make everyone happy–a real party animal. But after that first forty-five minutes, he was out like a light, falling asleep, just completely out of it. Like I said though, he wasn't belligerent at all, he was a loveable drunk, but he was still a drunk and that caused him a lot of problems in his life and in my life from being so close to him."

Maloney continued to try to help Johnson, and sometimes it paid off. But the successful ventures were few and far between. More often than not, Maloney found himself caught in the middle trying to explain Johnnie's behavior to irate club owners and disappointed friends and fans consistently let down by the pianist's irresponsible antics. Finally, he had to give up. "I realized after a while that the only person who could change Johnnie was Johnnie," Maloney says over coffee. "It had to come from within him. And I'll be honest with you, at his age, I couldn't see it happening. I really couldn't."

In 1985, Maloney put himself on the line for the last time. Through perseverance and a good reputation in the musical community, he was able to secure an enviable gig at the St. Louis History Museum's black history exhibit *From Ragtime to Rock*, playing for the most influential members of the local artistic community. It was an opportunity not just for Johnnie to achieve recognition as a local legend, but for the whole band to move to the next level. When Johnson failed to show up, Maloney and Thornton were livid.

"For over a month, I was on the phone almost every day with this woman from the museum, planning things out and getting everything ready for the big night," Maloney says. "They went ahead and had stuff printed out way in advance—this was no joke, man. It was the real deal.

"Then a week before the big day, Johnnie gets a call from Chuck to go to Las Vegas and he leaves at the last minute—just goes! And the thing was, he didn't do it out of meanness, he was just irresponsible. But I was angry and embarrassed and I was just..that was like the last straw, you know. I wasn't going out on a limb anymore. I mean I still cared about the guy and I wanted to play with him, but you just couldn't count on Johnnie, and so I just backed off. If he didn't want it himself, I wasn't going to push it on him."

At the start of 1986, Johnnie Johnson seemed headed for disaster and there wasn't anything his friends Tom Maloney or Gus

Thornton could do about it. Equally disturbing to Maloney was Johnson's strange relationship with Chuck Berry, and the fact that Berry was content to let his partner suffer in poverty while he raked in millions of dollars from royalties. Maloney could not understand why Johnnie didn't stand up for himself. "Everybody in St. Louis knows the truth about Chuck and Johnnie. It was like Johnnie had given up, you know. They still played together...it was just very weird, very strange."

Maloney goes on to tell of one instance in particular when Johnson invited his former partner on stage to jam.

"Chuck Berry was at a gig we were playing once and Johnnie, who was half-drunk at the time, leans over from the piano and tells me to bring Chuck up. 'Tom,' he says 'Call Chuck up here.' I said, 'What?' He says, 'Call Chuck up and have him play.' So I get on the microphone, 'cause I was doing all the announcing at that time, Johnnie hadn't started singing yet, and I said something like, 'Ladies and gentlemen we are honored and privileged to have a legend in the house tonight...' I mean I went all out—gave him this great introduction and ended it up with, 'And now please welcome to the stage, Chuck Berry!' And everybody goes crazy. But Chuck doesn't move. He just sits there like a cow on a railroad track staring at me with this look that said, 'Try and move me, punk.' So I'm thinking to myself, 'Oh, shit. Now what.' You know? Meanwhile, Johnnie's getting impatient and starts motioning at me, 'C'mon Tom, get Chuck up here. Let's play.' But Chuck ain't moving an inch.

"I tried three more times and I was just mortified you know, completely embarrassed, and so I finally said something like, 'We're real honored to have Mr. Berry here with us. Now the next song we're gonna do is....' And that was how it went. But I tell you man, I felt really bad about that, 'cause you know, Johnnie would get up and play with Chuck anytime. But that was the way Chuck came off, man.

"I remember another time, we did this thing at Blueberry Hill after

Chuck's book came out–some kind of a book signing party, you know. So he's sitting there signing books and we break into 'Johnny B. Goode,' which I have to say was really weird, you know, playing my guitar and singing 'Johnny B. Goode' in front of Chuck Berry himself. But anyway, half-way through the song I ask everyone to sing along and I know this sounds corny, but if you could have felt the love in that room, the complete adoration that the people in Blueberry Hill felt for Chuck Berry, it would have blown your mind. And the sad thing is he is such a standoffish bitter-type person who doesn't seem to want anything to do with that kind of emotion. I remember thinking that it just seemed kind of wasted, you know. All that love wasted on someone who doesn't give a shit."

Berry may not have "given a shit" per se. But in the eyes of the world, and the rock community specifically, he was an icon, the "Father of Rock & Roll," the man who started it all. On October 18, 1986, he would turn sixty years old and as a tribute to his accomplishments, a collection of rock and blues stars would gather to pay tribute to Chuck Berry in the form of an all-star concert. Maloney felt that Johnson should be honored during the show as well. But at the same time he realized the implausibility of the suggestion. To the average fan, Johnnie Johnson was just a sideman, and that was if they knew him at all.

"Can you name the Crickets?" Maloney asks. "Everyone knows Buddy Holly but can you name the members of his band, the Crickets? How about Elvis Presley's guitar player? Nobody knew Johnnie Johnson. They may have seen his name on a box set or something, misspelled 'Johnny Johnson,' but other than that he was just Chuck Berry's piano player. That's all.

"See rock and roll, in fact popular music in general, is a frontman's game. The frontman gets all the credit while the guys who really did it all end up like Johnnie or even worse. They could have done the concert without Johnnie and nobody except those of us who know what's really going on from a musical standpoint, would ever miss him. They'd be seeing stars and hearing the music, and although it wouldn't be close to as good, they could have pulled it off.

"But Keith Richards, who knew what was going on, got Johnnie on the bill and that changed everything. I really don't think Chuck would have called him otherwise—I really don't. He'd been hacking it alone for so long. Then again maybe he would have because he wanted to sound good and Johnnie always brought out the best in him. Whatever the case, Johnnie's life was forever changed that night."

Fate had cast its spell again for Johnnie Johnson in the familiar form of Chuck Berry. But whether or not he would capitalize on his chance remained entirely up to him; based on his past, it was not likely. What little ambition Johnnie Johnson had inside had been destroyed by alcohol, and he accepted the tragedy of his life with solemn resignation. As Tom Maloney recalls: "He just didn't seem to care anymore."

"Tom and Gus were always there for me," Johnnie says. "Not only are they great musicians—Tom can play anything and so can Gus—they are great friends. They tried to help me when I was down, but at that time there wasn't nothin' they could do. I needed a miracle."

Johnnie Johnson was sixty-two years old—and for all intents and purposes the concert was his last chance to pull himself out of the void. In other words, his life depended on it.

XI

HAIL! HAIL! ROCK 'N' ROLL

Even an adult would shy away from the naked truth when approached by a lie neatly dressed.
—Chuck Berry, *Chuck Berry: TheAutobiography*

On January 16, 1986, Charles Edward Anderson Berry was inducted as the first member of the Rock and Roll Hall of Fame during the Hall's inaugural ceremonies at New York's Waldorf Astoria Hotel. Keith Richards, serving as Berry's presenter, acknowledged his influence with an admission: "I lifted every lick he ever played."

The induction was the crowning achievement in the career of the man the world called the "Father of Rock & Roll." A year earlier he had received a Lifetime Achievement Award at the twenty-seventh annual Grammy Awards, where he was hailed as "one of the most influential and creative innovators in the history of American popular music, a composer and performer whose talents inspired the elevation of rock and roll to one of music's major art forms." The year would also see him inducted into the Songwriters' Hall of Fame at the seventeenth annual awards dinner held at the Hotel Plaza Grand Ballroom in New York.

In a decade of synthesized rock and empty-headed lyrics, the world seemed eager to embrace Berry as an example of a time long gone when rock was new and the performers actually played their own instruments. But as usual, the public knew only half of the story.

Shortly after Berry's induction, Delilah films executive Stephanie Bennett approached the legend after a concert at the Lone Star Café with an offer to produce a video celebrating his music. According to Berry, he had been receiving similar but "unattractive" offers for some four years before Bennett's proposal aroused his interest. Most likely it was Bennett's assurance that Berry himself would be co-producer of the film that provided the incentive for agreement.

The two camps began discussions, and before long, the proposed "video" had grown into a feature-film documentary, with an all-star concert as the centerpiece. Said Berry of the preliminary negotiations, "Before we got far, we merged the video musical production agreement into a full-length motion-picture contract for over double the fee and proceeded to arrange for the concert that was to be the apex of the movie. It was decided that we would shoot the concert in my hometown at the Fabulous Fox Theater, just a city block from where I had tried to break the black-and-white ice in 1959 by running my 'mixed' nightclub, Club Bandstand."

Acclaimed director, Taylor Hackford, signed on to direct and Keith Richards of the Rolling Stones was hired as the musical director and put in charge of assembling a top-notch band. For Richards, assembling a solid veteran backing band for Berry was something he had always wanted to do based on his own disappointment with the legends' consistently poor live performances.

"I wanted to serve Chuck up with a good band," said Richards. "I've never heard him play in tune, you know. I've been disappointed in Chuck Berry's live gigs for years and years and years whenever I've seen him. 'Cause he didn't give a damn, you know, and if he made a mistake he'd blame it on the band, you know, and he'd just wing it and get through. And he has such a powerful personality that he's managed to get away with it. I mean, I know everybody says I was mad to take the gig on. But if anyone was going to do it, I wanted it to be me— not so much a musical director as an S&M director—Social and Musical Director is the polite way to say it. Social director of the S&M band!"

S&M, in the classical sense, was an apt description of Berry and Richards's relationship leading up to the documentary. In Richards's biography, Victor Bockris sums up the highlights, or rather 'lowlights' of the two guitar innovators' run-ins with each other. As Richards said, "Every time him and me got in contact, whether it's intentional or not, I end up wounded."

> The most memorable thing Keith could remember Chuck Berry ever saying to him was 'Fuck off,' and their history had been, to say the least, uneven. Berry's attitude toward the Stones' appropriation of his work had always been ambivalent, even though they had increased his sales all over the world and earned him countless royalties. Sometimes he would act grateful, name 'Satisfaction' among his favorite songs, and say he loved them; at other times he would refuse to acknowledge their impact. In 1972 when Keith had guested on a couple numbers during a Berry concert in Hollywood, Chuck had him thrown off the stage for playing too loudly (claiming he had not recognized him.) In 1981 Chuck had punched Keith in the eye backstage at the Ritz in New York (using a similar excuse.) In 1983 he had dropped a lit match down Keith's shirt at Los Angeles International Airport.

"Chuck doesn't give a shit," Richards said matter-of-factly. "Chuck only thinks about himself. I like Chuck, but I feel sorry for him. He's a very lonely man. Also, after living that secluded one-man show for so many years, he probably wasn't prepared himself for how he was gonna act. He kind of played it by ear. I talked my way into it. Now get out of it."

Richards had a plan going into the project. He was going to honor Chuck Berry by making him sound as good as possible with an appropriately chosen all-star band—and he was also going to set things right based on his own conscience and a friend's dying words.

* * *

On December 12, 1985, the Rolling Stones were busy completing their album *Dirty Work*, when pianist Ian Stewart, suffering from respiratory problems, left to see a specialist in a West London medical clinic. There, while waiting to see the doctor, Stewart suffered a massive heart attack and died. He was forty-seven years old. The Stones were devastated by the loss. Said Richards, "What a hole he's left, such an obvious gap. He would always be there to comment on everything, and sometimes you would think he was crazy. But then you'd go and realize he was right all along. I mean, no one had a bad word to say about him. I'd had other friends pass on, and you go, 'Gee, it's a shame,' but Stu was different. I could think of a hundred other fuckers who should have gone instead of him! He wasn't even on my list!"

On February 23, the same day Berry began negotiations for his movie, a tribute concert was performed by Stewart's friends at the 100 Club in London, playing sets of R&B covers that Stewart had loved most. No one moved until Keith Richards himself walked out and started the jam, playing with a "power that was devastating," according to Eric Clapton, a friend of Stewart's who attended the show. "He's an unbelievable player," raved Clapton of Richards, "one of the best ever."

As a final nod to Stewart's influence, the Stones added thirty seconds of Stewart's boogie-woogie piano to the end of *Dirty Work*.

A haunting blues eerily similar to another pianist living thousands of miles away in St. Louis, Johnnie Johnson. It was no coincidence.

Richards was determined to carry on Stewart's legacy and with the Berry gig, he had a chance to honor one of Stewart's final wishes: To find and restore Stewart's own hero, a man neither had met, to his rightful place in the rock pantheon.

"Just before Stu died, without any real reason, he'd said, 'Keith, never forget Johnnie Johnson is still alive and playing,' recalls Richards. "There's an eerie feeling to that boogie Johnnie's got. His hands are like a big bunch of overripe bananas. Sometimes I was so fascinated I actually stopped playing and just watched those great big bananas bouncing around doing this incredible brain surgery. Other times I had an eerie feeling that it was Stu playing, but at the same time I felt he was up there, beaming down at me from his cloud: 'Well done, son.'"

Richards's first task upon meeting at Berry's mansion at Wentzville the following summer was to inquire about Johnnie Johnson. Berry informed him that there would be no problem getting Johnson to join up as he played regularly around St. Louis. Then quickly he turned to one of the video screens in his living room. According to Richards, Berry had two large video screens in the room, one that showed whatever he wished, the other that ran constant footage of naked white girls throwing pies at each other and falling over. Berry supposedly pointed to a tape of the January Rock and Roll Hall of Fame jam session and asked about the drummer, Steve Jordan. "This guy sounds pretty good," said Berry and Richards immediately called his good friend Jordan and informed him that he had gotten the job.

From there it was a matter of building a supporting cast. For his part, Richards recruited two Rolling Stone tour musicians, keyboardist Chuck Leavell, whom he slotted on organ, and Bobby Keyes on saxophone. Then Steve Jordan suggested NRBQ bassist Joey Spampinato be added for his uncanny ability to produce the sounds of a Willie Dixon upright from an electric bass. This selection irked Berry's regular bassist Jim Marsala to no end, as he had hoped to play. Finally, blues great Robert Cray tossed his hat in the ring, which filled out the guitar section considerably.

The assemblage of talent was impressive to say the least and the group of backing musicians were as solid as could be. But for Richards, the band was made when he got a hold of Johnnie Johnson who was playing in town with Tom Maloney and Gus Thornton.

"I got the key member in Johnson," said Richards. "I knew nobody else was going to get Johnnie Johnson together with Chuck Berry...I mean, you're talking Johnnie Johnson—Chuck Berry, you're talking Lennon—McCartney, you're talking Jagger—Richards, you're talking those great rock and roll teams, Leiber—Stoller, except that Johnnie never got any credit or any money."

Johnson's lack of credit touched a personal chord in Richards. For years he had served a similar function within the Rolling Stones as Johnson had with Berry, creating music behind the lyrics of frontman Mick Jagger and receiving much less notoriety than his flamboyant bandmate. But unlike Johnson, the salty Richards was well aware of what could happen if he did not lay claim to his share. Former Stones manager Andrew Loog Oldham recalled Richards's vital role in the band and the often subtle reminders he gave to Jagger and the others of his importance.

Said Oldham, "Mick may have thought he was running the show, but Keith was always in charge of the music. When I was remastering one of the tracks for CD I came across something I had not noticed at the time. There was a song where the key was easy for Keith's voice, but had caused Mick trouble and he could hardly sing it. I said to Keith: 'Did you pick the key for that song?' And he just looked at me and smiled."

* * *

It was spring of 1986, when Johnnie Johnson received the call from Berry's secretary, Francine Gillium, inviting him out to Wentzville for rehearsals. He was more than happy to participate.

"I was sitting watching television in my apartment," remembers Johnnie, "when the phone rings and it's Chuck's secretary, Fran. She says that Chuck is makin' a movie 'bout his career and that they were gonna have a concert and would I like to be part of it. I said, sure, 'cause I had been a big part of that career and it seemed like it would be fun. 'Sides that, I never turn down a chance to play."

The concert was set for October 16, 1986 at the Fox Theater in St. Louis, and the band went into rehearsals for a week at the honoree's own Berry Park studio–the same studio in which he and Johnnie had recorded *Rockit* in 1979. Between rehearsals, formal interviews were done with key band members, including Johnnie, who conducted one interview from his Area Citywide Transportation bus, bedecked in his fishing hat and corduroy jacket. Puffed up and weary, his eyes sallow, his teeth rotten, Johnnie explained how he allowed Chuck to take over the band because he thought it would bring them greater success. Speaking in his usual matter-of-fact tone, Johnnie seemed completely oblivious to the sad irony in what he was saying.

"Johnnie is not a bitter person," reminds Tom Maloney. "I don't think he even comprehends the emotion. He is extremely easygoing and humble—but humble to a fault in a lot of cases. I mean, he looked like a homeless man in that interview and he almost was or at least not far from it. It breaks your heart to see it now, but that is how I remember Johnnie. That's the Johnnie I knew. That's how he looked."

Unfortunately for Johnnie, he had no idea himself how he looked until after the movie came out. Having never seen himself on film and rarely if ever photographed, the reality of his appearance came as quite a shock.

"I'll never forget, after he saw himself in the movie, he got real self-conscious over his teeth," Maloney continues. "He used his V.A. deal and started going to the dentist. I was the one who drove him, two or three times a week for a month to the V.A. Hospital. He'd come out afterwards with his mouth all packed and bloody. I remember I'd come to pick him up and he'd get in the car and say, 'Take a right, Tom.' The dentist was to the left but Johnnie didn't want to go there. He'd take me out and show me where Chuck Berry's house used to be or where he first met his second wife, and I'm loving it 'cause it's history for me, but Johnnie was just trying to get up the courage to go 'cause he knew he was gonna have to get his teeth pulled. When he finally got his new teeth, he was like a kid. He said, 'I'm gonna go right out and get me a steak dinner.' He felt a lot better about himself after that."

The week of rehearsals at Berry's mansion was full of surprises. Berry's daughter Ingrid came out to sing a few numbers and as various stars signed on for guest appearances, the studio became the site of a regular rock and roll reunion. Etta James dropped by, as did Linda Ronstadt, Julian Lennon (son of Beatle John Lennon), and the great blues/rock master Eric Clapton.

Clapton had been part of a similar televised tribute to rockabilly legend Carl Perkins the previous year and was excited by the chance to pay homage to one of his biggest influences. Yet, despite the playful banter seen in the movie where Berry, Clapton, and Richards light-heartedly harmonize on "It Don't Take But A Few Minutes," Clapton was bitterly disappointed by Berry's attitude to the point that it marred his appreciation of the music.

Clapton recalls his first meeting with the guitar legend. "Chuck appeared and he sat down next to me on the couch and he said, 'Hi, I'm Chuck Berry, you're Eric Clapton. Nice to meet you.' Then he said, 'Hang on a second!' and shouted out, 'Bring the camera in!' So the next thing I knew, this person holding a camera and microphone walked into the situation. Then Chuck turned to me and said, 'Okay, so when was it you really got into my music?'

"I still love his music but meeting him in some senses took the edge off it for me. I found out bit by bit that he was so concerned with money and himself, and he is such an ambitious man, that in a way it kind of spoiled the feeling for the music."

Nevertheless, Clapton's scorching take on "Wee Wee Hours," with Johnson pounding away his familiar solo, is one of the highlights of the movie. And his insightful analysis of Berry's double-string guitar style (a style born of necessity due to the size of Berry's hands) served to reaffirm his status as one of rock's foremost stylistic historians.

For Johnnie, the whole affair was strange and rather intimidating. While Berry had made several movie appearances during their tenure together, Johnnie never once appeared on any of the films. He was not used to having cameras around and lights in his face. Nor was he used to the concept of dramatic embellishment, as demonstrated by his incomprehension of staged conflict.

"They had this one argument," says Johnnie of the movie, "Chuck and Keith, it's on the film, somethin' 'bout Chuck's amplifier and him not wantin' Keith to touch it. Well, that was all made up beforehand. The director, Taylor, he came in and set the whole thing up so it would look good for the movie. I couldn't understand why they felt the need to do all that. I guess I understand it now. Back then though...most of us just wanted to play the music and get on out of there."

While the "fight scene" may have been embellished somewhat, the tension between Richards and Berry was all too real. During a rehearsal of "Carol," Berry continuously stopped the song to correct Richards's playing of the signature opening slur, chastising the younger man with condescending statements such as, "You want to get it right? Let's get it right." As Richards's jaw muscles throb with suppressed rage, the camera focuses on Johnson who sits stoically behind the piano with a look of resigned disgust.

"That's Chuck's way of showing who's boss," Johnnie says. "He knows in his heart that he ain't near the guitar player that Keith is, but he always has to be in control. Doesn't matter who it is either. It could be the president of the United States and Chuck would try to tell him what to do."

Unlike Johnnie Johnson, Richards was not so accepting of Berry's idiosyncracies. After years of working with Mick Jagger, who could be just as temperamental as Berry, if not more so, when things did not go his way, Richards was an old hand at ego wars and refused to be intimidated by Berry's behavior. "I've worked with two of the toughest bitches of all time," bragged Richards to writer Stanley Booth, referring to Jagger and the late Brian Jones. "That's why I could handle Chuck. You know who I've been working with the last twenty years? You're chicken feed!"

But despite his bravado, Richards was far from immune to Berry's baiting. In later interviews he revealed just how close to the edge he had come.

"I played the straight man out of necessity," he said frankly. "My job was to get both Chuck and the band together, even though I was dying to turn around and let him have it. Never mind that the cameras were present, but I knew if I allowed myself to rise to the bait, it would have fallen to pieces. When I went into the rehearsals I'd take a .38 bullet and actually chew on it."

As for the "Carol" situation, Richards recalls being pushed to the point of violence by Berry's demeaning behavior. "Most of the band, the guys behind me, are going, 'Keith in this situation is going to pull out the blade and just slit the motherfucker's throat,' recalled Richards. "I'm biting bullets because I'm trying to show the band that, in order to get this gig together, I am going to take some shit that I wouldn't take from anybody. I'm not gonna let Chuck get to me that much. Whereas anybody else, it would have been toilet time. Nobody can touch me in that way. In the film you can see me chewin'. I'm on the edge. At any moment I could have turned and downed the motherfucker. But Chuck doesn't understand 'cause he doesn't deal with people. He's the only guy who's hit me and I haven't done anything about it. Far worse things have happened to me in my life than Chuck Berry trying to fuck with me."

Richards decided that the best way to handle Berry's outbursts was by being straightforward and not backing down. "If it takes shouting, fine," he said. "It ain't different from working with anybody else. If he's wrong, he's wrong, and you let the guy know it. 'Cause if you go around crawling, licking ass, 'Oh, Chuck, please, please,' you'd never get anything done, but under those frantic circumstances, you get to know someone a little better."

As for Berry, he supposedly attributed his difficulty and mood swings to what he labeled as "controlled schizophrenia." "At times I become very hot and cold, moody and very schizophrenic," Berry explained. "It's really controlled schizophrenia, and I'm controlling it."

By the time the show came around, the band was a well-rehearsed, cohesive unit, with each member comfortable in his position. Yet even up until showtime, Berry was still being difficult and refusing to yield to Richards's wishes. In a 1988 interview, Richards revealed that Berry's insistence on using his ancient tour amplifier forced him to have to secretly hook the canankerous legend up to a superior unit down in the basement area under the stage. "Worked like a charm," Richards laughed, "and unless Chuck himself gets wind of this conversation, he'll never be the wiser."

Regardless of the difficulties leading up to the event, the music produced during the night of October 18 was splendid, a testament to the power of rock and roll. Thousands crammed into the Fox Theater for the celebration of the music of Chuck Berry and—although few knew it at the time—Johnnie Johnson as well. Tom Maloney remembers vividly the night he and Gus Thornton drove to the Fox and watched with pride as their legendary bandmate took his first steps towards redemption.

"It was an unbelievable night," says Maloney. " I'll remember it for the rest of my life. It was magical. See, at the time of the concert with Chuck, Johnnie was still playing with me and Gus and the Sounds of the City, and we had a gig in Springfield, Missouri, that weekend. This was on a Wednesday.

"Well Johnnie had been sequestered up at Berry Park for the last week and we couldn't get a hold of him—they wouldn't take our calls. So naturally, Gus and I had to get a hold of him to tell him about the gig. Well, it was pretty late and we figured the show was over already. So we decided to drive on down and try to catch Johnnie, maybe see a few rock stars. 'Cause it was a big event in St. Louis, and we didn't know who was gonna be there, you know. The Beatles could have been there for all we knew.

"So we're driving along and all of a sudden we hear on the radio that they've finished filming the first show and the second show is about to begin. We were like, 'Great! We can still catch him!' So we drive down to the Fox and we go up to the ticket office, the show has been sold out for a long time, and we tell the guy the truth— that we're in a band with Johnnie Johnson and we have a gig this weekend that he needs to know about, you know, fully expecting the guy to be like, 'Sure fellas, c'mon in, Johnnie's in the back.'

"Well he looks up at us with this smile on his face and says, 'I gotta tell you guys that's the best one I've heard all night.' So we're screwed, right? Well, for some reason I say, 'Hey Gus, let's take the alley back around.' So we go down the alley and I notice this door that isn't completely shut. I say, 'Gus, c'mon, man' and we go inside—right into the foyer. And as soon as we get inside we can hear the music and it sounded great, man. Joey Spampinato is playing bass and it sounds just like an old upright fiddle. Steve Jordan had one of those old drum kits like Ebby Hardy used to play. I mean, they were going for tradition, you know. Sounding great! And there's Johnnie, right in the thick of it. The stage...everything looked great. Well, we're standing there checking out the music when this buddy of mine walks up and says, 'Hey, Tom, save our seats will ya'? We're going to the beer line.' So I said, 'Where are they?' And he looks back and says, 'Second row, second aisle.' So I look at Gus and we both say it at the same time, 'Second row!'

"So we go down there and as luck would have it, the seats are right in front of Johnnie's piano, which means it was stage right. At the Fox they have an orchestra pit right in front of the stage and that's where they put all the camera equipment and the lights and all. And the lights are all on. And there's Johnnie, our buddy, our piano player up on stage. It was too much.

"Anyway, it wasn't long after we got there and they just stop the music all together. The announcer gets on and says something like, 'Ladies and gentlemen, we have to stop and reload the cameras, we'll have the music back on shortly.' So everybody is all impatient. The guys in the band are just standing there, Johnnie, Keith Richards, Robert Cray—Chuck, of course, would leave as soon as they turned the cameras off—Steve Jordan, Bobby Keyes, Chuck Leavell from the Stones, all just standing there with nothing to do but wait. So I get this idea: Johnnie can't see me 'cause of the lights, but I yell out to him, 'Soft Winds!' which was a song we used to play—and Johnnie doesn't look out at me but he hears and starts playing it–'Soft Winds,' you know...by himself...just him and the piano.

"Well the band hears this and they join right in. Next thing you know, this great jam starts and from then on there was a bunch of them all through the night—mostly instigated by Johnnie. And it was great. Eric Clapton is running out on stage and jamming, you know. The audience is just loving it, man. Screaming for Johnnie, you know.

"And the best thing about it was the timing. See, we were playing all the time, Johnnie, Gus, and me. We weren't making any money but we were playing every night and sometimes twice on Saturdays and Sundays. Four hours every night. We worked our butts off. So Johnnie's chops were really good, you know what I'm saying? In other words, he wasn't some rusty old drunk piano player—he was a guy who was already great to begin with, playing five, six nights a week, every week, and loving it. And Johnnie could do it. I mean here's this guy at the end of his life up in this lonely little apartment and it gave him something to do to be out playing with us, you know. He was doing what he loved. Music was everything to Johnnie.

"And I'll tell you it was really weird for me because a year before when we'd hired him into the band, I remember driving home and thinking that guys like Eric Clapton and Keith Richards would give their right arms to be in my shoes, playing every night with Johnnie Johnson. And here just a year later, Johnnie's up on stage with both of those guys. And I'm here to tell you, he impressed the hell out of both of them. It just all fell into place. There he is, working his ass of every night and his chops are up, and then he's put in front of the right people who would go, 'Holy shit! Did you hear that?' And recognize it for the genius it is. I mean, Keith Richards loves Johnnie and rightly so because Keith Richards' guitar style was built on Chuck Berry, and Eric Clapton, being the connoisseur of blues that he is, can immediately hear what Johnnie is saying. And to hear him doing it with such power. I mean you turn Johnnie loose on a slow blues in G, he'll be raisin' the roof. There's not many people who can touch Johnnie on a slow blues in G. He's got that one thing he does in G, and when he does it there's no one in earshot that isn't impressed by it—that isn't moved by it. I don't care if we're playing in an all-black club in East St. Louis or playing for a bunch of white college intellectuals at a bookstore—he always does it. Johnnie knows how to touch that inner thing in people. When he did it in front of Richards and Clapton—Robert Cray already knew about Johnnie from when he was playing with Albert Collins and Johnnie was coming out with Albert King; but when he did it in front of those two–Richards and Clapton—it really freaked them out.

"So anyways, Gus had to go home to pick up his wife, and I'm walking out by myself on the side where I see Chuck Berry's RV parked when who should walk out but Johnnie. I said, 'Hey Johnnie! You sounded great!' He turns around and he's got his drink in one hand and a cigar in the other. 'Tom, baby! Come on in, you're going to the party!' So I was like, wow! You know what I mean. The Rolling Stones, Etta James, Eric Clapton, I couldn't believe it. And Johnnie's introducing me to everybody, 'This is Tom, he's my guitarist, he's great!'

"Finally he brings me into this back room and there's Keith Richards, Keith's manager Jane Rose, and this buddy of mine who owns a club we used to play at all the time. I don't know how he got in there. And Keith's sitting there just like in the movie and he's looking at Johnnie saying, 'Johnnie you were the mortar between the bricks tonight. You held this whole thing together. We just love you, mate. Anytime you want to come on tour we'd be glad to have you.' And Jane Rose is saying, 'Keith's right, Johnnie. Anytime you want to come out.' So Johnnie's hearing this and the whole time he's kicking me like, 'Listen to this shit, Tom. I've heard this a million times.' Only he had no idea that this was the real deal. He had no idea how big they were.

"And even when he did know how big they were—years later when the Stones came to town on the Steel Wheels tour and Johnnie got up and played with them, Johnnie just....I don't know. See, at the time, Johnnie was piss poor, in debt up to his eyeballs–didn't even have a car–and he and I are backstage with them–Jagger, Richards, Wood, Watts, Wyman...Jane Rose–and they're telling Johnnie how much they love him and Richards tells Johnnie, 'Anything I can do for you. Anything you want, Johnnie.' I mean Richards could have laid down the cash to buy Johnnie a brand new Rolls Royce–and I truly believe he would have. But Johnnie didn't ask for anything. He knew what he could get, but he didn't say a word. Through it all, Johnnie still had his pride. You have to admire him for that.

"So getting back to the party...I mean, the whole thing was great. I was expecting this wild party with drugs everywhere and naked women hanging from the rafters, but I didn't see any of that. Everyone was just real laid back—it was real classy sort of like a family reunion—no ego trips, nobody trying to outdo anyone else. It was beautiful, and like I said, I'll never ever forget it. That was the start of Johnnie Johnson's comeback, and I was really proud of him that night. I think everyone was."

* * *

The final product–made up of the concert and interviews—was edited into a ninety-minute documentary called *Hail! Hail! Rock 'n' Roll*. Richards took time out from his solo projects to edit both the film soundtrack and the subsequent album at the Electric Lady Studio in New York while Berry helped with the "dubbing and looping for the final editing of the film." Unfortunately, as they were not filmed, the impromptu jams will be forever lost to those of us who were unable to attend the concert. Berry makes a small reference to the success of the second show in his autobiography.

"The second show that was added after the first sold out," writes Berry, "lasted over two hours and was said by many to be the most enjoyed although I was nearly pooped when it began."

Hail! Hail! Rock 'n' Roll premiered on September 15, 1987, at the New York Film Festival at Lincoln Center, where Richards and Berry shared a private box. Johnnie Johnson did not attend. In an interview, Richards recalled the awkwardness he felt sitting next to Berry during the films more controversial scenes.

"I suddenly realized we were coming to the point in the movie where I suggested that maybe Chuck didn't write the music, that Johnnie Johnson actually provided the melodies, which I'm still firmly convinced of," Richards said. "So I'm sitting there in the balcony and I realize that I want a parachute. I wanted to get the hell out of there. But he thought it was all great. Loved the fight (in which Berry refused to play and Keith shouted at him), saw it for what it was. Since then, he's been a sweetheart. Asked me to work with him again. And now that we broke the ice, I say why throw it away? Asshole that he can be, I still love him. I'm still fascinated by what he does. I wouldn't have missed it for the world."

The film was released to the public the following month along with the album, and based on its success and his past musical contributions, Berry was presented his own star on the Walk of Fame on Hollywood Boulevard. For its part, *Hail! Hail! Rock 'n' Roll* will go down in history as a rare glimpse into the life of an intensely private man, a glimpse that will likely never be repeated.

Observes Richards, "He decided to write a book and make a movie, right? And he opened the door and thought he could just let a few people in and goddamn it—the whole world came in. He thought he could control them. The outside world flooded in. That's maybe what's so intriguing about him. The more you find out about him—the less you know about him."

Berry has his own ideas about public opinion. "I figure it like this," he said in an interview with Tom Wheeler. "What does it matter what they think of me as a person? I've already had some idea of what they think of me as a product, as a music inspiration, so what they think of me as a person has nothing to do with my music. The person who would condemn someone for their personality, and infiltrate that condemnation into their product—well it doesn't really matter."

Chuck Berry was on top of the world once again. But now, for the first time, Johnnie Johnson was beginning his own long overdue climb up from the depths of obscurity. People began to recognize him on the street, he looked better than ever, Keith Richards asked him to play on his solo album and, most importantly, he conquered his lifelong fear of flying ("I just woke up one morning and I wasn't scared no more.") and was now able to tour Europe and Asia and even Australia. Consequently, he found himself in the unfamiliar role of celebrity, which he faced with his usual self-effacing good humor and innocent wonder.

"For the first time in my life people began to take an interest in me," he recalls fondly. "Just about everyplace I played, there'd be someone askin' me 'bout the movie. I started signin' autographs. It was just very nice and I appreciated it very much that people took the time to come up and talk with me."

After nearly forty years as a professional musician, Johnnie Johnson stood on the brink of stardom for the first time. Before he could take the next step, however, he had to face down the demon that had plagued him since he was seventeen years old—alcohol.

Luckily for Johnnie, angels do walk the earth to help combat those demons. And he was about to meet his soul mate—a two-fisted, no-nonsense woman with a heart of gold. Her name was Frances.

XII

FRANCES

"Next to his talent and God-given ability, the best thing that ever happened to Johnnie Johnson was Frances Johnson."
—Don Abrams

Like the eye of a hurricane, Frances Johnson is stalwart amongst the swirling mass of children, grandchildren, dogs, pet birds, and visitors that fill her small St. Louis home to the point of overflow. She is the supreme mother; the undisputed queen. And she rules her kingdom with an iron fist.

"Ten-thirty every night. That's when Frances finishes watching her news and goes to bed, and if you don't live here, I want you out," she declares as she surveys her brood. There is a smile on her face but she is not joking. At 10:30, her house is empty.

"My kids all tell me, 'We could not stand you growing up,' she says. "But every single one of them—I have four kids Dale, Zheda,

Jerri, and Chastity—every one of them has thanked me for raising them the way I did. They are a loving set of children, ain't a dope addict or alcoholic among them, and when one of them has a problem they all get together to help out. That's what being a family is all about."

* * *

She had a life before him, she is quick to remind, before she was his wife. Frances Miller was her name; "Pudgy" to the folks she grew up with in the projects of St. Louis. She had spirit even then, an indomitable presence of being that seemed to lift her above her situation. She did not walk with the weight of oppression on her back, although it was there. Instead, she carried her head high-secure in the love of the Lord. And she was not afraid to speak her mind, even when her views elicited anger and the occasional threats of bodily harm. The bullies learned quickly that Frances was not one to be messed with. She always fought back. And she did not back down.

Frances finished high school, married early, and like her father before her, bought into a tavern. The tavern was called Pudgy's, and she tended bar herself–pouring drinks, chatting the regulars, and when necessary, enforcing the law. It was well understood that when Frances said you were cut off, you were cut off. No one challenged her. In all her years tending bar, only one man dared lay his hand on her. And while it was lust, not anger, that led him to touch her thigh, his intentions were irrelevant to the principle of the situation. And it was the principle that mattered to Frances. She did not hesitate; she grabbed him by the shirt, pulled him in real close, whispered something in his ear. The man never bothered her again. Frances knew how to handle a drunk.

In fact, Frances knew how to handle just about everything, or so she thought. Then her only son Dale, the oldest of her brood, graduated high school and joined the Navy. He was the first to go and she was proud of him. But the grief wore at her soul. She had been a protective mother—a lioness wielding a Louisville Slugger like the sword Excalibur—keeping her family close. You had to watch your kids in St. Louis, she always said. Watch them every second, because danger lurked around every corner and if you could hold on to them–through the drugs, and the guns, and the gangs–then you knew you had done your job. Then you could relax.

But it was never that simple. You got so used to holding on that when the time came to let go it just tore your guts out.

So she went a little crazy after Dale left. She admits this now. The day he left for basic training she packed her husband's clothes and dropped them on the front porch. He hadn't done anything wrong per se; he was a good man. She just decided she didn't want to be married anymore, and that was all there was to it. He was hurt at first, but never held a grudge. They remain friends to this day.

Frances carried on. She continued raising her kids while sharing a home with her mother and stepfather. She'd long since sold the tavern and was now working as a secretary for the University Drug Company in downtown St. Louis. That was good enough for her. She didn't need a man to support her or her children. In fact, she had lost interest in men. Sure, sometimes she dated. But men were all the same; all wanted the same things; and she was neither ready nor willing to give that part of herself. It just wasn't worth it. Not at her age.

* * *

"I seen her by the water fountain and I just had to talk to her," says Johnnie, smiling in spite of himself at the memory of seeing Frances Miller for the first time. Something about Frances pulled him to her immediately. She was different than the women he met at the clubs. Stronger. The way she carried herself left him at once intrigued and intimidated. She was a mystery. And he was in love.

He would never have seen her at all had he not taken the side job

He would never have seen her at all had he not taken the side job delivering senior citizens' taxes to a CPA named Ceola Sinclair. Sinclair's business was in the same building as University Drug and it was while leaving her office he first saw Frances.

The next few weeks were spent watching from a distance, studying her every move, trying to find the courage to actually speak to her. And while he thought he was being covert in his attentions, Frances was aware of him from the start.

"I could see him," she says. "He'd wait out by the water fountain for me to come out. Real pathetic, you know, but cute. He was always finding excuses to come in the office. On Valentine's Day he brought me a heart-shaped eraser. I could tell he liked me, but I wasn't interested at the time."

Frances's reluctance wasn't the only problem. The relationship between Johnnie and his "employer," Ceola Sinclair, extended beyond the boundaries of the working environment, and Sinclair was none too happy when her man began flirting with Frances.

"Johnnie and Ceola had a thing together," Frances declares. "I'm sure of it. But to this day Johnnie has never admitted it to me. As far as Johnnie is concerned, if he didn't marry the woman, it didn't happen. But I know he stayed with her and when a woman gives you looks and stops talking to you, that tells you something right there."

Tom Maloney confirms Frances' suspicions.

"Oh yeah, Johnnie and Ceola were together. In fact, a mutual friend of ours, Jimmy Miller–he was also friends with Ceola, and I remember he was pretty upset when Johnnie started dating Frances. I guess Frances was younger and cuter, you know? But it broke Ceola's heart. In fact Ceola, died suddenly not too long after Johnnie and Frances became serious. Johnnie was in Europe with Chuck at the time and couldn't get back for the funeral. So I sent a huge expensive flower arrangement to the funeral home in Johnnie's behalf because he couldn't be there. He loved me for that. Ceola was good for Johnnie. She really cared about him, I know helped him buy a keyboard and amplifier. I know Johnnie thought the world of Ceola and I think he felt a little guilty when she died."

Despite his relationship with Sinclair, Johnnie grew steadily more persistent trying to woo Frances. "He was always bringing me gifts, flowers, the whole deal," she recalls. "He really wanted to take me out." Finally, after months of refusals, Frances relented to Johnnie's urgings and agreed to see a movie with him.

"He kept saying, 'I want to take you to a movie and talk. I got something to tell you,'" Frances remembers. "That was what he always said. So finally I said that I would go and we went out. Well, we get to the movie and Johnnie just sits there—doesn't say a word the whole time! I don't know if he was nervous or shy or what. But I thought that was strange."

Nevertheless, Frances enjoyed his warm, self-effacing personality and the two continued dating. Completely enamored, Johnnie began showering gifts upon his new flame. "He'd pick me up after work and he'd have a pot of something in the trunk that he had cooked up," she recalls. "Then we'd have dinner together. It was really very sweet. Johnnie was like that. If he heard I liked something he would just load me up with it.

"Like cotton candy for example. I didn't know that you could buy cotton candy all year round. I thought you could only buy it at the fair, and I looked forward every year for the fair to come so I could get some cotton candy. Well, we have a store here called Venture that sells it all year round. I didn't know about this.

"So anyway, Johnnie found out how much I liked cotton candy and he started piling me with it. At first I would hide it from the kids, but then it got so much that I would let them share with me. Finally even they started getting sick of it. So after I don't know how many weeks of two cotton candy cones a day, I had to tell him to stop. He was gonna make us all sick."

Johnnie was a self-conscious and clumsily overzealous suitor when it came to Frances. And while these traits could be considered charming, at times his absentmindedness led to embarrassing charming, at times his absentmindedness led to embarrassing situations for both of them.

"I love fifties music," Frances says. "That's my thing. I'll put it on and dance all around the house. Back when Johnnie and I were first starting out, before we were serious, Johnnie decided that he was gonna make me a tape of my favorite fifties music off the radio. So he gets out his little tape recorder and makes the tape for me, right? Well, I put it on and I'm listening, really getting into it, you know, dancing all round the house while I'm cleaning. Then I start hearing these voices on the tape. So I walked over and pushed rewind, turned up the volume and listened to it again.

"Well come to find out that Johnnie had left the tape running while he was going about his business and you can hear him there in the background while the music's on trying to comp some other woman! He swore up and down that it wasn't him. But c'mon! I knew it was him. Ain't no man in the world with a voice like Johnnie's. I still have that tape somewhere and I still laugh about it to this day."

The two shared quite a bit of laughter during their early years together. But the one thing Frances never laughed about was Johnnie's drinking. As the daughter of a tavern owner and having run her own tavern herself, she'd spent a good deal of her life watching grown men throw away their lives for the bottle. She refused to allow any man of hers to make the same mistake. "I knew a drunk better than a drunk knew a drunk," she says. "I wasn't about to get mixed up with one.

"See, I don't know if it was a man thing or what, but Johnnie figured he was gonna change me. I remember the first date we had he came to pick me up at my house and he brought a bottle of Harvey's Bristol Creme, which he dropped on the sidewalk on the way in. I said, 'Johnnie don't worry about it, I'm not a drinker.' 'Oh no,' he says, 'I'll go get another one.'

"So off he goes to get another bottle, and I'll tell you, that bottle is probably still behind the bar at the house. I'm not a drinker and I never will be. Johnnie figured he was gonna get me out partying and drinking with him. Well, he was wrong. That ain't me. And if that's what he was expecting...well, he had another thing coming."

And that thing was religion. A God-fearing woman, Frances attended the St. Paul's Lutheran church every Sunday and before long she began inviting Johnnie to the services. Johnnie feigned interest at first, but the idea fell flat. Not because of any lack of respect for the church or religion, but rather the opposite. Johnnie felt he didn't belong in church because of his lifestyle. He had never been particularly religious, even as a child. But he did have a certain esteem for the church. Consequently, he would not play hymns like "When the Saints Go Marching In" or "Amazing Grace" at gigs. "I lost quite a few jobs cause I wouldn't play religious music," says Johnnie. "But as far as I'm concerned, club music don't belong in a church and church music don't belong in a club."

To fend off Frances's insistence, Johnnie continually fed her excuses as to why he could not join her in the pews. At first he refused on the basis that he could not play a late-night gig on Saturday and then get up early on Sunday. Frances's response to this assertion was to stay out with him all night on Saturday and then still get up herself and go to church. Johnnie tried to stay with her a few times, but was miserable. Finally he told Frances he couldn't stay awake and that he would rather sleep on Sundays. "My answer to that was real simple," recalls Frances. "If he didn't make it to church then I'd be gone all Sunday and he wouldn't be able to get a hold of me. He learned real quick that if he was gonna keep up with me on Sunday, he was gonna have to get his lazy butt out of bed and go to church."

That was in 1984. By 1986, Johnnie and Frances were a serious item, and Johnnie was becoming a frequent guest at the Miller home, although, much to his chagrin, he was never permitted to spend the night. "The kids started getting irritated because when Johnnie would come to visit I'd make them stay up in the living room until he left," Frances laughs. "It became like a game, you

I always went to bed at 10:30 and he'd have to go home. So I'd tell them before Johnnie even got there not to leave 'til he was gone. They'd say, 'Momma, why do we have to stay in here?' I'd say, 'Don't you leave me alone with that man.' 'Cause I knew he was wanting to do the 'kissey-kissey thing' and I wasn't wanting to do no 'kissey-kissey.'"

In September of the same year, Johnnie invited Frances's youngest daughter, Chastity, to accompany him out to Wentzville during the rehearsals for *Hail! Hail! Rock 'n' Roll*. It was his first effort at bonding with the children. For Frances, it was her first clue as to who Johnnie really was.

"He never talked. I mean, I knew he played with Chuck Berry, but that was all he ever really told me," admits Frances. "Then they invited him up to Wentzville–up in that mansion of Chuck's. I started to wonder a little then about the man's history. And as far as Johnnie taking Chas–that was real sweet. Chas was real excited. She got to meet Keith and all them and she was taking piano lessons at the time, so she and Johnnie played together on the piano. It was special for her. I remember when Johnnie first came around, the kids laughed at him 'cause he brought a bottle of whiskey to the house. They'd never seen anyone do that—and to drop it and have it break everywhere. They thought he was real funny–a fool, you know. Then once they got to know him, it was all over. They fell in love. My kids all love Johnnie to death and he loves them like his own. And the same thing with the grandchildren, they all love each other, so it's a good thing, you know."

Later, on the night of the concert taping, Frances gave her two tickets away to her sister and Chastity. She never regretted her decision. "I'd already been to the rehearsal the night before," she recalls, "and I knew Chas really wanted to go back and see all the guys from the band. So she went and I stayed home."

The concert came and went, and Frances, while still curious, let her questions about Johnnie's relationship with Chuck Berry fade away. It wasn't until over a year later when she and Johnnie attended the film's St. Louis premier, that Frances finally learned once and for all, the truth about the quiet man's role in rock and roll history.

"I remember going to that movie with Johnnie and hearing what Keith said, about how Johnnie gave Chuck all the music to them songs. Well, as you can probably guess, I was shocked. But I wasn't shocked that Johnnie had let it happen. Johnnie was all the time letting people take advantage of him. So I asked Johnnie about it and he said, 'Yeah, it's true.' I said, 'Why Johnnie? Why you gonna let that man do that to you?' He said—and I'll never forget this, 'If you're supposed to have it, then it will come to you.' That's what he thought. He was fine just setting back and letting things happen to him. Johnnie never worried about what he didn't have. He just lived his life one day at a time. For so many years, all that man cared about was playing his piano and drinking. He never put any money away—he was barely surviving in that little place of his. He had nothing. But he didn't seem to want anything more. That's how Johnnie was.

"And I wanted to save him. I had to. He looked like a big ol' drunk bear up on the screen. Here he was getting filmed for a movie....and he was drunk. He was drunk during the show, I'm sure of it. Get the movie and watch him. That's when I really started to realize how bad his problem was. Something had to be done."

* * *

"I consider booze to be far more harmful than any other available drug, Keith Richards once said. "Far more damaging to the body, to the mind, to the person's attitude. The way some people change on it is amazing, and then, goddamn it, every morning when you wake up you've got a cold turkey whether you like it or not. You know, just because it's called the 'hangover.' It seems to me the most uneconomical and inconvenient high you could possibly have, 'cause every morning you've got to pay for it. I mean, even a junkie doesn't have to do that unless he decides to stop or runs out of stuff, but even if you've got bottles of booze in the morning you've still got a hangover. And it just seems so vague putting yourself through those constant incredible changes. That's what I think really does you with booze."

Richards would certainly qualify as an expert. By 1988, he had been in the rock and roll business for twenty-five years and in that time had ingested more drugs in both variety and content than perhaps any other living musician. His constitution was legendary. And like Johnnie Johnson, he too was known to down two fifths of whiskey every performance, without breaking a sweat nor losing his skill. Richards understood the addiction. He also knew that Johnnie Johnson, twenty years his senior, was killing himself and needed help to break out of his situation.

"Keith was the first person that called me after *Hail! Hail! Rock'n'Roll*," remembers Johnnie. "He said he wanted to work on a project with me and flew me up to New York so I could play on his record *Talk Is Cheap*. The song they used was called 'I Could Have Stood You Up,' and it sounded a lot like what Chuck and I did back in the fifties, so I didn't have no problem playin'. It was fun. Me and Keith get along real well–Steve Jordan, too. Them fellas was great to work with."

Johnnie Johnson's comeback had begun. His impressive performance during *Hail! Hail! Rock 'n' Roll* had started the wheels in motion and the call from Richards would be the first of many to come from other artists who seemed to be discovering the pianist for the first time. Says Johnnie, "That really was the beginnin' of it all. The movie, and then Keith callin' me up to play on his record. After that I started gettin' calls from people like Jimmy Rogers and John Lee Hooker to play on their records. People really started to take an interest in me for the first time."

Based on his dramatic re-emergence into the music world, it was inevitable that he be asked to do a solo album. Oliver Sain, a St. Louis musician who had managed Little Milton and discovered both Fontella Bass and Bobby McClure, approached Johnnie in mid-1988 about producing a solo album for him. The shy pianist was taken aback by the offer. He'd been propositioned before by the Chess brothers, but had been too intimidated to make the attempt. Now with good friend Sain in his corner, he found the courage to try. "I guess the time was right," he says, "and I figured that I probably wouldn't get the chance again if I turned it down this time. So I told Oliver I would do it."

The album, *Bluehand Johnnie*, would be financed by Sam Valenti of Evidence Music, who planned to release it on his label. He, along with Sain, would produce the album, and they brought in a group of top-notch studio musicians to back Johnnie up, including Herb Sadler, guitarist for the Ike and Tina Turner Revue during the sixties, and Johnson's future bandmates, guitarist Steve Waldman and drummer Keith Robertson. A local group called the Bel Aires stopped by to lend their chops to the mix, and former Chess artist Barbara Carr and local Stacey Johnson provided the vocals.

Things were changing on Johnnie's personal front as well. Shortly before the recording, Johnson and Frances were engaged to be married and Frances began to take an even more active role in the dealings of her betrothed. Not surprisingly, what she saw at that time, she did not like.

"Anyone who wanted to use Johnnie had liquor for him," she observed. "It wasn't too hard to figure out. During the time he made *Bluehand Johnnie*, for example, Johnnie would leave my house and say, 'I gotta go. I have a meeting with Sam Valenti about the album.' And off he'd go and a few hours later he'd come back drunk as a skunk. Johnnie was drinking a hell of a lot, and when I say hell of a lot, I know what I'm saying. Johnnie would drink two big ice tea glasses of gin in no time; I'd think it was water until he tried to stand up. Then I knew. I once saw him go through an entire quart of Tanqueray by himself in less than an hour. The man could drink.

"So anyway, Johnnie would go and come back drunk, and he'd be the onliest one coming back drunk. Now I didn't mind Johnnie drinking as long as he did it at home and not when he was going to be out on the road—Johnnie has been very lucky with cars. I also told him I didn't want him drinking before shows. My father, who owned a tavern, told me: 'Frances, you can't be drunk and take care of business.' And he was right. Johnnie was going to these 'meetings,' and I know he had no idea what was going on 'cause he was in a stupor.

"So finally I had enough and I went ahead and called Sam. This was the start of me becoming a big B. I called him and I asked him, 'Sam, do you have a life insurance policy on Johnnie?' He said, 'No.' I said, 'Then why you trying to kill him?' And I went on from there. I wasn't very ladylike about it—I basically threatened him. I told him the next time he sent that man back around here drunk he'd have to deal with me. I'd had enough of watching Johnnie get used. If he wasn't going to do something about it, I was."

Bluehand Johnnie was recorded at Archway Studios in St. Louis with Sain overseeing the production. In total, ten tracks were laid down including two original compositions by Sain himself, "Slow Train" and "Way South"—and three by Fats Washington—"O.J. Blues," "Black Nights," and "Talkin' Woman" (with Lowell Fulson). The rest of the album was filled out by Ma Rainey's "See See Rider," Bill Doggett's "Honk Tonk Part 1," Jimmy Reed's "Baby What You Want Me To Do," and a retooled version of "Johnny B. Goode," which the producers took the liberty of re-spelling 'Johnnie', with Barbara Carr twisting the original vocals to suit the occasion (Johnnie in the song became a piano player instead of a guitarist). Johnson's only original contribution was his own "Johnnie's Boogie" which he had been playing since he was a teen. In retrospect, he wishes he had put more original material on the album.

"I've been makin' up my own songs for years and years," he says. "Since before Chuck and I ever got together. The only problem is that none of them have titles and none of them have words. It was nice when I was with Chuck 'cause he could always come up with lyrics to put with the music I did, like 'Wee Wee Hours,' for example. I'd been playin' that for a while, foolin' around, but it didn't have no title or nothin' and it didn't have no words. With that first album, I guess it was just easier to do the standards, and since I didn't sing, I just let Oliver do whatever he thought was best. I was real intimidated by the whole thing. I wasn't used to bein' the frontman in the studio, havin' to make all the decisions, and everything. Oliver took care of all that."

Oliver Sain remembers that Johnnie found his common-sense approach to playing and recording a welcome alternative to the usual musician's way of doing things.

"Johnnie was tired of fooling with musicians," says Sain. "I think that was one of the things that drove him away from Chuck Berry and that whole rock and roll scene. As long as I was running things he was happy because he knew I was reliable and that I would take care of things for him."

Bluehand Johnnie was released in 1988 to mixed reviews. Some critics felt the piano sound was too "tinkling" on the final product and others found Johnson's lack of original material and the complete absence of his vocals to be detrimental to any attempt at star status. Nevertheless, Johnnie's considerable skills could not be denied, and it was that fact that kept the album in circulation. In that year's *Rolling Stone* Critics' Poll, Johnnie was voted best keyboardist, a long-overdue title presented more on the basis of his *Hail! Hail! Rock 'n' Roll* piano performance than as a result of his album.

Frances thought *Bluehand Johnnie* did not accurately represent her husband at all. "He was drinking throughout the whole thing. You look at the cover of the album—there's his drink sitting up on the piano. He certainly did not live up to his potential on that first album and I think it was because of his drinking. In fact, I'm sure of it."

Following the release of his first solo project, Johnnie traveled with Oliver Sain to Europe and toured with Sain's band. He had been to Europe before with Chuck Berry in 1984, but now he was experiencing it from a different perspective. In America he was a sideman; in Europe he was a star.

"We opened up for Johnny Copeland in Italy and I came out and played with him durin' his set," Johnnie recalls. "Well, the folks in the audience just went crazy. And afterwards, Johnny was jokin' around and he said, 'Don't ever put me on the same stage with Johnnie Johnson! Don't do it, not nowhere! He just stole my whole damn show!' That was the first time I'd ever really gotten a compliment like that from a showman like Johnny Copeland. It was real nice."

Says Oliver Sain, "They loved Johnnie in Europe. Everywhere we played, they just loved him. See, Europeans have much more of an appreciation for the piano than Americans do. They have a respect for the piano and the piano players that you just don't find here. I remember in Germany they were asking all kinds of questions about Johnnie. He won himself a lot of fans on that tour."

He also won himself an agent. Based on the pianist's skill and his association with Chuck Berry, *Bluehand Johnnie* producer Sam Valenti introduced Johnnie to a New York talent agent named Glen Knight who would take over the piano legend's publicity and booking—a job Johnson had been doing for himself with little or no success.

"Sam Valenti got me hooked up with Glen Knight and right away he got me my first gig, at the Lone Star Cafe in New York," recalls Johnnie. "I took Tom Maloney, Gus Thornton, Stacey Johnson, and Keith Robertson and that was my first gig with an agent being booked as a frontman instead of the sideman. We did two shows opening up for John Mayall and Johnny Copeland."

Knight's plan as he told Johnnie and Frances, was to "sell Johnnie Johnson to the public." According to Knight, this meant that sometimes Johnnie would have to take less pay until he began to get a bigger name. Then and only then, said Knight, would he be able to request top-price gigs. To Johnnie, Knight's philosophy made perfect sense and he took to him immediately. Frances, on the other hand, had her doubts.

"Glen was a good agent in the beginning," she admits. " I didn't like the fact that everyone seemed to make money except Johnnie, but Glen insisted that you had to start out that way before you started making any headway in the music business. Then he'd tell me that he had to 'sell Johnnie' and that was just the way it was done. Johnnie believed every word he said and I went along with it because he was getting Johnnie more jobs than Johnnie had been able to get on his own. But I still had my suspicions, if you know what I mean."

Knight's greatest accomplishments as Johnnie Johnson's agent occurred in 1990. While browsing through a music magazine, Knight stumbled upon an interview with Eric Clapton in which the guitarist expressed a desire to have Johnnie Johnson as his pianist during the blues night at his annual Royal Albert Hall concerts. Smelling the opportunity for exposure, Knight immediately contacted Roger Forrester, Clapton's manager, and set up a deal to have Johnnie fly out to London for the event. Johnnie was thrilled.

"I was real excited when Glen called me up and told me about playin' with Eric Clapton at Royal Albert Hall. When I found out Buddy Guy and Robert Cray was gonna be there, that made it even more excitin'. I couldn't wait to get out there and I didn't think nothin' bout flyin' or anything. It was one of the highlights of my career."

Eric Clapton began performing his consecutive shows at Royal Albert Hall with six dates at the venue in 1987. In 1988 he performed nine. Then in 1989, he stayed for twelve concert dates, playing to an audience packed full of his adoring fans. The 1990 show would feature four different programs with three different bands and run eighteen nights over the course of a month from January 18 to February 18, and although both the rock band (ranging in size from four to thirteen pieces) and the sixty-piece orchestra were both successful to varying degrees, it was the three blues nights that really stole the show and left concertgoers shaking their heads in disbelief.

A purist, Clapton had assembled an all-star band for his interpretation of classic blues standards by artists such as Muddy Waters, Otis Rush, and Elmore James. Besides Johnson on piano, Clapton had invited both Buddy Guy and Robert Cray to back him on guitar, along with the tasteful rhythm section of Robert Cousins on bass and Jamie Oldaker on drums. The band was solid and needed little rehearsal time before they were off and running. Or as Johnnie remembers—running late. The band got along so well together and Clapton was having such a good time, that he was actually fined by the hall for playing seventy-five minutes over the scheduled time the first show.

"We had a lot of fun together," remembers Johnnie, "and I really got to know those guys better, especially Eric and Buddy Guy. I had already met Robert Cray, but I hadn't seen too much of those other two. Eric is a real quiet fella like me. So he and I understood each other pretty well. Like I said, it was a lot of fun."

The fun on the stage was evident in the smiles and chemistry between the musicians. The fun off stage, however, was just as plentiful. Too plentiful, for Johnnie. After fifty years of drinking, he finally met his match in a bottle of Cognac–a stiff after-dinner drink meant to be taken in small doses. Based on his history, Johnnie Johnson should have died that night in 1990. Right behind the piano.

* * *

The stagehands noticed it first. The bleeding. A steady drip of crimson rolling down the old man's goatee and spattering the ivories as he played the blues with an intricacy only a handful of others have ever achieved. The bass keys were smeared with quarter-sized fingerprints. Johnnie never noticed. He was too drunk.

He'd started the bottle backstage before the show—a fifth of Cognac slowly disappearing by the glassful. It was strong stuff, tasted like fire going down, but the steady burn made it pleasant to Johnnie's desensitized tastebuds. Everyone told him to slow down, including Clapton and Clapton's manager Roger Forrester, who were no strangers to the bottle themselves. But Johnnie did not listen and continued to down the Cognac like water until showtime.

The glass went with him onto the stage, and for a long time he did not see the smattering of red spots swimming in lurid contrast with the fierce yellow liquid. The blood began sometime during the middle of the set. Jeff Dillon, a devout Clapton fan and a good friend of Johnnie's, was in the audience that night. He remembers watching the stagehands bring him towels and ice cubes. He saw the look of bewilderment on Johnnie's face as he stared at the scarlet-drenched towel. And he recalls the mélange of awe and horror he felt as Johnnie played one of the greatest live piano solos in blues history with one hand while holding that same towel to his nose with the other (captured forever on the *Eric Clapton 24 Nights* home video), after which he stood in the middle of the next song and walked off the stage on unsteady legs. When he returned moments later, the bleeding still had not stopped. Johnnie should have left the stage for good then and gone to the hospital. But the old man continued to play–and drink—without considering the consequences. He did not think. He was too drunk.

They finally stopped it. After the show, Johnnie went back to the hotel and fell asleep. He'd finished the entire fifth of Cognac before moving on to Tanqueray and that last bottle put him out. He got up the next morning and boarded the plane back to St. Louis, the previous night's calamity a blurred recollection. He drank some more on the plane and slept.

Fourteen hours later, he awoke upon landing with a mouthful of blood. The change in altitude had set it off again. Borrowing a towel from the stewardess he pressed it to his nose and stumbled off the plane. They asked if he needed help. He said no. Somehow he made it through the wait for baggage. Somehow he found his car. He drove down the highway, blood streaming down his face, saturating his shirt and jacket. He began to feel light-headed. Something was wrong. Something serious. He had to find Frances.

She met him at the door, eyes blazing in anger. Immediately, she smelled the liquor on his breath and would hear no explanations. He begged her to let him in. She refused. He said he was bleeding. She gave him a towel; told him to go sleep it off and come back in the morning. He turned around, got in the car, and nearly fainted behind the wheel. He could not drive. Staggering up the walk he ran into Frances' daughter Jerri, a nurse. She took one look at him and felt her breath catch in her throat. Only her training kept her composed as she helped him to sit down. Then she walked up to her mother who had come back out on the porch to send him away once and for all. "Momma," she said to Frances calmly, "Johnnie's hemorrhaging. And if you don't get him to a hospital right now he's gonna die."

The car screamed down Carrie Street at one a.m. The man in the passenger seat lolled with the momentum–he was losing consciousness fast. Frances pushed on with fear in her heart. "Don't you die on me, Johnnie Johnson!" she yelled. "Stay awake now, you hear?"

Frances looked out the windshield and felt her heart sink. "Oh shit," she said. Johnnie turned weakly towards her. "Whaa...?" "Nothing Johnnie. Nothing but a bunch of kids."

The kids, a local gang of delinquents, had gathered for a nightly convention right in the middle of the street. This happened sometimes. Part of life in the city. Most people either turned off on a side street if possible or on last resort slowed down–a dangerous option in itself that unfailingly resulted in harassment or worse, depending on the gang's mood and degree of intoxication. Frances shook her head in disgust. They were young men— teens mostly—

but still dangerous despite their youth. Perhaps more so because of it. Frances readied herself and continued on.

They paid little notice to the approaching car until it was already upon them, whereupon they made a show of standing defiantly still—a backstreet version of chicken—daring the woman to part their ranks. Frances had expected this. She stared them down, considered for a split second, then slammed down the gas pedal and plowed through at full speed, sending them scattering like bowling pins for the safety of the sidewalk where they stood cursing her as she drove away. Frances watched them gesturing in her rearview mirror and in spite of the grave situation, she smiled.

* * *

The doctor could not believe Johnnie Johnson was walking. He stared at the blood pressure gauge in amazement. Shook it. Tested him again. It read 250 over 155. The man should have had a stroke, he thought. The blown vessel in his head—the one that had caused the hemorrhaging—saved his life. Had the vessel held, he would have been lost. It was the drinking that caused it, the doctor informed him. "You're lucky to be alive," he said frankly. "Few people get second chances. Make the most of it."

Johnnie took it all in. The time had come to make a decision. He sent everyone out of the room, sat by himself, and reflected on his life. Then he made up his mind.

"The doctor told me," Johnnie recalls, "that if that blood vessel hadn't of busted in my nose, I could have had a stroke and died. My brother, Jack, had died right about that time from liver disease and that was on my mind, too. Wasn't none of us left. It pretty much scared me away from drinkin'. I decided right then and there to leave the bottle alone."

Johnnie says he stopped drinking immediately following the incident and has not touched any alcohol since. But overcoming addiction is not that easy–it is a battle–and Frances remembers a much more gradual phasing out of the bottle from Johnson's life than he admits.

"Johnnie was still drinking when we got married in 1991," she recalls. "Now he had cut down, but he was still doing it. He was just trying to hide it from me. One time he was in Chicago. Johnnie and I have this thing where when he gets where he is going, he calls to tell me that he's made it all right.

"So he gets to Chicago and he calls me, 'I'm here.' Well, I immediately heard it in his voice. I said, 'Johnnie, have you been drinking?' 'Oh, no! I ain't been drinking! I'm on the forty-second floor so I just sound funny.' Like I'm gonna believe that lie. But what could I do? I wasn't there. I couldn't prove nothing. I said, 'Okay, Johnnie. See you later.' And we hang up.

"Well he calls me back five minutes later and this is when I know for sure. He said, 'You know that red dress I've been wanting you to get?' Johnnie had been wanting me to get a red dress since he first met me and since he was starting to make a little more money he wanted me to have it. I said, 'Yes, Johnnie, I know the red dress.' He said, 'Go find that red dress!' I said 'Okay, Johnnie.' And hung up the phone.

"Now I can't kill him, so I just let it go and got back to whatever I was doing. Sure enough, he calls me back ten minutes later. 'Have you found the red dress?' I said, 'Johnnie, if you call me one more time I'm gonna kill you when you get back to St. Louis!' He was about to drive me crazy. So I yelled at him some more and he apologized and that was that.

"Well I thought that was it. Over with. Uh-uh. Ten minutes later he calls back again. I said, 'Johnnie!' And he cuts me off real quick, 'Don't get mad! Pops Staples from the Staples Singers is in my room and I showed him your picture, he wants to say hi!' Well now I see he's drunk as a skunk, you know, and I'm just shaking my head. But that's the kind of stuff I heard when Johnnie was trying to pretend that he wasn't drinking anymore. He has never been able to lie.

"And like with the airports. I don't know if he started before he got there or afterwards but he'd come home looking like he got hit by a Mac truck. I'd be there to pick him up and he'd look just awful. So I'd ask him, 'Johnnie, you been drinking?' 'Oh, no! I fell asleep on the plane.' Well, I got tired of hearing that lie, so after a while when he came home looking funny, I'd start kicking him and hitting on him in the airport and it embarrassed him. Johnnie never liked to make a scene and he didn't want nobody seeing him getting beat on by his old lady.

"So finally he realized that he had to stop drinking the day before he got home or else, and from there I guess it just kind of faded away. Pretty soon he had stopped drinking altogether. It got down to where it was a matter of the liquor or me and Johnnie cared too much to lose me. He'd messed up three marriages drinking and I think he was just tired of it. He stopped because he cared and if he hadn't cared about me and about living he would still be doing it his way to this day."

* * *

The wheel kept turning. A month after his recovery, Johnnie was approached about doing another album, this time by producer Daniel Jacoubovitch, who proposed a teaming of Johnnie with two other great St. Louis pianists, Clayton Love and Jimmy Vaughan. The album would be called *Rockin' Eighty-Eights*, and as an extra incentive, Jacoubovitch secured a backing band of Tom Maloney, Gus Thornton, and Kenny Rice with Vernon Guy to provide the vocals for Johnnie's number. Based on his chemistry with the others, Maloney was hired as both the musical director and pre-production coordinator.

"I'll never forget when I told Jimmy Vaughan about having to play on the same album with Johnnie," remembers Maloney. "He said, 'I got to play with Johnnie Johnson! Oh, man!' Here was this great piano player and he was actually intimidated about playing with Johnnie. That's the kind of reputation he had around the area. Johnnie was bad."

From his point of view, Johnnie saw the chance to record with two other great pianists as a once-in-a-lifetime chance. However, if he'd had his way, he says, the album would have been made with his good friend, Joe Buckner.

"Clayton and Jimmy...they was good. But Joe Buckner was my man," praises Johnnie. "Ain't nobody ever heard of Joe, but he was just about the best jazz pianist I ever heard next to Oscar Peterson. He and I used to hang out together a lot and we'd have these little contests with the bands that came through town. If one of them had a good jazz piano player, I'd say, 'You think you can take him, Joe?' 'I 'spect I probably could.' And then he'd go up there and just play the lights out of the joint. Same thing if a good blues piano player came to town. Joe would say, 'Hey Johnnie, why don't you go up there and show that fool he ain't as good as he thinks he is.' It was all for fun, we didn't cause no fights or nothin'. But that was my man, Joe. A couple years back, I was coming back from a long tour, and I saw Joe's son in the airport. We was talkin' and he said, 'You know, daddy gone.' I said, 'Nobody told me!' 'Cause I would have caught the first plane home if I knew. Joe was my friend. I wish I could've done some records with him."

The *Rockin' Eighty-Eights* recordings took place in the Executive Room at George Edick's Club Imperial, in St. Louis, Missouri, from April 20 to April 22, 1990. Johnnie laid down four tracks, of which only two were original compositions. Tom Maloney, well aware of Johnson's big-band background, brought in a full horn section featuring Willie Akins on tenor sax, Albert Hunter on baritone sax, Dave Caputo on trombone, and Jim Rosse on trumpet, along with himself, Rice, and Thornton.

The album opens with an instrumental entitled "Frances," after the then future Mrs. Johnson who dropped in during several of the sessions to keep an eye on her man. Maloney arranged the song and then, as he says, "gave Johnnie the key and turned him loose." The result was a powerful stop-start big-band swing boogie with Johnnie playing the music he loves and showcasing his trademark rolling sixteenth-note triplets.

Maloney and Johnson teamed for one more composition–a song based on one of Johnnie's piano licks that the two men adapted into a nearly six-minute instrumental called "Slidin' Serenade." "We put a lot of work into that one," remembers Maloney. "Johnnie really got into it and I love how it came out on record."

For his last two numbers, Johnnie chose Isaac Hayes's "Bluebird" and the song he'd made his own—Avery Parrish's "After Hours" co-written by Ace Harris, and originally performed by Parrish. Most musicians who have heard Johnnie Johnson's version say that there is no comparison between the two. "Johnnie plays the best 'After Hours' I have ever heard," says Kenny Rice. Tom Maloney agrees. "Johnnie does incredible things with 'After Hours.' Just incredible. The dynamic aspect of the song is perfect for Johnnie's style. It was made for him."

Following the recording of *Rockin' Eighty-Eights*, Johnnie was propositioned again, this time by Elektra Entertainment, who felt his music would be a welcome addition to their American Explorers series showcasing little-known regional artists who had an influence on their particular genres. A few months out of the studio and Johnson was right back in. "Here I'd been in the music business almost fifty years and never made a record on my own," says Johnnie. "Then all of a sudden, in just two years, I got two records and one on the way. That nutted me up, boy!"

The first ten tracks of *Johnnie B. Bad* were recorded in November and December of 1990 at the Ultrasonic Studios in New Orleans. Joey Spampinato, who had played bass during *Hail! Hail! Rock 'n' Roll*, recruited the members of his own group, NRBQ, to back Johnnie: rhythm guitarist Al Anderson, drummer Tom Ardolino, harpist/pianist Terry Adams, and lead guitarist Steve Ferguson.

A prolific writer, Ferguson would pen four of the first ten songs, including the instrumentals "Johnnie B. Bad" (with Terry Adams) and "Fault Line Tremor." He would also lend vocals to both his own composition "Can You Stand It" and the Jimmy Reed standard "Baby What's Wrong." As a finale, Ferguson would compose the hilarious misadventure of a ripe-smelling Romeo, "Stepped In What!?" marking Johnnie's long-awaited vocal debut. Knowing of the self-imposed sideman's reluctance to vocalize–Ferguson wrote the lyrics so that Johnnie could rhythmically narrate the tale in a laconic, grandfatherly sort of way without actually having to sing. "I was deathly afraid of the microphone," Johnnie admits. "I couldn't say my own name."

Finally, after laying down the tracks for the Roosevelt Sykes/ Pearl King collaboration "Hush Oh Hush" and Charles Davenport's "Cow Cow Blues," which he had been playing since he was six-years-old, Johnnie began working on his own compositions. The three instrumentals, called "Creek Mud," "Movin' Out," and "Blues #572," would boast a surprise guest on lead guitar.

"Eric Clapton came and played on a couple of my songs, one which was called 'Blues #572' and then another called 'Creek Mud'," Johnnie remembers. "I didn't expect it, so it was a really nice surprise to have him come all the way from England just to play with me. I really liked how those songs turned out, too. Eric is real good."

In January, Johnnie moved to Sorcerer Sound in New York to lay down the last part of his album with Keith Richards and His X-pensive Winos, with whom he had recorded *Talk Is Cheap* in 1987. At the time, Richards had just finished mixing the new live Stones album *Flashpoint*, and he was glad to get back to the basics of blues with Johnson. The first song the group recorded was the old Muddy Waters tune "Key to the Highway," which Richards provided the vocals for. Then, as he had done many times before in the studio with Chuck Berry, Johnnie began to play around on the piano during breaks. Listening to his hero inventing entirely new songs one after the other, Richards got an idea.

"It was kind of like what Chuck Berry used to do, 'cept Chuck would take what I was doin', put some words to it, and keep it for hisself and all," says Johnnie. "Keith heard me playin' and he said, 'You got to make a song out of that.' So I said, 'Okay.' And I started waitin' for him to come up with some words and sing them. He said, 'Oh, no, Johnnie. You got to sing this one.' I 'bout died.

"See, I can play piano in front of the whole world without a second thought, but I couldn't even sing in the shower. Now Keith and the guys are twistin' my arm, beggin' me to sing, and I keep tellin' them that I can't sing—never have sang a song in my life. Finally, I decided that I would do it so they could see how bad it was and then they wouldn't bother me about it no more.

"So I sit down and I start playin' then I just start makin' up words as I go along. The whole time I'm singin' one verse, I'm thinkin' 'bout what to say in the next verse—tryin' to rhyme, you know. 'Listen to me baby and hear what I gotta say. I'm goin' 'round the corner and get a drink of Tanqueray.' I didn't know what I was doin' at all. I don't know how Chuck did it, comin' up with all those words. I was as nervous as I had ever been. I figured now they'll see I ain't no singer. But it backfired on me 'cause Keith and the guys are lovin' it and sayin' that I'm doin' great. I thought I sounded terrible, but the next thing I know, we're recordin' it."

"Tanqueray," a song about Johnnie's notorious love affair with gin, would become his signature song and critics would applaud his efforts as a reflection of his gentle and self-effacing humor. But as far as the subject matter was concerned, the song about a man trying to get his baby to "settle down" with him "and have a drink of Tanqueray," was an ironic tribute to the end of one cycle in his life and the beginning of a new one.

On February 14, 1991 after returning home from his second consecutive year playing with Eric Clapton at Royal Albert Hall, Johnnie Johnson married Frances Miller, inheriting four stepchildren, and a new life as a church going, dog-walking, family man. Most importantly, for the first time in his adult life—Johnnie Johnson was sober.

"Quittin' drinkin' was 'bout the hardest thing I ever did," he says. "You do something for fifty years, it becomes a part of who you are. But I'll tell you this much, quittin' that bottle has changed my life for the better and I'll never go back. I owe it all to Frances. She made me a better man."

Says Frances, "I can always tell the folks who really love Johnnie because they come up to me and they say, 'Thank you.' I'll say, 'What for?' They say, 'Thank you for making Johnnie stop drinking. You saved his life.' I always tell them that it was Johnnie's decision to stop and they should be applauding him. I gave him some strength when he needed it, but the will to stop came from inside of him."

Aside from sobering up her husband, the new Mrs. Johnson's most important accomplishment was encouraging him to reestablish contact with his own children whom he had barely spoken to in years.

"Family has always been very important to me," she says. "My parents were separated, but every Christmas we got together and had two celebrations—one with my father and one with my mother. All those years, drunk ol' Johnnie hadn't even sent a birthday card or a Christmas card—nothing.

"Of course, part of that had to do with the fact that his second wife, Rose, told the kids that their father was dead. They didn't make no effort to him because of this. Fact, they didn't even know he was alive until they saw him at a funeral for some other relative. They were angry at Johnnie and they had a right to be. His sons don't even call him daddy and his son, Johnnie Johnson, Jr., will tell you that his name is not Johnnie Johnson—it's Michael. The oldest son, John David, the real tall one (by the way all Johnnie's boys are taller than him, and three of the four girls too) I had Johnnie call him just two months before he died and they had a nice conversation. John David was his son from his first marriage to Marguerite, who is just a lovely woman. But his two other sons—uh-uh. The one boy, Peter, he called Johnnie up one time sayin' he needed to be bailed out of jail. Johnnie didn't ask no questions, he went ahead and got an advance on a gig to get him out. Wired him the money. And we didn't have no money ourselves, you know. Johnnie couldn't afford to spare it. But he did 'cause in his heart he loves his children and he feels guilty. Well, he got him out and that was that. No 'thank you.' Nothing. I don't think things will ever be right between Johnnie and his boys.

"The daughters, though, they're starting to come around. He talks to all of them and he's even starting to get close with a couple of them. His daughter Althea came up to a gig Johnnie was doing in Chicago and I just left the room, let them sort things out. They needed to talk and it wasn't none of my affair. That was something they needed to do alone. And there was tears, and hugs, and forgiveness, and understanding that passed between them. The girls see that their father is a different person now. They see that he isn't drinking anymore and that he's got his act together. His daughter Connie even had a ballcap made that says 'Connie Loves Daddy' and he wears that thing all the time. 'Connie Loves Daddy.' It made me feel so good when she did that for him 'cause I know how much he hurts over the whole thing with his kids. When they call, it just makes his day and that makes me happy because I love him. I'm proud of Johnnie and I'm proud of his children for giving him a chance to come back into their lives."

* * *

On February 25, 1992, Johnnie Johnson traveled to New York to attend the thirty-fourth annual Grammy Awards held at Radio City Music Hall. Much to his surprise, *Johnnie B. Bad* had been nominated for Best Traditional Blues Recording. At the same time, John Lee Hooker's *Mr. Lucky*, an album to which he had contributed two tracks—"I Want To Hug You" and "This Is Hip"—was up for the same award. Earlier in the year, Johnnie had performed with Hooker on a live A&E television special during which the bluesman announced to the audience that not only had Johnnie started the career of Chuck Berry—he was in fact "Johnny B. Goode." It was the first time this fact had been made public, and the crowd whooped in surprise.

To be associated with two nominated albums is a great achievement, and Johnnie was flattered by the recognition–a rare moment of pride for a meek and humble man. Dressed in the best outfit he could afford, Johnnie sat shy and unnoticed amongst the stars and big-name performers both old and new who had come to receive their awards. Fifth and sixth-generation rock stars pranced about exalting in their own splendor, completely unaware that their great-grandfather sat among them, alone in the corner with a glass of orange juice. "I didn't know none of the young fellas," remembers Johnnie, "and none of them knew me. So I just tried to find somebody my own age to talk to. I felt kinda lost."

Then the Kentucky Headhunters arrived.

Founded in the bluegrass state by the Young brothers, Richard and Fred, their cousin Anthony Kenney and friend Greg Martin, the Kentucky Headhunters burst on the scene with a sound all their own, a wild mix of rock and country called too hick for L.A. and too bold for Nashville. However, following the release of their first album, *Pickin' On Nashville,* and the hit "Walk Softly On This Heart of Mine," America caught on to the band's fun-loving, down-home style and the Headhunters won themselves a fiercely loyal legion of country music fans.

But the Kentucky Headhunters were much more than just a country band. Each member had been raised on rhythm and blues and rock and roll, and all were well-versed in both styles. Recalls Richard Young, "We all knew each other growing up and we spent years in my Grandma's barn practicing these old rock and roll and blues songs—Chuck Berry, Jerry Lee Lewis, Albert King, Albert Collins, Muddy Waters. Of course we played a lot of Hank Williams, too. But that's what we grew up on—rhythm and blues.

Most people don't know that."

It was complete serendipity that on the day of the Grammys, the Headhunters discovered *Johnnie B. Bad*. But it was the skill of the pianist and his celebrated place in music lore that had them listening to the CD repeatedly the entire trip up from Kentucky, all the time unaware that Johnnie Johnson had been nominated and would be there at the Grammys when they arrived.

"We were getting ready to go to the Grammy Awards in 1991," Richard Young explained during an interview on the television show *Crook & Chase*, "and Greg came in and had this album and said, 'Ya'all got to check this out. Johnnie Johnson's got a solo album out.' So all the way to New York we are all just raving and having the best time in the world listening to this album.

"Well, when we get there...they always have this big party before the Grammys, you know? And we walk in and, of course, people were clambering over the stars. They had Madonna, and everybody was there and everybody was over here doin' all this, and we walked in and we saw Roy Rogers and Les Paul and Johnnie Johnson sittin' in the same area. Well we'd already met Les Paul, and we'd done an album with Roy Rogers, his last one called *The Cowboy*, so we went running across this room like a bunch of idiots and jumped on Johnnie's table and were just asking him questions real fast. And it was just some kind of rapport started from that and we just got to be good buddies that night."

Johnnie recalls the evening as pleasant—due for the most part to the Headhunter's company.

"They was just great, Richard and them. They came up and started talkin' to me right 'bout the time I started feelin' out of place. I didn't have nobody to talk to with all them young musicians. I'd seen that fella M.C. Hammer on the TV jumpin' all around with them big britches, but he didn't know me and I didn't know him. So like I say, it was great that the Headhunters came over 'cause they really made the night for me."

Following the Grammys, where he lost to B.B. King's album *Live*

At The Apollo, Johnnie was back on the road again. And although he continued to play with Tom Maloney, Gus Thornton, and Kenny Rice around St. Louis, he had formed his own touring band consisting of guitarist Steve Waldman, drummer Keith Robertson (both of whom played on *Bluehand Johnnie*) and bassist Frank Dunbar who can be seen rocking with Johnnie and Chuck Berry at the reopened Cosmopolitan Club in *Hail! Hail! Rock 'n' Roll.*

Dunbar wasn't his only renewed contact from that film. In 1993, Johnson got a call from Berry himself, who invited his former partner to join him on stage at Bill Clinton's inauguration in Washington, D.C. After the gig, an inspired Chuck asked Johnnie to join him in the studio for another album. Jim Marsala remembers the session.

"Chuck had Johnnie come in to the studio down on Woodson Road about five years ago because he was wanting to make a new record," says Marsala. "It was going to be a double album. I think as of now we have twelve songs and five of those are from that live show *Live at the Roxy* with Tina Turner and a bunch of other people. I've listened to some of the early mixes and I have to admit that I don't like the way it sounds. It just isn't mixed right or something. Maybe someday we'll release it, but I don't know. It depends on Chuck."

Over thirty years after his first record made him a star, Chuck Berry had little time for music. As well as the nineties started out for Johnnie Johnson, they were somewhat less than wonderful for his former partner. On December 27, 1989, a civil suit for invasion of privacy was filed against Berry by Hosana A. Huck who had worked as a cook at the Southern Air restaurant, which Berry bought in 1987. Ms. Huck alleged that over the course of a year, Berry had secretly installed video equipment (which turned out to be state-of-the-art fiber optics) in the ladies toilet stalls to record, from various angles (including ariel views), women and girls relieving themselves. From these recordings, two videotapes were allegedly made which were painstakingly edited—allegedly in

Berry's own advanced video workshop—"for the improper purpose of the entertainment and gratification of the abnormal urination and coprophagous sexual fetishes and sexual predilections of Defendant Chuck Berry," as alleged the Huck's attorney.

Berry denied owning these tapes, though twenty more were found by Huck's husband Vincent (who worked as a handyman for Berry) in a dumpster outside Berry's home. These tapes featured Berry with an assortment of busty blonds, some of whom he urinated on before allowing them to defecate on his face. To add to the embarrassment, Vincent Huck sold eight full-frontal nude stills of Berry and his women to *High Society* magazine, prompting Berry to file a lawsuit stating that the Hucks and their attorneys "entered into illicit negotiations with video distributors...to capitalize upon Mr. Berry's status as a world-class performer." Berry also accused the Hucks of trying to blackmail him by threatening lawsuits and prosecution and demanding $10 million for the return of the tapes.

What happened next, according to an affidavit filed by an agent of the Multijurisdictional Enforcement Group, was that Vincent Huck, who had been working as an informant for the D.E.A., tipped them off that Berry had made nine million dollars over the years as a cocaine trafficker and would often carry as much as twenty-five kilos at a time back to Wentzville in his guitar case.

At five a.m. on June 30, 1990, St. Charles County drug-enforcement agents raided Berry Park while Berry was in Massachusetts. According to police records published in a 1993 SPY magazine article, the officers seized bags of marijuana, hashish, two rifles, a shotgun, seven trays of pornographic slides, fifty-nine VHS videotapes, three paperback books and newspapers described as "sexual in nature," and $122,501 in cash. No traces of the alleged cocaine were found on the premises.

Despite the fact that investigators found no traces of cocaine, county prosecuter William J. Hannah held a press conference in which he declared that, "Chuck Berry is involved in cocaine trafficking, earning millions a year." However, the lack of evidence allowed for only one count of possession of marijuana and three counts of child abuse (due to some of the women in his videos being under age), charges which were filed while Berry was on tour in Sweden. Upon his return, a dejected Berry turned himself into authorities, but denied both making the tapes and using or selling cocaine. He posted a $20,000 bond and was released. But the trouble was far from over.

Based on the existence of the bathroom tapes, Berry was faced with a class-action suit brought against him by 200 women who had visited his restaurant during the year the tapes were supposedly made. Berry fought back, suing for the return of the tapes, both the plaintiffs and their lawyers, and *High Society* magazine for publishing the photos. He also brought a suit against William J. Hannah for his "maliciously baseless" charges and the contention that Hannah was "basically trying to run for reelection at Chuck Berry's expense."

On November 20, 1990, after extensive negotiations, Berry's suit against Hannah was dropped as were the charges of child abuse. Berry was given two years probation for the misdemeanor marijuana charge and forced to donate $5,000 to local substance-abuse programs.

Once again, Chuck Berry had been made the target of intense prosecution by legal authorities. Three years later, an embittered Berry would argue to the Missouri Supreme Court that he has been the victim of a conspiracy to destroy him financially, "tantamount to an economic lynching of a uniquely American cultural icon."

Indeed, Berry seems to be unable to avoid trouble with the law and his frequent run-ins (six altogether) and three prison terms have left him, as his former guitar player Billy Peek says, "very bitter."

"Chuck had a lot of negative things happen, man," says Peek. "I mean, he gets busted at the pinnacle of his career for violating the Mann Act and then the whole tax evasion thing in the seventies. You know they were trying to get him eleven years for that in

Missouri? Eleven years, man! And then the bathroom tapes. He paid a fortune for that—something like $1.5 million total. Luckily, it was only a civil suit. He is a two-time loser with felonies. If he ever gets convicted of a felony again, he'd be gone forever. Now I'm not saying he didn't do some bad things. But if you got busted that many times, you'd be protective, too."

Nonetheless, despite yet another batch of legal troubles, Berry was all business in the studio, and Johnnie recalls no deviations in the guitarist's behavior.

"When he and I got together again to work on that new album, he was right in the middle of all that mess with the bathroom pictures and all that. But Chuck never brought his problems into the studio. That's one thing you could always say 'bout Chuck. When we got down to makin' music together, that was where it was at. Just like it had always been. Just me and Chuck, the piano and the guitar."

* * *

At the start of 1993, Johnnie met up again with his friends from the Grammy Awards, the Kentucky Headhunters. The Headhunters's manager Mitchell Fox and Elektra Records representative Nancy Jeffries had been privy to the pleasant conversation between the rural rockers and their rock and roll godfather, and after talks with both Johnnie and Glen Knight, it was decided that the Headhunters would be the perfect choice to back Johnnie on his fourth solo album. Richard Young remembers the call.

"Nancy Jeffries called up Mitchell Fox, our manager, and asked if we would be interested in doing the next Johnnie Johnson solo album," he says. "We were like, 'When?' I mean this is Johnnie Johnson! So she tells me that they—meaning Elektra—wanted him to come down and stay with us in Kentucky, they wanted us to write the songs with him, and then they wanted us to produce the record. I guess what they were looking for was a self-contained unit that made a lot of records together and that worked well together;

someone Johnnie could fit in with, you know?

"Well anyway, Johnnie Johnson is coming to Kentucky, and Mark Orr, who was our singer at the time, he's gonna pick Johnnie up and bring him over to the house. Man that was the greatest feeling. I'll never forget what it felt like sitting on the front porch of that house waiting for Johnnie Johnson— anxiety at the fullest. But a great anxiety. Here's this place where we grew up for twenty years playing music–playing his music—and here comes the man himself, Johnnie Johnson, up the walk. It was unbelievable, man. Just unbelievable.

"So Johnnie comes up and he says, 'Okay they sent me down here to do a record with you fellas. But I heard you was a country-western band. We better play a couple and see if this is gonna work.' So we played 'Carol,' and 'Little Queenie,' and Johnnie looks up from the piano and says, 'Okay, I'm in the Headhunters.' Just like that. Johnnie Johnson is the sixth Headhunter!"

Had Johnnie known more about the band's history, he would not have been surprised that they had such a handle on his music. The entire group was raised on Chuck Berry records and they were well familiar with Johnnie's rhythm—thanks to Richard Young—who stumbled upon the key to rock and roll years before while trying to determine his role in the band.

"When we were about thirteen, maybe fourteen, playing together in the barn, I started to realize that Greg Martin was gonna be a better lead guitar player than I was," recalls Young. "I'd always wanted to be lead, but Greg was just headed in that direction. And I thought, 'How can I can contribute to our band at the same level that Greg could as lead guitar?' So I started listening to a lot of records and then I narrowed it down to the Chuck Berry records. And what I got out of that was Johnnie. I didn't get my style from other guitar players—I got it from Johnnie Johnson's left hand. I practiced and practiced until I figured out a way that I could play guitar like Johnnie Johnson's left hand. Just like Chuck had and Keith Richards and John Lennon. And I used to wonder if it was really helpful or not. Then one night my amp went out on stage and the whole bottom fell out of the song. It just went dead. And I remember saying to myself, 'Oh, so there's Johnnie Johnson!'

"'Cause, I knew who he was by that time. I first saw Johnnie's picture in a magazine around 1968 and it was like,'That's the guy!' And the name 'Johnnie Johnson,' J.J. That was easy to remember. But we all knew, 'cause...see back when the Beatles came out we were listening to them pretty heavy. And while we were listening, we were trying to figure out who each Beatle's main influence was. I mean, George Harrison was obviously Carl Perkins. And Paul McCartney was Little Richard. And they were all Chuck Berry, but Lennon especially. You could tell that Lennon had dug the deepest into Chuck Berry. But there was something else besides Chuck Berry. Something about the feel. And that was Johnnie Johnson. Lennon may not have even known that's who he was copying, but it was.

"And when he'd start playing the piano on some of the Beatle songs—it wasn't like Johnnie exactly, but it...how can I explain this...it had the same attitude. The same air. And that was what Johnnie contributed to the following generations and especially to Chuck's music. Johnnie gave us the dance. Take Johnnie away from those songs and watch the dance go away. That's what made Chuck Berry's music happy was Johnnie. Johnnie Johnson's piano. It made it a happy-go-lucky, danceable, irresistible, infectious music. 'Up in the morning and out to school!' And of course, the lyrics were very important because the lyrics caught the attention of young white people. Chuck Berry knew how to get into the heads of young white kids. That's what he added to those songs. But that groove–the dance–that was Johnnie Johnson. Chuck Berry was the voice of rock and roll, but Johnnie Johnson was rock and roll music. That's why we were so in awe of him and keyed up about working with him. I mean there ain't another guy like Johnnie Johnson. I mean who contributed more to rock music? He's the one and only!"

The twelve tracks for *That'll Work* were cut within the span of a week. In order to take the pressure off, and to make the sessions as fun and democratic as possible, the group decided that regardless of who actually wrote the songs, everyone would share equally in the credits. Writing music with Johnnie Johnson, recalls Young, was something that had to be experienced first-hand. "It all makes sense to me now," he says. "How he does it. I can't really explain it except to say that he's always there and the music just seems to come out of him. 'Okay Big Mouth, watcha' want to do now?' That's what he calls me, 'Big Mouth.' And he just goes. It was just a week–we did it in a week. It's like it takes no effort at all. I guess that's why the sessions were so quick. You start working at Johnnie's pace and you realize what you can do as a musician."

For Young, collaborating with Johnson on songs like "Bummed About Love" and "The Feel" were a great challenge to him as he had little experience in jazz. But under his leadership, the band jelled together and were soon producing authentic jazz numbers much to Johnson's satisfaction.

"Johnnie wanted to do a record with a lot of jazz and blues, as opposed to rock and roll," Young says. "I think he was just burned out on the fast stuff. He said he wanted to get back to the basics–back into Billie Holiday. And that was hard for me because my least amount of education as a musician is in jazz. But when we set to writing 'Bummed About Love,' I was hoping we could come up with something that didn't sound like a ripoff, but like an old unreleased song from Billie Holiday's time. Something that got dug up out the vaults, you know? And I think we succeeded. In fact, the coolest thing about that song was that we did it in one take. Johnnie had his coat on and his briefcase ready to walk out the door and get on a plane. But he sat down right there and knocked it out–one time was all it took. It was great. And it brought us together as a band playing that type of music. Johnnie was real happy with the result. In fact, he told me later that Fred and Anthony were one of the best rhythm sections he'd ever worked with. That blew me away–I mean if you're fishing for compliments you can stop right there. That's the best you can do. It made me feel real good because we grew up together and I knew how much work Fred and Anthony had put into it. He made my day with that one."

Of the several songs recorded that week, ten others made it onto the album including "That'll Work," sung by Johnnie himself, and a down-and-dirty blues, "Back To Memphis," kicked off by thirty-seven seconds of the legend's boogie piano. For the Headhunters, experiencing Johnnie's famous groove first hand in the studio was a thrill and they relished every second. But for the man himself, having played it all his life, the sound was old hat—a lesson Young and the band learned early on in the sessions.

"We'd just got done recording 'Stumblin',' which is a fast, rock and roll type song, and we're listening to the playback. And it's just crazy. We were all dancing around, hopping, leaning on the console. And I turn back to Johnnie who's sitting in this lean-back recliner with his sunglasses on and I say, 'Johnnie ain't that great?' SNORE!!! He's out like a light. I mean, to us it was like the first naked woman we ever saw, and to Johnnie it was just another groove. He's sitting there sleeping with his big ol' eyes half shut, looking like a mud turtle."

With the songs completed and Johnnie on his way home, the band sat down to discuss royalties with their collaborator. What Richard Young learned that day shocked him to no end. Johnnie Johnson, despite recording three previous albums, the last of which had been nominated for a Grammy, had never received a single penny in royalties.

"We were all listed as songwriters on the album," Young says. "So I ask Johnnie when it comes time to make the arrangements, 'Johnnie, are you a BMI writer or an ASCAP writer?' Those are the two main organizations that see to it that songwriters get their royalties from record play and televison appearances, you know. It's standard. Every songwriter is either one or the other. Well I ask

Johnnie which one he belongs to, and he looks at me like I just asked him what planet he was from. 'Well, Richard, I don't think I'm either one. I mighta-used-to-been once, but I don't think I am. I ain't never heard of 'em.'

"Well, what happened was that Johnnie had been writing songs and doing these solo albums. But in all that time he hadn't received any income from airplay, and 'Tanqueray,' I know for a fact, was played quite a bit. Like with that album *Johnnie B. Bad*. Clapton and Richards–they were in and out and it was hard trying to get everyone together at one time. And I think that in all the hassle, no one took into consideration that Johnnie might not have his part taken care of. I don't guess Keith and them ever dreamed. They just assumed.

"So anyway, I got to digging and found out that Johnnie Johnson was not a member of either affiliation—ASCAP or BMI. So I called my good friend Charlene Wilheim down in Nashville and she said, 'Richard he has to have other records.' So she punches it up on the computer and all these songs come up from those three other albums. Songs that he hadn't made a thing on because he wasn't registered. Johnnie just figured he got paid once for making the record and that was it.

"So I went ahead and got Johnnie signed up and helped him collect some of the back royalties on those songs. And I tell ya man, it was a great feeling—he called me up one time and said, 'Man I just got a check on 'Tanqueray' and I just wanted to thank you for setting everything straight.' I was like, 'My pleasure.' And it was. To me it was like the cherry on top after doing that album. I'd been ripping off all his licks for years, and it made me feel a little better about it. You know, I took it for granted that Johnnie's name was on all those Chuck Berry records as co-writer, but it's not. Everybody knows he had a lot to do with the writing of Chuck's music, but no one ever thought to check if he was a member of ASCAP or BMI until 1993. It's tragic, man."

Johnnie Johnson and the Kentucky Headhunters continue to play together occasionally and Johnnie and Richard Young stay in close contact over the phone. Yet despite the band's familiarity with Johnnie, the thrill of playing with the piano legend live has lost none of its luster.

"You know, I'll tell you about what it's like to play with Johnnie," says Young. "A couple years ago we had a gig in St. Louis and Doug Phelps who is singing with us now, he had never played with Johnnie. And ever since he joined up, we'd been telling Doug about Johnnie. 'If you ever play live with him you'll get it–you'll know what it is.' We kept trying to explain, but he just didn't get it. So we figured next time we were in town, we'd have Johnnie up to play with us.

"Well, we call up Johnnie and he was exhausted 'cause he'd been on tour with Bob Weir and them guys. But Frances made sure he got to the gig. And we had a piano set up on stage all ready for him to set in. So here comes Johnnie and he walks up on stage and says, 'Okay, let's take it easy fellas, I'm tired.' So I said, 'Okay then, let's play little 'Little Queenie.' And Johnnie says, 'That'll work.'

"So we broke into it, and I never will forget–you know the guitar starts it out–but the minute the rest of the band came in it was like Johnnie reached out and touched everyone's shoulder. And he pulled us back into this groove—this funk—that I just cannot explain. I looked over at Doug Phelps and he was white around the mouth like he's just seen someone murdered. And it was so funny to all of us and such a great moment, because we all knew, but Doug had never witnessed it before. But that's Johnnie. When you play with Johnnie Johnson, it's like he has his hand on your shoulder the whole time you're playing together. He completely takes over the whole mode of what's going on stage. And he's not the type of person who gets in your face and does that. It's not aggressive at all. It's just like your grandfather putting his hand on your shoulder—'I want to tell you something,'—you know. It literally pulls you into a different groove. He turns any band into a superstar-sounding group. So you can understand why Chuck Berry, Eric Clapton,

Keith Richards, all those guys—why they just live to play with him. Because there's a certain thrill from playing with Johnnie Johnson on piano that I never felt with any other piano player. It's kind of spooky sometimes.

"And the funny thing is, he's such a passive person when he's not behind those keys. I mean, all the man wants out of life is to just fish and live a simple life. And he never really aspired to be a big star or anything himself—he just wanted to play music based on his love of jazz and big band music and blues. It just amazes me the contributions he made to rock and roll music. I think about the tons of people that I talk to in the industry that say, 'Man I was so influenced by that guy.' Johnnie is a national treasure. A real national treasure. And he's been overlooked by the general public for so long. Most people don't even know who he is. We have to educate them. It's been wrong for forty years. How about making it right?"

* * *

When Johnnie received his first copy of *That'll Work*, he called Frances over and sat her down. "I wrote this song here for you. It's called 'I Know You Can.' Mark helped me with the words."

And indeed it was true. Johnnie had asked that he write the lyrics to the song, and Kentucky Headhunter singer Mark Orr had sat down with him and aided him in composing the verse. In all his years as a musician, Johnnie had never written a love song. Frances listened in astonishment and then she cracked a smile big enough to swallow St. Louis. And afterwards she let Johnnie go right ahead with the "kissey-kissey thing."

> *Well I know she'll be there with me*
> *When trouble's coming down*
> *Leave it to my baby*
> *She'll pick me up off the ground*

You know she's used to bad love
But she's the type to understand
And if I tell her, I can make it rain, baby
Well she just says I know you can

Frances Johnson had picked Johnnie up at his lowest point and changed his life forever. Healthy, settled-down, and sober, it was time for the forgotten legend to step up to the next level and reap the long-overdue rewards for his incalculable influence on the whole of modern music. Consistent with the theme of his life, a twist of fate, a situation born purely out of accident, would bring him into contact with George Turek, a businessman who would make it his life's ambition to secure Johnnie Johnson his rightful place amongst the founding fathers of rock and roll.

XIII

GEORGE'S JAM

"George Turek—what can I say? He's an angel. That's the best way to put it. He's my guardian angel."

—Johnnie Johnson, 1997

"I guess my life really began when I was fourteen years old," says George Turek. "The summer after my freshman year in high school. And it wasn't just any school. Not to me, anyway. It was Catholic Central, an all-boy high school in Detroit. I'd wanted to go there since I was in grade school. CC was the best in academics and athletics–still is. *US News and World Report* ranks them at the top every year. The kids were rich–at least in my eyes–'cause my family didn't have a pot to pee in. It meant everything to me when I got in and my Pop scraped up the money for the tuition. My folks, too. Especially my mother. She became very active in the parent organizations–had the priests over for dinner–the whole bit. She was proud to have a son there, you know?

"Well, I got so into being part of the school my first year that I forgot what I was there for, and my grades went straight into the gutter. Next thing I know, the end of the year rolls around and my parents get this call from the assistant principal, Father Stoba. Tough ol'guy he was. Mean but fair. He says he wants me and my parents to come down to the school for a conference about my grades.

"I knew I was in over my head. So we wait until my Pop gets home from work in the afternoon, and we all head down there you know, the whole Turek clan. Well, Father Stoba brings us all into his office and closes the door. Then he sits down behind his desk and throws my grade report down right in front of me and my folks. Two big fat F's. One in Algebra and one in Latin.

"You flunked out Mr. Turek."

"That's all he said. 'You flunked out, Mr. Turek.' Well, my mother just burst into tears, you know? And I can just feel my Pop's eyes burning into the back of my neck, but he ain't saying nothing. Everyone is looking at me with these disappointed faces and I feel like I want to crawl right under that desk and die. Then my Pop speaks up.

"What's he got to do to get back in?'

Father Stoba doesn't take his eyes off me.

"Summer school. Eight weeks. If he passes both classes with a 'C' or higher, I will see about reinstating him as a student here. Otherwise, this will likely be our last meeting together. I wish you luck, Mr. Turek."

"And that was it. We walk out and my mother is sobbing and I'm bawling, too, just like a baby. Because I loved that school, you know? That school meant everything to me. Well my Pop, he's real quiet until we get outside the school. Then he tells my mother to go get in the car and while she's walking away, he takes me back around the building, out of sight, and puts me up against the wall.

"Now you got to know my Pop—George Sr. He was an ex-Navy

man, a WWII vet, used to box in the amateurs, tough as leather, you know? And naturally, I was scared to death of him. So he's holding me there by the shirt and he's tired and dirty and he still has his uniform on 'cause he'd just got back from work. My father like his father before him was a janitor. I come from eighty-years of Detroit public school janitors. And he's so pissed that his face is turning beet red. He gets right up in my face and says–I'll never forget it for as long as I live–he says, 'You screwed up, George. I worked my ass off all year, every single day, to send you to this school. I never made it past the ninth-grade. I never had that chance. What do you do? You fail. You humiliated me. Humiliated yourself. I've got a vacation coming this summer. Your mother and I are going up north and I'm goin' fishing. The house will be locked up when we leave 'cause we ain't gonna be there. You find yourself a place to stay this summer. You find a job and pay for summer school. And if you make it back in that school, you find a way to pay the tuition. I ain't spending another dime on you.' And that was the last we ever talked about the subject 'cause from then on it was up to me. Sink or swim.

"So there I am, fourteen years old, and my Pop tells me that I gotta find a place to live for the summer 'cause he's going on vacation. Screw you. Adios. Good-bye. He wasn't fooling around. So I call up my best friend, Joe McElligott, who lived one block over and also went to CC, and I tell him what's going on. Then he puts his mom on the phone and I tell her what's going on and she says sure, I can stay with them for the summer. I had a place to stay.

"After that I went looking around for jobs. I found one caddying at Western Golf and Country Club, and that's how I spent my summer. Hitchhiking to class because I couldn't afford bus fare, going to work, studying and sleeping. To this day, I've still got a dent in my shoulder from carrying those golf bags, and I'm not much of a golf fan. But to make a long story short–I aced both those summer classes. And when the fall semester came around, I got another job on the weekends so I could earn my $240 a year tuition.

I paid for my own school from then on out with no help from my folks. Pop meant what he said. And I did well enough my next three years to earn a scholarship to college. Cutting me off was the best thing my old man ever did for me. It made me strong, self-reliant. I grew up quick."

Turek eventually graduated with a Bachelor of Science degree. But he did not make it to his commencement ceremony. While his friends were walking on stage in cap and gown to receive their formal proof of education, George Turek was on a commercial plane bound for Pensacola, Florida, to pursue his dream of being a Naval Aviator. Flying a Navy jet had been his ambition ever since he was nine years old and saw the Blue Angels at an airshow. He decided then and there that he was going to be a pilot, and unlike most children, who let go of their budding ambition as easily as their stuffed animals, Turek remained true to his goal despite the fact that until the day he boarded the flight to Pensacola, he had never been inside of an airplane. "I knew what I wanted to do and I stuck with it," he says. Eventually he graduated second in his primary flight-training class and was assigned the coveted jet pipeline–a rewarding but extremely perilous position.

"My first training hop in basic jet at NAS Meridian, an instructor and his student crashed on take off right in front of me as I pulled up to the hold-short line." Turek remembers. "The instructor hadn't de-iced the wings, and when they got out of ground effect–bye bye birdie. 'Mishaps'–that's polite Navy talk for getting killed–happened on a routine basis. You just lived with it. You are on the edge all the time in carrier aviation. There is nothing on this earth that will scare the crap out of you more than night landing on an aircraft carrier—especially in foul weather. The pressure is intense. You train, you build up confidence, and believe me, you find out about yourself. Catholic Central and the Navy made me what I am today. I was lucky. I wish every young man could go through those experiences.

Following his discharge from the Navy, Turek went back to

school on his V.A. benefits and obtained his masters degree from the University of Michigan. The path to a comfortable future seemed clear for Turek. However, he chose not to accept the numerous job offers he received. For some reason, he felt he could do better on his own.

In 1978, Turek sold his home and used the $5000 profit to start his own business. He worked seven days a week trying to make his business work. Before long, he recalls, strange things began to happen to him. "I'd go to restaurants and glasses would explode right in front of me without me even touching them," he remembers. "Ink pens would blow up in my shirt pocket all the time. I never really believed in ESP or anything like that, but I do think that those things could have happened because of the energy I was letting off. I was a very intense young man."

Finally, the strain was too much. Six years later, after completing a demanding work week, Turek collapsed in a Los Angeles restaurant. He was rushed to USC Medical Center, where he spent the next week undergoing a complete battery of neurological tests. Thankfully, all the results were negative. But as he says, "God gave me a warning." The Professor of Neurology at USC sat down with Turek shortly before his discharge and told him he had to slow down and warned him to take better care of himself. "I realized that I was pushing the envelope and that I had to get things into perspective," he recalls. " I had to prioritize my life, or I might not be around to enjoy the fruits of my labors."

By 1992, Turek's one-man operation had grown into a full-fledged corporation spanning eight states with thirty-five offices nationwide. He had, by then, retired both his parents and donated tens of thousands of dollars to his high school alma mater. He gave money to many charities, especially anything to do with kids. Yet, despite all this, he still he felt something else remained to be done. Something outside his current realm of knowledge and understanding. There existed somewhere, one last challenge, and it was up to him to find it. "I knew I had something left to do, I just didn't know what," recalls Turek. "Then I met Johnnie Johnson and it all fell into place. The whole pattern of my life. Everything I'd done up to that point had prepared me for the great task at hand. No one else was gonna do it. No one else could do it. The entire history of rock and roll was built on a lie, a man's legacy had been denied him, and it was my job to help him find redemption. That was where I stood. And God help anyone who blocked my way because I would tear through them like crap through a goose."

* * *

It's six a.m. on Monday morning and George Turek is running. He's done three miles so far this day and he will do three more before he is through. The sweat pours off his body in rivulets, soaking his cotton T-shirt and drips onto the worn sable of the treadmill. He likes to think when he is running, he tells me. That's where he comes up with all his ideas and inspirations. "Either when I'm running or in the shower," he laughs. "That's when I do my brainstorming."

There is something eerie about being in a room with George Turek. Especially up close. You can almost feel the energy radiating from his body. All the stories about the pens and glasses exploding in his presence; his employees insist they are very true. Many, in fact, claim to have seen this phenomenon first-hand. "George literally exudes intensity," claims best friend and company president Patrick Cohan. "You can actually feel it walking by his office—especially when he's preoccupied with something. And the pens—yeah I've seen it happen. Many times. In fact, I don't ever let him borrow my shirts because they always come back with ink stains. I don't know if it is a good thing or not—all that energy. But the thing is, he can't help it, that's just him."

For his part, Turek is unphased by the odd happenings around him.

"I believe in four things," he says between breaths. "God, timing and location, and persistence. And I think all of those things have come into play in my relationship with Johnnie Johnson."

Morning has broken. The first rays of sunlight peek through the blinds, catching their shape and striping his face with a graceful radiance. Turek meets my eye and smiles.

"A lot of people have asked me how Johnnie and I got together. At various times I've said jokingly that it was Elvis who brought us together. At other times, I've said it was the love for my wife that brought us together. But if I were to pin it down—I'd say the real thing that brought us together was fate. I think God brought us together. He brought us together to make things right before Johnnie leaves this earth for the other side."

* * *

It began with a pilgrimage to Graceland. In June of 1992, Turek and his younger brother Howard, both Elvis fans, flew to Memphis along with Turek's fiancé Linda, Howard's wife Jodie, and their friends Dr. Paul and Rose Drouillard from Detroit.

The day promised to be a long one indeed. And nine hours later, after spending the afternoon sweating through long lines at Elvis Presley's refuge and final resting place, the six friends journeyed to Beale Street, hoping to relax and maybe catch some live music at one of the area's famous nightclubs. By eleven that evening, they'd visited two establishments, had dinner, and were just about to call it a night when Turek saw B.B. King's club and decided to check it out.

"As soon as I walked inside, the music just hit me," he recalls. "This guitarist, an older black man, was up there with his band playing good ol' Chicago Blues and everyone in the place was dancing. We ended up staying the whole rest of the evening and having a blast. In fact, Linda and I literally danced all night."

As it turned out, the show was a turning point. And although Turek did not know it at the time, his last minute compulsion to visit

B.B. King's would change his life forever.

"After the show we were going back to the Peabody Hotel where we were staying, and we started talking about how much we loved the music. That whole blues sound. Well, what happened was, Linda and I were planning a huge wedding celebration for the following year. So I thought it would be a great idea to hire the band we'd just seen to play our wedding. A great majority of the guests would be employees of the company, all of whom I consider family, and I wanted to share the great experience that we had in Memphis with the people who provide my livelihood. So I brought this up to Linda and she agreed. We decided right then and there to hire the band."

Immediately upon returning to Detroit, Turek asked his administrative assistant, Mary Bradley, to find the band he and Linda had seen at B.B. King's. After a few days of digging around, Bradley found out the name and booking information of the guitarist. His name was Jimmy Johnson. And not only was he a genuine Chicago bluesman—he was one of the best and most well respected.

Jimmy Johnson, born Jimmy Thompson in 1928, never reached the same level of national prominence as his fellow Chicagoans Son Seals and Buddy Guy. But his laid-back style and unconventional chord structures had made him a sellout attraction within the Windy City for decades and consequently, a huge draw in blues cities like New Orleans and Memphis. At the time Turek and party saw him in 1992, Johnson was in the middle of a comeback of sorts following the tragic deaths of his keyboardist and bassist in an Indiana car accident which had left him injured as well. When Bradley asked his manager if Johnson would be interested in the gig, his first response was, "Jimmy doesn't usually play weddings." But Bradley assured him that the wedding was not typical and that nearly a thousand people would be in attendance. She promised that Jimmy and the band would have a good time and that they would be well compensated for their efforts. A week later, Johnson agreed to perform.

"I was like, 'Yes! Yes! We got him!'" recalls Turek. "I figured if everything else went to hell, we'd still have a great band to keep everyone on the dance floor."

Meanwhile, Howard Turek had been so taken with Jimmy Johnson's performance that he went out and bought what he thought was Jimmy's CD. During a conversation the following week, he told his brother how much he enjoyed the CD and that he and Paul Drouillard listened to it almost everyday. "This guy is a great pianist, George," Howard Turek supposedly said. "You have got to hear this CD."

George Turek, hearing "pianist" instead of "guitarist" was quick to correct his younger sibling's mistake.

"I said, 'Hold it, Howard. The guy we heard is a guitarist. What CD do you have?' He says, 'Johnnie Johnson.' I said, 'No, Howard. It was Jimmy Johnson–not Johnnie Johnson. Jimmy Johnson is a guitarist from Chicago. But like a typical Turek he wouldn't give up. 'No George, I think it was Johnnie Johnson.' I said, 'Howard, I know for a fact that it was Jimmy Johnson because I had Mary call up to find out who the guy was and he's playing at Linda and I's wedding! 'Well, whatever,' he says, 'this CD is great.'

"So I figured that was it and we never talked about it again. Seven months go past and the wedding is in the final stages of preparation when a bomb is dropped. Jimmy Johnson had been given an opportunity to take his band to Europe for a summer tour and had called to cancel the wedding gig. Talk about last minute! I was pissed. But in the end, I understood the reasons behind it. There are no problems, only solutions. We decided that we would simply extend the time of the opening act—a twenty-two piece Glen Miller-type band called the Ambassadors—and leave it at that.

"Well, later in the day, I was driving home from work, and a thought struck me. I called up my brother from the car. When he answered I asked him, 'Howard, do you remember that Johnnie Johnson CD you were telling me about last summer?' He said,

'Yeah, I listen to it all the time. I said, 'Great. Bring it to work tomorrow—I want to hear it.'

"Well, the next morning he brings this Johnnie Johnson CD into my office and I put it on. I only had to listen to it one time. I got chills. *Johnnie B. Bad* was the album he'd bought, and when I heard the beginning of "Tanqueray," that was it for me. I walked outside of my office and I said, 'Mary, find this guy.' She gave me one of her looks like, 'Boss, you're nuts,' but as usual she tracked him down. We got a hold of Johnnie's booking agent in New York, Glen Knight, and he of course told Mary right off the bat what Jimmy Johnson's manager had told us—'Johnnie doesn't play weddings.' So once again, Mary had to go through the whole spiel and Knight told her he would get back to her in a couple of days. Well, to make a long story short, Johnnie, or I should say Glen Knight, eventually agreed to do our wedding and that is how it all started."

The following month, George and Linda flew out to Los Angeles for business. When it came time to return to Detroit, the two lovebirds decided on a whim to forego the usual plane ride in order to drive one of the company cars back across country to sightsee and enjoy a little time together. It was a Saturday evening while driving through St. Louis that George remembered about Johnnie Johnson.

"We'd just gotten into St. Louis and we're driving along and all of a sudden it hits me. I said to Linda, 'Doesn't Johnnie Johnson live here?' She said, 'Yeah. I think he does.' I said, 'Well, I got his phone number, let's see if he's playing anywhere in town tonight.' So, I call up his house and a woman answers. I said, 'Is this the Johnnie Johnson residence?' She said, 'Yes.' It was Frances, Johnnie's wife. So I told her my name was George Turek and that Johnnie was supposed to play at my wedding in July. 'Oh yeah,' she says, 'you're the couple that Johnnie's going to be playing for! Just hold on!' And then I hear her in the background calling for him, 'J.J.! J.J.! Come back here! Don't go nowhere! The young couple from Detroit is on the phone!' So a few seconds later this deep voice says, 'Hello.' I said, 'Hi, Johnnie this is George Turek, you're going to be playing at my wedding.' He said, 'Oh, yeah! How are you?' I said, 'Fine, Johnnie. Just fine. You won't believe this, but we're driving through St. Louis right now and I just decided to call you and see if we can get together.' So Johnnie kind of laughs and says, 'Well, believe it or not, I just got back from being on tour yesterday and I was just walking out the door to play at a club here in town called Blueberry Hill. Why don't you come out and see me? Where you at right now?' I told him we were coming up on such-and-such an exit. 'That's exactly the exit you need to take to get to Blueberry Hill. Just pull off right where you at and I'll get you the rest of the way there.'

"So Johnnie gives us directions and we meet up with him at the club. When we ask the doorman where he's going to be playing, he sends us—get this—to the Elvis room! Can you believe the coincidence? Anyway, we spent a wonderful evening with Johnnie and Frances and the band. The music was just unbelievable—Johnnie is even better live than on CD—and both he and Frances turned out to be such great people that we had an absolute blast. We laughed about how I came to find Johnnie, about what an unbelievable quirk of fate it was that my brother happened to pick up the wrong CD and that Johnnie just happened to be in town that night after touring all month. We also found out that Johnnie and Linda grew up just a few miles away from each other in West Virginia, and that he had been living in Detroit when I was born there as well. I know this sounds corny, but it was as if we had known each other all our lives.

"Now as usual, I couldn't make it through the night without embarrassing myself, although I wouldn't find out about my goof until much later. The subject of the wedding came up and well...I had this little request. See, Linda had been singing for years, not professionally, but for fun around the house and at the occasional piano bar, and I loved her singing so much that I told her I wouldn't marry her unless she sang three songs at our wedding. One of these songs I enjoyed hearing her sing was 'Back in the U.S.A.,' which as everyone knows is a Chuck Berry song.

"So we're all sitting there and I, having no clue who Johnnie is other than that he is a great blues player, ask him if he had ever heard of the song 'Back in the U.S.A.' Johnnie and Frances just kind of chuckled and Johnnie said, 'Sure I've heard of it.' I figured they were laughing because everyone had heard of the song. So I said, 'Well, do you think you could accompany Linda on the song? We could get you the sheet music if you need it.' Somehow he kept a straight face, although he told me later that he thought I was putting him on. Looking back I have to laugh–how was I supposed to know he'd helped write the damn thing? I thought he was a blues pianist! But that just goes to show how little notoriety Johnnie has gotten throughout his career. I grew up listening to those records and I had no idea who Johnnie was!"

The wedding was held on July 3, 1993, in a hanger at the Oakland, Michigan airport. Over 750 guests showed up for the event. And due to the size of the nuptial party, the Independence Day/WWII theme (guests dressed in 1940s costumes and the bride was flown to the altar in a vintage Billy Mitchell B-25 bomber), the quirky additions of an Elvis impersonator who claimed to be the illegitimate son of the King, and the fact Linda's wedding dress was the exact dress model Stephanie Seymour had donned in the Guns 'n' Roses video "November Rain," (Turek had bought the dress directly from the production company), CNN, ABC, CBS, and NBC broadcast clips from the event on all the local evening news programs. As Johnnie would say after it was all over, "That was one of the most incredible things I ever did see. I ain't never played a gig with an airplane sittin' on stage with me. The guys in the band had their cameras out filmin' it all. That nutted me up, man."

Later that evening, with the reception winding down and the guests watching fireworks exploding in the distance, Johnnie, who had rented a tuxedo for the occasion, approached the elated Turek alone and asked if he could talk to him.

"I said, 'Sure, Johnnie. Have a seat,' Turek remembers. "Then he asks me, 'Where does Linda sing?' I said, 'What?' He says, 'Where does Linda sing?' I said, 'In the shower.' 'She doesn't sing anywhere?' I said, 'No, Johnnie, she's not a professional.' He said, 'Well, that woman can sing and we need to get her in the studio.' 'You're kidding!' I said. 'No. She's got a great voice, and she should be singing professionally.' I almost fell out of my chair. After that, Johnnie got back up and went over to get some barbecue and I could see Linda surrounded by all these guests, so I knew she was busy. But I tell you I wanted to run over to her. 'Guess what! Guess what!' But I kept my cool. It was hard, though. I mean, I wanted to tell Linda so badly, but it just wasn't the time. It was very exciting. What an evening that was–the happiest of my life."

Johnson and Turek stayed in contact over the next few months, talking on the phone every couple weeks. And Turek remembers that during each conversation, Johnnie would remind his new friend that his wife should be singing professionally and that he would be glad to back her up in the studio. "I knew he was serious," recalls Turek. "He kept talking about it and so I decided that although I needed Linda in the company–she was running our Texas operation at the time–her dreams were more important to me. So I called Johnnie up and told him I was interested in getting Linda in the studio and when would be a good time. This was in the fall."

The following Christmas, Johnnie sent the Tureks an autographed copy of *That'll Work*. George immediately turned on the stereo and popped the CD in while he and Linda set to work decorating the tree. "Some people listen to 'White Christmas' and 'Jingle Bells' while they're putting up the Christmas Tree," laughs Turek. "I listen to Johnnie Johnson and the Kentucky Headhunters!"

Before long, Turek noticed his wife and her daughter Jessica dancing and singing along with the record. A feeling overcame him and he decided to give Linda her present a little early.

"I couldn't wait any longer," he recalls. "She was getting into the music so much and I'd been keeping the whole thing a secret so long. I just decided to tell her right then and there. I went upstairs while she was talking to the kids—Linda has two children, a son and a daughter—and got her the card I'd written. When I gave it to her she said, 'What is this?' I said, 'It's your first Christmas present. Open it.' She said, 'But it's not Christmas yet.' I said, 'Just open it, will ya!'

"So she opens it up and the kids are craning their necks trying to see what it says. Well she reads it once, reads it again, and then breaks down in tears. The card informed her that she was going to be heading up to St. Louis to record in a real studio with Johnnie Johnson and his band. She was thrilled. That was her dream. She'd never sung professionally before, and now she was going to make an actual CD with this great blues pianist and his band. Which was all we knew about Johnnie, you know? The guy never talks! I mean, I knew he played with Chuck Berry and Keith Richards, and Eric Clapton, but I figured those were just gigs. I had no idea.

"But anyway, Linda's just flying over the whole thing and I call Johnnie up right then and tell him how she reacted and he's laughing, so I put Linda on the phone and she's crying again, 'Thank you, Johnnie. Thank you so much for believing in me.' I mean, she's really happy. And let me tell ya, I was pretty excited for her, because I knew how she must have felt. I mean this was the real deal man."

But as time wore on and the summer recording date grew closer and closer, Linda's feelings of elation quickly grew into apprehension. Having never recorded with a band before–much less one of Johnnie's caliber–she found the whole prospect intimidating. "I'd never done anything like that before," she remembers. "And while I was really excited, I was scared to death at the same time."

Turek's solution was to purchase a small microphone setup in order that his wife would have a place to practice beforehand. Knowing nothing about music himself, Turek enlisted friend and employee, Howard Weinstein, a guitarist and former writer for

ROCK magazine, who had installed his own home recording studio in his basement years earlier. Through Weinstein's expertise and Turek's enthusiasm, the humble microphone setup grew into a full twenty-four track studio, and Weinstein soon found himself in over his head. He needed help installing and figuring out the system. That's when Harry Bartholomew came into the picture. "They called me out to teach them how to use the equipment almost four years ago—and I'm still running everything!" laughs Bartholomew.

"My mother, Molly Smyth, has been involved in the entertainment industry my whole life," he continues. "So my brother Gene and I grew up around the business, and as we got older we knew that's what we wanted to do. I sort of gravitated towards sound-engineering when I was in my teens working in theater and I just stayed with it—touring with *Phantom of the Opera*, doing live shows—mixing records at SugarHill Studios in Houston. I had no idea what I was getting into with the Tureks. When I heard about the job and pulled up to the house, I expected some overprivileged know-it-all who was going to try and tell me how to do my job. I'd run into that quite a bit on past jobs like this. But George wasn't like that at all. He brought me right in and offered me lunch and a cold drink and ever since then we have been close friends. Like I said, I had no idea what I was getting into, but let me tell you, it has been quite a ride these last few years."

Building the studio took time, and much to Linda's relief, the recording session was pushed back until the following summer.

In the early part of the year, Johnnie joined Buddy Guy in the studio to record *Slippin' In*, which would win the 1994 Grammy for Best Contemporary Blues Album. Afterwards, super-producer Eddie Kramer, who mixed the sessions along with Brian Sperber at Electric Lady and RPM Sound Studios, praised Johnnie, calling him "the best blues pianist I have ever worked with and a real pleasure to have around. I'd do anything for Johnnie Johnson."

December found him heading back into the studio, this time to record his next solo album, *Johnnie Be Back*. A year earlier, *Bluehand*

Johnnie had been rereleased on the Evidence label with two additional tracks, "Back In The U.S.A." and the live "Son's Dream" recorded with Tom Maloney, Gus Thornton, and Kenny Rice at the 1990 Missouri River Blues Festival, and Johnnie was drawing bigger and bigger crowds to his shows. For *Johnnie Be Back*, the piano legend would be using the group he had come to refer to as his "New York band": guitarist Jimmy Vivino, bassist Michael Merrit, and drummer James Wormworth. Both Vivino and Merrit worked a regular gig as members of the Max Weinberg Seven, providing music for NBC televison's *Late Night with Conan O'Brien*. As a solo artist, Vivino had also served as musical director for the film *Sister Act 2* with Whoopi Goldberg and was well-versed in a wide variety of blues, jazz, and R&B.

Johnnie first met Vivino when the guitarist backed him up during a gig in 1990—a gig that Vivino mentions in an interview with *Blues Review* magazine, as the turning point in his musical career.

"Before that I hadn't played with any real cats," he admits. "With a guy like Johnnie Johnson, you'll learn in one night where it's at. It was an amazing feeling playing with that great groove of his, like I hadn't felt before. I won't say I wasted all those years, but I wish it had hit me when I was fifteen years old."

Johnnie Be Back was recorded over the span of three days in three different studios—Clinton Recording Studios, the Magic Shop and Sear Sound—all in New York City. Special guests Phoebe Snow, Al Kooper (on whose albums *Soul Of A Man* and *Rekooperation* Johnnie had played during the course of the year), John Sebastian, Buddy Guy, Steve Jordan, Jimmy Vivino's brother, the great sax man Jerry Vivino, and Vivino and Merrit's *Late Night* bandleader, drummer Max Weinberg, all made appearances. Johnson co-wrote two of the albums twelve tracks—the instrumental "Johnnie & John" and the semi-autobiographical "Goin' Fishin'," which he wrote with Jimmy Vivino. As per his contract with Musicmasters, who released the album, Johnnie would sing the majority of the songs, providing for seven of the album's eleven vocal tracks with Phoebe Snow and

Jimmy Vivino adding two each to fill out the CD. Vivino produced the album, and it came out sounding tight and professional. *Johnnie Be Back* would become Johnson's most well-known recording, if not his best, and the opening track, a reworking of James Van Buren's "Real Good Woman" became his standard opener for live gigs. "The way it starts, it just makes a good introduction, gives you time to warm up," Johnnie says. "I like the feel of it."

In the next year, he would receive countless introductions, not just on the stage, but on televison as well. Due in large part to the fact that a majority of Conan O'Brien's band found their way on to his album, Johnnie began appearing on the show periodically to perform songs from *Johnnie Be Back*. "Conan is wonderful," says Johnson of the late-night host. "He really makes you feel welcome."

The year of 1994 was extremely busy for Johnnie, and he was loaded with additional recordings and live performances. But despite his schedule, he still found time to talk to George Turek every now and then. He also remembered George's wife Linda, and the fact that he wished to get her in the studio to record.

"During the time I first met George, I was pretty busy with tourin' and workin' with different folks," he recalls. "But I was serious about Linda comin' to record with me. She had talent, and I knew if I got her feelin' comfortable enough, we could even make a record."

Turek's answer to the comfort issue was to bring Johnnie down to Houston so that he could work with Linda in their own studio. "We had the same studio setup that Willie Nelson had in his house, and we had one of the best sound engineers in Texas, Harry Bartholomew, running the mixing console. So I knew we could at least get something usable down on tape and get Linda relaxed. All we needed from that point on was a band, and that's where Harry came in."

Through Bartholomew, Turek met Texas guitar legend Bert Wills, a contemporary of both Jimmie Vaughan and ZZTop's Billy

Gibbons. Somehow despite his incredible talent and a Grammy-nominated album, *Mr. Politician*, Wills had never become a household name. Bartholomew suggested that Turek hire Wills and his band to back Linda and Johnnie in the studio. After hearing Wills play live at a Houston club called Billy Blues, an enthused Turek agreed and arrangements were made to have Wills and his band provide the music. All Turek had to do next was bring Johnson down to Houston.

"I called Johnnie at his home in St. Louis in early April of 1995 and asked him whether or not he would consider coming down and working with Linda and a band at our home for a long weekend. He thought it was a great idea and thought it would be a lot of fun. I told him that we couldn't wait to see him again. That's when he said that if we wanted to see him, he was going to be playing with Chuck Berry at the New Orleans Jazz Festival during the last week in April, and if we would be interested in flying over for the day, we would be backstage guests of his, and we could meet Chuck Berry. This was the very first time I learned that he had any relationship with Chuck other than just a few gigs. I asked him, 'Johnnie, how do you know Chuck Berry?' He chuckled and said, 'He and I have been makin' music together for forty years.' Well, it goes without saying that I was excited to see them play together."

On April 30, 1995, Turek and his family flew down to New Orleans for the annual Heritage Fair Jazz Festival. They met Johnnie backstage and he promptly introduced them to his agent, Glen Knight, and an assortment of other musicians, including boogie-pianist Mitch Woods, who had also come to visit the legend. They were in the midst of chatting with Woods when a silver Cadillac rolled to a stop on the back lawn and a tall, thin black man in a white shirt, tan slacks, bolo tie and sunglasses stepped out and began making his way towards the trailers. Chuck Berry had arrived.

"I watched Chuck walk right past all these people who were trying to get his attention and go right up to Johnnie and throw his arms around him," recalls Turek. "At that time I had no idea of

Chuck's temperament, so I didn't understand how special and unique this show of affection was. Chuck said something to Johnnie and they laughed and then Johnnie introduced us. Chuck gave a short hello without really looking at us and rushed off to his trailer. He seemed to be in a better mood after talking to Johnnie and he actually stopped to take a couple pictures—one with our new friend Mitch Woods, before he disappeared around back. That was my introduction to Chuck Berry."

At show time, Knight led Turek's group up onto the stage, just outside the view of the crowd and right behind Johnson's piano. For Turek, it was the thrill of a lifetime and quite a surprise as well.

"There must have been a good ten thousand people in the audience sitting there waiting for Chuck Berry," he remembers. "And then the announcer comes on and introduces him—just him—and he walks out with Johnnie behind him. The crowd goes crazy and Chuck has changed his clothes—he's got this outfit—red pants, red Hawaiian shirt, and he's carrying his guitar and Johnnie's right behind him in a sweatshirt and jeans with a black George Thorogood & the Destroyers baseball hat, looking like any old guy on the street.

"So imagine my surprise when Johnnie starts playing this amazing rock and roll piano. And it's that sound. Anybody who grew up in my generation, back when rock and roll first came out, would know what I mean. It was that sound–that piano. I realized then that it was Johnnie I had been hearing on all those records. And my jaw is just hitting my knees because I'd only heard him play blues and I had no idea, you know. The guy never talks! Besides, I didn't know anything about music. I can remember the dates when certain albums came out like *Sergeant Pepper's Lonely Hearts Club Band* or the Beach Boys's *Pet Sounds*. But I don't play any instruments or anything and I never really got into rock and roll trivia, so I was completely ignorant. I knew who Chuck Berry was—who doesn't? But I didn't know of the relationship between him and Johnnie.

"Well anyway, my stepson, the rock and roll buff is sitting beside me and he's about to have a coronary he's so excited, and he's telling me, 'This is the man. This is rock and roll! These two guys made rock and roll!' So then it started to dawn on me what I was seeing. History. And through it all, Berry was deferring to Johnnie. Johnnie would be taking a solo and Chuck would come over to the piano and just lean on it and watch him play with this look of respect, you know, like he was paying homage to him. I'll never forget the end of the show when Chuck and Johnnie stood arm in arm, bowing to the audience while all these people screamed for more. It was great.

"After that, I was hooked. One of my good friends, Marvin Brown, who used to be lead singer in a band that opened for the group War some years ago, sent me a clip from a movie that had Johnnie and Eric Clapton and Keith Richards and Chuck Berry, but he didn't tell me what it was, and it was just a clip. So I started showing people the clip and asking them if they knew anything about it, but no one did and I couldn't get a hold of Marvin. Well, luckily my stepson came home from school around that time and he took one look at it and said, 'Oh yeah, that's from *Hail! Hail! Rock 'n' Roll*. It's a documentary about Chuck Berry.' I said, 'Where can you find it?' He said, 'Blockbuster.' I said, 'Go get it.'

"So off he went, and he brings it back and I'm on the Stairmaster watching this movie when all of a sudden I hear Keith Richards say that Johnnie Johnson, the old blues pianist I had known for two years, gave Chuck Berry his music, and that without Johnnie those great songs would have been 'just a bunch of words on paper.' I got off the Stairmaster. Then the interviewer starts talking to Johnnie and I can't believe it's the same guy—he just looked terrible, like he'd been drinking—and the guy asks him if it was true that he had written the music. Well the first thing Johnnie says is no he didn't write the music—but then he spends the next couple minutes explaining what he did do and that explanation sounded a hell of a lot like he did help write the music. It was like a lightning bolt. That day the lid to the Pandora's box was blown off its hinges. I started turning over rocks left and right. I asked my stepson what he knew, which was basically the same thing I was getting from the movie—Johnnie had a lot to do with writing that music. Finally, I said, 'Screw it, I'm going to the horse's mouth. I'm calling Johnnie right now.'

"So I called him up right then and there–forget the workout—and asked him point blank: 'Johnnie did you write those songs with Chuck?' And he said, 'I didn't write them—I just made up the music for them.' 'What do you mean?' I asked him. He said, 'Chuck wrote the lyrics and I gave him a lot of the music that he put behind those lyrics to make the song.' I said, 'Johnnie that is writing music!' He said, 'No it ain't–that's makin' up music. Writin' music is when you write down what you're doing and I don't know how to write down notes or nothin'. So finally this was making sense. I said, 'Which ones did you do?' And he starts giving me this list of songs—rock and roll classics, man! I said, 'Jesus, Johnnie! Did you do all of them?' He said, 'Just about.' I said, 'Well which ones didn't you do?' He said, 'Johnny B. Goode.' I said, 'Why not?' He said, 'Because Chuck wrote it as a surprise for me.' Then it dawned on me. I put the phone down for a minute to catch my breath, 'Oh, my God.' Then I all but yelled into the phone, 'You're Johnny B. Goode? Holy cow, Johnnie! Why didn't you tell me...let me guess...I didn't ask, right?' He kind of chuckled. I couldn't believe it. Here I had known this man for two years, and he was *the* Johnny B. Goode! Unbelievable!"

In June of 1995, Johnnie Johnson came to Houston and began working with Linda Turek on overcoming her studio-fright. Sitting behind the piano with Linda by his side, Johnnie became the quiet schoolmaster, leading by example with encouragement and the occasional correction. "He made me feel very at ease," recalls Linda of singing with Johnson. "He helped me get a feel for the music, to put the right inflections in the right places, and most of all to have confidence in myself. I made a lot of mistakes in front of Johnnie, but he never made me feel foolish. He would just say, 'That's all right. I make mistakes, too.' He was just so very kind and patient."

After a day of Linda and Johnnie getting used to each other, Turek brought the band in to rehearse. Self-conscious at first, Linda began to relax as the day wore on. She was especially hesitant when the band arrived but she soon realized that Bert Wills was every bit as patient and kind as Johnnie Johnson.

"Bert reminded me so much of my family in West Virginia—we could have been cousins," she marvels. "He and Johnnie and I were sitting around talking, making references to things that nobody else in the room really understood. Things you would only know about if you had lived in the country. Bert really throws you off at first because he comes in with this beard and sunglasses and leather jacket, like a biker—which he is—but he doesn't have a mean bone in his body and he knows so many songs. Songs my grandmother used to sing. We had a great time. If you ask me, you couldn't have two better teachers than Bert Wills and Johnnie Johnson."

Turek wasn't the only one impressed with Wills. During his long career, Johnnie Johnson had jammed with some of the best guitarists in the world—Albert King, Eric Clapton, Buddy Guy, Matt "Guitar" Murphy. In his eyes, Bert Wills was as good as any of them–perhaps even better. "Bert Wills comes the closest to T-Bone Walker as anyone I've ever played with, " he says frankly. "I couldn't believe how good that man was when I first played with him. Just goes to show you that the best aren't always the ones who are famous. Whatever you want played, Bert can play it, and on top of that he's got his own style. He might be able to play like T-Bone Walker or Albert King, but when you hear him you still know it's Bert Wills. That's what I always tried to do with my playin'. Bert and I understand each other just like me and Tom Maloney do. How Chuck and I do. I know where he's comin' from and he knows where I'm comin' from."

Following the succesful first sessions, Linda began sitting in with Johnson and his band all over the country in places as diverse as

Boston and Chicago and at B.B. King's blues club in Memphis. Finally, tired of traveling around the country to catch up with his famous friend, Turek proposed a show in Houston. "And so began my short foray into promotion," he laughs. "Once was all it took. I'll never do it again."

On September 1, 1995, with an army of his own employees and friends, Turek took over the Satellite Lounge in Houston, billing the show "Under a Houston Blue Moon" and teaming Johnnie Johnson and Bert Wills together for the first time on a live stage. Recalls Turek, "I had my secretary and the kids outside selling T-shirts, I had my wife on stage singing, and I had a bunch of other employees and friends in the audience. The whole thing was like an office party."

A profitable office party. Despite the disadvantage of having Bobby "Blue" Bland playing right next door at Rockefeller's, Turek was able to attract enough people to turn a profit—which he promptly turned over to Johnson and the band. "I didn't need any money. I got to have all the fun," laughs Turek. "It was bad enough that Johnnie was working for door money. The happiest day of my life will be when I can't afford to hire Johnnie. That's what he deserves. So I gave it all to Johnnie, and I gave him and the guys a bonus as well."

Following the Satellite show, the band traveled to New Orleans for a gig at the House of Blues. While the show came off without a hitch, the problems beforehand were enough to convince Turek that booking and managing musicians was not his bag.

"We'd played B.B. King's in Memphis and they hadn't given us any trouble about recording the show," remembers Turek. "I'd been told that it wouldn't be a problem in New Orleans. So I brought Harry to record and another guy named Chris Laurel to film it. Next thing I know, I've got this psycho sound guy named Scooter or something, screaming at me because I insisted on talking to his manager. Meanwhile one of our group is being held back by our sound engineer because he's going to clock the guy for getting in my face. It was ridiculous. On top of that, they almost didn't let the kids in to see their mom sing because they were under age. Everyone was so pissed off and agitated that I'm surprised the show went as well as it did. I decided right then and there that I was through trying to play booking agent. Too many nuts to deal with out there."

Despite his intentions, Turek would continue to become more and more involved, as would his family and close friends, in the life and career of Johnnie Johnson. Before long, the pianist's redemption became his cause—a mission that took on all the more relevance to him based on the events of a single evening following the New Orleans show.

"It was the evening after we'd gotten back from New Orleans and Johnnie was staying over an extra night. While we were gone, Paul Bradley, Mary's husband, who also works with us, had set up his VCR to record the opening ceremony for the Rock and Roll Hall of Fame which had been broadcast the night before. We were having a late dinner, the night after we got back, Harry, Johnnie, Linda and I, and the kids. There wasn't much going on conversation-wise. We were all pretty worn out from traveling. So Harry suggested that we watch the tape Paul had left at the house.

"Anyway, so we're all sitting there watching the opening ceremonies, and the helicopter flies over the stadium in Cleveland, and there's all the screaming fans. Then the camera pans the crowd and comes to a stop right on this huge stage and who should be there but Chuck Berry. 'Look Johnnie,' I said. 'There's your buddy, Chuck.' Johnnie just smiled. Chuck was there to commence the festivities and open the show which would begin the ceremonies for the inauguration of the Rock and Roll Hall of Fame. As it's first inductee, Chuck was going to kick off the show. And what did he play? That's right. 'Johnny B. Goode' the song he had written for his partner.

"I think it all kind of hit us at the same time. Where was the guy he had written this tribute for? His partner and musical collaborator for all those years? Not on stage with Chuck and Bruce Springsteen, who was backing him up. Not behind the piano where he belonged. He wasn't going in the Rock and Roll Hall of Fame. Johnnie Johnson was sitting at our dining room table. He was sitting there with his head bowed, unable to look at the television screen. We all became very uncomfortable as we realized the situation. We were all quiet. And when I say quiet–I mean nobody even breathed. It was really very, very awkward. My wife left the table and went to the bathroom—she told me later it was because she didn't want to cry in front of Johnnie. My heart hurt for him. His eyes never left his plate the whole time Chuck was singing, 'Go Johnnie Go!' Finally Harry made up some excuse and got up to turn the damn thing off. But the damage was done. It was like a black cloud had settled over the table and things were pretty much low key for the rest of the dinner. I'd made up my mind, though.

"Later that night when Johnnie had gone upstairs to bed, we all sat back down and talked about what had happened. We all agreed that Johnnie had been cheated out of his place in history. We decided from that day forward that we would all be committed to helping Johnnie get the recognition he deserves for the monumental contributions he made to music. None of us were extremely religious by any means. But we decided as a group–as a family— that God had given us an opportunity to help a wonderful man who had given us all so much and received almost nothing in return. There have been so few deserving martyrs in history. I knew right then and there that something had to be done. That this wrong had to be righted. It was time, I told them, to get involved."

XIV

THROWING STONES

"If I'm in the Hall of Fame and he's not, there is something wrong there."

—Bob Weir

It was mid-September, 1995, when George Turek began assembling the group of people affectionately known as "Team Johnnie." Besides his family, Harry Bartholomew and Mary Bradley, Turek organized and funded a squad of attorneys, financial officers, secretaries, and artists, to back Johnson. He proposed several endeavors meant to rectify what he saw as very significant historical injustices—the first and foremost being Johnnie Johnson's induction into the Rock and Roll Hall of Fame.

"I wrote Suzan Evans from the Rock and Roll Hall of Fame Foundation shortly after I decided to take up Johnnie's cause and naturally she never wrote me back," recalls Turek. "So then we started calling the office, Mary Bradley and I, and all we ever got from them was a bunch of double talk. They wouldn't tell us the rules or qualifications—it was all this top-secret bullshit.

"So after a couple of these useless calls, the head of our legal department, Bob Toohey, came up with the brilliant idea of forming the Johnnie Johnson Nominating Committee made up of Johnnie's friends in the music industry. After meeting with everyone, we came up with a letter format and a list of names, most of whom were already in the Hall of Fame, and began searching them out and asking them to support Johnnie."

Turek was loaded with responsibility, trying to organize Johnnie's committee while running his company at the same time. He was also feeling the pressure from another source, Johnson's wife Frances, who was completely fed up with booking agent Glen Knight. She insisted that Johnnie had reached a plateau with Knight and that it was time to move on. But despite it all, Johnnie remained fiercely loyal to Knight and would not listen to his wife's pleas. Frances hoped that as Johnnie respected his opinions more than anyone's, Turek could convince her husband to sign with another agent.

"Glen had Johnnie so brainwashed that he thought he worked for Glen instead of Glen working for Johnnie!" recalls Frances. "I couldn't say nothing to Johnnie about Glen. Johnnie is a loyal person—that man's been going to the same barber since 1952! And that's good in some ways, but you can look at Johnnie's life and see that he's been crazy loyal to people who keep ripping him off. All you had to do was fill Johnnie with drinks and he'd smile at you while you stole the shirt off his back. Now I don't know if Glen was doing anything way out of line, but I know Johnnie was coming home from these gigs and after he paid the band he didn't have no money left for himself. So I called Glen and he kept giving me the same thing about "selling Johnnie" and "that's the way we do things." He didn't like me asking questions.

That was the first strike.

"The second strike came when Johnnie played the *Vicky Lawrence Show* and they mailed us a letter that said they were holding Johnnie's check. There is this union called AFTRA that takes care of performers when they go on television—makes sure they get paid right and all that. Well, Glen had to call all the way to California to find out what it was! He was supposed to be Johnnie's agent and he didn't know about that stuff? I started thinking that maybe he had never had someone under his management that had made it to the level Johnnie was getting to. I gave Glen the benefit of the doubt and figured that maybe Johnnie had grown past him and that Glen was doing his best to rise to that next level.

"Then Richard Young from the Kentucky Headhunters calls me up directly and tells me that Johnnie doesn't know anything about royalties and that he has never been a member of ASCAP or BMI. Richard said that this was unheard of. Glen was supposed to be in the entertainment business. Johnnie hired him to look after his best interests as far as the music business, and the man hadn't even told him about the most basic part of being a musician. Johnnie had already made four albums and he had no idea that royalties even existed! Here we thought he got paid for an album and that was it. We had no idea!

"The third and final strike—-the last straw—-was when he started playing one against the other. He'd tell me one thing on the phone and then he'd get on and tell Johnnie something completely different. When I brought this up to Johnnie he wouldn't believe me at first—-that loyalty thing, you know? But then I started taping the conversations and that's when he finally heard what was going on. But by then we'd had all kinds of fights about it. So I told Glen that I wasn't gonna stand for no one causing these kinds of problems in my house. It told him that if he was thinking about playing one against the other it wasn't gonna work 'cause I was gonna beat Johnnie's brains out if he didn't back me up. Me and Glen, we didn't like each other from then on out."

Following the argument, Frances claims that Knight attempted to sabotage Johnnie by canceling his annual Australia tour. "Neil Mumme, the fella who promoted Johnnie in Australia called me at the house and said that Glen was going to cancel Johnnie's trip to Australia. Johnnie had been going to Australia for three years, and he absolutely loves it down there. The man looks forward to going, and Glen is gonna mess that up for him out of spite—-spite towards me. When Neil asked him what he was going to tell Johnnie, Glen told him he was going to blame it on him! That's why Neil called, 'cause he was steamed about the whole thing and he didn't want Johnnie blaming him. I tell you, I was ready to kill that man."

Finally, after months of cajoling by Frances, George Turek decided to help Johnnie find a new booking agent.

"I was concerned about getting involved with Johnnie's career on the business end because I knew nothing about the music business," he recalls. "But every time I talked to Frances, she went on about Glen Knight and how bad he was for Johnnie. Now I didn't know anything about artist booking or managing or anything like that but I figured that if Frances was that adamant about finding a new agent for Johnnie, I would help her. So I asked her what kind of contract Johnnie had signed and she tells me that Johnnie hadn't signed anything! I said, 'What's the problem? If he doesn't have a contract, then leave.' It didn't make any sense."

But unbeknownst to Frances, Johnnie had signed a contract—Knight faxed Frances a copy of the agreement. It was a single page declaring Knight to be Johnnie Johnson's manager and agent and there on the bottom line was her husband's signature.

"Johnnie swore up and down that he hadn't signed anything with Glen Knight and then here comes this contract with Johnnie's signature on it. And see, Johnnie wasn't lying—-he honestly thought he hadn't signed anything. The reason was 'cause he'd been in one of his damn drunken stupors. I said, 'Johnnie, you were drunk when you signed this. I told you not to do business while you was drinking.' And I had so many times. Glen was one of the people I called and told not to let Johnnie drink, which was sad because here was this woman calling all over the country telling people not to let this grown man drink. But I had to for this very reason—Johnnie would sign away his soul to the devil if the devil got him drunk enough. He just wanted to make everyone happy when he was drinking and that was what did him in."

In December, Johnnie flew to Chicago to play on former Chess stablemate Bo Diddley's *A Man Amongst Men* album. Margo Lewis, Diddley's manager, had been interested in Johnnie for years and had approached him several times about becoming his agent. Each time the pianist had refused out of loyalty to Glen Knight. But with pressure mounting at home, Johnson finally relented during the recording session and gave Turek's phone number to Lewis. At that moment, George Turek unknowingly became Johnnie Johnson's personal "consigliore".

Says Johnnie, "I knew I could trust George with business-type deals, and everyone was tellin' me I needed a new agent. I knew Margo pretty well and I knew she was a nice lady, so I decided to go ahead and have her call George. He knew what he was doin'. If he liked her, I was gonna join up with her."

Frances was pleased.

"Johnnie wouldn't listen to me, but he would listen to George," she says. "He trusted George. All of us did. As you can tell, I don't trust that many people. But there was something about George, in the way that he related to me, that made me feel relaxed, and I never doubted him. Maybe it was the excitement in his voice when he'd find out something new about Johnnie—I don't know. It was like a sixth sense telling me that this man was good. George is a Godsend person, which makes me nervous sometimes because God don't usually let people like that stay around with us down here on earth for too long. But because he is a Godsend person, I knew he would never lead us astray."

Through Lewis, Turek secured the services of entertainment attorney John Rosenberg, who helped Johnson sever the ties with Knight and retain Lewis. By January, Johnson had joined Lewis's stable of entertainers which included, among others Bo Diddley and soul legend Wilson Pickett, and for the first time, he began making money. "He did better that first year with Margo than in all his years as a musician combined," says Frances. "It was definitely the right decision."

Throughout the course of the management upheaval, Turek continued to press the Rock and Roll Hall of Fame with little success. "I finally got them to tell me when they would be meeting to vote," he remembers. "They told me it would be sometime in July or August."

Meanwhile, Turek had secured a list of fourteen stars including Keith Richards, Rod Stewart, Eric Clapton, John Lee Hooker, Dick Clark, and Little Richard, to sign a petition for Johnson's induction. By all accounts, shipping the petition around the world was a perilous undertaking and George remembers sweating each time the original copy left his hands.

"You know in *The Blues Brothers* when Dan Ackroyd's character Elwood Blues is completely convinced that everything will work out because he is on a 'mission from God.' That's how I was with that letter. I should have taken it personally to every musician—instead I just sent it in the mail trusting that it wouldn't get lost. And it didn't. Everyone signed it that we asked—except for B.B. King and Bonnie Raitt. We know that they both would have signed it in a second—we couldn't get past their managers. Bonnie loves Johnnie. I know that for a fact. Other than that, with the exception of a couple scares, we got the original letter back with all fourteen signatures. Its one of a kind! Nothing like that had ever been done before for any candidate. I figured that there wasn't any way in hell that the Rock and Roll Hall of Fame could possibly deny such a petition."

But deny they did. Turek was outraged. "They had told me July or August, right? Well, I called in May just to be sure. To check up on whether or not they had an exact date. And do you know what they told me? 'We've already voted on the nominees—we decided to do it early this year!' I hit the roof. 'But you told me July or August.' 'Sorry Mr. Turek, things change.' Boy, was I pissed off. So of course Johnnie wasn't even on the ballot and therefore couldn't be voted in. We got snookered on our first try!"

Yet things were not all bad for Johnnie Johnson. Despite the misfortune with the Rock and Roll Hall of Fame, his career was once again about to take a turn for the better. During the time Turek was preparing his nomination letter, Johnson called from Marin County, California with a very strange announcement.

"I was in my office when Jackie, my administrative assistant, tells me that Johnnie is on the phone," recalls Turek. So, I say, 'Johnnie, how are you?' He says, 'Great George. I'm out here playing with a bunch of dead guys. They want me to join their band.' I said, 'Whoa. Hold on a second. Dead guys?' He said, 'Yeah, the Dead Guys.' Okay. Then he says, 'Well, we're about to start rehearsing again. Just calling to say hi!' You know the usual stuff. Meanwhile, I'm thinking who in the hell are the Dead Guys? So I call up Chris Tuthill, who is Margo's assistant, and he tells me that Johnnie is playing with a group called RatDog. I said, 'Well, where is he getting the Dead Guys from?' He just kind of laughed and said, 'RatDog is Bob Weir's band. The guitarist from the Grateful Dead.' Johnnie had absolutely no idea who they were."

Long before they became the cultural phenomenon known as The Grateful Dead, Weir, lead guitarist Jerry Garcia, drummer Bill Kreutzmann, bassist Phil Lesh, and organist Ron "Pigpen" McKernan were the Warlocks, an R&B band covering the Rolling Stones and Chess Records artists around San Francisco's Bay Area. Bob Weir was only eighteen when elder member Jerry Garcia, five years his senior, renamed the band the Grateful Dead, after seeing the name in the Oxford English Dictionary.

In December of 1965, deeply immersed in the Haight-Ashbury hippy culture, the band members began experimenting with the still-legal hallucinogen LSD, taking part in a number of author Ken Kesey's "Acid Tests." The band's experiences at these "tests" would serve to shape the future of their music. Leaving the R&B covers behind, the Grateful Dead began developing a new sound for a new audience—the flourishing drug culture of sixties youth. Using a customized PA system designed by financial benefactor Owen Stanley, a chemist and wholesale manufacturer of LSD, and with an intense amplified conglomeration of country, bluegrass, rhythm and blues, and rock and roll bursting forth from the stacks of speakers, the Grateful Dead became the heroes of the new subculture sprouting in the communal atmosphere of the Haight-Ashbury area in San Francisco: the flower children.

Soon the Grateful Dead had grown so popular as to have their own legion of fans—a veritable tribe of VW nomads know as Deadheads, who spent months at a time following the band from show to show in a communal caravan. Remaining true to their generous principals, the band would perform several free concerts and always allow for concertgoers to record their performances, going so far as to provide a section in every arena for the "tapers."

"They're acting out their version of how much freedom there is in America to go for a wild ride," said Jerry Garcia of the loyal Deadheads in a *Musician* magazine interview. "What's left is, well, you can follow the Grateful Dead on the road. You can't be locked up for that, yet. So it's an adventure. And an adventure, as part of the American experience, is essential."

By 1989, the Grateful Dead had become the twenty-ninth highest-grossing entertainment act in the world pulling in $12.5 million dollars annually. During the nineties, this number would rise to over $50 million. Thirty years after they first began laying down their own particular brand of laid-back rock and roll, a new generation of fans had embraced them just as their parents had before. An amazed and appreciative Garcia would quip in *Rolling Stone* magazine, "What do they find fascinating about these middle-aged bastards playing basically the same thing we've always played?"

The answer in part, was Jerry himself. Always beloved for his cuddly demeanor and self-effacing humor, Garcia was the focal point of the band. When he died suddenly of a heart attack in August of 1995, the Dead and their fans were shattered. Four months later, the remaining members of the band would meet and decide to dissolve the group permanently. Bob Weir could not believe it was over.

As the little brother of the band, the babyfaced Weir had worked hard to earn his respect slowly and gradually over time. At one point during the early years, the group's sound engineer was so disrespectful of him as to turn Weir's guitar down to such a level that it was barely audible. "I was definitely low man on the totem pole," Weir told *Rolling Stone*, "especially at the beginning. And for a long time, I just had to shut up and take it."

Eventually, Weir would find his own voice and secure his place as an invaluable member of the group. In the seventies he had branched off into two different side projects—Kingfish and Bobby & the Midnights—and with various members of the Dead coming and going, became the unofficial second in command to Garcia in the band's pecking order.

Now with Garcia gone and the Grateful Dead no more, Weir began to explore the idea of starting a new band. In 1992 he had played a few dates at the Orpheum Theatre in Minneapolis, Minnesota, with former Lou Reed and Ricky Lee Jones bassist Rob Wasserman. The shows had gone well and in 1996, Weir decided to contact Wasserman about putting an R&B band together.

The result was RatDog, an eclectic conglomeration of musicians spanning three generations. First Weir recruited harpist Matthew Kelly whom he had played with in Kingfish. Then Wasserman introduced drummer Jay Lane, a Generation X'er, and a founding member of the groups Primus and Sausage. Finally, both men decided that Johnnie Johnson, although twenty-five years their senior, would be a perfect addition to the group being not only the father of rock and roll piano, but arguably the best blues pianist in the world as well. Johnnie remembers the phone call that sent him out to Marin County.

"Bob and them got a hold of me through Margo, and I went out to California to rehearse with the band. We had a great time, and they really set me up nice. I stayed in this place that was like a mini-apartment, and every day they came and picked me up and took me out to Bob's place, which was just beautiful, with all the trees around, and we'd rehearse out there in his little studio, playin' the blues."

Blues in general was what Weir had hoped to play with RatDog, along with a smattering of songs from his solo career. He considered the performance of Grateful Dead tunes as "living in the past" and he was primed to move on and explore roots rhythm and blues. The first Furthur Festival or "Deadapalooza" as it became known to fans, debuted in the summer of 1996. As the headliners, RatDog topped a list of talented acts including Los Lobos, Bruce Hornsby, and former Dead drummer Mickey Hart's Mystery Box. Dead fans poured out in droves to see their beloved Weir and Hart jamming with their new bands. For Johnnie, the tour was an enlightening and enjoyable experience.

"People just went crazy over Bobby," he remembers. "He'd walk out on stage and they'd start screamin' and hollerin'. Didn't matter where we went. We had a great time. They had a tour bus you wouldn't believe with a TV in every bunk, just like a house on wheels, and everyone was real nice. I'd play some of my songs durin' the show like 'Tanqueray' and 'Goin' Fishin' and people seemed to really enjoy it."

Indeed, although few fans recognized Johnnie Johnson as one of the founding fathers of rock and roll, he was nonetheless welcomed into the fold by the kindhearted Dead fans, who cheered him wildly every time he took the stage and complimented him with regularity on the Grateful Dead web sites.

These web sites were filling up with comments–but not the kind

Weir had hoped for. More common than the raves about Johnnie Johnson, in fact, more common than anything else, were the requests for more Grateful Dead material. The appeals were understandable. Garcia had been gone less than a year and he was still missed terribly. And while the Deadheads understood Weir's desire to explore other types of music, they could not be satisfied. Before long, promoters began to call for the Dead songs as well. Obstinate at first, Weir eventually came to terms with the fact that he "wasn't yet able to give some of the material up." By Spring, he was performing Dead songs on stage again.

Bob Weir's decision to revisit the Grateful Dead catalogue marked the beginning of the end for Johnnie Johnson's tenure in RatDog. For despite Weir's best attempts, which included buying Johnnie a transcribed piano so that he could play every key in C, and bringing in former Jefferson Starship and Hot Tuna bassist/keyboardist Pete Sears to work with him, the old pianist was falling short learning the Dead standards. Frances Johnson recalls her husband's frustrations.

"It wasn't that Johnnie couldn't learn those songs—he wouldn't learn them. They were a different style from what Johnnie liked to play and he didn't want to put in the time to learn them. Bob was very patient with him, but it got to where they decided that Johnnie would just leave the stage when they started playing Grateful Dead stuff."

By the spring of the following year, RatDog had hired another pianist, Jeff Chimenti, to play along with Johnnie on tunes such as "Throwing Stones," "Truckin'" and various other Bob Weir/Grateful Dead songs. Johnnie continued to play the blues and R&B. But with the second Furthur tour fast approaching, it soon became painfully obvious that Johnnie was no longer needed in the group, and Weir was forced to let him go. Tom Maloney spoke to Weir about his decison.

"He said part of the reason was that Johnnie didn't play the Dead songs which the public was really putting the pressure on to play.

But he said that wasn't as much a factor as was Johnnie's health. He said that he worried about Johnnie on such a strenuous tour at his age and that he'd had difficulties climbing in the bunks on the tour bus and things. But they still paid Johnnie, even when he wasn't playing, and they still brought him up to play as a special guest. Bobby is a smart guy; he knows that Johnnie is still the best when it comes to rock and roll and blues-type stuff. But the Dead stuff was different, you know, and Johnnie just didn't have the feel for it. Bob still thinks Johnnie is just the greatest and is really gung-ho about getting him in the Rock and Roll Hall of Fame. He also wants to do a blues album with him."

In the meantime, Weir was finally forced to put RatDog on the shelf temporarily in favor of rejoining former bandmates Mickey Hart and Phil Lesh for the 1998 Furthur Festival tour. Calling themselves the Other Ones, they performed a repetoire of Grateful Dead tunes for equally grateful fans who seemed to have never been able to let go of the music that had united them thirty years before. As long as Weir, Hart, and Lesh were alive, the Grateful Dead could never die.

For Johnnie Johnson, life went on as usual and he spent the summer of 1997 touring, though somewhat sparingly due to the scheduling problems caused by the last-minute cancellation of his Further Festival plans. True to his character, he holds no hard feelings towards Weir or RatDog, saying simply, "It was fun while it lasted and hopefully we can get together again."

Meanwhile in Houston, Turek had assembled his troops for a second assault on the Hall of Fame. A new addition to the group was a multi-talented twenty-eight-year old drummer/video/computer expert named Spike "the Percussionist" Longoria, whom Turek had met through Harry Bartholomew. It would be Longoria's job to film Johnnie at various shows, including the Furthur Festival, and gather other bits of material suitable for a highlight film of Johnson's career. During late summer of 1996,

Longoria collaborated on what was to become the first of three drafts of the *Johnnie Johnson Nomination Video*, highlighting Johnson's career and contributions to rock and roll music. At the same time, Longoria's other skills in the computer department were called in to play as he began preliminary designs for johnnie.com, the Johnnie Johnson webpage. Longoria himself would maintain the page, updating touring schedules and happenings on a weekly basis. A musician as well, he was more than willing to join the cause. "There are so many unsung heroes in music," Longoria says. "Even today with bands like Tad and Dif Juz who never get the recogniton they deserve. To me...I don't know...I guess I saw it as my duty as a musician. The guy put everything in motion. There's a little bit of Johnnie in all of us."

Turek was taking the Johnnie Johnson campaign to another level. The frustrations of the preceding year had caused him to rethink his strategy and he began attacking from another another angle—inside. "The Rock and Roll Hall of Fame Foundation," as he says, "is like this private club. The country club, you might say. Outsiders are not welcome. I had to find a connection on the inside. That was the only way I could find out what was going on"

One Hall of Fame Foundation employee who sympathized with Johnson's plight was Marc Bronitt—administrative assistant to Suzan Evans. Bronitt informed Turek that he would help as much as he could, but was limited in the information he could provide. "Marc was a big help," lauds Turek. "I found out that the head of the committee was Jon Landau, Bruce Springsteen's manager. I also found out about how many people were on the nominating committee, the basic requirement for nomination, which was that the artist had to have a charting song at least twenty-five years prior, and the approximate date they would be meeting again to decide on the new nominees. I decided to talk to the man in charge–Landau–about putting Johnnie in."

After several unsuccessful attempts at trying to contact Landau, Turek relented and called Margo Lewis for help. A move that led him to hire his first–and only–publicist.

"After getting nowhere with Landau, I realized that I didn't have enough clout to get what I wanted in the music business," he remembers. "So I called Margo up and she suggested I hire a publicist to handle Johnnie and monitor the situation within the Hall of Fame Foundation."

Lewis suggested Rogers & Cowan, one of the largest public relations firms in the world, whom she believed might be interested in Johnnie's story. Turek agreed and flew to New York in order to meet with one of the agency's representatives, Paul Freundlich.

"Margo thought we could get somewhere with Rogers & Cowan and it only made sense that we could," says Turek. "They were huge. I met with a fellow named Paul Freundlich who was a heavyweight in the business, did publicity for the Beatles, Rod Stewart, Bonnie Raitt, you name it. Well, after hearing Johnnie's story, Paul seemed very interested and agreed to take on the account. I was very pumped up over the whole thing. I figured this was it—Johnnie was going to make it. Freundlich had an inside contact at Landau's office and he said he would watch that situation for me. In the meantime, he suggested we try to get Chuck Berry to write a letter to Ahmet Ertegun, who was in charge of the whole shebang, asking that Johnnie be nominated. I'd met Chuck a few times since and I knew by then that he wasn't the type to be bothered. But I figured I would try anyway."

Turek had first met Berry when he and Johnson had played together at the New Orleans Jazz Festival in 1995. He ran into him again at the St. Louis Music Awards in December of 1996 when Johnnie was honored with the "Slammy" Award for Lifetime Achievement—the second of its kind ever awarded by the committee. The first had been given to Berry, who made a surprise appearance in the audience to watch his old partner receive the award.

"They had just finished up with the nomination video when we found out about the Slammy awards," recalls Turek. "The coordinator for the event got in touch with me about showing part of the video during Johnnie's segment of the ceremony and so I had them edit the tape down to about ten minutes of footage—most of it from *Hail! Hail! Rock 'n' Roll,* including the part where Keith Richards' talks about Johnnie giving Chuck the music. So anyway, the show is going great and it was really interesting—Johnnie was sitting beside me the whole time and he would tell me who he thought was going to win the awards before they were announced, and he was right every single time! Then they get to best pianist and he didn't say anything at all. Of course, he won that one himself!

"Well, anyway, they are about to start the Lifetime Achievement award section and who should walk in but Chuck. We see him come in and sit down to the left of the stage. Then they start playing the video and it gets to Keith Richards's part—and the way we have it spliced together, with Bruce Springsteen talking about Chuck 'playing in strange keys like B-flat, E-flat' and then Keith coming in with this answer 'piano keys, horn keys, jazz keys, Johnnie Johnson's keys,' it was pretty obvious what we were getting at. Frances and I looked at each other like, 'Oh, shit!'

"But the thing was, after the ceremony, Chuck comes right up to the table and slaps Johnnie on the back and hugs Frances. He was very gregarious. He didn't talk to us at all, but he was very friendly with Johnnie and his family and he was looking at Johnnie with this strange look—see, Johnnie had really gotten decked out for the ceremony. He had this real sharp brown suit and a matching hat and he just really looked great. I took a picture of Johnnie and Chuck which, all modesty aside, I believe is the best picture ever taken of them together."

Frances Johnson agrees. "That was a great picture George took of the two of them. They look so good together. You know, in all the times I've seen Chuck, and I've seen him in some bad moods, he has always been nice to Johnnie. But I have to tell you I was on guard that night. I told my girls, if he says something bad to my baby—I'm gonna go crazy. But he was still just as nice as could be afterwards. And the way he looked at Johnnie that night. Chuck once said to me, 'I love the way you watch Johnnie.' I said, 'Well, he pays me to do it.' And we laughed. But that night he looked at Johnnie like, 'How the hell did you make it?' It was like he was in awe of Johnnie for still being around and looking as good as he did. I mean, Johnnie had it goin' on—smelling good, nice clothes, nice shoes. See, for years the man was buying second and third-hand clothes, you know. He was always clean but you know... two-pairs of shoes for twenty-five dollars, and they never fit right on his big ol' fat feet. But that night and even a little before and since that night I'll catch Chuck just staring at him like, 'How is this possible?' It makes me feel good that he can see the difference in Johnnie. It really does."

For Turek, the full realization of Johnnie's humble lifestyle hit home when upon asking the pianist what style of instrument he owned, Johnnie replied matter-of-factly that he did not own a piano because he could not afford one.

"He said, 'George, I ain't got a piano.' I said, 'You, Johnnie Johnson, do not have a piano in your home?' He said, 'That's right, I can't afford one.' I said, 'Well, how do you practice? How do you come up with all that music?' He said–and I'll never forget this as long as I live–'I do it all in my head.'

"I can never put into words the rush of emotions that went through me at that moment: amazement, awe, sorrow, anger. The fact that the greatest blues and rock and roll pianist in the world could not afford his own piano to practice on, but yet at the same time was such a genius that he practiced and composed in his head. In his *head!*

"And then there's Mr. Berry living it up in his mansion with all that money–money Johnnie Johnson made for him–and he didn't even have the decency to throw Johnnie a crumb. Not even a crumb. I mean, anyone else in Berry's shoes would have thanked his lucky stars that he had the good fortune to team up with Johnnie Johnson. Would have been more than willing to share fame and fortune with his partner. But not Chuck Berry. I have a wonderful and wise friend who once told me, 'George, people have a tendency to let you know exactly who they are without even knowing they are doing it. All you have to do is listen to what they say and read what they write.'

"Well, I read Chuck's autobiography and you know the thing that gets me? That story about the drunk and the mugger. Pages thirty-nine and forty. I wrote it down because that one story, in my mind, sums up Berry's personality, his outlook on life, his morals, and his comprehension of right and wrong. In that story he lets all of us know that he feels there is nothing wrong with using anybody or stealing from anybody to supplement his own gain—even if that person be his partner and friend. Everything about the man made me absolutely nauseous.

"Anyway, I could tell Johnnie was embarrassed about the situation, so I let it drop. But afterwards I walked into Linda's office and I said, 'I'm going out right now and getting Johnnie a baby-grand piano and have it delivered to his house.' She said, 'Hold on! Don't do anything crazy. They couldn't fit a piano that big in that living room—it would fill up the whole house!' I knew she was right. So I started calling around and eventually settled for one of those smaller uprights—a Yamaha. Johnnie likes Yamahas. That way, Johnnie could fit it up against the wall and still be able to walk through his living room.

"So, I bought the piano and had it delivered as a surprise for Johnnie. Well, he calls me up after they deliver it and he's in tears. 'Thank you, George. Thank you. This is the best thing anyone's ever done for me.' And I said, 'Johnnie, this is the least you deserve. Thank you for your wonderful music.' And I meant that with all my heart. He's done so much, and he never asks for anything. I'm afraid that he's going to end up like Van Gogh—ignored in life and worshiped in death.

Shortly after the Slammy Awards, Johnson and Berry were

slotted to play together at Blueberry Hill, the same club where the Tureks had met Johnnie for the first time four years earlier. Joe Edwards, the owner and proprietor of the club, was good friends with both Johnson and Berry. So good, in fact, that Berry had donated the guitar he'd used to record 'Johnny B. Goode' to Edwards's memorabilia collection.

"Joe Edwards has always been good to me and to Chuck," says Johnnie. "He lent me money many times when I was in trouble with bills and things, and I always had a place to play at his club. He's done a lot for the city, too. We've been friends for quite a while."

As special guests of Johnson, the Tureks were invited to a pre-show dinner at Edwards's home with Johnnie, Frances, Jim Marsala and his wife, and Berry. Berry was the last to arrive, several hours late, accompanied by a blond assistant named Sherry.

"It was interesting that night," says Turek. "Chuck was very late and so we sat around talking for quite a while before he arrived. I got to know Chuck's bass player Jim Marsala, who turned out to be a fabulous guy and the Edwardses were very nice. Finally, Chuck arrives and we get ready for dinner, and that's when the first kind of awkward moment happened. See, in addition to working on gettting Johnnie in the Hall of Fame, I had also explored the idea of doing a tribute concert for him, similar to the one in *Hail! Hail! Rock 'n' Roll* at one of the major national venues. In doing so, I had looked into various places including Radio City Music Hall and Carnegie Hall. When I went to Carnegie, the person who met with me about renting was a fellow by the name of Jim Rose, who ironically had gone to high school in Wisconsin with Keith Richards's manager Jane Rose, although they were not related. Well, Jim and I started talking about Johnnie and he tells me that not only did he know Johnnie really well—he had also been Chuck Berry's road manager for several years! In fact, Jim said that Chuck used to say he was the only white man he trusted to handle his money. I thought that was quite a coincidence.

"So anyway, I'm talking to Chuck at dinner and I bring up this guy

Jim Rose. Chuck just looks at me like I'm crazy and says, 'I don't know any Jim Rose.' He wasn't mean about it or anything. He just said, 'I don't know the guy.' So I'm sitting there feeling foolish. And you know, later that night before the show at Blueberry Hill, Jim Marsala pulls me aside and says, 'I just wanted to tell you, George, you're not crazy. Chuck knows Jim Rose very well. He was our road manager. I don't know why Chuck said that. He just does it sometimes. Don't worry about it.' So he walks away and I'm feeling real confused. Why had he lied? I couldn't figure it out.

"That evening at dinner he was entertaining but kind of aloof towards Linda and I, even though before dinner I had given him that great picture of him and Johnnie, which I had framed, as a present. Sort of like a peace offering. I didn't like the guy. Don't get me wrong. But I figured that I could get more accomplished for Johnnie with Chuck as an ally, although I could barely stand to look at him for what he did to Johnnie. So I swallowed my feelings and made my best effort.

"That evening, he and Johnnie played together, and although I had Spike bring the camera, we were not allowed to film the show per Chuck's demand. I thought that was shitty of him. But oh well, that was to be expected.

"Then not too long afterwards, about four months or so, we once again had dinner with Chuck at Joe Edwards's house. This time he came by himself and was much more outgoing. Joe introduced us again and said something like, 'Hey Chuck, this is George Turek, Johnnie's friend. He gave you the picture of you and Johnnie from the Slammys.'

"Well he looked at me for a moment and I could tell he remembered me. But then he just shrugged his shoulders and said, 'I don't remember any picture.' He acted like he'd never seen me before in his life! So I'm thinking, 'Jim told me he does this sometimes, no big deal.' But it was very strange.

"At dinner he was the life of the party, telling stories about him and Johnnie on the road, even about the robbery that had gotten him thrown in prison the first time and how his gun had fallen apart in his hand while he was pointing it. Funny stuff. Of course, that led into a very strange discussion where he talked about getting in trouble every seventeen years. I remembered reading that in his book, so I said, 'Well, looks like your about due for the next one.' It just slipped out. He kind of laughed it off and meanwhile Linda's kicking me under the table like, 'What were you thinking saying something like that?'

"But I wasn't the only one guilty of starting an awkward moment. Chuck was talking about writing another book and he was reminiscing over all these road stories with Johnnie. Then he gets this whimsical look on his face all of a sudden. Very contrived, you know? And then he says something like, 'All the time we've known each other, Johnnie and I only had one fight. We were coming back from the club and I guess I got out of line and took a swing at Johnnie and he threw me against the wall and had me by the throat. I always thought no one could whip me. But when I felt how strong Johnnie was, I knew then I wasn't ever gonna mess with him again. But that was years ago and I don't even remember what it was about now.' And he's laughing and about to say something else when Johnnie says kind of quietly without even looking up from his soup, 'I remember.'

"Well you should have seen the look on Frances's face—it was classic. Everyone kind of quieted down because for Johnnie to speak up like that...it just never happened, you know. Then he goes on: 'You took all the money for yourself and you weren't gonna split it up with me and Ebby.' Johnnie was actually speaking up! I didn't know what was going to happen after that, but Chuck just kind of laughed it off, the same way he laughed off my little comment, and then they were off talking about other things. But I was proud of Johnnie."

Johnnie recalls the conversation. "Yeah I said that about rememberin' the fight we had. And I got to admit that for a long time I never would have. Sometimes Chuck will say somethin' in front of me that we both know isn't true and I'll just keep my mouth shut. But things was changin'. Like with the whole thing playin' at Blueberry Hill. Used to be whenever Chuck called me up, I'd go and he'd pay me whatever he was payin' the rest of the sidemen. Well, he tried that on me at the Hill. It got time to talk about the dead presidents and Chuck asked me how much I wanted. I said what I usually said which was, 'Whatever you think is right.'

"Well Chuck takes out a piece of paper and says, 'I was thinkin' about this.' The paper said $300. I just kinda looked at it and he said, 'Is that about right?' Well I'd been playin' with all kinds of folks, and ain't none of 'em paid me any less than that. John Lee Hooker paid me over a thousand just for playin' on a couple songs of his. So I told Chuck that and he said, 'Well I ain't gonna let any of them beat me.' And he paid me a thousand for the gig. But after that, he has still tried to get me for three or four hundred dollars, and I always tell him no. It just ain't worth it. Not anymore it ain't."

Back in Houston, George Turek was rethinking his plans. After witnessing Berry's behavior at the dinners, he was concerned that the mercurial rocker would not sign the letter to Ahmet Ertegun. "The way he seemed at dinner with all the lying and narcissism," says Turek. "I figured there wasn't much of a chance."

But Joe Edwards assured him that there would not be a problem as long as the letter was worded appropriately for Berry. Turek penned the first draft of the letter himself and sent it off to Edwards to review and make any necessary changes. Finally, the two men agreed on a format and the letter was sent to Wentzville for Berry to sign. "I got what I wanted which was the part about them being 'musical collaborators,'" Turek remembers. 'I figured it was pretty gutsy, but we could hope."

To further insure success, Turek asked Johnnie Johnson to call Berry personally and ask him to sign the letter. According to Johnson, Berry answered "I'd do anything for you, Johnnie."

For days afterward, Turek and company sweated over the return of the letter. Finally, he could wait no longer and asked Johnnie to call. "I told him to tell Chuck that the letter was on its way and could have possibly arrived already," recalls Turek, "I basically left it up to Johnnie to make sure we got it."

Johnnie remembers: "I called Chuck up a second time to tell him that George had sent the letter. He said that it must have got lost with all his other mail and that he would find it right away and send it off. Sure enough, he did. He was real nice about the whole thing and said he hoped I got in 'cause I deserved it as much as him and all that kind of stuff.

With letter in hand, Turek began the final preparations for the 1997 campaign. Through Freundlich, he was able to secure a fairly recent list of the nominating committee members and their addresses. The website was up and running as well, and the nominating video was mass-produced and packaged for shipment. Turek knew from his conversations with both Freundlich and Marc Bronitt that the committee would be meeting sometime in July, and by June first, Turek and his team were stuffing overnight envelopes with copies of both letters and the nominating video.

"I put everybody to work stuffing envelopes, packaging the tapes, in a big assembly line," remembers Turek. "We all came together, joined in this single purpose, to get Johnnie in the Hall of Fame. Everyone was gung-ho. It was the topic of almost every conversation. Every day people were asking me 'Did you find out anything?' And every day I'm asking Paul Freundlich the same question. 'Did you find out anything?' 'We know that Landau has the tape on his desk,' he would say. Or, 'Kurt Loder has gotten his copy.' Things like that. And the whole time I'm telling him, 'Stay on top of it, Paul.' And he's telling me, 'I am George. I am.' 'Are you sure they haven't met yet?' 'I'm sure, just relax.'"

In late June, Turek began talking about publishing the first letter in an advertisement form asking publicly on behalf of the fourteen signees that Johnson be nominated. He eventually decided that *Billboard* magazine would be the best choice as, according to Paul

Freundlich, it reached the desk of every major player in the industry. By the time Spike Longoria had worked his artistic magic, adding quotes and pictures of Johnnie Johnson with various signees, the ad was quite a sight to behold.

"We were extremely proud of the *Billboard* ad," remembers Turek. "Not just because it was good—Spike did a wonderful job—but because of what it represented and the fact that nothing of the kind had ever been done before. It caused quite a sensation."

When the full-page ad was published in the July 12, 1997 issue, Turek's phone rang off the hook for the next week. " I had people from Reuters calling me, televison stations, other artists's managers, even studio executives," he says. "They especially loved it in Cleveland because a lot of people in that city really resented the fact that a bunch of New Yorkers had come into their city, had them build the Hall of Fame, and then completely shut them out of the picture as far as the selection procedure was concerned. I was basically this nobody, a goofball from Houston who wasn't even in the music business, taking on this private club. And I think the thing that caught the most attention was that I wasn't part of the music scene—they couldn't blacklist me or shut me up. I called them, I wrote them, I stuffed their mail boxes with letters and videos, and now I was going public. Nothing takes the place of persistence. I was in the right and I wasn't going away until they acknowledged the problem and fixed it. Period."

Meanwhile Johnnie Johnson waited on pins and needles, hoping to hear of his nomination.

"George told me that there was a good chance that I might get into the Hall of Fame and I got real excited," he says. "People were comin' up all the time askin' me about the ad and could I believe that all those people had signed the letter and all that. But I just tried to keep from gettin' my hopes up too high. I figured if they ever saw fit to let me in then I would be honored. But if they didn't then that was their decision. I was more excited for George than myself 'cause he had taken such an interest in me and was workin' so hard that I didn't want to see him disappointed."

The phone call came in the early afternoon while Turek was finishing his lunch. "Monica, who is one of our secretaries, gets on the intercom and tells me that Mike Kappas is on the phone," remembers Turek. "Mike was Robert Cray's and John Lee Hooker's manager and he'd always been helpful to me. So I said, 'Hey Mike, how ya doin.' Usual hellos, exchange of pleasantries. Then he hits me with it. 'George, I just called to tell you how sorry I am that Johnnie didn't make it on the ballot this year.'

"I got dizzy for a second. Then I remembered Paul was keeping tabs on everything. 'But the committee hasn't even met yet,' I said confidently. Mike was quiet for a minute then he said, 'Well I'm afraid you were misinformed, George. I've seen the ballot for this year and Johnnie isn't on it.' Well, I basically dropped the phone. It was like getting hit with a sledgehammer. I don't even remember the rest of the conversation with Mike, I just remember hanging up the phone and sitting there trying to catch my breath. How? That's all that kept running through my mind. How?"

For Turek's friends and family, the day he learned of Johnnie's second consecutive snubbing by the Hall has gone down in infamy as "D-Day." George had not taken the news well and he was ready to go to war.

"I came around the corner and it was like walking into a funeral," Linda Turek says. "I immediately knew something was wrong. I thought something had happened to one of his parents, or worse, to one of the kids. I mean, that's how bad it was. You could actually feel his pain in the air. The whole office just kind of went into a daze. He was sitting there and his face was red as a beet. I had never seen George so upset in my life. I think he was near tears if he hadn't already been crying. He looked up at me from his desk and he was holding a copy of the *Billboard* ad in his hand. That's when I knew. 'They screwed him,' he said. He just couldn't believe it."

For Turek, the black rage in his heart stemmed not from his own disappointment–although that was part of it–but from the fact that he would have to tell Johnnie himself that he had been denied a place on the ballot.

"The thought of having to call Johnnie and tell him—the thought of having to hear him tell me how he was fine but know that he was really hurting inside. The thought of having to let him down—that's what sent me over the edge," recalls Turek. "The first person I called was Freundlich. I had paid him thousands of dollars to keep me updated with what was going on and I find out from someone else that they've already met? I don't remember exactly what I said but I told him we weren't going to be using him anymore. Then I called the Rock and Roll Hall of Fame Foundation. I think Bronitt answered, I don't remember, I was too angry. I said, 'Johnnie Johnson is seventy-three years old, he belongs in the Rock and Roll Hall of Fame as much as anyone you have ever inducted, and he continues to be passed over year after year! He's going to die never having been inducted and then it will be too late no matter what they do!' I was absolutely furious. I've never been that angry before or since.

"After that, I hung up the phone and called in my attorneys Bob Toohey and Scott Orr for an emergency meeting. When I had finally calmed down enough, I started to call around and get the scoop on exactly what had happened."

Over the course of the next few days, Turek found out that the committee had met and that Johnson's dilemma had been discussed in-depth. So in-depth in fact, that Bronitt had been sent out of the room and only the committee members were allowed to remain. Turek also found out that only a fraction of the eligible committee members had voted and that Johnnie was left off the ballot by way of two no votes. In the end, the committee had chosen to follow the letter of the law— "Artists become eligible for induction twenty-five years after the release of their first record." Although Johnnie Johnson had collaborated with Chuck Berry on the hits that defined rock and roll, his name did not appear on any of the records, nor had he received writing credit. Based on that criteria, he was not eligible for nomination into the Rock and Roll Hall of Fame.

"It was a hard pill to swallow," recalls Turek, "especially since almost everyone we talked to, including Ahmet Ertegun, who is the Co-Chairman of the Rock and Roll Hall of Fame Foundation, along with Jann Wenner, publisher of *Rolling Stone* magazine, has been sympathetic to the cause. But in each and every case, they pull the old Pontius Pilot routine, stating that they would love to see Johnnie get the credit due him, but that they are only one of many and have little individual say in the matter. No one wants to take a stand. Those are the kinds of things that drive you crazy. But I take solace in the fact that at least they know and maybe one day, if enough people like me keep beating them over the head with the truth, one of them will stand up on behalf of Johnnie Johnson and all the unsung heroes of rock and blues and jazz. All the uncredited geniuses who provided us with such gifts and were never thanked. There are more out there, I know this for a fact. Since I've started campaigning for Johnnie, I've gotten countless stories about other musicians just like him who have never been acknowledged. I chose Johnnie because he was my friend and because his accomplishments in particular were so influential and so unique in regards to creating a whole new type of music, that I felt he would serve as a model and a source of hope for others equally dedicated as myself to setting things right."

The months following Johnson's second rejection by the Hall were not spent in mourning over the defeat, but rather in preparation for the next year's quest. Turek knew that in order to get Johnson inducted he would have to keep up his same level of intensity. "I had some moments of self-pity," he admits, "but I look at every failure as a learning experience. I would have never made it in business if I had given up after every time things didn't go my way. We hadn't achieved our objective, but we had made an impact and that was enough to keep me in the fight."

For his part, Johnnie Johnson was discouraged at the way the events had unfolded, but nevertheless he was ever more appreciative of his friend's efforts.

"George took it real hard. But he told me he was goin' to keep tryin' and I said, 'You go.' 'Cause if anyone can do it, George can. Sure I was disappointed, but I had to put it out of my mind and keep on playin' music. You can't go through life worryin' bout what you don't have. As long as I had my family and the ability to play piano, that was all I needed to keep me happy."

Turek meanwhile, was determined to further Johnson's career, even if that meant losing money himself. During the course of the previous year, Turek and company had produced a CD for Johnson, *Johnnie B. Live*, recorded with Jimmy Vivino's band at the Bottom Line in New York. It would be Johnson's sixth CD and the first to capture him in an entirely live setting. Harry Bartholomew, who recorded, mixed, and co-produced the CD, recalls that the Bottom Line show was recorded for the purpose of updating the nomination video–not for a CD.

"It was a great show. Johnnie did some amazing things and the band was smokin'—Jimmy Vivino, Mike Merrit, James Wormworth, and Al Kooper on Hammond—Spike and I were sitting there like 'Damn! This would make a great album.' But that wasn't realistic and, like I said, we weren't even thinking in those terms. Then I guess George caught wind of it, because the next thing I know, he's asking me to mix the thing for an album and he's got Spike working on the cover layout with this artist Jim Kersey who is just incredible. It was work, but when all was said and done I think we were all pretty happy with it."

Following the completion of the album, Turek's plan to release it to the public ran into a roadblock in the form of MusicMasters, the company that had released Johnson's last CD, *Johnnie Be Back*, in 1995. According to MusicMasters, Johnnie was not allowed to release any songs previously performed on their album for sales purposes until a three-year period had elapsed. As *Johnnie B. Live* was a live album, Johnson had played several songs from his previous recordings, including three from *Johnnie Be Back*. MusicMasters threatened a lawsuit if Turek sold any CDs commercially before the three years were up. Turek's solution was simple, but completely unconventional.

"They told me they would sue me if I sold any of the CDs before June of '98," recalls Turek. "So I said okay—I'll give the damn things away!"

And so he did. For the next year, Turek gave away *Johnnie B. Live* to anyone who would have it: friends, business acquaintances, it didn't matter. "I'd give them away to people I met in airports," Turek laughs. "The goal was not to make money, I was just trying to get Johnnie's music out there." But the well-meaning ploy soon backfired when Longoria announced on Johnnie's website that the new Johnnie Johnson CD was being distributed for free.

"I was calling the office for something and I got a busy signal," Longoria recalls. "I was like, 'What?' So I checked the number, dialed again, same thing. I don't know how many lines they have in that office but there are several, and every single one was busy. I didn't know what was going on."

Says Turek, "I think what happened was some deejay in St. Louis got wind of what was happening from the website and announced over the radio that we were giving away Johnnie's new CD. I'd never seen anything like it—the whole switchboard almost blew out with all the phone calls. My administrative assistants Jackie and Monica were about to kill me. Finally we had to call the radio station in St. Louis from a cellular phone and have them announce that we were out of CDs because I had a company to run and none of our clients could get through. But that just goes to show how many people love Johnnie, especially in St. Louis. The guy has a million fans. It was unbelievable."

Eager to jump back into the Hall of Fame campaign, Turek began 1998 with his boldest initiative yet. The week before the nomination ceremony at the Waldorf Astoria, he released his second full-page ad in *Billboard*, the published Chuck Berry "collaboration" letter—complete with his own picture of the two taken at the Slammy Awards in December of 1996. Then, by way of Margo Lewis, Marc Bronnit, and $4000 dollars of his own money, Turek sent Johnson and Lewis to the 1998 Rock and Roll Hall of Fame Induction Ceremony.

"I wanted them to see that Johnnie was for real, that he was with a real talent agency, that he had support," recalls Turek. "But mainly I wanted Johnnie there in the audience when they inducted those other artists, a great majority of whom owe their careers to him, and yet somehow deserve induction more than he. I wanted them to see his face in the crowd. The guy who created the music they are celebrating."

What Turek got for his efforts, however, was much more than he could have ever expected.

"Margo called me after it was over and told me that as they entered the ballroom she saw Paul Shaffer, who was the bandleader that evening, and told him that she had Johnnie with her and would he be interested in having him sit in with the band," says Turek. "She didn't have to ask twice. Shaffer immediately invited him up on stage to play during Lloyd Price's number. Even better, Schaefer had actually introduced Johnnie beforehand which Margo said caused an uproar from the crowd. She also said that during the solo section, all the musicians on stage had gathered around Johnnie, pointing to him as he played so that the camera would pick up on him. So I ask Johnnie about it and he says, yeah, he got on stage and played and, yeah, he had a great time. I was so happy.

"Then the next day, I turn on MTV and they're showing highlights from the ceremony and who should be on the screen—Johnnie Johnson. I got a lot of calls that day asking me if I'd seen Johnnie on MTV. All of us, everyone involved in this campaign, felt a sense of pride seeing Johnnie up there playing and receiving so much respect from his peers. As far as I was concerned we had taken another step towards making the dream a reality."

But time was running out. In early 1998, Turek began noticing a drastic change in Johnson. He was urinating frequently and had little control over his bladder, to the point that he was regularly leaving the piano during gigs to visit the toliet, sometimes twice or three times a night. Concerned, he called Frances, who admitted that she had noticed the same thing. Johnnie was not himself.

"I knew then we had a big problem. Johnnie had been going to the V.A. Hospital for checkups because he had no health insurance and they had a file on him. And it just so happened that he'd had a checkup the month before. So I got permission from Johnnie to talk to the V.A. people about his test results. Well, they started running off all these results. He had diabetes, which I knew, and high blood pressure. But everything else was basically okay. So they go through the list and when they're finished, I say, 'What about his PSA test?' The PSA is the test for prostate cancer that men go through after they get to a certain age. Well, Ms. Martha Deady, the V.A. patient advocate I had been speaking to regarding Johnnie looked into his file and read off the number–13.5. I almost lost it. Anything over a four is extremely high–cancer zone. I'm a one. Most guys are ones, maybe twos. I said, 'Jesus! He's got prostate cancer! We've got to get him biopsied right now!'"

The results of the biopsy done at the V.A. Hospital in St. Louis confirmed Turek's fears.

"We didn't know how bad it was. I had the biopsy slides sent to Dr. Edward Kim, a top urologist at Baylor College of Medicine in Houston, and he had the pathology department render a second opinion. Dr. Kim told us that yes, Johnnie did have cancer of the prostate and that it was time to discuss treatment options."

Johnnie recalls his fear upon learning of the gravity of his disease: "They told me I had cancer. That's somethin' nobody wants to hear. They gave me all kinda tests and whatever and they wasn't too comfortable–goin' all up inside. I was pretty scared. The doctors at the V.A. said that 'cause of my age, maybe I shouldn't have treatments at all 'cause it would be hard on my health. But me and George and Frances talked, and we went ahead with gettin' the radiation treatments. They wore me out pretty good, but at least they got rid of the cancer."

Indeed, the weekly radiation treatments had forced the cancer into remission for the time being. But as Turek knew, remission did not mean relaxation. The threat of a relapse would loom over the seventy-three year-old's head for the rest of his life. "Once you have cancer, especially at Johnnie's age, there is always the chance that it will come back," he says. "Sometimes even worse than before. Luckily, we caught it in time, before it metastasized. But I tell you what, for all of us involved in Johnnie's life, especially Frances and the kids, it was a scare and a half. I mean, we could have lost him.

"And I tell you, it really lit a fire under my butt as far as getting things put right. Johnnie isn't a young man anymore; it's not like we have twenty or thirty years to play with here. There is a sense of urgency. I really feel strongly about Johnnie being alive to see his redemption. I want him on stage when he is inducted into the Rock and Roll Hall of Fame, and I want him to make the speech, not Keith Richards or somebody speaking on his behalf. And I know that I may come across as pushy or overly aggressive. But I won't apologize for that. I've been involved with the music industry for going on four years now and I've dealt with all kinds of musicians and artists. And the one thing I've noticed is that while a lot of times their intentions are good, they tend to procrastinate. 'Oh yeah, we'll get together, man.' 'Oh yeah, we talked about doing an album together five years ago, but I haven't heard anything about it.'

"And they'll have great ideas, and they'll actually be sincere, but nothing ever gets done. I mean, if you have any kind of business sense, you know that you don't just wait around for things to happen. Five years? Well I don't have five years with Johnnie Johnson. I can't sit around and wait for the idea to just occur to one of the industry's who's who. 'Oh yeah, Johnnie Johnson. You mean he's not in the Hall? Oh man, somebody has got to do something about that. That's not right, man. Somebody should fix that.' I don't have the time. Johnnie doesn't have the time. We have got to move, and if I wait for the music industry to do something about it, we are going to lose him. It will be too late. Look what happened to poor Bill Monroe, who died only months before his induction. So yeah, I bang on their heads. Yeah I'm a nuisance. But I'll tell you what— I'm not asking for anything that isn't due that man. They should be honored to put him in the Hall. And until they decide to do something about it, I will be right in their faces. Writing letters, making phone calls, putting out full-page ads in *Billboard* and *USA Today* and *People*. I'll do whatever it takes and I will not stop. Because Johnnie Johnson is the most influential artist in rock and roll history. Because he is a good and humble man who has been cheated out of that place in history. And most of all, because he is my friend. And I love him."

As we leave the office and walk out to the parking garage, Turek reminds me that summer is nearly here and that the committee will be meeting again soon to vote. He shows me a letter he is composing to the members of the nominating committee. Handwritten on a yellow legal pad, it is both heartfelt and to the point, the speech of a man entirely convinced of the rightness of his cause.

Dear Nominating Committee Members:

Since September of 1995, I have been involved in the life and career of Mr. Johnnie Johnson. During that time I have had the opportunity to meet and talk to literally hundreds of people around the country and around the world who truly love Johnnie and consider him not just a wonderful talent but a wonderful human being as well. We have talked to musicians. We have talked to producers. We have talked to record executives, songwriters, managers, and recording engineers. And out of these hundreds of individuals who have made music their lives, not once have I met anyone who expressed anything but the utmost respect for Johnnie Johnson and his contributions to music. The truth is out there. Johnnie Johnson changed the course of music history by creating the sound known as rock and roll. We have in our midst a cultural treasure—an unrecognized, underappreciated cultural treasure. Please do the right thing and put Johnnie Johnson's name on the ballot this year.

Sincerely,

George C. Turek

When I finish, Turek tells me that it is only the beginning. "I want him inducted into the Blues Foundation Hall of Fame. He deserves to receive the Lifetime Achievement Award from the Rhythm and Blues Foundation. He should be inducted into the Songwriter's Hall of Fame. He should receive the Lifetime Achievement Award from the Grammys. He should get both the National Medal of Arts Award and induction as a Kennedy Center Honoree. I even think he should receive a Pulitzer Prize for Music–Wynton Marsalis got one for jazz composition. Johnnie should have one. He should have all of these and more."

"But on top of all that, I want the world to know what a vital role he played in the creation of rock and roll music. Every time I hear someone say, 'Who is Johnnie Johnson?' it makes me even more determined to do these things I have set out to do. I mean, I still have people saying things to me like, 'What about Lafayette Leake, Chuck's other piano player?' Well, what about him? If he really did play on some of Chuck's records as some suggest, then how come Chuck never mentions him in his own autobiography? Not once. Does he ever talk about him in interviews? No. It's always Chuck talking about Johnnie. Johnnie this and Johnnie that. Berry always goes on and on about Johnnie and he also talks about Ebby Hardy, Willie Dixon, Billy Peek, L.C. Davis, and Jaspar Thomas. But he never ever mentions Lafayette Leake.

"And even if Leake played on some of the released versions, who cares? Johnnie and Chuck wrote those songs together, and they recorded the original versions together. If the Chess brothers decided to release a subsequent version with Lafayette Leake or whoever, who cares? The bottom line is that Johnnie Johnson wrote the music; Johnnie Johnson collaborated with Chuck Berry to create those songs. George Gershwin wrote, performed, and recorded "Rhapsody In Blue." Just about every major classical pianist since has played it, has recorded it, but there is only one person who created it—Gershwin.

"But that's why I do what I do for him. He's the man in the iron mask, the rightful king, and I will do everything in my power to restore him to his rightful place and ensure that he receives in his lifetime, all the respect, accolades, and honors that are due him." Johnnie would never call himself the Father of Rock & Roll–he's way too humble. But he is. You want to call Chuck something–call him the Poet Laureate of Rock–because that's all he is and ever was. Rock and Roll is a type of music–not a poem. And Johnnie created that music.

"Lots of people have said, 'But George, rock and roll was around way before Johnnie and Chuck Berry. What about Bill Haley? What about Elvis? What about Little Richard? What about all those doo-wop groups?' And you know what I tell them? I say, 'When the Rolling Stones play rock and roll who are they playing? When the Beatles played rock and roll who were they playing? How about Bob Seger, Bruce Springsteen, Elton John, or Eric Clapton? What about Pearl Jam and Nirvana? All those modern groups? The answer is Chuck Berry. They play Chuck Berry–because there really isn't any other way to play rock and roll. And when you play Chuck Berry, my friend–you play Johnnie Johnson. Because that's who Chuck Berry played when he played rock and roll–Chuck Berry played Johnnie Johnson.'

Now I'm no rock and roll historian. I will be the first to admit it. I don't play an instrument, nor can I sing. I am a businessman who just fell into this crazy situation. Hell, the only song I know all the words to is the National Anthem. Actually I'm an engineering-type by profession. I'm analytical by nature, and so to me it's just math. Simple mathematics. You strip away, and strip away, until you find the one common denominator. Take everything else away–the electric guitars, the bass, the drums, strip it all down to its very core and what do you have? You have Johnnie Johnson's left hand."

"Johnnie's left hand. Johnnie's fills. Johnnie's groove. That's what stuck through all the generations of rock and roll. I mean a woman can have sex, but if she gets pregnant, only one man can be the father. And that was the man who passed on his genes. This is a crude analogy, but it is true. There were others before and at the same time as Johnnie–but his were the genes that passed on–in the name of Chuck Berry of course–but they were still his genes. His influence. That, my friend, is why Johnnie Johnson is the Father of Rock & Roll."

"Why are you doing all this?" I ask him. "Why all the time, the money, the effort?"

Turek stops his double-time pace, puts his briefcase down and looks at me. "Travis," he says, "Most of the guys who get to my fortunate position in life spend their spare time either doing things that entertain them or spend their time with the 'right people' or mingling in the 'right circles'. I'm not into golf, because it just makes no sense to me to spend a whole day hitting a little ball with a stick and not getting any exercise. Nor am I into buying cigarette boats that go around in circles, make a lot of noise, and guzzle gas. I've never been into rubbing shoulders with the 'right people.' I'm not a club-joiner. I think I know who I am, and I don't need others to remind me. My Pop once told me, 'George, you come into this world bare-assed and you leave the same way. It's what you do in between that counts.'

"So I would much rather spend any extra time I have with my family or doing something I think will make a difference. That is why I spend time helping Johnnie and Frances. I know in my heart that a wrong has been committed and it needs to be corrected. Johnnie is a national treasure who will be with us only a little longer. My satisfaction will come when he gets what is due him. I am going to make sure Johnnie gets into the Rock and Roll Hall of Fame. I'm going to make sure that he receives all the accolades and honors he deserves. I'm going to make sure he gets enough money to buy that little house and garage he always wanted."

"How are you going to do all of this with such little time left? What's the secret?"

Turek responds with a white-toothed grin, "It took me a little while, but I finally figured it out. Now I know what I've got to do. And when I do it, everything will fall into place. It's just as simple as that."

"But what's the secret?"

Turek shakes his head. "Travis, a secret isn't a secret anymore once you tell somebody. Do you remember when I was talking about business?"

"Sure."

"Well, I learned something years ago when I first started in business that has helped me more than anything else. No matter what you have planned—never show your trump card."

And with that he is gone. I watch him go, hurrying down the walkway, briefcase in one hand, car keys in the other. A man with so much to accomplish. And so little time.

XV

BLUE ON BLUE

"Please Mr. Johnson. Don't play them blues so sad."

—Chuck Berry

It's Thursday night at Blueberry Hill and Michael Williams arrives early, shaking off the December cold. He does not stop to talk but instead begins wading through tables and chairs to get to his regular spot, located a few rows back, stage right, facing the piano. Always facing the piano. Before he takes his seat, Williams sheds his heavy coat, revealing a black T-shirt, somewhat faded but immaculately pressed. As he turns around, I am shocked to see Johnnie Johnson staring back at me, his face magnified and covering the entire area of Williams's upper torso. *Johnnie Johnson* the shirt says in bold type. *Johnnie B. Bad.* "This is one-of-a-kind, man," he says proudly. "Johnnie gave it to me after he got back from Australia. Everyone asks me where I got it. They all want one."

By showtime, a noisy crowd has gathered near the back of the club, hovering expectantly. As the opening act leaves the stage, they begin to push boisterously forward until every seat is filled and we are surrounded by a sea of St. Louis music fans.

"That's why I like to get here early," Williams says, eyeing the mass of humanity around him. "By the time they get started, you won't be able to find a place to stand, much less sit."

Michael Williams is just an average guy, he tells me. No different than anyone else here. In fact, he says, the only thing that sets him apart from anyone else in the room is that he happens to be Johnnie Johnson's number one fan. "You're lookin' at the president of the Johnnie Johnson fan club," he laughs. "I come out to all the shows and scream for Johnnie. I love him. He's a great man."

There is electricity in the air tonight. Feeling antsy I run a mental check on my materials. Notepad–check. Pen–check. Camera–check. Video recorder–check.

Staring at the latter perched gently in my lap, Williams shakes his head.

"Awww man, I hate to tell ya, You can't use that in here."

"What?" I ask, surprised.

"Chuck don't let nobody film his shows. He'll stop right in the middle of playing and start yelling until all the video recorders are shut off. Don't worry, though. I record 'em all on my tape machine." With that, Williams pulls out a small black cassette recorder–the kind used by college students to record lectures. "The quality ain't too good, but you get the idea."

I certainly do, I say. I certainly do.

* * *

The band takes the stage at 9:30. Jim Marsala comes out first, his cheery Matthauesque hound-dog face off set by a droopy moustache. He has been through a lot during his twenty-five-plus years as Berry's bass player. Yet through it all he remains a kind and loyal sideman; just like Johnnie was. When asked why he sticks around, Marsala simply smiles. "I've seen a lot from behind my bass. I've been all over the world as Chuck Berry's bass player. I guess I can't complain too much."

The drummer, Bob Spitzfadden, comes out next behind Marsala, and settles in behind the kit. He's young, but he knows the music. He picks up his sticks and watches gleefully as Johnnie Johnson lumbers on stage to a deafening ovation.

"Johnnie!" Williams screams beside me. "Johnnie!"

The old man waves to the crowd, squinting in the glare of the lights, and settles behind the piano, the bench slightly askew, just as he likes it.

"He's looking good tonight!" Williams shouts happily.

I agree. He does look good, dressed immaculately in a dark suit and cap. I study the face for a moment and notice that his eyes are fixed across stage. I search the darkness trying to see what he is staring at. Then I see them— Frances and George Turek. Johnnie has brought his family. I catch Frances's eye and she gives me a smile and the thumbs-up sign. Then she motions with her eyes to the opposite side of the stage. Chuck Berry is coming.

Suddenly Joe Edwards's voice fills the room. "Ladies and gentlemen, introducing the incomparable Chuck Berry!"

He walks on stage strumming a G-chord. His thinning hair is pushed back, the blood red Gibson ES-357 slung ponderously low around his hips. The audience roars. He lets the last notes resonate for a moment, then glances back at Johnnie. The communication is brief and completely unspoken.

Stomp-stomp-stomp. *Duh–nuh–nuh–NUH-na-nuh-na-nuh-na-na-nuh-na-nuh*–and then it begins. The undercurrent. The groove. I have never heard them in a small room with equal amplification before. Johnnie begins to swing the bass–*dun-duh-dun-duh-dun-duh-dun-duh*—and the sound reverberates throughout Blueberry Hill with the force of a locomotive. God he is powerful, even at seventy-three. I can hardly imagine him in his younger days, how he must have filled up the Cosmopolitan Club with that sound.

Then Berry jumps on the groove. I watch his hand form a G-chord again, but this time the little finger begins bouncing back and forth, alternating on the fifth and sixth, mimicking Johnnie's left-hand. He approaches the microphone for a moment as if about to sing, then changes his mind and continues the groove. He is beaming in satisfaction. Turning towards the piano, he begins to strut towards his former partner, slurring notes, as Johnnie begins to solo. He will take most of the solos tonight, his hands flying nimbly up and down the keys while Berry watches with undisguised adoration, leaning on the oddly placed pole in the middle of the stage, strumming along absentmindedly. Perhaps too absentmindedly. Somewhere in the middle of "Sweet Little Sixteen" he turns back to Johnnie and quietly asks, 'What key are we in?' Johnnie doesn't answer, but raises his right hand and forms a 'C.' Berry nods and continues playing.

"Is it always like this?" I ask Williams towards the middle of the show.

"Like what?"

"Does Johnnie always run the show?"

"Oh yeah. Johnnie's always in charge on stage. He runs the music. Chuck just calls the songs beforehand."

"Really?" I ask.

"Yeah. That's why we all come to see 'em play. It used to be just me, but now they got all kinds of Johnnie fans coming in here. We all come 'cause we love Johnnie. And 'cause when you come here to see Chuck and Johnnie play together in a little place like this, you get to hear what them records would have sounded like if they had given Johnnie a microphone instead of turning him down in the background."

I nod in understanding.

The number ends and the audience applauds wildly. For a moment all is quiet on stage. Berry walks to the microphone, guitar at his side. He looks back at Johnnie for a moment, at the aged and gentle face watching from behind the keys, the plaintive shadowed eyes. "Please Mr. Johnson," he says. "Don't play them blues so sad."

As if in answer, the thick hands begin to roll out the intro to "Wee Wee Hours"—a symphony of desolate pain–crawling slowly along like a lost soul on a long and lonely highway. Berry closes his eyes. And at that instant, standing there awash in sentiment, he is a young man again. A young man with a chance to make it all right. If only for a moment.

"This is the theme song," he says, "of the Johnnie Johnson Trio."

* * *

The rain-slicked street glows brightly under the glare of the headlights as Tom Maloney drives me back to the hotel. It is night and we have spent the entire day together talking about Johnnie Johnson. For a while the topic changed to politics, then family matters, business affairs. We've learned much about each other, Tom and I. But inevitably, we always returned to the pianist. This ride however, Maloney is oddly quiet and I sense something is on his mind. I ask him to unburden himself.

"You know what it is?" he says. "We've been talking about Johnnie and it's like we think we know him really well. But the thing I just can't stop thinking about–maybe this is a little too weird for you–but the thing I can't stop thinking about is that Johnnie has been holding out on us for all these years."

"What do you mean?" I ask.

"Well, it has to do with this contest a couple years back. See, there's a place here in St. Louis that wanted to do a battle of the pianos. There's a younger guy in town from L.A., pretty good pianist, and he's kinda made a name for himself playing with some great blues artists. I don't want to mention any names. And this guy he wanted to play with Johnnie for charity. Now, normally I don't get into that kind of thing because I don't believe that competition belongs in music. But that's the American mind-set: 'Who's better,' you know? And besides, it was for charity, so I agreed to be in the backup band.

"Anyway, they had this whole thing set up in dramatic fashion with two baby grands on stage–the whole works. And this guy, the younger pianist, he just lives for this. Then here's Johnnie sitting at home, 'Well, it's 8:30, I better get on down to the show.' And he puts on his suit and goes. To him it's just another gig. You know what I mean?

"Well, we're doin' the gig and he and Johnnie are taking turns soloing, and it's really fun, not at all what I expected. And Johnnie's just playing real laid-back, letting this young guy do his thing you know? So we get into playing 'Route 66,' and it's going real good, when all of a sudden, the young guy puts up his hand and stops the band. But he doesn't tag the ending–he just stops. And I said to myself, 'Uh oh.' Sure enough, he starts back into the song–double time–playing as fast as he can at this break-neck pace. And I'm thinking, 'If I had a pie I would throw it in this guy's face–Three Stooges time.' Because there really wasn't any need to do that–it was just showing off. And yes, it was exciting. And yes, the crowd got into it. But I felt he was dragging Johnnie into something that he didn't need to be involved in at his age and in his position.

"So what happens is the guy plays everything he knows twice then looks over to Johnnie like ,'Take it.' I couldn't believe it. I was standing right by Johnnie's piano and I was ready to tell him to forget it. Not that I didn't think Johnnie could handle it. But just out of principal. I mean you don't put a guy in that position on stage–especially someone as renowned as Johnnie Johnson. I admit I can be protective of Johnnie sometimes, but I really felt that was out of line. Disrespectful, you know?

"Well like I said, I was about to tell Johnnie to forget the whole thing when all of a sudden he gets this look on his face, stiffens back his shoulders, and goes into this solo that is just jaw-dropping. I mean we were playing mostly acoustically and I was standing right by the piano, so I got the full force of it. And I mean to tell you that it was on another level entirely from anything I had ever heard on a piano. I thought I knew Johnnie's style. He tends to use the same patterns as springboards for his improvisations. And while it's always fresh and he's a virtual encyclopedia of old songs, I usually know where he's going. But this was completely different, and it was so fast and so intense, that I swear to you right now if he played that way all the time there is not another pianist on this planet who could stay on the same stage with him. I know the guy he played with that night didn't feel like playing anymore. It was unreal. Supernatural almost, what he did that night. And the thing was, afterwards, he went right back to his normal style, which is still the best in the business right now and that was all there was.

"But I've never been able to forget that night–that solo. That's what I mean by 'he's holding out on us.' It had to come from somewhere. I mean, he has that music inside of him. And I can't help but think that there is even more in there that he hasn't shared with us. I'd love to bug his house so we could hear what he practices when he's all alone. Do you see what I'm getting at?"

"That he's even better than we think he is?"

"Exactly. And do you know what else?"

"What."

"I think he knows it."

* * *

May 17, 1998.

Joe Edwards stands on a makeshift stage outside Blueberry Hill under a canopy of trees. The sun is cruel today. Burning. From my seat in the second row I can see Edwards's brow awash in sweat and I feel my own fair skin reddening. Regardless, hundreds of spectators have braved the heat to bear witness to the day's proceedings. Looking forward, my view of the stage is momentarily blocked as a tall, thin black man and his wife take the seat directly in front of me. Then as the dixieland jazz band finishes their number, Joe Edwards walks to the podium.

I notice that Edwards is unusually formal today in khakis and a pink button-up shirt, his long graying hair pulled back into a pony tail. He seems proud; regal almost. Eyeing the audience, he lowers his bearded face to the microphone and utters a single name.

"Johnnie Johnson." The crowd erupts. They have been waiting hours for this moment. Edwards waits for the torrent to subside, then continues.

"Born July 8, 1924. Self-taught pianist Johnnie Johnson settled in St. Louis in 1952 and formed the Sir John's Trio. He asked Chuck Berry to sit in that New Year's Eve, and a magical, half-century collaboration was born. Johnson provided the driving undercurrent on many Berry classics. His inspired piano playing in the 1987 film *Hail! Hail! Rock 'n' Roll* earned him a new generation of fans, including Keith Richards and Eric Clapton, both of whom played on his album *Johnnie B. Bad*. Other albums and international tours followed. Always a loyal sideman, Johnnie Johnson emerged as a star in his own right."

Edwards finishes reading and looks out at the crowd. "It gives me great pleasure to induct into the St. Louis Walk of Fame, a humble man, and a great boogie pianist–Johnnie Johnson!"

He walks to the podium shyly, eyes downcast. He does not like to speak in public. He hates the sound of his voice, especially when he is nervous. Looking out over the sea of expectant faces, he loses himself for a moment. His palms sweat, his mind races, instinctively he reaches for the piano and finds his only reassurance absent. He is not used to being on stage without his piano. Lowering his head to the microphone, he begins to speak.

"Thank you," he rumbles softly. "There ain't enough ink or paper to write down all the people I got to thank. I've had several highlights in my career–playin' the president's inauguration, my first time playin' with Eric Clapton at Royal Albert Hall in London, playin' with Chuck Berry. But out of all them, this takes the cake.

And maybe someday if they see fit to let me in, I'll make it to the Hall of Rock and Roll Fame. Thank you."

The man in front of me stands and begins clapping. The first to do so. And I realize with a start that it is Chuck Berry. He turns towards the crowd and I could have sworn that there were tears in his eyes. But I'm not so sure, for I could hardly see through my own.

Afterwards, Johnnie and I sit in the back room of Blueberry Hill reflecting on the day's events. Most of the guests have gone home, but a few still linger around the buffet spread, picking at the entrees and talking with each other. At the table adjacent to us, Chuck Berry holds court with a group of friends, entertaining them with his humorous quips. He seems not to notice Johnnie at all. His behavior perplexes me.

"I was pretty nervous up there," Johnnie confides as he munches on a slice of buttered bread. "I ain't used to talking in public."

"You did just fine, Johnnie," I reassure him.

"I remember when they gave Chuck his star," he says. "I never thought they'd want to put me out there. Now I got my own star down by the bank. I guess things are startin' to change for me."

"I hope so, Johnnie."

Suddenly we are interrupted by a man approaching the table.

"Mr. Johnson, I just wanted to say congratulations on your induction and that you've been a great influence not just on me and a lot of other musicians in the area, but on the whole music world."

Johnnie smiles warmly. "Thank you."

"And another thing–I'd like to let you know that I named my new son after you. His name is Johnnie."

At that moment, Berry turns around in his chair and fixes us with a quizzical look. "Johnnie?" he says. "There's a lot of folks named Johnnie."

The man, caught by surprise, is flustered for a moment. Then as the words sink in he bristles noticeably and seems prepared to launch a retort when Berry continues.

" I got a song named after you, Jack!"
Johnnie laughs and fans dismissively with his huge hand.
"Awwww..."
The four of us, including the man who realizes then that Berry is not insulting his taste in names, laugh heartily. Then Berry speaks again and this time he is not laughing. He blocks us out. Silences us. Stares directly at Johnnie. The man and I sense immediately that this is between them. Something Berry needs to tell him. The two men lock gazes; Berry's eyes gleam.

"I got a career named after you. " And there was no more to be said.

* * *

He wakes at dawn the next morning. Rolling out of bed carefully so as not to disturb his wife, he makes his way to the bathroom and relieves himself. The prostate cancer had made the process quite difficult. But he isn't complaining. Not when he is so lucky to be alive.

Dressing in the half-light filtering through the bedroom window, Johnnie glances at his sleeping wife and smiles to himself. Counts his blessings. Then he shuffles out to the living room to find Sabu bouncing excitedly on the couch.

"Okay Sabu," he whispers. "Okay."

The dog wags its fuzzball tail furiously.

"Okay, we gonna go out. Okay, now."

He reaches out to pet the little animal and laughs as a pink tongue flicks his hand. "All right then, Sabu."

Johnnie walks to the mantle and retrieves the tattered leash from its hook by the door. Certain of his destination, Sabu paws and twitches uncontrollably as the big man bends slowly towards him and deftly fastens the leash to his collar. Raising up, Johnnie notices a tinge in his back but pays it no mind. Aches and pains are common when you're almost seventy-four years old. He shrugs and steps towards the window.

The curtains are drawn tight and he moves them aside only slightly to gaze outside. Even at this early hour, the streets are alive. But not how he would hope. Through the thin glass he can hear the shouting, and the cursing. The rumbling of car stereo speakers. The distant sirens.

He considers waiting a few hours, but then Sabu has to go like anyone else and he wouldn't want to make him wait. As if reading his mind, the little dog barks impatiently.

"Hush now. We goin'. We goin'."

Leaving Sabu behind, he returns to the bedroom where he is relieved to find Frances still asleep. She'd just worry, he thinks to himself. Then as noiselessly as he possibly can, Johnnie opens the drawer under the nightstand and pulls out a pistol. He checks the chamber, flips the safety, and quickly pockets the weapon. Frances does not stir as he plants a light kiss on her cheek.

Moments later in the light of a new mourn, amidst the ever-present dangers of the inner city, an old man steps hesitantly outside, locks the door behind him, and takes his dog for a walk.

ACKNOWLEDGMENTS

When I began this project, I had no idea how long it would take, nor did I realize the amount of work that would be put into its completion. I had, with all seriousness, predicted a finishing date of January 1997. Now as I write the last words of my first book some two years past my goal and four years since its inception, I can laugh at my own naivete.

There are a lot of memories tied up in this book. All but a semester of my entire college career has been spent either researching or writing, and I've made more than a few sacrifices along the way. But I would go through it all again: the stress, the moments of self-doubt and fear. Life is full of opportunities, opportunities that many of us miss because we are afraid, or because we see them as beyond our capabilities. I have missed my share. But regardless of

ACKNOWLEDGEMENTS

how this book is received, I will always be glad that I took the chance to write it.

The acknowledgment page is included in books for a very good reason. No matter whose name is on the cover, the process of taking a manuscript from a stack of typewritten pages to an actual book is always a team effort. I have so many people to thank for helping me along the way. The following is a list of those individuals.

First and foremost, I believe that there is a God up there looking down on us all with love and guidance. And I would like to thank Him for the gifts He has provided me. I also believe that there is no love like the love of a parent for his or her child. For that reason, I would like to thank my parents John and Linda, and my step-parents George and Marie. Dad, you always inspired my imagination and encouraged me to learn, even through the tough times. I love you very much. Mom, you are a beautiful person and a gift to the world. I feel your arms around me wherever I am and I love you very much. George, what can I say? You've given me so many opportunities and treated me like a son. But most of all you've made my mother happy and that I can never repay. I love you very much. Marie, you took me into your home at the toughest point in my adolescence and I'll always love you for that. You also gave me two little sisters who have added so much to my life. Speaking of sisters, Jessica, you are my pride and joy, so beautiful and talented. I watched you grow up and blossom and now as you approach womanhood, I have to let go. Every time I watch you perform on stage, I have to fight back the tears because I am so proud of you. Erin, my step-sister, you too took me in at a very awkward time in my life. You are so vibrant you just fill up the room when you walk in. I always admired that. I'm sorry I didn't

ACKNOWLEDGEMENTS

tell you that I loved you enough. You are in a fight right now, but it is a fight I know you will win because you are strong. Allison and Kasey, my baby sisters—one shy, the other spunky, both beautiful—watching you grow up has been so wonderful for me. There is nothing as valuable as seeing the world through the eyes of a child. Grandma and Grandpa Fitz, how could I ask for anything more? Your home was always a creative environment. The same goes for Grandma and Grandpa Nutter. Thanks for all the bedtime stories, Grandma. Uncle Bob, I'll always appreciate you teaching me to draw and supporting my creativity. Uncle Dave, we fought like cats and dogs growing up, but in the end we became great friends. Thanks for letting me listen to all your albums. That's one of the main things I would like to thank my entire family for: the music. My family has always been musical, and without their influence, I would have never become involved in this project at all. Thank you all.

I have been blessed with a number of great friends in my life. Some have come and some have gone, but I will always remember them. My absorption in this project put a lot of stress on my personal relationships. But a few friends stuck with me through it all. Jenny Tallant, my girlfriend, was a pillar of strength and love throughout. Steve Kapp and Tony DeFalco—I could always count on you. If you look up the word "friend" in the dictionary, your ugly mugs would be right there. Thanks for the Pain Cave. Eric Gooden, my best buddy from high school—I don't have the words to thank you for all you've done for me over the years. Barry Griffiths and Simon Smith are both from Britain (actually Barry is technically from Wales...he's very sensitive about that) and they expanded my horizons quite a bit and taught me about other cultures. Thanks guys.

Lastly, I'd like to thank someone I haven't seen in years. Aaron Hill was my best friend when I was a child, and I have to say he taught me more than anyone else. Through him I learned that the color of someone's skin means nothing. It is the soul of the person that counts. In this day and age, that is something I'm very proud of. Thank you, Aaron.

Now to the technical end of things. The following people were directly involved in the making of this book. Johnnie and Frances Johnson and their family. Do I even need to explain? This is their life. I hope I did it justice. Harry Bartholomew and Spike Longoria: I'd put you in the friends category, but no one is allowed to be mentioned twice, and you guys have just done too damn much not to be in this section. Without Spike, you wouldn't have anything to read. Without Harry, you wouldn't have anything to listen to. That's how important these guys are. Spike helped me format all of this into book form and Harry mixed and mastered the CD that is included at the end. Their help and friendship have been invaluable. Daniel Durchholz, my content editor, you taught me so much. Thanks for everything. Of course I wouldn't have been ready to let Daniel go to work without the help of Patrick Cohan and Mary Bradley who went through my first drafts and gave me all kinds of great suggestions. So I have them to thank as well. Jacqueline Rodriguez, how could I even begin to thank you. You were mission control through this whole thing. Scott Orr and Teresa Ford, you guys made this all official. Scott, you saved my butt at the last minute, I owe you one. Thanks Al Wagner, Joe Chartier, and the Polish Prince John Salatka, the finance guys: I owe you all literally. Finally, I'd like to give special mention to the genius Marc Norberg, who volunteered his time and talents to support the project. Thanks Marc—you'll always be part of the tribe.

Before I sign off, I'd like to make mention of the a number of other individuals who lent their time and support to this project. Paul Bradley, Monica Serna, Marcia Udin, Bob Toohey, Don Abrams, Tom Maloney, Kenny Rice, Harold White, Billy Peek, Bert Wills, Eric Demmer, Nuri Nuri, Jim Marsala, Robby Parish, Chuck Tillman, Marguerite Johnson, Elvira Simms, Phil Chess, Jeff Dillon, Gus Thornton, Laura Harris, Paul Pointer, Otis Woodard, Bob Weir, Dennis McNally, RatDog and the entire Grateful Dead family, Pete Sears, Roger Forrester, Oliver Sain, Richard Young, Mitchell Fox, and the Kentucky Headhunters, Frank Dunbar, Steve Waldman, Keith Robertson, Neil Mumme, Margo Lewis, Chris Tuthill, Gary Graff, Bruce Pegg, Janice Kite, Chuck Moebius, Liz Bolen, Rachel Shepherd, Joe Edwards, Clayton Love, Mike Williams, Barbara and Isabel Bevins, Debby Hastings and the Bo Diddley Band, John Lee Hooker, Mike Kappas, Eddie Kramer, Jimmy Vivino, Michael Merritt, James Wormworth, and Al Kooper. Thank you all.

Lastly, I'd like to thank Keith Richards and the late great Ian Stewart for recognizing Johnnie Johnson's influence before anyone else. You started the wheels in motion. Thank you.

DISCOGRAPHY

- *Bluehand Johnnie* (Pulsar, 1988/Evidence, 1993)
- *Rockin' Eighty-Eights* (Modern Blues, 1991)
- *Johnnie B. Bad* (Elektra Nonesuch American Explorer Series, 1991)
- *That'll Work* w/ the Kentucky Headhunters (Elektra Nonesuch American Explorer Series, 1993)
- *Johnnie Be Back* (MusicMasters, 1995)
- *Johnnie B. Live* (Father of Rock and Roll Music, 1997)

ESSENTIAL LISTENING

- Berry, Chuck. *Chuck Berry: The Chess Box* (Chess/MCA, 1988) Contains 71 classics and covers the entire span of Berry's Chess career with and without Johnnie Johnson.

DISCOGRAPHY

- Berry, Chuck. *Rock 'n ' Roll Rarities* (Chess, 1986) Includes the original versions of several Berry/Johnson songs. Of note is the first recording of "Sweet Little Sixteen"which features Johnnie's unmistakable sixteenth note triplets.

- Berry, Chuck. *Chuck Berry Is on Top* (Chess, 1959) Perhaps the greatest and most influential album in the history of rock and roll. Contains "Maybellene," "Roll Over Beethoven," "Carol," "Johnny B. Goode" and "Little Queenie"–the five songs that defined rock and roll for the next generation.

- Berry, Chuck. *Hail! Hail! Rock 'n' Roll: The Soundtrack* (MCA, 1987) Recording of Berry's 1986 sixtieth birthday concert at the Fox Theater in St. Louis. Keith Richards and an all-star band back Berry and Johnson as they roll through a melange of their greatest hits.

- King, Albert. *Let's Have a Natural Ball* (Modern Blues, 1989) Covers Johnnie's tenure with Albert King and the power house St. Louis band that would shape the latter's sound, jumpstarting his magnificent career.

- Davis, Larry. *Funny Stuff* (Rooster Blues,1982) "Texas Flood" originator Davis' comeback record and Johnnie Johnson's first non-Berry related album in twenty years. This great record has never been made available on CD.

- Richards, Keith. *Talk Is Cheap* (Virgin, 1988) Richards' first solo album and the beginning of Johnnie's career resurgence following *Hail! Hail! Rock 'n' Roll.* Johnnie rocks on the fifties style "I Could Have Stood You Up."

- Clapton, Eric. *24 Nights* (Reprise, 1991) Another contact from *Hail! Hail! Rock 'n' Roll*, Clapton requested that Johnnie be part of his all-star blues band during his live shows at London's Royal Albert Hall. Note the stinging piano solo on "Worried Life Blues" that Johnnie managed to lay down while hemorrhaging on stage! An amazing achievement to say the least.

- Hooker, John Lee. *Mr. Lucky* (Charisma,1991) Johnnie rips it up on the rollicking "I Want To Hug You" and "This Is Hip" while adding tracks to this 1991 Grammy nominated album by the elder statesman of the blues. Ironically,

Johnnie's own album, *Johnnie B. Bad*, was competing for the same Best Traditional Blues Album award.

- Guy, Buddy. *Slippin' In* (Silvertone, 1994) Johnnie ripples through this Grammy Award winning album by good friend and former Chess stablemate Buddy Guy.

- Thorogood, George & the Destroyers. *Live: Let's Work Together* (EMI, 1995) "He helped shape the way of rock and roll as we know it," praises Thorogood while introducing Johnnie to a hometown crowd at Mississippi Nights in St. Louis. Johnnie then procedes to rock the house, joining Thorogood and his band for raucous versions of "St. Louis Blues" and "Johnny B. Goode."

- Woods, Mitch. *Keeper of the Flame* (Viceroy, 1996) Johnnie joins protegee Mitch Woods for a number of great piano duets. Of particular note is the white hot "Full Tilt Boogie" which features both pianists trading licks at lightning speed overtop a classic rolling bass line. A barrelhouse purist's dream.

- Diddley, Bo. *A Man Amongst Men* (Code Blue/Atlantic, 1996) Johnnie joins up with fellow rock pioneer Bo Diddley and the combination is something to behold.

- Rhythmtown Jive. *On the Main Stem* (Globe, 1998) This Bay Area band led by Johnnie's good friend, Tim Eschliman, had used the pianist sparingly on their 1991 album *Retrogroove Artifact*. On this recording, however, Johnnie plays on seven of the album's twelve tracks, three of which he wrote himself. A solid example of Johnnie with an excellent hardworking band.

- Rogers, Jimmy. *Blues Blues Blues* (Atlantic,1998) This was the great Chicago bluesman's last album and what a legacy he has left behind. Johnnie is brilliant throughout, leading Rogers' top-notch backing band through all-star renditions of blues classics.

VIDEO

- *The Blues Rock Piano of Johnnie Johnson* (Homespun Tapes Ltd., 1999) Take a full hour lesson on rock piano with "The Father of Rock & Roll Piano®."

BIBLIOGRAPHY

Amburn, Ellis. *Buddy Holly: A Biography.* New York: St. Martin, 1996.

Berry, Chuck. *Chuck Berry: The Autobiography.* New York: Harmony Books, 1987.

Bockris, Victor. *Keith Richards.* New York: Poseidon Press, 1992.

Booth, Stanley. *Keith: Standing In The Shadows.* New York: St. Martin, 1995.

Burdon, Eric. *I Used to Be an Animal but I'm All Right Now.* London: Faber and Faber, 1986.

Chuck Berry: The Chess Box. Universal City, CA: Chess/MCA Records, 1988.

Clarke, Donald. *The Rise and Fall of Popular Music.* New York: St. Martin, 1995.

Crampton, Luke and Dafydd Rees. *Encyclopedia of Rock Stars.*
New York: DK, 1996.

Davidson, James West and Mark Hamilton Lytle. *After the Fact: The Art of Historical Detection Volume II, Third Edition.* New York: McGraw-Hill, 1992.

Davies, Dave. *Kink: An Autobiography.* New York: Hyperion, 1997.

Davis, Francis. *The History of the Blues: The Roots, the Music, the People: From Charley Patton to Robert Cray.* New York: Hyperion, 1995.

Dawson, Jim and Steve Propes. *What Was the First Rock 'n' Roll Record?* Boston: Faber and Faber, 1992.

Dinnerstein, Leonard and Kenneth T. Jackson. *American Vistas: 1877 to the Present.* New York: Oxford University Press, 1995.

Dixon, Willie and Don Snowden. *I Am the Blues: The Willie Dixon Story.* New York: DaCapo, 1989.

Escott, Colin, and Martin Hawkins. *Good Rockin' Tonight: Sun Records and the Birth of Rock 'n' Roll.* New York: St. Martin's Press, 1991.

Escott, Colin, with George Merritt and William MacEwen. *Hank Williams: The Biography.* Boston: Little, Brown, 1994.

Faragher, John Mack, Mari Jo Buhle, Daniel Czitrom, and Susan H. Armitage. *Out of Many: A History of the American People.* New Jersey: Prentice Hall, 1995.

Goldman, Albert. *The Lives of John Lennon.* New York: Morrow, 1988.

Goldrosen, John, and John Beecher. *Remembering Buddy: The Definitive Biography of Buddy Holly.* New York: Penguin Books, 1986.

Graff, Gary and Daniel Durchholz *MusicHound Rock: The Essential Album Guide.* Detroit Visible Ink, 1999.

Graff, Gary, Josh Freedom du Lac and Jim McFarlin. *MusicHound R&B: The Essential Album Guide.* Detroit: Visible Ink, 1998.

Guralnick, Peter. *Last Train to Memphis: The Rise of Elvis Presley.* Boston: Little, Brown, 1994.

Halberstam, David. *The Fifties.* New York: Villard Books, 1993.

Lewis, Myra, with Murray Silver. *Great Balls of Fire: The Uncensored Story of Jerry Lee Lewis.* New York: Quill, 1982.

Manzarek, Ray. *Light My Fire: My Life With the Doors.* New York: G.P. Putnam's Sons, 1998.

Miller, Jim. *The Rolling Stone Illustrated History of Rock & Roll.* New York: Random House, Rolling Stone Press, 1976

Palmer, Robert. *Jerry Lee Lewis Rocks!* New York: G.P. Putnam's Sons, 1981.

Passman, Arnold. *The Deejays.* New York: Macmillan, 1971.

Perkins, Carl, with Ron Rendleman. *Disciple in Blue Suede Shoes.* Grand Rapids, Michigan: Zondervan Publishing House, 1978.

"Roll Over, Chuck Berry." *Rolling Stone Magazine*, June 14, 1969.

Rucker, Leland. *MusicHound Blues: The Essential Album Guide.* Detroit: Visible Ink, 1998.

Ryan, Thomas. *American Hit Radio: A History of Popular Singles From 1955 to the Present.* Rocklin, California: Prima, 1996.

Sager, Mike. "Sex and Drugs and Rock 'N' Roll Especially Sex." *SPY Magazine*, February, 1993.

Santelli, Robert. *The Big Book of Blues.* New York: Penguin, 1993.

Schaffer, Nicholas. *The British Invasion.* New York: McGraw-Hill, 1983.

Schumacher, Michael. *Crossroads: The Life and Music of Eric Clapton.* New York: Hyperion, 1995.

Silvester, Peter J. *A Left Hand Like God: A History of Boogie-Wooge Piano.* New York: DaCapo, 1989.

BIBLIOGRAPHY

Sokolow, Fred. *Chuck Berry: Authentic Transcriptions with Notes and Tablature.* New York: The Goodman Group, 1991.

Tosches, Nick. *Hellfire: The Jerry Lee Lewis Story.* New York: Dell, 1982.

Townsend, Charles R. *San Antonio Rose: The Life and Music of Bob Wills.* Urbana: University of Illinois Press, 1976.

Turner, Tina, with Kurt Loder. *I, Tina.* New York: Avon, 1986.

Ward, Ed, Geoffrey Stokes, and Ken Tucker. *Rock of Ages: The Rolling Stone History of Rock & Roll.* New York: Summit Books, 1986.

Weinberg, Max. *The Big Beat.* New York: Billboard Books, 1991.

Wheeler, Tom. "Chuck Berry." *Guitar Player*, March, 1998.

White, Charles. *The Life and Times of Little Richard: The Quasar of Rock.* New York: Harmony Books, 1984.

White, Timothy. *Rock Lives: Profiles and Interviews.* New York: Henry Holt, 1990.

Wilkinson, Alec. "Friend of the Devil." *Rolling Stone Magazine*, July 9-23, 1998.

Wyman, Bill. *Stone Alone.* New York: Penguin, 1990.

Younger, Richard. Jimmy Vivino: The "Late Night" Man's Journey to The Blues. *Blues Review Magazine*, January/February 1998.

Index

A

"A Fool In Love" 87
A Man Amongst Men 341
A Night On The Town 224, 225
A&E 295
"A-Train" 19
ABC 322
Abrams, Don 213, 214-216, 269
Ackroyd, Dan 342
Adams, Terry 291
Ada's Lounge 56
Admiral 170
"After Hours" 18, 27, 30, 170, 291
After School Session 142
AFTRA 339
Akins, Willie 290
Alan Freed Rock and Roll Jubilee 98, 100, 101
Albert King Band 165, 168, 169, 170, 173, 175, 179, 181, 182, 217, 240, 244
Algoa State Reformatory 73
"All My Loving" 192
"Almost Grown" 127, 151, 152
Alsup, Tommy 153
"Amazing Grace" 275
Ambassadors, The 319
American Bandstand 149
American Explorers 291
"American Pie" 153
Anderson, Al 291
Andrew Tibbs 86
Animals, The 138, 197-199
Anka, Paul 144
Apollo Theater 98
Arc Music 104, 105
Ardolino, Tom 291
Aristocrat 86, 87, 93
Armstrong, Louis 55
"Around and Around" 148, 196

Art Rupe's Specialty Records 107
ASCAP 305, 306, 339
Ashby, Harold 92
Atco 231, 232
Atilla & the Huns of Time 205
Atlantic 231
Average White Band 209

B

B.B. King's 333
"Baby Doll" 121
"Baby What You Want Me To Do" 280
"Baby What's Wrong" 292
Back Home 208
"Back in the U.S.A." 151, 321, 325
"Back To Memphis" 305
"Bad Luck Blues" 162
Baker, Laverne 100
Bankhead, Tommy 221
Barnes, Lee 238
Barracudas, The 33-35, 43
Bartholomew, Dave 210
Bartholomew, Gene 325
Bartholomew, Harry 325, 327, 333-335 337, 348, 363
Basie, Count 18, 33, 34, 170
Bass, Fontella 279
Baylor University Medical School 366
"Be on Your Merry Way" 162
Beach Boys 104, 192, 193, 329
Beatles, The 137, 191-196, 199, 208, 303, 350, 370
"Beautiful Delilah" 149
Beech Church 23
"Beer Drinkin' Woman" 78
Bees, The 210
Bel Aires, The 279
Belafonte, Harry 140
Below, Fred 94, 132, 147
Bennett, Alvin 59, 67, 69, 70
Bennett, Tony 99
Bennie Clapper's Universal Recording Services 86

Berry, Chuck 19, 53, 54, 62, 63, 65, 67-81, 89-110, 113, 119, 120, 130, 132, 134, 135, 137-159, 163, 164 168, 169, 173, 174, 176, 177, 179, 192, 194-205, 207, 211, 213, 215, 217-219, 222-227, 231-234, 240-242, 247-261, 263, 264, 266, 267, 272, 276, 277, 280, 281, 282, 292, 293, 295, 296, 298-303, 306, 307, 321, 324, 328-330, 332, 334, 335, 350, 350, 358, 361, 364, 369-371, 373-376, 380-382
Berry Park 204, 215, 217, 222, 231, 257, 262, 299
"Berry Pickin'" 143
Billboard 128, 137, 358-360, 364, 368
Billy Blues 327
Biloski, Count 43
"Black Nights" 280
Black Sabbath 208
Blackwell, Robert "Bumps" 107
Blake, Eubie 7
Blakey, Art 170
Bland, Bobby "Blue" 4, 182, 333
Blondes Have More Fun 224, 230
Bloomfield, Mike 171
"Blue on Blue" 151, 152, 176
Blue Rhythm Swingsters 28, 30
"Blue Suede Shoes" 108, 109
Blueberry Hill 248, 321, 353, 355, 357, 373, 375, 379, 381
"Bluebird" 291
Bluehand Johnnie 279, 280, 281, 282, 298, 325
"Blues #572" 292
Blues Brothers 245, 342
"Blues For Hawaiians" 148

399

INDEX

Blues Foundation Hall of Fame 369
Blues Review 326
BMI 113, 305, 306, 339
"Bo Diddley" 89
Bobbin 175
Bobby & the Midnights 345
Bockris, Victor 253
Booker T. and the MG's 177
Boone, Pat 140
Booth, Stanley 260
Born Under a Bad Sign 182
Bottom Line Club 363
Boy", Arthur "Big Crudup 108
Bradley, Mary 318
Bradley, Paul 334
"Brenda Lee" 187
Brenston, Jackie 87
Briggs, Lillian 99
British Invasion 192
Bronitt, Marc 349, 358, 361
Brooklyn Paramount 99
Brooks, Lawson 43
Broonzy, Big Bill 51, 127
Brown, Clifford 28
"Brown Eyed Handsome Man" 104, 124
Brown, Henry 61
Brown, Marvin 330
Brown, Myra 153
Bucket of Blood 43
Buckner, Joe 290
"Bummed About Love" 304
Bunch, Carl 153
Burdon, Eric 197, 198
Butterfield, Paul 243
"Bye Bye Johnny" 104, 157

C

"California" 232
"Can You Stand It" 292
Capitol Records 192
Caputo, Dave 290
Carnegie Hall 354
"Carol" 149, 196, 204, 259, 302
Carr, Barbara 279, 280
Casa Loma Ballroom 106
Cash, Johnny 109
Catholic Central 311, 314
CBS 192, 322
Charles, Ray 238
Chauvin, Louis 60
Checker 89

Cherokee Studios 225
Chess 51, 53, 54, 84-86, 87-90, 92, 93, 94-97, 101, 103, 104-106, 108, 110, 117, 128, 137, 142, 144, 147, 150, 151, 176, 188, 200-202, 205-207, 227, 228, 231-233, 279, 341, 343, 370
Chess, Leonard 51, 84-86, 90, 95, 117, 118, 124, 143, 145, 146, 150, 152, 158, 185, 188, 201, 205, 206, 227
Chess, Marshall 195, 205
Chess, Phil 51, 52, 85, 89, 92, 94, 95, 104, 117, 146, 147, 148, 200, 202
Chicago Defender, The 50
Chicago Tribune 86
Chimenti, Jeff 347
"Chopsticks" 18
Christian, Charlie 43, 125
Chuck Berry on Stage 197
Chuck Berry Trio 97, 98, 99, 100, 106, 179
Chuck Berryn Combo 97
Chuck Berry's Golden Decade 210
Chuck Berry's Golden Decade Vol. 3 151
Chuck Berry's Golden Hits 201
Clapton, Eric 171, 204, 254, 258, 259, 263, 264, 283, 292, 293, 307, 324, 330, 332, 342, 370, 380, 381
Clark, Dick 342
Cleftones 100
Clinton, Bill 298
Clinton Recording Studios 326
Club Bandstand 149, 155, 156, 158, 252
"Club Go Go" 198
"Club Nitty Gritty" 201
CNN 322
Cochran, Eddie 154
Cohan, Patrick 316
Cohen, Al 104
Cole, Nat King 124, 140

Collins, Albert 296
"Confessin' the Blues" 71
Conner, Chuck 136
"Cookin' at the Continental" 170
Copeland, Johnny 282
Cosmopolitan Club 59, 61, 62, 66-69, 76, 80, 90, 91, 96, 97, 106, 118, 125, 158, 163, 204, 206, 215, 298
Couch, Bert 238
Cousins, Robert 284
"Cow Cow Blues" 8, 292
Cozy Corner 37, 43
Crawford, Big 86, 93
Cray, Robert 256, 263, 264, 283, 284, 360
Cream 203
"Creek Mud" 292
Crickets, The 249
Crook & Chase, 297
Cropper, Steve 182, 225
Crosby, John 218
Culph, Richard 97

D

"Danny Boy" 71
Dave Clark Five 194
Davenport, Charles 8, 292
Davies, Dave 154
Davies, Ray 154
Davis, Francis 50, 54
Davis, Jesse 225
Davis, Jim 30
Davis, Larry 240-243
Davis, Leroy "L.C." 106, 110, 117, 124, 155, 190, 370
Davis, Walter 61
Dawn Patrol 18
Deady, Martha 366
Dean, Tommy 112
"Dear Dad" 201
"Deep Feeling" 142
DeLay, Paul 41
Delvons 213
Densmore, John 203
Diddley, Bo 88, 200, 206, 341, 342
Dif Juz 349
Dillon, Jeff 285
Dirty Work 254
Dixon, Willie 51, 87, 88,

INDEX

91, 92-95, 117, 125, 147, 195, 196, 206, 256, 370
Doggett, Bill 280
Domino, Fats 67, 210, 223
"Don't Throw Your Love on Me So Strong" 177
Doors, The 202, 203
Dorsey, Tommy 33
Dorseys 28
Dowd, Tom 225, 226
"Down South Blues" 93
"Down the Road Apiece" 157, 196, 200
"Downbound Train" 106, 123
Drifters, The 144
"Driftin' Heart" 124, 128
Drouillard, Paul Dr. 317, 319
Drouillard, Rose 317
Duke 240
Dunbar High School 27, 28
Duncan, Al 92
Dunn, Donald "Duck" 182
Dylan, Bob 192, 202
"Dyna Flow" 176, 177

E

Ed Sullivan Show 192
Eddie Johnson Band 143
Edwards, Joe 354, 355, 357
El Dorado 112
Electric Lady 325
Electric Mud 206
Elektra Entertainment 291
Eric Clapton 24 Nights 285
Erskine, Bill 97
Ertegun, Ahmet 37, 350, 357, 362
Escalanti, Janice 155, 156, 157, 159
Evans, Suzan 337
Everly Brothers, The 144
Evidence Music 279, 625

F

Faces, The 209
"Fault Line Tremor" 292
"Feel Like Going Home" 87
Ferguson, Steve 291
Filmore West 182
Five Blazes, The 86
Flashpoint 292

"Fly Right Little Girl" 86
Ford, Frankie 154
Ford, Tennessee Ernie 110
Forest, Jimmy 162
Forrester, Roger 283, 285
Four Fellas, The 99
Fox, Mitchell 301
Fox Theater 252, 257, 261-263
"Frances" 290
Fratto, Russ 103
Freddy and the Dreamers 194
Freed, Alan 97, 99, 102, 130, 134, 144, 150, 153
Freundlich, Paul 350, 358, 361
From Ragtime to Rock, 247
Fulson, Lowell 280
Funny Stuff 241
Furthur Festival Tour 102, 346, 348

G

Gale Agency 98, 133
Gales, Billy 165, 241
Garcia, Jerry 343, 344
Garner, Errol 44
Gene and Harry Goodman 104
George Edick's Club Imperial 290
"Georgia On My Mind" 118
Gershwin, George 370
Gibbons, Billy 327
Gillespie, Dizzy 44
Gillium, Francine 149, 158, 189, 257
Go, Johnny, Go 150
"Goin' Fishin'" 326, 346
"Goin' To California" 175—177
Goldberg, Whoopi 326
Goodman, Benny 104
"Got To Be Some Changes Made" 180
Graceland 317
Grammy 251, 295-297, 301, 305, 325, 369
Grateful Dead 102, 343-348
"Green Dolphin Street" 19
Grice, Kirk 244
"Guitar Boogie" 145, 146

Guitar 201
Guns 'n' Roses 322
Guy, Buddy 283, 284, 325, 326
Guy, Vernon 289

H

Hackford, Taylor 68, 252, 259
"Had You Told It Like It Was (It Wouldn't Be Like It Is)" 181
Hail! Hail! Rock 'n' Roll 68, 81, 90, 111, 121, 135, 140, 211, 215, 266, 267, 276, 278, 281, 291, 298, 330, 351, 354, 380
Haley, Bill 143, 370
Hank Williams 296
Hannah, William J. 299
Hardy, Ebby 59, 67, 68, 70, 75, 76, 78, 80, 81, 85, 90, 92, 94, 95, 96, 97, 98, 99, 101, 102, 110, 117, 123, 125, 127, 129-134, 130, 132, 179, 369
Harmony Kings 162
Harpo, Slim 196
Harris, Ace 291
Harris, Ben 35
Harris, Ira 72, 74
Harris, Laura 239, 240
Harrison, George 303
Hart, Mickey 346, 348
"Havana Moon" 121, 124
Hawkins, Coleman 55
Hawkins, Erskine 18
Hawkins, Screamin' Jay 102
Hayes, Isaac 291
"Heartbreak Hotel" 109
Hendrix, Jimi 43, 171, 175, 204, 215
Herman's Hermits 194
High Society 299
Hilton 224
Hines, David 165
Hines, Earl 55
Hogan, Carl 125, 140, 141
Holiday, Billie 304
Holland-Dozier-Holland 196
Holly, Buddy 89, 144,

401

145, 152, 153, 154, 249
"Honey Don't" 109
"Honeydripper" 44
"Honky Tonk Part 1" 280
"Honky Tonk Train" 119, 142
"Hoochie Coochie Man" 88
Hooker, John Lee 37, 42, 43, 48, 49, 55, 63, 127, 197, 278, 295, 342, 357, 360
Hope, Bob 33, 34
Hopkins, Harry 21
Hopkins, Lightnin' 127
Hornsby, Bruce 346
Hot Tuna 347
Hotel Plaza Grand Ballroom 252
House of Blues 333
"House of the Rising Sun" 198
House, Son 51
"How High the Moon" 47
Howlin' Wolf Album 206
Huck, Hosana 298
Huck, Vincent 299
Huff's Garden 62, 74, 75, 76
Hunter, Albert 290
"Hush Oh Hush" 292
Hutchinson, Lawrence "Skip" 73
Hutton, Betty 33

I

"I Can't Be Satisfied" 86
"I Can't Get No Satisfaction" 194, 253
"I Could Have Stood You Up" 278
"I Get Evil" 180
"I Saw Her Standing There" 192, 194
"I Walked All Night Long" 164
"I Want To Hold Your Hand" 192, 194
"I Want To Hug You" 295
"Ida Red" 84, 85, 89, 90, 210
Ike and Tina Turner Revue 279
"I'll Do Anything You Say" 180
"I'm a Man" 89
In the Groove Boys 162
"Ingo" 148
Irving Field's Biggest Show of Stars 144, 145
"It Doesn't Matter Anymore" 154
"It Don't Take But a Few Minutes" 148, 258
"I've Made Nights By Myself" 164

J

Jackson, Al 182
Jacoubovitch, Daniel 289
Jagger, Mick 103, 196, 200, 256, 260, 265
Jagger—Richards 256
"Jambalaya" 84
James, Elmore 284
James, Etta 152, 258
Jazz On a Hot Summer's Day 154
Jefferson Airplane 203
Jefferson, Blind Lemon 43, 51
Jefferson Starship 347
Jeffries, Nancy 301
Jennings, Waylon 153
Jimi Hendrix Experience 203
Jimmie Vaughan 327
"Jingle Bells" 323
"Jo Jo Gunne" 150
John, Elton 370
"Johnnie & John" 326
Johnnie B. Bad 291, 295, 319, 373, 380
"Johnnie B. Bad." 306
Johnnie B. Live 363, 364
Johnnie Be Back 325, 326, 327, 363
Johnnie Johnson Nomination Video 349
Johnnie Johnson Quartet 54, 56
Johnnie Johnson (or Sir John's) Trio 59, 65, 75, 77, 79, 96, 97, 377, 380
"Johnnie's Boogie" 119, 125, 142, 280
"Johnny B. Goode" 94, 101, 125, 147, 148, 149, 157, 204, 221, 248, 280, 331, 334
Johnson, Althea 166, 295
Johnson, Andy 229
Johnson, Barbara Jean 49
Johnson, Buddy 9, 11, 12
Johnson, Connie 45, 295
Johnson, Dorothy 23, 24
Johnson, Frances Miller 268, 269, 282, 283, 286, 287, 293, 294, 307-309, 320, 321, 338-342, 347, 351, 354, 356, 366, 367, 372, 375
Johnson, Jack 10, 106
Johnson, James "Stump" 59
Johnson, Jimmy 318, 319, 320
Johnson, John David 39, 294
Johnson, Johnnie Jr. 166, 294
Johnson, Lonnie 51
Johnson, Marguerite Rolls 29, 30, 39, 40, 45, 56, 294
"Johnson Machine Gun" 86
Johnson, Maudell Powell 204, 205, 217
Johnson, Peter 133, 294
Johnson, Pless 10, 11, 12, 25, 26, 57, 58
Johnson, Priscilla Banks 9, 11
Johnson, Robert 42, 53, 55, 204
Johnson, Rose Hill 67, 133, 166-168, 294
Johnson, Syble 149
Johnson, Stacey 279, 282
Johnson, Willie "Jack" 10, 11, 12, 19, 25, 26, 287
Jones, Booker T. 182
Jones, Brian 260
Jones, Ricky Lee 345
Joplin, Scott 60
Jordan, Steve 255, 262, 263, 278, 326
Jump Jackson's Orchestra 86
"Just A Shy Guy" 124

INDEX

K

Kappas, Mike 48, 360
KDKA 18
Kelly, Matthew 345
Kendall, Ben 104
Kennedy Center 369
Kenney, Anthony 296, 304
Kentucky Headhunters 296, 323, 339
Kersey, Jim 363
Kesey, Ken 344
"Key To The Highway" 292
Keyes, Bobby 255, 263
Kim, Dr. Edward 366
"Kind-Hearted Woman" 93
King, Albert 122, 159, 161-166, 169-182, 222, 242-244, 296
King, B.B. 39, 166, 170, 297, 342
King, Ben E. 193
Kingfish 345
Kinks, The 138, 154
Knight, Glen 282, 283, 301, 338-341
Kooper, Al 326, 363
Kramer, Eddie 325
Kreutzmann, Bill 343
Krieger, Robby 202
Krupa, Gene 131

L

LaBostrie, Dorothy 108
Landau, Jon 349, 350, 358
Lane, Jay 345
Langdon, Chris 104
Late Night with Conan O'Brien 326
Laurel, Chris 333
Leake, Lafayette 92, 147,-149, 369, 370
Leavell, Chuck 263
Led Zeppelin 208
Leiber—Stoller 256
Lemp, Edwin 237
Lemp III, William 236
Lemp, John Adam 236
Lemp Mansion 235, 236, 238, 239, 244
Lemp, William, Jr. 236
Lennon, John 192, 196, 199, 258, 302, 303
Lennon, Julian 258
Lennon—McCartney 256

Lesh, Phil 343, 348
"Let it Rock" 154
"Let's Have a Natural Ball" 170
Lewis, Jerry Lee 75, 143, 153, 226, 296
Lewis, Joe 59, 67, 68, 77, 130
Lewis, Margo 341, 343, 346, 349, 350, 365
Liberace 118
Life 153
Lincoln Center 266
"Little Marie" 200
"Little Queenie" 151, 302, 307
"Little Red Rooster" 88
Little Walter Jacobs 87
Live At The Apollo 297
Live at the Roxy 298
Loder, Kurt 358
Lone Star Café 252, 282
Long, Son 60
Longoria, Spike 'the Percussionist" 348, 349, 355, 358, 359, 363, 364,
Los Lobos 346
Love, Clayton 289
"Love for Sale" 19
Lutheran Outreach 219

M

M.C. Hammer 297
MacLean, Don 153
Macomba Lounge 85, 86
Madison Square Garden 217
Madonna 297
Mae, Ethel 93
Magic Shop 326
Magnificent Six, The 182, 183, 204, 217
Maloney, Tom 235, 242-247, 249, 258, 250, 256, 257, 261, 272, 282, 289-291, 297, 325, 347
Mandy's Lounge 106
Manhattan Club 62, 163, 169
Mann Act 156, 159, 164, 300
Manzarek, Ray 202, 203
"Maple Leaf Rag" 60
Marsala, Jim 232, 233, 256, 354, 355, 374
Martin, George 199
Martin, Greg 296, 302
"Mary Jo" 68, 76
Mathis, Joan 157
Max Weinberg Seven, The 326
Mayall, John 282
"Maybellene" 67, 83, 90, 92, 95, 97, 99, 100, 101, 103, 104-107, 149, 163, 190, 210
McCartney, Paul 199, 303
McClure, Bobby 279
McElligott, Joe 313
McKernan, Ron "Pigpen" 343
McPhatter, Clyde 100, 144, 149
McShann, Jay 71
Melrose, Larry 51
"Memphis" 104, 200
Memphis Horns 182
Mercury 185, 201, 202, 205
Merrit, Michael 326, 363
"Merry Christmas Baby" 150
Mickey Hart's Mystery Box 346
Midnight Special 224
Miller, Chastity 270, 276
Miller, Dale 269, 270, 271
Miller, Glenn 18, 34, 319
Miller, Jerri 270, 286
Miller, Jimmy 272
Miller, Mitch 110
Miller, Zheda 269
Milton, Little 163, 169, 238, 279
Monroe, Bill 368
Montgomery, Donald 29
Moonglows, The 103, 152
"Moonlight in Vermont" 244
Moore, Judge George H., Jr. 157
Morrison, Jim 202
Moseby, Albert 106
"Most of All" 103
"Mother's Little Helper" 194
Motown 196
"Mountain Dew" 84
"Movin' Out" 292
Mr. Lucky 295

INDEX

Mr. Politician 328
Mr. Rock and Roll 144
MTV 365
Mumme, Neil 340
Murphy, Matt 'Guitar' 245
Musician 344
MusicMasters 363, 364
"My Ding-A-Ling" 209, 210

N

"Nadine" 114, 187, 190, 196, 223
Nallum, Floyd 130
NAS Meridian 314
National Medal of Arts Award 369
NBC 322
Nelson, Willie 327
New Orleans Jazz Fest 328, 350
New York Film Festival 266
Nick Manaloft's Book of Guitar Chords 72
Nighthawk, Robert 93
"Night Train" 162
Nirvana 370
"No Money Down" 106, 123
"No Particular Place to Go" 187, 197, 200
"November Rain" 322
NRBQ 255

O

"O.J. Blues" 280
O'Brien, Conan 327
"Oh Baby Doll" 104, 143
"Oh What a Thrill" 232
"Old Man River" 71
Oldaker, Jamie 284
Oldham, Andrew Loog 256
One Dozen Berrys 150
O'Neal, Jim 241
Orpheum Theatre 345
Orr, Mark 302 308
Orr, Scott 361
Other Ones, The 348
Otis, Johnny 89

P

Palladium 84

Palmer, Earl 107
Park High School 222
Parker, Charlie 44
Parrish, Avery 18, 291
Parrot 162
"Pass Away" 232
Paul, Les 297
Pearl Jam 370
Pearl King 292
Peek, Billy 201, 215, 222, 224, 228, 229, 232, 300, 369
Peek-a-boo Inn 222
People 368
Perkins, Carl 107, 109, 187, 258, 303
Pet Sounds 329
Peterson, Oscar 55, 290
Peterson, Roger 152
Phantom of the Opera 325
Phelps, Doug 307
Phillips, Sam 87, 108, 109
Pickett, Wilson 342
Pickin' Berries 150
Pickin' On Nashville 296
Pointer, Dick 238, 239
Pointer Sr., Dick 237-239
Pointer family 237-239
Pointer, Paul 237-239
Powell, Bud 55
Presley, Elvis 107-109, 118, 128, 137, 154, 192, 194, 199, 249, 317, 321, 322, 370
Price, Lloyd 210, 365
Primus 345
"Promised Land" 114, 187, 200
Pudgy's 270
Pulitzer Prize 369

R

Radio City Music Hall 295, 354
Rainbow 225
Rainey, Ma 280
Raitt, Bonnie 342, 350
RatDog 102, 343, 345-348
RCA 108
"Real Good Woman" 327
Red", Rufus "Speckled Perryman 61
Red, Tampa 51
Reed, Jimmy 112, 162, 280

Reed, Lou 345
Reed, Teddy 98
Reeder, Eskew "Esquerita" 107
"Reelin and Rockin" 104, 143, 210
Reese, Della 102
Rekooperation 326
Rektor, Milton 52, 54
"Rhapsody In Blue" 370
Rhythm and Blues Foundation 369
Rice, Kenny 161, 165, 166, 170, 172, 173, 175, 177-182, 289, 291, 297, 326
Richard, Little 75, 102, 107, 108, 109, 118, 136, 137, 153, 194, 199, 226, 303, 342, 370
Richards, Keith 103, 111, 121, 136, 192, 195, 211, 228, 249, 251-256, 258-261, 264-267, 277, 278, 292, 302, 306, 307, 324, 330, 342, 351, 354, 367, 380
Richardson, J.P. "The Big Bopper" 152
Ritz 253
Roach, Hal 150
Roach, Max 170
Robertson, Keith 279, 282, 298
Robinette, Freddie 165
Rock and Roll Hall of Fame 88, 334, 342, 348, 361, 365, 367, 372
Rock and Roll Hall of Fame Foundation 337, 361, 362
"Rock Around the Clock" 143
ROCK 325
"Rock 'n' Roll Music" 104, 143, 196, 223
Rock 'n' Roll Rarities 148
Rock, Rock, Rock 137
Rockefeller's 4, 243, 333
"Rocket 88" 87
"Rockin' at the Philharmonic" 145, 146
Rockin' Eighty-Eights 289-

INDEX

291
Rockit 232, 233, 257
Rock'n'Roll House Party 99
Rodgers, Erskine 97
Rodriguez, Jackie 343, 364
Rogers & Cowan 350
Rogers, Jimmy 89
Rogers, Roy 297
"Roll Over Beethoven"
    104, 110, 121, 124-
    128, 141, 148, 196
Rolling Stone magazine
    207, 224
Rolling Stones, The
    75, 89, 102,
    138, 194-
    197, 199, 200,
    213, 225, 228, 252-
    256,
    263, 264, 265, 281,
    292,
Rolling Stones, The(cont.)
    343-345, 362, 370
"Roly Poly" 143
Ronstadt, Linda 258
Roomfull of Blues 243
Roosevelt, Franklin 21
Roosevelt Sykes 292
Rooster Blues Records 241
Rose, Jane 265, 354
Rose, Jim 354, 355
Rosse, Jim 290
"Route 66" 378
Royal Albert Hall
    283, 293, 381
RPM Sound Studios 325
"Run Rudolph Run" 150
Rush, Otis 284
Ryan, Thomas 83

S

Sabu 22, 382, 383
Sadler, Herb 279
Sain, Oliver 278, 281, 282
Sam, Washboard 51
San Francisco Dues 209
Santelli, Robert 65
Satellite Lounge 3, 333
"Satin Doll" 59
Sausage 345
Shaffer, Paul 365
"School Days" 104,
    114, 119, 140-142
Scott, Levi 29
"Sea Cruise" 154

Sear Sound 326
Sears, Pete 347
Sebastian, John 139, 326
"See See Rider" 280
Seger, Bob 370
"September in the Rain"
    44, 47
Sergeant Pepper's Lonely
    Hearts Club Band
    199, 329
Serna, Monica 364
Seymour, Stephanie 322
"She Loves You" 192
Sherman, Joe 74
Shirelles, The 193
Silver, Horace 170
Silvercloud 238
Silvester, Peter J. 7, 60
Sims, Elvira 12
Sinatra, Frank 140
"Sincerely" 103
Sinclair, Ceola 272
Sister Act 2 326
"Sittin' Here and Drinkin'"
    93
"Slidin' Serenade" 291
Slim, Memphis
    52, 53, 55, 197
Slim, Sunnyland 86
Slippin' In 325
"Slow Train" 280
Smith, Bessie 18
Smitty's Corner 56
Smyth, Molly 325
Snow, Phoebe 326
Snowden, Don 93
"Soft Winds" 263
Soklow, Fred 127
"Son of the Father Neptune"
    35
Songwriters' Hall of Fame
    252, 369
"Son's Dream" 325
Sooner or Later 241
Sorcerer Sound 292
Soul Of A Man 326
Soulard Blues Band 243
Sounds of the City 244
Southern Air restaurant 298
Spampinato, Joey
    256, 262, 291
Spaniels, The 102, 112
Spann, Otis 94, 177, 203
Spector, Phil 192, 193,
    195, 198
Sperber, Brian 325

Spitzfadden, Bob 375
Springsteen, Bruce
    334, 349, 351,
    370
St. Louis History Museum
    247
St. Louis Music Awards 350
St. Louis Symphony 182
St. Louis to Frisco to
    Memphis 210
St. Louis to Liverpool 201
St. Louis Walk of Fame 380
St. Paul's Lutheran Church
    275
Stafford, Joe 34
Stanley, Owen 344
Staples, Pops 288
Staples Singers 288
"Stardust" 59, 244
Status Quo 205
Stax Records 177, 182
Steel Wheels 265
Stephanie Bennett 252
"Stepped In What!?" 292
Steve Gibbons band 208
Steve Miller Band 210
Stevens, Tommy 62, 70-
    72, 74,
    75, 123
Stewart, Ian 213, 254
Stewart, Rod 209, 224-
    230, 342,
    350
Stoba, Father Richard 312
"Stormy Monday" 39
"Stumblin'" 305
"Stupid Girl" 194
Subway Lounge 56
SugarHill Studios 325
"Summertime Blues" 154
Sumner High School 71, 72
Sun Records 87, 108
"Surfin' Steel" 148
"Surfin' U.S.A." 104
Suzan Evans 349
"Sweet Little Rock 'n'
    Roller" 104, 150
"Sweet Little Sixteen"
    104, 145,
    146, 376
Sweet Little Sixteen 150
"Sweet Sixteen" 170
Sykes, Roosevelt
    61, 223, 242

# INDEX

T

Tad 349
Talk Is Cheap 278, 292
"Talkin' Woman" 280
"Tanqueray" 279, 285, 293, 306, 320, 346
Tatum, Art 44, 55
Taylor, Eddie 162
"Texas Flood" 240, 242
"That'll Work" 308
"That's Alright Mama" 108
"The Buggy Ride" 78
The Cowboy 297
"The Feel" 304
The Johnnie Johnson Nominating Committee 338
The Jungle Book 218
The London Chuck Berry Sessions 209
The Milton Berle Show. 109
The Rock and Roll Hall of Fame Foundation 349
"The Wild Side of Life" 226
"Thirty Days" 106, 123, 149
"This Is Hip" 295
Thomas, Andrew 'Boots' 54
Thomas, Jaspar 94, 95, 137, 143, 147, 149, 150, 151, 154, 155, 157, 190, 191, 200, 370
Thomas, Rufus 196
Thompson, Charles 60
Thompson, Wilbur "Buttercup" 165, 180, 181
Thornton, Gus 171, 244, 245, 247, 256, 261-264, 282, 289, 297, 325
Thurston, Larry 244
"Till There Was You" 192
Tillman, Cornelius "Chuck" 111, 112, 116, 117, 122, 171
"Too Much Monkey Business" 104, 113, 114, 124, 141
"Too Pooped to Pop" 155
Toohey, Bob 338, 361
"Toy Bell" 209, 210
"Train Fare Home" 93
"Tulane" 187, 208
Turek, George 5, 6, 309, 311-320, 322-325, 327-329, 331-333, 337, 340, 341, 355, 357-369, 371, 372, 375
Turek, George Sr. 311-314, 372
Turek, Howard 317-319
Turek, Jessica 323
Turek, Jodie 317
Turek, Linda 317-325, 327, 328, 331, 332, 334, 353, 355, 356, 360
Turk, William 7
Turner, Ike 87, 88, 127, 163, 165, 169, 175, 177, 222, 241
Turner, Joe 96
Turner, Tina 87, 298
Tuthill, Chris 343
"Tutti Frutti" 107

U

Ultrasonic Studios 291
University Drug Company 271
University of Michigan 315
Upchurch, Phil 207
US News and World Report 311
USA Today 368
USC Medical Center 315

V

Valens, Ritchie 152
Valenti, Sam 279, 282
Van, James Buren 327
Vaughan, Jimmy 122, 164, 289
Vaughan, Stevie Ray 242
Vaughan, Willie 10
Vaughn, Stevie Ray 171
Vee Jay Records 84, 112
Vicky Lawrence Show 339
Vivino, Jerry 326
Vivino, Jimmy 326, 363

W

W.C. Handy 241
Waldman, Steve 279, 298
Waldorf Astoria 251, 364
"Walk Softly On This Heart of Mine" 296
Walker, T-Bone 39, 40, 43, 123, 125, 140, 327
Wallace, Sam 164
Waller, Fats 178, 223
Walsh, Joe 225
War 330
Washington, Fats 280
Wasserman, Rob 345
Waters, Ethel 18
Waters, Muddy 84, 86, 88, 92-94, 140, 169, 194-196, 200, 202, 206, 207, 228, 242, 284, 292, 296
Watts, Charlie 200, 265
"Way South" 280
"Wee Baby Blue" 96
"Wee Wee Hours" 96, 97, 99, 101, 114, 151, 176, 244, 259, 281
Weinberg, Max 326
Weinstein, Howard 324
Weir, Bob 103, 307, 337, 343, 345-348
Wenner, Jann 362
"West End Blues" 55
WEW 74
"What Can I Do To Change Your Mind" 180
Wheeler, Tom 201
"When the Saints Go Marching In" 275
Wilheim, Charlene 306
"White Christmas" 323
White, Harold 162-166, 169, 173, 174, 177, 179, 180-182, 217
Williams, Big Joe 52
Williams, Cora 12, 17, 29, 30, 31
Williams, Ernest 12, 14, 20, 21
Williams, James 73
Williams, Michael 373, 374
Williamson, Sonny Boy 197
Wills, Bert 327, 328 332, 333
Wills, Bob 209
Wilson, Brian 104, 192, 193, 195, 198
WMMN 19
Wolf, Howlin' 87, 88, 92, 140, 169, 170, 206, 242

Wood, Ron 209, 224, 265
Woodard, Otis 219, 220, 221, 240
Woods, Mitch 328
Wormworth, James 326, 363
"Worried Life Blues" 157
Wright, Lee Otis 165, 166 181, 182, 217
Wright, Tom 204
Wyman, Bill 195, 200, 228, 265

X

X-pensive Winos 292

Y

Yardbirds 200
"You Can't Catch Me" 106, 137
"You Never Can Tell" 187
Young, Fred 296, 304
Young, Richard 296, 297, 301, 302, 305, 306, 339

Z

ZZTop 327

ABOUT THE CD

Some years ago, during an English class, my fellow classmates and I were presented with a difficult assignment. "Imagine that you are composing a letter to a person deaf from birth," our teacher instructed. "Then, as best you can, describe to that person the concept of music."

We all picked up our pens at the same time and began racking our brains, hoping to find that one magical adjective that would somehow transcend the senses and explain the unexplainable. In the end, our attempts were futile. Although there were some very creative responses, none of us was able to verbally capture the essence of music. We all learned an important lesson that day. The power of words is not infinite, and some things can only be defined through subjective experience.

ABOUT THE CD

A few months after I began writing Johnnie Johnson's biography, I realized that I was faced with a similar dilemma as the one that had so challenged me in English class years before. How do I explain the music? I could pull out my entire arsenal of similes and metaphors, but even the clearest could not compare to hearing a single note of Johnnie's piano. I knew what I had heard. But how do I make someone who has never heard Johnnie understand? The solution was simple.

I am pleased to present to you the *Father of Rock & Roll* companion CD, featuring 14 tracks of Johnnie Johnson's music. With the exception of tracks 4, 9 and 10, these are all original versions, introduced by the legend himself, and recorded especially for the book by Johnnie's own sound engineer Harry Bartholomew. Harry and I made sure that all of Johnnie's styles and influences are represented in this collection—from big-band swing to gut-bucket blues—and naturally we threw in a heap of rock and roll as well. It was a daunting task to try and authentically reproduce those great Johnson/Berry collaborations—the songs that virtually defined rock and roll during the 50s and early 60s—but try we did, with one exception—this time the piano would be out front. No more mixed down keyboards behind boosted guitars and vocals. This is rock and roll as it was meant to be heard—a rollicking good time music powered by the man who started it all, Johnnie "B.Goode" Johnson. So sit back, relax and enjoy the music. I'm sure you'll be pleasantly surprised.

Best Wishes,

Travis Fitzpatrick

CD LINER NOTES

1. **JOHNNIE'S BOOGIE** / 2:30 (J. Johnson)
Father of Rock & Roll Piano® Publishing, ASCAP

Johnnie Johnson (piano)

2. **CALL IT STORMY MONDAY** / 6:18 (T-Bone Walker)
Gregmark, BMI

Johnnie Johnson (piano and vocals)
Bert Wills (guitar)
Terry Dry (bass)
SPIKE the Percussionist (drums)
Travis Doyle (organ)
Eric Demmer (saxophone)

3. **MAYBELLENE** / 2:22 (C. Berry) Arc Music Corp., Isalee Music Pub. Co., BMI

Johnnie Johnson (piano)
Bert Wills (guitar and vocals)
Nuri Nuri (bass)
SPIKE the Percussionist (drums)

4. **WEE WEE HOURS** / 3:48 (C. Berry) Arc Music Corp., Isalee Music Pub. Co., BMI

Johnnie Johnson (piano)
Clara McDaniel (vocals)
Charles Jones (guitar)
Tom Maloney (guitar)
Gus Thornton (bass)
Kenny Rice (drums)
Arthur Williams (harmonica)
Erskine Oglesby (saxophone)

5. **SCHOOL DAYS** / 2:56 (C. Berry) Arc Music Corp., Isalee Music Pub. Co., BMI

Johnnie Johnson (piano)
Bert Wills (guitar and vocals)
Jim Marsala (bass)
Robbie Parrish (drums)

CD LINER NOTES

6.**CAROL** / 3:32 (C. Berry) Arc Music Corp.,
Isalee Music Pub. Co., BMI

Johnnie Johnson (piano)
Bert Wills (guitar and vocals)
Jim Marsala (bass)
Robbie Parrish (drums)

7.**JOHNNY B. GOODE** / 2:44 (C. Berry) Arc Music Corp.,
Isalee Music Pub. Co., BMI

Johnnie Johnson (piano)
Bert Wills (guitar and vocals)
Jim Marsala (bass)
Robbie Parrish (drums)

8.**NADINE** / 2:37 (C. Berry) Arc Music Corp., BMI

Johnnie Johnson (piano)
Bert Wills (guitar and vocals)
Nuri Nuri (bass)
SPIKE the Percussionist (drums)
Eric Demmer (saxophone)

9.**DYNA FLOW** / 2:49 (A. King)
Conrad Music, Fort Knox Music Inc., Trio Music Co. Inc., BMI

Johnnie Johnson (piano)
Albert King (guitar)
Harold White (tenor sax)
Freddie Robinette (baritone sax)
Lee Otis Wright (bass)
Wilbur Thompson (trumpet)
Kenny Rice (drums)

10.**FRANCES** / 4:10 (J. Johnson/T. Maloney)
Modern Blues Recordings ASCAP

Johnnie Johnson (piano)   Dave Caputo (trombone)
Tom Maloney (guitar)   Jim Rosse (trumpet)
Gus Thornton (bass)
Kenny Rice (drums)
Willie Akins (tenor sax)
Albert Hunter (baritone sax)

11. **TANQUERAY** / 6:12 (J. Johnson/K. Richards)
J.F.J., ASCAP/Promopub B.V., PRS

Johnnie Johnson (piano and vocals)
Jimmy Vivino (guitar and backing vocals)
Michael Merritt (bass and backing vocals)
James Wormworth (drums and backing vocals)
Al Kooper (organ and backing vocals)

12. **GEORGE'S JAM** / 3:33 (J. Johnson)
Father of Rock & Roll Piano® Publishing, ASCAP

Johnnie Johnson (piano)

13. **CHITTLINS CON CARNE** / 5:40 (K. Burrell)
Elliot Music Co., ASCAP

Johnnie Johnson (piano)
Bert Wills (guitar)
Terry Dry (bass)
Eldridge Goins (drums)
Travis Doyle (organ)
Gordon Marsh (sax)

14. **HOW MANY MORE YEARS** / 2:57 (C. Burnett)
Arc Music Corp., BMI

Johnnie Johnson (vocals)
Bert Wills (guitar)
SPIKE the Percussionist (boot and crate)

All songs produced by Travis Fitzpatrick and Harry Bartholomew except tracks 4, 9, and 10.

This book was generated on a Power Mac.
Three different fonts were used in the printing of this book:
Palatino, **AGaramond Semibold**, and Utopia.

AGaramond Semibold was used for the dustcover.
Palatino was used for the body of the text.
Utopia was used for the page headers.

All dustcover pictures were produced using a unique quadtone process from the original black and white prints.

The companion CD was recorded, mixed and mastered using a Mackie Digital 8-Bus, Genelec 1029 Nearfiled Monitors, Lexicon 300 Reverb, and Tascam DA-88s. All vocals were recorded with an original Telefunken U67 microphone.

ORDERING INFORMATION

ALPHA PUBLISHING GROUP

12651 Briar Forest Dr., Suite 155

Houston, TX 77077

Credit Card Orders

Call Toll Free: 1.800.235.6646

All major cards Accepted

Visa, Mastercard, American Express, Discover

Visit Johnnie Johnson Online at:

johnnie.com

Here you can find out about:
- Tour Dates
- Albums
- JJ Merchandise
- Upcoming Special Events